DOCS THAT ROCK, MUSIC THAT MATTERS

by Harvey Kubernik

DOCS THAT ROCK, MUSIC THAT MATTERS

by Harvey Kubernik

Otherworld Cottage Industries
Los Angeles

First Printing, July 2020

Kubernik, Harvey
Docs That Rock, Music That Matters

   1. Music History. 2. Music Festivals. 3. Music Popular, (Songs, etc.)
   4. Motion pictures, Documentary.
   I. Harvey Kubernik. II. Title.

780.9

ISBN-13: 978-1-892900-09-8
ISBN-10: 1892900092

Printed in the United States of America
Cover Design by Linda Snyder

Otherworld Cottage Industries
1746 South Kingsley Drive, Los Angeles, CA 90006

For Gower Gulch

Acknowledgments, Credits and Support:

Harvey Kubernik would like to thank his filmic partners and contributors: Travis and Judy Pike at Otherworld Cottage Industries, spirit guide and photographer Henry Diltz, the yeomen efforts of archivist/ artifact librarian Gary Strobl and his brother Greg Strobl, Dr. David B. Wolfe, Michael McClure, Andrew Loog Oldham, Daniel Weizmann, Rodney Bingenheimer, Bobby Womack, Chris Darrow, David Carr, Gary Stewart, Ian Whitcomb, Gary Schneider, Ron Lando, The Pan-Pacific Theater, Lauren Blum, Gary Pig Gold, Andrew Solt, Greg Vines and SOFA Entertainment for all their help, David Peck and Reelin' In The Years Productions, Brad Pye, Jr., Curtis Mayfield, Ram Dass, Stephen J. Kalinich, Jim Kaplan at *Record Collector News* magazine, David and Jan Kessel at cavehollywood.com, Kent Kotal at www.forgottenhits. com, Andy Morten at *Shindig!* magazine, Mike Stax at *Ugly Things* magazine, Peter Piper, Nolan Gallagher at Gravitas Ventures, Mark Nardone at musicconnection.com, Elliot Kendall and Crystal Ann Lea, David A. Barmack, Walter E. Hurst, Nancy Rose Retchin, Barry Gordon, Harry E. Northup and Holly Prado, Dr. James Cushing and Celeste Goyer, Jim Salzer, Lisa Roth, Musso & Frank Grill, The Hollywood Ranch Market, Matty Simmons, Michael Simmons, Michael Ochs, Sherry Hendrick and Mick Vranich, Dr. David James, Allan Arkush, Vicki Shigekuni Wong, David Leaf, Brad Elterman, Jimmy Steinfeldt, Russ Regan, Jim Nelson, Bob Merlis at M.f.h., ABKCO, Carol Kaye, Jam, Inc., THC Exposé, Roy Trakin at *HITS,* Pat Prince at *Goldmine, Treats!,* Martin Banner, Paul Tarnopol, John Van Hamersveld and Alida Post, Hal Blaine, Richard Williams, D.A. Pennebaker, Michael Hacker, Steven Gaydos, Eva Easton Leaf, Ethan James, Richard Bosworth, Frank Zappa, Ron Furmanek, Lanny Waggoner, Denny Tedesco, Sarah Mary Cunningham and Michael Esposito at Columbia Records, Alex Del Zoppo, Elizabeth Darrow Jones, Amelia Cone, Tom Cording, Frank and Anthea Orlando Tony Funches, Michael Posner, Clay Travis, Helen Marketti, Paramahansa Yogananda, Dr. Robert Klapper, Barney Hoskyns Joel Selvin, Marko Budgyk, Frazer Pennebaker at Pennebaker/ Hegedus Films, Steve Binder, Kim Hendrickson and Abbey Lustgarden at The Criterion Collection, Barney Kessel, Phil Bunch, Jim & Cynthia Keltner, Nik Venet, Del Shannon, Dan and Kelly Bourgoise, Brian Young, Mark Bentley, Todd Thompson, Bob "Deacon" Kushner, Jan Alan Henderson, Keith Richard, Michael Macdonald, David N.

Pepperell, Larry LeBlanc, Leslie Ann Coles, Maria Malta at Sony Music, Leonard Cohen, Sarah Kramer, George Harrison, Ravi Shankar, Randy Haecker, Stuart Cornfeld, Howard Kaylan, Rebecca Baltutis, Morgan Neville, Anton Kline, Drew Steele, Dennis Dragon, Bruce Gary, Velvert Turner, Rosemarie Patronette and Scott Stoddard, Greg Franco, Rob Hill, Steven Van Zandt, Dick Clark, Jack Good, Don Webster, Carol Schofield and MsMusic Productions, Lou Adler, Howard Frank, Sujata Murthy, Tim Plumley, Megan McLean Corso, Todd Nakamine at Universal Music Enterprises, Kirk Silsbee, Roger and Mary Steffens, John Cassavetes, Roger Corman, Samuel Z. Arkoff, James Harvey Nicholson, André Previn, Jack Nicholson, Dennis Hopper, Guy Webster, Lisa Gizara, Barbara Berger, Clint Weiler, Jeff Goldman and Santa Monica Press, Wanda Coleman, Pat Baker, Johnny Mandel, Gene Aguilera, Robert Sherman, Brian Skyra, Ray Coleman, Dave Diamond, Humble Harve, Real Don Steele, Hal Lifson, Kevin Gershan, Dr. Cindy Summers, Bob Sarles, Rudy Ray Moore, Mike Johnson, Ben McLane, Ray Manzarek, James Douglas Morrison, Pat Baker, Edith Wolfe, Christopher Allport, David M. Berger, Art Fleischer, Jim Roup, Robby Krieger, Lonn Friend, Brian Jones, Guy Webster, Lisa Gizara, Max Crook, The Dark Bob, Laurette Hayden, The Nu-Art Theater, Toho La Brea, Erin Ediken at Jigsaw Productions, Scott Aitkin, Lenny Bruce, Marko Budgyk, Bob Say at FreakBeat Records, Wallichs Music City, The Frigate, Lewin Record Paradise, Grelun Landon, Justin Pierce, Dave Kephart, John R. Wooden, Dan Patrick, Colin Cowherd, Denny Bruce, Buddy Colette, Kim Fowley, Jack Nitzsche, Phil Spector, Brad Ross, Jonathan Rosenberg, Paul Body, Robert Marchese, Slash, Alicia Malone and Ben Mankiewicz at Turner Classic Movies, *The Twilight Zone, The Outer Limits, The Fugitive, Naked City, Route 66,* Herbert B. Leonard, Stirling Silliphant, Nelson Riddle, Gil Grau, Billy May, George Maharis, Martin Milner, Glen Corbett, Pete Rugolo, Diane Baker, Lois Nettleton, Susan Oliver, Lois Smith, David Janssen, Ann Francis, Jim Nelson, Jill Fraser, the Soft Machine, John Densmore, Pooch, Tom Johnson, Heather Harris and Mr. Twister, Cantor Nathan Lam, Rabbi Yoshi Zweiback, Jeremy Gilien, Steve Kerr, Mark London, Cake, Dean Dean the Taping Machine, Vee-Jay, Stax and Motown Records, Melissa, Bill Walton, Vivian Sisskin, the Pasadena City College record swap meet, Dr. Ronald Saltman, Bones Howe, Marina, Johnny Cash, Vin Scully, Chick Hearn and especially Kenneth, Marshall & Hilda Kubernik.

Table of Contents

Prologue: Writer in Quarantine

Having spent 2019 and the first quarter of 2020 writing, assembling and completing a music, recording and pop culture book on Jimi Hendrix with my brother Kenneth for last quarter 2020 publication by Sterling/Barnes and Noble, I then received a heartfelt email from my longtime editor who politely informed me that the company's offices in New York were currently closed.

Our tome and additional 2020 titles were abruptly being re-scheduled for year 2021 owing to the coronavirus pandemic. All Hendrix-related plans for 2020 are now post-poned indefinitely. Thankfully, I was simultaneously developing *Docs That Rock, Music That Matters.*

It follows the 2006 publication of *Hollywood Shack Job: Rock Music in Film and On Your Screen*, my conversations with Melvin Van Peeples, D.A. Pennebaker, Paul Thomas Anderson, Ice Cube, Mel Stuart, Jim Jarmusch, Andrew Loog Oldham, Jessie Nelson, Baz Luhrmann, Harry E. Northup, Clem Burke, writers, and music supervisors.

Docs That Rock, Music That Matters is a compilation of 1975-2019 director/producer/artist interviews, dialogues with Academy Award recipients, never previously published multi-voice narratives, new essays and non-edited content from my catalog and archives, tributes to television music hosts, plus examinations on outdoor festival culture, events and movie soundtracks.

It's not lost on me that in the last few years we have entered a golden age for a variety of documentaries. Cradle-to-grave portraits, snap shots of moments, docuseries deep dive unknown expeditions, *This Is Your Life* type witness testimonials, DVD's, multi-cultural products booked at theaters, on PBS, network and cable TV channels, digital streaming outlets and ever-growing platforms inviting us into a relationship with heralded cinema.

This century I've touted music documentaries for *Record Collector News* magazine and cavehollywood.com while occasionally an interview subject, consultant, writer or producer on domestic and international documentaries.

In 2018 I gave a lecture in Cleveland, Ohio, at the Rock and Roll Hall of Fame as part of their *Distinguished Author Series* discussing my book *1967 A Complete Rock Music History of the Summer of Love.* I had a very enjoyable Q. and A. session with the venue's curator and audience.

Afterward, a woman introduced herself, and mentioned her friend in Los Angeles had been at my campus appearance in 2008 at the University of Southern California School of Cinema and Television for Dr. David James' course *Cinematheque 108* where I showed the class D.A. Pennebaker's films on Bob Dylan and David Bowie.

"I'm a marketing executive at an educational book distribution company that services universities and colleges. When are you going to do another book on rock documentaries?" she asked, and continued before I could answer, "Child of Hollywood let me give you a tip. Besides readers, active retail foot traffic consumers who buy musical recordings, and avid movie buffs, gear it also to film school students, their professors' curriculum required reading lists, department chairs, teaching assistants, and the rockademic demographic."

What has emerged is a gathering of connection.

We got squad!

Harvey Kubernik
Los Angeles, California

Heather Harris:
20 Genuine Rock 'N' Roll Movies That Matter

Heather Harris' photographs of musicians have been published in *Rolling Stone, MOJO, Billboard, Los Angeles Times, Rock&Folk, Creem, Music Connection, Warner Brothers, Penguin Books, St. Martin's Press* and many more. Spanning Buffalo Springfield to Starcrawler, her work includes many of the most important

Heather Harris, Still Photographer (photo © Kurt Ingham)

figures in Rock that came through her native Los Angeles throughout the past five decades. She went to the Westlake School for Girls.

She has photographed covers for *New York Times* top ten best-selling books, has enjoyed three solo exhibitions of her photographic work in Los Angeles, has provided still photography for Warner Bros. television advertising, for assorted films and video productions and garnered awards for music books that were designed, photographed and written by her. She authored the books, *Punk Rock 'n' Roll* and *Bob Marley: Rastaman Vibration,* for A&M Records in the mid-1970s, and her popular *Fastfilm* blog, http://fastfilm1.blogspot.com, currently attests to her skill annotating these photo shoots in lively terms.

Last decade, I was housesitting for photographer Heather and her husband, Mr. Twister, former lead singer of Chainsaw and Christopher Milk. Heather, one-time editor of *The UCLA Daily Bruin* entertainment sections has always been one of my video/DVD librarians.

Over the two-week period, I was given the assignment of viewing a few dozen rock music-driven titles Heather owned, that she felt had been overlooked and not extensively reviewed.

After my binge and upon her return from a vacation, I asked Heather to list and comment on some of them.

Heather Harris: Everyone's caught *DIG!, Some Kind of Monster, No Direction Home,* Mark Wahlberg's weird turn in *Rock Star*, etc. Here's the best rock 'n' roll films, both fiction and non-fiction, that you've never seen and should. Some are readily available, others require deep Googling.

STILL CRAZY (comedy, fiction). Didja like *This Is Spinal Tap*, comrades? *Still Crazy* is its companion film, done Brit-style, and with a soulful redemption story at its core. Rife with musician in-jokes galore like the former, it follows a reunion of 70's Brit-rockers 25 years later, which prompt fist pumping yells of "rock and roll!" to be immediately followed by doubling over in back pain, as we geezers are wont. And it forecast the Chainsaw reunion tour of Italy I later photographed with Mr. Twister 28 years after their punk glory days disturbingly accurately, venue-wise.

Great cast with Bill Nighy (*Pirates of the Carribean*, and far better, with expansive screen time and more authentic as a rocker than in *Love Actually*), Timothy Spall (*Harry Potter* and assorted movies), Chris Rea (*The Crying Game*, the surprised one) Juliet Aubrey (*Primeval's* mad Jurassic scientist) amongst others, and a mysterious Syd-Barrett/ Richie Manic character buried in ghosts from the past. Everything rings true, rare as we know in films about rockers. Treat yourself to a parallel universe *Spinal Tap*.

24 HOUR PARTY PEOPLE (comedy, non-fiction). I photographed the *Happy Mondays* in 1990, the film about the subject, its origin and expanded universe of its surrounding phenom, first came out in 2002, and the film's real life main character died about two years ago . . . completely off the map to my fellow Americans. I just saw the movie for the first time recently on cable. Are we all too late to the dinner table?

Nosirree. Share the fun in retrospect, for the film *24 Hour Party People* remains one of the all-time best music films ever, wholly successful in conveying its subject matter accurately, despite its Python-esque edge, and bringing to life a specialty music understandable to the *non-cognoscenti*. It's also hilarious, insider-joke-heavy which matters not a whit to non-insiders cinematically overall, and features a commanding, intellectually fun and dry as champagne performance by its lead, Steve Coogan (already godhead to myself and others for his "Alan Partridge" satire on punitively vacuous talk shows.)

24 Hour Party People traces the beginning, full flowering and decline of the Rave phenom, first pollinated in Manchester, England before germinating worldwide, and as it was engineered by a single human being, Tony Wilson. Wilson found the bands, started the music label with assorted deranged partners, owned the main music/dance club and held it all together, all the while keeping his "day job" as a British television personality, both reporting features and even helming the UK *Wheel of Fortune!*

2

The movie follows Wilson's dry-humored (over-educated Oxbridge bombast as sound bytes, and solumnly intoned asides with narration like "This is my date Miss United Kingdom. I like her for herself. I know what you're thinking, and we're still together,") ascent and decline, and that of his colleagues, while being utterly true to its subject and as entertaining as if Monty Python fashioned a music documentary.

Biographical depictions include Ian Curtis and Joy Division, *Happy Mondays* and *New Order*, all ascending and declining as well. Actor Andy Serkis' (Gollum) turn as a renegade producer is a hoot, and the music is to die for (as Curtis unfortunately proved). My personal ethos of non-censorship comes into play in recommending this picture whole-heartedly, since there's an animal cruelty scene that I personally must fast-forward, and a LOT of (don't do as we did boys and girls, do as we should have done) drug-taking, but these, indeed, further the story.

And it's a singularly fascinating one of a lone, creative man finding himself, as he puts it "in the right place, with the right music, the right bands, the right record label, the right partners, the right club and the right drugs, all at the right time." The place was Manchester, England, the man was Tony Wilson, and the movie was *24 Hour Party People*. They are still yours to enjoy immensely.

EDGEPLAY (documentary). Former bassist of subject turned director Victory Tischler-Blue ("Vicki Blue") cajoles the Runaways, their associates and family to explain what went right and what went wrong in the legendary teen girl group who were monster players as well as jailbait.

Shot without legal authorization of Joan Jett, copyright holder of most of their original songs, it fills this vacuum very cleverly with a soundtrack wafting in and out of the few Runaways' live numbers in a dream-like fashion, very apt for hazy by nature recollections of thirty years ago that can be pleasant or genuinely nightmare-like, depending on the memory invoked. You're not going to envy the Runaways...

SUNSET STRIP, (comedy, fiction), 2000, should be viewed as a character study companion piece to *Almost Famous* with far more accurate verisimilitude. *Famous* is a wondrous pastiche, lotsa entertaining bang for your buck. But *Sunset Strip* represents the real shit. I know. I was there. And here's why you should take my anonymous word for it.

When I first saw this movie I was astonished that I didn't recognize the name of its writer, for I recognized every one of his characters, literally as well as figuratively. The writer obviously was exactly the

The Runaways at the Whisky a Go Go, 1975 (photo by Heather Harris)

same age I was, worked in the exact aspects of the entertainment industry that I did, at the exact same time in the early 70's at the exact same spots in Hollywood and knew the exact same people I did (or knew of). Anna Friel was Genie the Tailor, who did in fact die in an auto accident with several members of British band Fairport Convention. The geeky manager/producer was seemingly an early Geffen clone. The dissolute songwriter was a Warren Zevon-like, while Jared Leto was, dare I say, a completely interchangeable popstar type of the era. Stephanie Romanov played a Catherine James type, musician's muse beautiful both outside and inside. My own future beloved, glampunk rocker of that era, lived in the exact same Laurel Canyon mountain aerie depicted in the film (replete with same benevolent landlord), while I worked as a music photographer amongst the same scenes as the main protagonist's doppelganger.

And I did know who he was. He was one of the names you'll recognize on photo credits of essential music shots of the era, who now owns a major restaurant here. But he didn't want his name on the writing credits, so I'll respect that. *Sunset Strip* is a highly entertaining character study that is unbelievably accurate in its depiction of an assortment of characters on the perimeter, or the earliest stages of ascent, of the music scene in Los Angeles in the early 1970's. It's all true. And we did go out there every night. . .

I JUST WASN'T MADE FOR THESE TIMES (documentary). Producer, eccentric musician and genuine good guy in the business,

4

Don Was fashioned a documentary about the mid-1990's Brian Wilson that explained the latter's genius to musicians and fans alike better than anyone ever has. You'll actually grow to understand the enigma, as rare in films as it is in real life.

I WANNA HOLD YOUR HAND (comedy, realistic fiction). It really is a must for music fans and popculture historians of all ages (barring the odd sociopath who despises the Beatles). This 1978 comedy about events surrounding the Beatles' 1964 U.S. arrival and first televised gig in NYC is Robert Zemekis' well nigh perfect first film, cast with engaging young talent, and licensing 17 genuine Beatles songs bombarding the era as would have been real life soundtrack.

I witnessed the West Coast version of Beatlemania amongst teens and can attest that however outrageous this comedy seems, it's practically a documentary. Why this behavior, some still ask? The obvious answer through the ages has been that Beatlemania (a perfect storm of ad hoc promotion and new music worthy of such plaudits) allowed an America still grieving from the JFK assassination to obsess about something obviously good and brand new in their lives. Seventy-three million people watched that live televised gig; in other words 43% of all American households whether or not they were regular TV viewers or not.

The less publicized reason has to do with Beatlemania's springboard to, yes, sexual awakening for the new 1960s generation of liberated teen girls. Although out of reach (except for some plot points in this movie, and select, well-connected girlfriends I knew in prep school), the Beatles had twofold allure. #1. The reinforcement of their music constantly heard on mass media and instantly recognizable, quite unlike anything that came before. #2. Their outgoing, witty personas on the newsbytes was a great introduction to just what these good looking young Beatles themselves wanted to convey in their art: personal sexiness, always the primal ingredient of real rock and roll.

Unforgettable images: actress Nancy Allen as a teen who has broken into the band's hotel suite while they are out, succumbing to feeling up and practically dry-humping all of the Beatles' possessions strewn about their hotel room as an orgasmic, vicarious thrill, way beyond her fan expectations. Personal trivia: 1) at their requests and for barter, I used to draw pictures of friends en flagrante with their favorite Beatle or Stone. 2) Reflecting how one made long distance calls in olden days of yore, my friend Sally McMahon used to call Liverpool, England repeatedly until she would get a young sounding

5

operator on the line, then query her or him at length about the latest Beatles' doings. Proud Liverpudlian operators gladly obliged her.

Last factoid actually on topic, the Beatles aren't impersonated in this film except in longshots, news footage and a few scenes from behind while they're conversing. My friend Rich Correll supplied the voice for Paul McCartney in this film!

ALL DOLLED UP (documentary). Bob Gruen and first wife Nadya Beck's video documentary of the New York Dolls, young, fresh, outrageous, believable show-offs, so alive. Probably the all-time best rock doc to show actual backstage shenanigans as normal, with priceless live footage. If you know nothing of the NY Dolls, you'll understand the appeal instantly; it's that good a documented depiction thereof.

Often misidentified as Corel Shields, sister of Sabel Shields who ended up coupling with Johnny Thunders that very night, my friend Evita Corby can be spotted backstage at the Whisky a Go Go scenes, a gorgeous young brunette with derriere-length hair. The one rock writer who, although tackling difficult subjects as in his compilation book *The Hard Stuff*, wrote with voluptuous Romanticism about all sorts of hardcore characters as well as the facts, Nick Kent makes a somewhat out of it appearance backstage there too.

This film was shot with what was then the *dernier cri* in video technology, a portable (only 25 lbs! I know, I wielded one available at UCLA in the early 1970s), video camera that could handle low light without need for supplemental lighting, initially intended for newsmedia. Gruen and Beck had shot 40 hours of Dolls footage, so all of the highlights of the band's career appear here alongside all those glittering backstage tableaux.

MC5: A TRUE TESTIMONIAL (documentary). Wow. Quite possibly the greatest rock documentary ever, and it's still held up in the courts unwatchable to you the public. Totally portrays historical context, personalities involved, greatness of and uniqueness for the times music canon, and the prototypical rise, fall and rediscovery of this rowdy band of late 60's, mega-influential Detroit legends.

Do you remember hard-assed smartypants John Lydon uncharacteristically being reduced to tears talking about his dead friend Sid Vicious in *The Filth and the Fury*, acknowledging they were all too young to know how to help their out of control chum? Multiply that times two and eat yer heart out Barbara Walters, for the interview honesty here, yet without any of the innate fun-ness of the band being surgically removed from the DNA.

Worth every second of the film and special features. Work this out already, litigators, it's only the best rock doc ever!

GIMME DANGER (documentary). Jim Jarmusch's well done Stooges' 2016 documentary, important because its subject was the Stooges plus Iggy and the Stooges, not just their outrageously colorful, witty survivor frontman, Iggy Pop. The Rock and Roll Hall of Fame finally acknowledged their collective influential greatness-- um, all hard rock genres owe them--in 2010, after 7 non-successful tries. Subjective trivia: my friend Evita Corby appeared in the film's visuals, as she was guitarist James Williamson's longtime girlfriend during the band's *Raw Power* era and also modeled for the back cover of the original *Kill City* album by Iggy Pop and James Williamson, plus I was thanked in the small print credits crawl.

1973 Iggy and the Stooges at the Whisky a Go Go (photo by Heather Harris)

None of my pics were in the film, but I had brokered the live *Raw Power*-era Stooges' footage in the film that wasn't Ivan Kral's, therefore 50% of the universe's known footage, which heretofore was unknown to the world (*Antiques Roadshow* moment!). Its only other public appearance, also brokered by me, was in Morgan Neville's *The Making of Raw Power* DVD that accompanied its re-release in 2009. Originally videotaped for a St. Louis, Missouri broadcast news TV program, the footage was 6 minutes long and silent. But extant, thanks to my archiving. I am guessing that despite my best efforts, Jarmusch's production company couldn't locate the original footage (mine was a copy of its maker's Betamax format that I had digitized as soon as one could. Apparently, even its maker hadn't done this, and it degraded.)

Why so rare? Virtually all live footage of that era, except for that of the televised, mighty Cincinnati Pop Festival (best rock footage ever, of anyone, Iggy walking impromptu on a sea of hands) was indeed subject to severe technical limitations of 1960s/70s low-light photography/ cinematography, and was silent unless you had a Hollywood Studio's well-funded production budget behind you. None of us did, of course, even those with great access, like photographer filmmaker Leni Sinclair. All the early footage in this film was augmented with all sorts of bootleg audio that is traceable to each show. Once a lip reader can sort out which song the singer is performing, it's not too hard to sync up the bootleg music...

30 CENTURY MAN: SCOTT WALKER (documentary) (Ed.- this review circa 2008, now available worldwide. Unfortunately Scott Walker isn't, having passed away in 2019.)

It's not released in the U.S. yet, but eventually should be. The subject is American, but his pre-eminence is strictly European. Fans of *Absolutely Fabulous* should remember Patsy's older sister claiming she was the subject of a Scott Walker song, fans of director Minghella's first (and best) film *Truly, Madly, Deeply* (comedy-tragedy-ghost story: deserves own eventual blog), should remember the woman and her ghostly dead lover singing a raucous cover of "The Sun Ain't Gonna Shine Anymore," while fans of oldskool retro-60's classics on classics radio should recall "Make It Easy On Yourself" plus many anthemic others done with the same sonorous baritone over an orchestral sweeping vista.

The film is *30 Century Man* and the subject is Scott Walker. Once upon a time in the 1960's, three typical tall, skinny Sunset Strip denizens with long hair and bangs past their eyebrows plus failed C.V.s as musicians moved to England, wherein the intrinsic lack of tall, skinny Sunset Strip denizens with bangs past their eyebrows would allow them to actually stand out. And they did, to eventual mega-stardom.

Precursors of the Ramones' hat trick, these unrelated chums named themselves the Walker Brothers, surrendered to mainstream pop, and had enormous hit after enormous hit there, with their flagship sound of Scott Walker's baritone crooning. However mushy the MOR slop tended to be, at least it was interesting having "one of our own" youth culturers singing this way, and all three looking so shaggable. Believe me, David Bowie was listening INTENTLY to this particular sound, and you can hear it every concert he sings to this day. (Ed. On his recordings. Sadly, David Bowie has also departed this planet.)

Huge hits written by the era's best other songwriters, genuine Beatles-esque fan mobbing, compromises, breakdowns, substance abuse, what photographer/director Larry Clark called "the usual betrayals in the music biz," then it gets weird. Prettiest boy and main voice Scott derails, joins a monastery, emerges as a Jacques Brel interpreter, then a techno-artist songwriter before there actually is techno, then avant-garde orchestrator cum performance artist for music that has no categorizing description, all of which he warbles the highest brow intellectual themes over. He releases his work maybe once a decade.

This is the story of Scott Walker, a man rightly called the most enigmatic figure ever in the history of popular music, depicted from infancy to 2006 in *30 Century Man*. The director gives us "listening heads" instead of the talking variety, what with David Bowie coming aboard, Radiohead, Brian Eno and others chatting about Walker's influence upon their own work. Even 60's compatriot Lulu inquires to the only director that's managed to snag an interview with Walker if he's still gorgeous (A: yes, in a tall, skinny, bit of receding hairline, wildly creative, intellectual mien way. Plus he's sober now for decades. The guy laughs a lot for a supposed morbidly reclusive type, too.)

Many depicted fans of old don't "get" his newest work, voicing Luddite disdain for something so far ahead of what's going on now (whenever "now" is: that's the beauty of the avant garde), that they fail to embrace pure innovation for its own sake. You'll see recent footage of him orchestrating in the studio (replete with a percussionist pounding a huge side of pork, or recording sounds under a wooden box), and explaining his difficult themes with assured ease and aplomb.

Scott Walker is one former pop star turned composer who is actually working at the peak of creative powers right here, right now, a massive achievement for anyone, but especially former popstars. Trent Reznor should be so lucky when he's Walker's age. Check out *30 Century Man* when it's released to watch a fascinating musical journey.

Folks are SO USED TO rock and roll films being inadequate or downright bad that the good ones slip by. *THAT'LL BE THE DAY* and *STARDUST* came out in 1973 and '74 respectively and were the most accurate fictionalization of Brit rock up until then. I know, I just re-watched them. Absolutely astonishing that they were released so closely on the heels of their musical reality, including the deliberately pretentious rock opera of the second. And they feature the likes of Ringo Starr, Keith Moon, Adam Faith, Billy Fury, Marty Wilde el al. in supporting roles, not cameos, to its lead David Essex. The 1973 one so inspired me at the time that I wrote an 18-page expose for *The UCLA Daily Bruin* Intro entertainment section on same. I may still have the passion but oh, to still have that energy!

9

DOGS in SPACE (1986), was fashioned by its scene's insiders to celebrate something very geographically site-specific-- the emergence of punk rock in the late 70s in Australia via an ensemble cast set in a squalid rental house -- yet its many fine attributes place it universally global, echoing nascent and emerging punk scenes anywhere and everywhere. It certainly mirrors all written tales of famed communal punk rock hovel Disgraceland in my own metropolis.

Its splendid casting certainly churns it all up effectively. Standouts in the large cast (all of whom are meant to represent genuine folks): as the beautiful blonde punkette, actress Saskia Post (who remained a working actress [and Facebook friend] but who sadly passed away unexpectedly this 2020 year), will break your heart by the film's end. Her love interest (and that's to be taken very literally, as he straddles her to the floor each time he sees her no matter what the setting, a very cute continuing sight gag throughout the film as both actors are quite appealing) was none other than the also now late but then extremely young Michael Hutchence (of INXS chart hittery.) Yes, he does his own vocals throughout.

The film's name derives not only from its fictional punk band, but also, with televised space exploration and falling Skylab debris of the era as Greek chorus throughout the flick, from the sad plight of the real dogs in space, unfortunates like the U.S.S.R.'s Laika, who was elevated higher than any sentient Earthling had ever been beyond the stratosphere and into the heavens by spacecraft, then left up there to die. Metaphor, ya see.

The right music helps as well. Do I know this very specific, regional Oz discography? No. But despite my own geezerhood, I did write the first book published in the US on the subject of punk rock which went to press the week the Sex Pistols broke up, and can accurately assess the intended veracity here. Which would be a resounding "yes."

Except for a final song that narrates the growth of one of the characters, the film is bookended and served well by Iggy Pop via his songs "Dog Food" and "Endless Sea." Do note in the film's special features a section on the real musicians depicted, the real Oz punk scene and its real influences, in which all agree on the standard Velvet Underground, New York Dolls and Iggy and the Stooges triumvirate. But when each is asked for specific songs special to their group, each separately repeats as if by rehearsed mantra "Raw Power," "Raw Power," "Raw Power" etc. etc.

10

My Afternoon with *American Bandstand's* Dick Clark

Dick Clark (November 30, 1929-April 18, 2012) was one of the most recognized personalities in entertainment in America. He hosted two nationally syndicated radio shows, *Rock, Roll and Remember* and *The Music Survey*, live *Good Ol' Rock 'n' Roll* shows, and various rock 'n' roll video collections.

Clark began his entertainment career at age 17 at WRUN Radio in Utica, New York. After graduating from Syracuse University, he became a news anchorman at television station WKTV. He later moved to Philadelphia to work for WFIL Radio and Television, where he became the host of the local

**Dick Clark, 1983
(Photo courtesy of Gary Strobl)**

television show, *Bandstand.* Clark convinced the ABC network to carry the show nationwide, and shortly thereafter *American Bandstand* was the country's highest-rated daytime show. *American Bandstand* holds the record as television's longest running music/variety program. VH-1 in the late 1990's aired select *American Bandstand* episodes weekly.

Dick Clark Productions was responsible for creating TV programs like *Where The Action Is* that constantly spotlighted regional and national rock 'n' roll sounds during 1965-1967. Some of the best proto-punk rock, pop, rock 'n' roll and soul music captured in black and white footage was from that influential short-lived series. I went to a *Where the Action Is* taping at Pacific Ocean Park.

Clark's company also produced *Happening '68*, a Saturday afternoon program hosted by Mark Lindsay and Paul Revere that followed *American Bandstand* in 1968, and a spin-off, *It's Happening*, a weekday show that ended in 1969.

In 1998 I talked to Dick Clark inside at his office in Burbank, Caliofornia, about production of his *25th American Music Awards* show that saluted Frank Sinatra.

11

Paul Revere and the Raiders on stage at *Dick Clark's Happening '68*
(Photo and ticket courtesy of Open Mynd Collectibles)

ABC TELEVISION NETWORK	SUNDAY MAY

ABC TELEVISION NETWORK
PRESENTS

HAPPENING
WITH
PAUL REVERE and MARK LINDSAY

NAME_____

THIS TICKET IS NOT TRANSFERABLE

Children under 14 will not be admitted. Guests over 14 need not be accompanied by an adult. Boys must wear coats and ties — Girls proper attire.

SUNDAY
MAY
25
1 9 6 9
12:30 p.m.
Doors Close
12 Noon

4 1 5 1
Prospect
Avenue
Hollywood

I asked Dick about his radio years and his extensive film and video music library, requested heartfelt reflections on the loss of Sonny Bono, the Rock 'n' Roll Hall of Fame, his insights into the early recording careers of the Beatles and Elvis Presley, and how to conduct an interview.

Clark also offered some candid reflections on early 60's music touring packages and racial obstacles the entertainers endured, as well as a fond remembrance for the late Ewart Abner, former Motown president and assistant to Berry Gordy, Jr., who Clark knew for decades.

12

As a native Angeleno and teenager in 1965 and 66, I danced for a brief season on *Dick Clark's American Bandstand* filmed in Hollywood at Fountain Ave. and Vine St. Teenagers from local high schools were occasionally recruited to occupy seats, dance to records and mingle with performers who lip-synced their hit songs.

One time the Mamas & Papas and Bob Lind were the in-studio guests. I was in the Slauson Line in May of 1966. I also danced occasionally on *Shebang!* another regional TV dance program that Clark produced and was hosted by deejay Casey Kasem.

My wingmen were Peter Piper and Bob "Deacon" Kushner. I still talk to them. We knew one of the regular dancers, Famous Hooks, who Clark was speaking to on the telephone just before I interviewed him.

Clark later served as executive producer on the weekly 2004 TV series *American Dreams* which licensed his *American Bandstand* library, often integrating his archive film clips and vintage *American Bandstand* footage of dancers into the era portrayals in *American Dreams.*

Author Eddi Fiegel, who penned the book *Dream a Little Dream of Me: The Life of Cass Elliot,* emailed me a telling look about the Mamas & Papas TV screen relationship that included a national debut on *American Bandstand,* a San Diego-shot *Where The Action Is* televised booking and when the foursome later did an appearance on *The Ed Sullivan Show.*

The Mamas and the Papas arriving for *Where the Action Is*
(Photo by Henry Diltz)

"The Mamas and Papas popularity stemmed almost as much from their unique image as their singular vocal sound, and so TV played a vital part in making them the stars they became. Although the freshness and originality of their sound leapt out at you from the radio, it was the crazy visual combination of four spectacularly different characters which stopped people in their tracks: Cass Elliot's psychedelic muumuus and gogo boots set against Michelle Phillips --the ultimate svelte blonde flowerchild; and beanpole behatted John Phillips alongside the hearthrob moptop Denny Doherty. You couldn't have made it up, and the arrival of colour TV helped bring the impact of their acid-trip visuals home even more vividly."

Dick Clark was the major prime mover and producer of the revolving celluloid aural groove tube not only exposing the Mamas and Papas but others on his TV shows. Film and video clips then still emerge today in countless network, cable documentaries and DVD's decades after the initial lensing. Only now do we truly begin comprehending the countless R&B pioneers, prototype garage rock bands, pop singers and the hit-makers Clark's *American Bandstand*, *Shebang* and *Where The Action Is* introduced to millions of people.

"Prior to that positively historic evening of September 12, 1966, when a certain cathode-powered quartet premiered over there on NBC, it was the one and only *Where The Action Is* which would deliver a daily California-kissed squint at the the fun fun fun of mid-Sixties pop 'n' roll to my folks' far-from-the-Action 23-inch living room Admiral," enthused Canadian small screen devotee Gary Pig Gold.

"Even though my nine-year-old sensibilities already wondered how a guitar plugged into a boulder on the beach managed to produce such an authentic vinyl-sounding jangle, beliefs could, and would happily be suspended for 30 minutes every afternoon in order to catch various Raiders, Robbs, and slews of guest rockers romping and rolling over their latest hit-bounder, as Dick Clark remotely yet calmly reigned over it all. Sand-drenched footage of sublime 'Rhonda' knock-off 'She's Just My Style,' Jr. Walker's 'Shotgun,' and the boldly Beatle-y 'Lies' by those Knickerbockers never failed to send me running out into the backyard, miming myself with one of dad's discarded tennis racquets hung Rickenbacker-style over shoulder before being called in for supper: These be the innocent, yet thoroughly inspiring moments which molded countless aspiring popsters down the path of skipping homework, staying up late, and eventually forsaking traditional life paths altogether in search of some authentic Action to call our own."

14

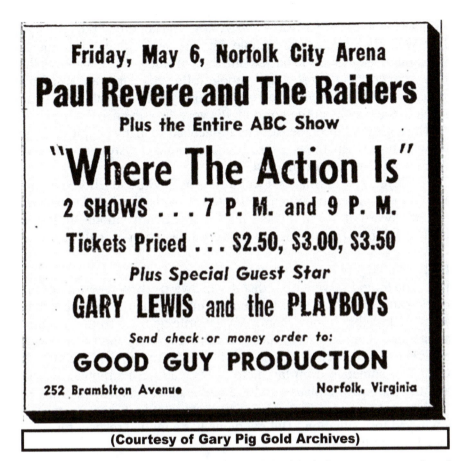

Friday, May 6, Norfolk City Arena

Paul Revere and The Raiders

Plus the Entire ABC Show

"Where The Action Is"

2 SHOWS . . . 7 P. M. and 9 P. M.

Tickets Priced . . . $2.50, $3.00, $3.50

Plus Special Guest Star

GARY LEWIS and the PLAYBOYS

Send check or money order to:

GOOD GUY PRODUCTION

252 Bramblton Avenue   **Norfolk, Virginia**

(Courtesy of Gary Pig Gold Archives)

Before 1998, I hadn't talked to Dick Clark in over a couple of decades. After our discussion, he sent me two different handwritten thank you notes.

I'll say one thing about Dick. Long after my teenage years, Clark would on occasion have his office call and invite me to various TV tapings and music specials he was producing. I was part of the window dressing and filler, but felt appreciated.

More than a few times, at some receptions over the years, Dick would walk across the room to say hello first, and always acknowledge me and Rodney Bingenheimer if we were in attendance at one of his functions.

A few times he'd introduce us to record label executives, ahead of the celebrities and stars in the room, long before Rodney had a radio show and I ever wrote a book. By the way, Clark's after-TV taping parties always had the best food.

15

HK: At the *American Music Awards Show* you honored Frank Sinatra.
DC: Well, there are certain people who are very influential in music throughout the years. Go back to the days of Rudy Valee, who was the first crooner, Bing Crosby, and people followed. Sinatra learned his style, I'm told, by listening to Tommy Dorsey play a trombone. If you listen to the way he crafted a song, it's very "trombonish."

I'm a great admirer, because he influenced so many people. I grew up with him when I was a disc jockey at an AC station in the days when it was 'middle-of-the-road.'

I played a lot of Sinatra. I was a Nelson Riddle and Billy May fan. So it's a real pleasure. When we started off with *The American Music Awards* Award of Merit, it was Bing Crosby, Benny Goodman, Irving Berlin. So this takes us back to the very foundation of it all.

HK: What do you leave with, when the show is over?
DC: The thing I leave with is that it's an awards show where all of the participants have fun. One of the few times in their lives where they all come together in one room. My favorite quote is from a country artist a few years ago, who said, "I do all the country shows and know everybody in our area, we hang out. This is the first time I ever met LL Cool J, or someone from far afield." They all have a mutual respect and there's equal applause and the audience is very enthusiastic. I don't want to get maudlin. It's not an evening of love, because there's a win and lose situation. But everyone has a mutual respect for what they bring to the party.

HK: Technically, what have been the changes in production over the 25 year period for the program?
DC: Well, early on we had a line of dancers. We had a house band. Now you bring your own band, bring your own sound mixer. The equipment was so primitive when we first started. When it began it was a 90-minute show. It was an experiment that grew to two hours, then to three hours. Consistently it's been the second highest rated show next to *The Oscars*. It's just a phenomenal growth pattern. And it's all due to the fact of asking ordinary folks who buy music what they like.

HK: Do you miss the actual physical hosting of *American Bandstand*?
DC: Yes, I'd be lying if I told you I didn't, but I knew at one point I had to leave the party when I turned 60. It would be inappropriate to be still doing the show. Not that I couldn't physically do it and pull it off, but you gotta know when to hang it up. It's a little bit like Jerry

Seinfeld saying, "I gotta leave after this year." It's a tough decision, but I do miss it.

HK: And you had *The Best Of American Bandstand* that aired last decade on VH-1?
DC: I did new wraparounds for it in the old studio. It makes me happy because it's been on in the 50's, 60's, 70's, 80's, and now the 90's. I only wish it had stayed on as a new production in the 90's. If I had kept it on another three months we would have made it into the 90's. But I didn't think about it historically.

HK: Did you ever think there would be a problem with recording artists lip-syncing their songs on live TV, or that it would have such an impact on viewers?
DC: Oh yeah. I've never relegated the lip-sync to a lower form of entertainment. Lip-syncing is an art unto itself. A lot of people can't do it. Jazz singers, improvisational singers just can't pull it off.

HK: What about the interviews you conducted on *American Bandstand*? Even today, what constitutes a good interview or technique between yourself and whoever you are talking to?
DC: In the old days, our interviews with the artists were short. Two to three minutes max. The way I patterned them - I've done 10,000 of them. 10,000 individual interviews. I had what I hoped was a beginning, middle and end. I tried to get something out of it other than "Where do you go next?" I always tried to get something you could hang on to. Sometimes totally frivolous. Sometimes very stupid. Sometimes not memorable. Maybe just show the humanity. The Prince interview was a failure. Huge, but most memorable 'cause he didn't say anything.

HK: Is there a different technique or style when doing a radio interview?
DC: I think radio is the most intimate medium there is, because it goes with you wherever. On radio I get background information, so I know what I'm walking into. On the flipside, what is this guy or woman on the radio for? To plug a record or a television show? Give them the courtesy of allowing them to get their plug in and then get what you want out of it. It's a very symbiotic relationship. We are using one another.

HK: You have some programs airing on the radio with you hosting.
DC: 15 years ago we started *Rock, Roll and Remember* when we started the united stations the first time. It's a four hour show that

replaces an air shift on the weekend when somebody has to get a day off. It works really well because it deals with music I love a lot. Roots music. There's only a certain number of radio stations that are formatted that can handle it, but it's been very successful. The other one is *US Music Survey*. There have been several spins of that. It's had several titles. That's a current AC countdown, a three hour show. I do both of them at the studio we have in my offices. The equipment we have is minimal at best. We have DAT and a few goodies. You can still send it over the air and put over the disc. It used to be tapes. Then CDs and someday it will go direct. *Rock, Roll and Remember* has a play list.

HK: You emerged out of radio?
DC: First job I had I was 17 years old. I was primarily the mail room boy at the radio station, an FM station. And in those days nobody listened to FM. It was a bastard medium that played classical music, and that was it.

I used to argue with my father, who was the manager of the station, "Why don't you play music that ordinary people would like?" In addition to classical, they had an FM rural radio network. Weather forecasts for farmers. So I did the area forecast and would relay it to Schenectady, knowing there were a few farmers and some geese listening. That's how I first got behind a microphone.

Later I was on WFIL. AM dial with 5,000 watts that covered the world because it was low on the dial. It was like a powerhouse 50,000 watt AM station in those days, owned by *The Philadelphia Enquirer.* The play list was highly restricted, based on the taste of the owner.

HK: When did you know or realize how valuable your film, TV and video archives were? Did you collect and document all performances, knowing one day the footage would be rare and valuable?
DC: I have no idea. I wasn't bright enough to know they had historical or money value. But I've always been a collector. Look around my office. I never throw anything away. I started when I was a child. I saved the returned kinescopes. I begged ABC to give me the old films. We have a huge file, second or third biggest in the world. Now I realize the historical importance of all of this.

HK: When did you know there was afterlife with this stuff? Clips of Fabian and Bobby Rydell?
DC: You've mentioned Fabian and Bobby Rydell. People think that's the file, but it's Chuck Berry, Little Richard, The Crows... It's

Jefferson Airplane, the Doors. That's what's so phenomenal about it. I knew it would have entertainment value. I didn't know it would have historical value until I got older.

HK: Who is the most popular requested music performer for licensing?
DC: Buddy Holly. The irony there was that we once did a retrospective show for ABC, and I had an editor in from San Francisco who lost the Buddy Holly footage. Never found it. The only Buddy Holly footage we have of him doing "Peggy Sue" is from *The Arthur Murray Dance Party*. I'm still a friend of Mrs. Murray and her former husband who passed on. I told her, "Let me have your tapes. You'll own them always, we'll just administer them. And we'll take good care of them and store them in various formats so they won't get lost."

Steve Allen's 'Hound Dog' performance with Elvis Presley was sitting in his closet in Encino. I said, 'Steve, let me make a dub of it. I'll put it in my file and give you an extra dub.' Two, three months later, he gave me a call. 'That tape I gave you, did I ever get it back?' I said, 'Yes. You signed for it. Here's the receipt.' 'I can't find it.' I struck another deal. Somebody has to be crazy enough to save stuff. The *The Tonight Show* is gone because NBC destroyed it.

When I called for the films of ABC, they wouldn't give them to me. Against company policy. I said, 'You're gonna scrap 'em like at ten cents a pound - let me at least buy 'em for that.' 'We can't. It's against company policy. It's against the rules'."

Ironically, a mail room boy called me one day and said, "I've got a truckload of stuff here. Cans of films and tapes that have your name on them. I'm gonna take it to the dump. Do you want it?" "DON'T MOVE THE TRUCK! I'll be down in a minute." We went to the truck and physically removed all those tapes that were going to be taken and burned, thrown in a pile somewhere, and saved them. So you have to cut through stupid organizational red tape. Sometimes they're human beings and know it has value.

All the clip requests come to me, the president of the company, and the archivist. The ball dropping at New Year's Eve is a big request. The night of *We Are The World* when everyone was on stage at *The American Music Awards*, prior to Quincy and the gang going to A&M to make the record. The reason they booked the studio date was because we had 'em all on *The American Music Awards*.

As far as requests for footage - unfortunately, anybody who is deceased we immediately get requests. The most talked about things are early Michael Jackson when he was with the Jackson Five.

19

Madonna's very first appearance is quite memorable. It all depends on the individual needs of the producers.

There were not a lot of sources for the early stuff. As time went on, and videos were made and other tape recordings were made of concert appearances, people saved them. There's more available. History gets shorter. You can get stuff from the '80's and '90's. '50's and '60's is scarce.

HK: What about the home video market? Did you and your staff anticipate the growing lucrative market for collections?
DC: It's not lucrative for us. The archives... I guess maybe this year they will be profit-making. It's not a big business. We've never ever been able to put a compilation together that was clearable. The rights clearances are horrendous. It's very difficult. Someday it will work.

HK: You were inducted into the Rock and Roll Hall Of Fame. What are your feelings about the honor? I know Phil Spector was one of the people lobbying for your inclusion. I saw your note to him at his home.
DC: Dion's speech is hanging framed on my wall. I needed his introductory remarks for my wall. It was a very big night, to be inducted into the Rock and Roll Hall Of Fame with all of your musical contemporaries. Colleagues, icons, idols. That's heavy duty company.

It took a lot of years for me to get in. There was resistance. I'm a non-performer. So you sort of have to wait in line, because they only put in a few each year. I was overcome with emotion because they finally let me in. I think I had an important role in that period of time. I know it doesn't sound very humble, but I was there from the beginning. I appreciate the honor.

HK: You know the thing that strikes me about your durability and longevity is, during research, it became apparent that you gave and presented a TV platform for many seminal rock and R&B figures years before you were identified with *The Philly Sound*.
DC: Well, one of the aggravations in life - and it really doesn't happen much anymore - but there was a period of time when young music writers took a stance that *American Bandstand* was the home to Philadelphia recording artists. Bobby Rydell, Fabian, Frankie Avalon, Chubby Checker. These are my very dear friends. I'm not demeaning their talent. That was one aspect of it. But they never really gave any thought to the fact that the Penguins, the Crows, Little Richard, Chuck Berry, Fats Domino, Bo Diddley, all made their first appearances on

American Bandstand. That aggravated me, but that's just stupid youth perpetuating an untruth. The truth has come out now and we don't hear much about that anymore. We've got smarter people writing.

HK: I know Paul McCartney appeared on one *American Music Awards* a few years back. And, looking around your office, I mean, photos of the Beatles, John Lennon, Stuart Sutcliffe artwork, and I realized at one time you had a record label, Swan that issued "She Loves You" b/w "I'll Get You" very early in the game.

Can we talk about the Beatles? The anthologies are selling, *The BBC tapes.* What impressed you about them? (Clark invited me on a tour of the photos on his office wall and showed me a Swan Records staff photo and a record presentation to the Beatles on their first American tour in 1964. And I got to see his fantastic Jackie Wilson photo!)

DC: You asked for it (laughs). Here's a ticket stub from November 1961 from a Beatles show which amounts to 42 cents US money. Here's the photo of Bernie and Tony, my former partners in Swan, with the Beatles when I was in the music business; after the government forced me out of the music business, they went on with it. The first record Bernie brought back was from these four kids from England with the funny haircuts. I put it ("She Loves You") on *Rate-A-Record* (an *American Bandstand* segment) and the kids gave it a 73. They didn't like it. I thought they looked strange. I didn't particularly care for it, because I thought it was derivative. It sounded like The Crickets and Buddy Holly, and a little Chuck Berry. Recycled old American music. I didn't focus in on the fact that it had a different thrust. I had no idea they would go on and make their own music and change the world.

The irony of the picture of Bernie and Tony with the Beatles and the record "She Loves You" was that, had Swan sold 50,000 copies of "She Loves You" that we played on *Rate-A-Record*, we would have had the rights to the Beatles ad infinitum. I said to Bernie years later, 'Why didn't you buy 50,000 copies?' (laughs) This was their second release. Vee-Jay and Ewart Abner had them first. Bernie was an alert guy. Someone called his attention and he went over to England to check the Beatles out. At the time, Capitol didn't want them in the US.

How fate changes things. I'm looking at Ringo Starr... We did *Birth Of The Beatles* and Pete Best got aced out of a drummer's job and I met him and talked to him. I wondered, how did this man walk around without being a total nutcase, knowing that he got aced out of a job as one of four musicians who changed the world?

He was the technical advisor on our show. A sweet man. I still hear from him.

HK: Did you ever see the band play live in the US or promote any of their live shows?
DC: I saw them in Atlantic City on their first tour here. The first time I saw them in the flesh. Several times thereafter.

HK: Did you like their stage show?
DC: It was interesting because it was like the first time I saw Elvis Presley. There was this shriek, this sound, which I think is part of the reason they gave up performing in person. It was very hard to hear the music. The audience reaction was phenomenally interesting. That's what I found about Presley. I saw Presley in the '50's at The Arena in Philadelphia, a 4,000 seater. It was the first time my ears rang after a concert. The same thing happened in Atlantic City when I saw the Beatles. So you knew something was going on. We later promoted them in Pittsburgh, I think. We had to pay them $25,000 for the night, which was just incredibly expensive in those days.

HK: You also put together touring packages that featured live bands from England during the initial English Invasion. Through my writing for *Melody Maker* and later employing some of these music-makers, I've gotten to hear some pretty tall tales of road life, and especially some of the insane racial scenes that existed when you presented and toured mixed black and white performers. What a minefield you all were walking into in the US.
DC: *The Caravan Of Stars* started in the late '50's and was derivative of Irving Feld's *Biggest Shows* concerts. Those were primarily black-oriented shows with a few white performers. Pretty much stayed the same for years. The headliners for years and years were blacks and whites, but primarily black. We would have a couple of teen idol white types as a closer for the white audiences.

We played to segregated audiences. That's all documented. But when it came time to bring the English over, they had no feel for the racism we had in this country. Because the Indian people had invaded their shores, the Pakistanis had been there, and I used to have long conversations and discussions with Eric Burdon of the Animals. We sat and argued about this for years (laughs).

He was such a fan of black music. I said to him, "You have no idea what this country has been through." His first introduction was on a rock 'n' roll tour. He found they couldn't eat with the black performers in public restaurants. They couldn't stay in the same hotels. It was a revelation. We'd run into posters like, "Don't Play Negro Music," "Don't Buy Negro Records." It was a very bizarre experience. And if you are a young person, it's gonna make an indelible impression on you.

HK: On those package tours, did you always like the concept of multiple performers on a bill? Many acts, a few hits, and that sort of production?

DC: I preferred multiple acts because I always had a short attention span, a plate full of a variety of things. I know that is offensive to an artist, I know there are artists that can command your attention for two hours. My personal preference is I'd rather have shorter bits and anticipate coming back for more at a later time.

TOMORROW (Sun.) ONLY AT 7:30 P.M.
DICK CLARK CARAVAN OF STARS
ALL IN PERSON
DICK CLARK

MAJOR LANCE	THE CRYSTALS
THE REFLECTIONS	THE DIXIE CUPS
MIKE CLIFFORD	THE SHIRELLES
BRIAN HYLAND	DEAN & JEAN
ROUND ROBIN	THE SUPREMES
GENE PITNEY	THE RIP CHORDS
THE COASTERS	BRENDA HOLLOWAY
THE KASUALS	GEORGE McCANNON
	M. C.

RPI FIELD HOUSE
SUNDAY JUNE 28 at 7:30 P.M.
All Seats Reserved $2.00—$2.50—$3.00
TICKETS ON SALE AT FIELD HOUSE ONLY
Phone Orders 274-0900 Troy, N.Y.

(Courtesy of Gary Pig Gold Archives)

HK: I couldn't help but ask you about Sonny Bono. Around the time of his funeral, you were quoted about his determination.

DC: Yes... I think it was his greatest asset. I've said for years, in a business that is a competitive one, young kids have said, 'How do I get or make a break in the music business?' I've said, 'Have bulldog determination.' Artistic people very often wait for the lightning to hit. Sonny made the lightning come to him. There's something to learn from that. Put yourself in the right place at the right time.

23

Be in the right city. Get to the right person. Hang in there. You have to be aggressive, or otherwise it will be a miracle if someone walks into the nearest Holiday Inn and finds you in the lounge.

HK: I met Sonny Bono. I knew Nik Venet, who died this week, and who signed the Beach Boys to Capitol after they recorded for Candix. And I interviewed Berry Gordy, Jr., and naturally met Ewart Abner, who also died this week, and who was president of Motown and, earlier, president of Vee-Jay Records, who released the Beatles' first record in America. Abner was a character. My dad even had lunch with him once. I mean, the Vee-Jay label had the Impressions, Jimmy Reed, and I know you have fond memories of him. All of these people were by-products of independent music.

DC: Yes. Ewart's contributions were overlooked. Abner was one of the unsung heroes of music. He was one of the most extraordinarily imaginative, colorful, pacifistic men. He was there during the days of integration, helping to bring that about. He could bring people together. That was his great role. He could spot talent. [Earlier at Chance Records, he joined with Art Sheridan to feature two new groups, the Flamingos and the Moonglows.]

I mean, as late as a couple of weeks ago, before he passed, I was irate about something. We were working on a project together with Berry and some other people. And Abner was my point man for Berry. I was ready to throw in the towel. "I can't put up with this anymore..." He said, "Let me call you back." 20 minutes later he calls me back, "Let's talk about this now that you're over this. Isn't this really the logical way?" He got me around to where I knew I'd get eventually. He was able to take me like a big brother and say, "Come on, let's get on with it." And he did that with everybody.

HK: I also feel the indie labels then - and still today, but talking about Vee-Jay, and the Swan effort with the Beatles, Sam Phillips with Sun also knew where the talent was.

DC: The independent guys found it and jammed it right up in their face. It was a very vibrant business in the early days. It was probably faster moving and more fun, because you weren't layered. You didn't have to go through the business affairs department, the accounting department, the promo department. Your fate was usually in the hands of one or two people who ran the joint.

It hasn't happened that way in years except in the area of rap now, where it's street guys instead of the multi-national conglomerates that pull the strings.

HK: What are your feelings about the internet and emerging new media communication and broadcast equipment?

DC: Some of the technology may have taken over and may have outstripped the appetite of the general public. I'm not against progress. I don't want to sound like some old fogey hanging on to the past, but I don't know what we're going to do with all of these improvements. I don't know if we really need direct-to-automobile transmission of non-commercial radio, for which you'll have to pay. I'm really not sure where the music business is headed, what the role of the retailer will be, when you'll just be able to call up for something for your house which we don't even know yet. It's a chip of some sort that will memorize your music for you.

But again, I can talk to more people, and communicate better, through radio than I can on the internet - for my purposes. I've been asked to spend time on the internet. I don't want to demean it, but who am I talking to, a handful of people? Give me the same 20 minutes and let me talk to three radio stations and I'll reach more people than you'll reach in a whole year that have hit on that internet website.

HK: Is any of this analogous to when *American Bandstand* went from a black and white program to color and maybe reached a wider audience?

DC: It was the last show on ABC to go in color because we were low man on the totem pole, a day time kids' show. What did they care? Probably one of the most colorful shows they ever had, but it didn't make the least bit of difference to the viewers.

D.A. Pennebaker: Reflections on Bob Dylan, *Dont Look Back, Monterey Pop,* David Bowie's *Ziggy Stardust,* and *Only the Strong Survive*

Widely regarded as one of the pioneers of rock documentary filmmaking, director/producer D.A. (Donn Alan) Pennebaker was born in Evanston, Illinois on July 15, 1925. He was educated at Yale and the Massachusetts Institute of Technology.

Pennebaker is the recipient of numerous awards including lifetime achievement recognition -- *The Gotham Award, the Platinum Music Network Award, The John Cassavetes Award from the Denver International Film Festival,* as well as career awards from the *International Documentary, Full Frame Documentary,* and *Hot Doc Documentary* festivals.

D. A. Pennebaker filming the 1967 *Monterey International Pop Festival* (Photo by Don MacSorley, courtesy Pennebaker/Hegedus Films)

On December 1, 2012, Pennebaker received a Lifetime Achievement Oscar for his six decades of nonfiction filmmaking from the Motion Picture Academy. He was the first documentary filmmaker to be given such an award. The 85th Oscars was broadcast worldwide on February 24, 2013 from Hollywood, California.

Author, deejay, and manager/record producer of the Rolling Stones 1963-1967, Andrew Loog Oldham in a 2017 email correspondence hailed the artist. "D.A. Pennebaker is an audio visual Walt Whitman of our musical heritage."

Pennebaker passed away of natural causes on August 1, 2019 in Sag Harbor, New York. His life and cinematic journey always had an intimate relationship to music, and his debut movie short in 1953 was *Daybreak Express*, a five-minute study about the train wedded to the Duke Elllington song of the same name.

In 1959, Pennebaker, Albert Maysles, Richard Leacock and Charlotte Zwerin began working with the New York-based Drew Associates, filmmakers assembled by Robert Drew and Time Inc, a team dedicated to broadening the merger of film in journalism.

Drew helped lead the direct cinema style that Pennebaker and others toiled in. The outfit helped birth the use of the first fully portable 16mm synchronized camera and sound system. The "direct cinema," or *cinema verité*, an unobtrusive style of filmmaking brought viewers right in to the action, by using hand-held cameras and techniques when they previously felt isolated from traditional narration documentaries.

In 1964 Leacock and Pennebaker formed Leacock-Pennebaker Films. They shot two songs at a Lambert, Ross & Hendricks recording session in New York at RCA studios. A month later Albert Grossman, Bob Dylan's manager, came to their office and suggested a documentary film on his client about Dylan's upcoming 1965 tour of England.

Their film *Dont Look Back* was released in 1967.

I saw it debut at the Los Feliz Theater in Los Angeles after it premiered in May 1967 at the Presidio Theater in San Francisco.

Jack Nitzsche, Denny Bruce and Buffalo Springfield's Neil Young were at the theater when *Dont Look Back* opened. The following evening, Neil went back for a second viewing.

"Los Feliz art house opening night," volunteered documentarian Andrew Solt, co-producer and co-director of *This is Elvis* and co-producer and director of *Imagine: John Lennon,* "transfixed Dylan on screen. Not stage. Docu verité window into a magical world— spellbinding moments, musical gems, beyond comprehension. Next day. Same time. Same place. Back in line for another shot," confessed the head of SOFA Entertainment. In 1965, then UCLA student Solt attended three Bob Dylan concerts in Southern California.

"I saw *Dont Look Back* in a Los Angeles theater—the Los Feliz,— when it opened, in May 1967," testified Dr. James Cushing, an English and Literature Professor at Cal Poly San Luis Obispo and a KEBF-FM deejay.

"We must remember that, as far as I or anyone in my circle knew, Bob Dylan's June 1966 motorcycle accident had left him either 1) dead, or 2) so permanently disfigured that he would never tour or record again.

"Like the *Bob Dylan's Greatest Hits* LP released that same season, Pennebaker's movie functioned within the context of the star's disappearance; this movie was as close as you were ever going to get to seeing this brilliant-but-now-vanished legend in concert. And the movie kept functioning that way until early 1974 when the legend returned to the boards.

"The movie is still astonishing, even if one's seen it a hundred times. I show it on DVD to students, and they identify with the young genius right away. When I watch the DVD myself, I'm always struck by Dylan's youth and self-confidence, and by the permanent power of these songs as evocative works of art. That Pennebaker included the non-Dylan scene with Albert Grossman and Tito Burns in the office is a tribute to his courage and sense of realism. (Has there ever been a similar scene in any music documentary?)

"Having no friends to accompany me, I saw it with my very conservative father (born 1920, Marine Corps in WWII), who detested everything about it; his main comment, as I recall, was that 'the whole movie was close ups of a bunch of really ugly-looking people!'

"That remark encapsulates the period's 'generation gap' as well as anything I can remember. In terms of blending concert footage with behind-the-scenes intimacy, it remains the best 'rockumentary' movie ever," Cushing insisted.

**D.A. Pennebaker and Chris Hegedus working on *The War Room*
(Photo courtesy of Pennebaker/Hegedus Films)**

In 1968, *Dont Look Back* won *Outstanding Film Of The Year* at The London Film Festival. In 1968, Ballantine Books published a transcript of the movie, with photographs.

D.A. Pennebaker's next celluloid undertaking was *Monterey Pop*, about the *1967 Monterey International Pop Festival* theatrically released in late 1968. Jimi Hendrix, the Mamas & Papas, Otis Redding, Hugh Masekela, Johnny Rivers, Janis Joplin, the Who, and Jefferson Airplane were now shown on tte silver screen.

I went to that premiere at The Fine Arts Theatre in Beverly Hills with Pennebaker and his partner/wife Chris Hegedus' collaborating with him since 1976. Their efforts on *The War Room* were nominated for an Academy Award.

In 2008 I presented a lecture under the direction of Dr. David James at the University of Southern California School of Cinematic Arts for the school's *Cinematheque 108* series and screened Pennebaker's epic documentary on Bob Dylan, *Dont Look Back*, to his students.

In 2017, a Director-approved edition of *Dont Look Back* was available from Criterion in a restored 4K digital transfer, with newly restored monaural sound from the original quarter-inch magnetic masters, presented uncompressed on the Blu-ray. Audio commentary from 1999 featuring Pennebaker and tour manager Bob Neuwirth *65 Revisited*, a 2006 documentary by Pennebaker audio excerpt from a 2000 interview with Bob Dylan for the documentary *No Direction Home*, previously unseen outtakes from *Dont Look Back,* a new documentary about the evolution of Pennebaker's filming style, a conversation between Pennebaker and Neuwirth about their work together, snapshots from the tour, never-before-seen outtakes from *Dont Look Back* plus a new interview with Patti Smith, along with a conversation between music critic Greil Marcus and Pennebaker from 2010 are included.

There is an alternate version of the film's "Subterranean Homesick Blues" cue card sequence five audio recordings of Dylan songs not used in the film trailer and a booklet featuring an essay by critic and poet Robert Polito.

There is a single DVD release of *Bob Dylan: Dont Look Back*. This format offers consumers the new digitally-remastered version from the *65 Tour Deluxe Edition* minus the two vintage collectable photo-laden books and second disc.

"Of course, there's really no way for film to catch the kind of wizardry that happens between Dylan and the English language," theorizes writer Daniel Weizmann. "His gifts are supernatural, invisible to the naked eye. He also famously refused to be photographed while writing because he considers it a private act. Fair enough.

"Still, there's a clip that Pennebaker shot for *Eat the Document* which appears in Scorsese's *No Direction Home* where we actually get to watch Dylan create in real-time, on the fly, and it's one of the most astounding things you'll ever dig. In a fast minute and fourteen seconds, you are zapped with the mental turbulence and psychedelic hopscotching of a great poet at the zenith of his powers.

"In the clip, a bedraggled, tour-weary Dylan is accompanied by Richard Manuel. At a glance, it's just a little bit of stony afternoon humor, but this crazed little minute pulls back the curtain to let us see the running gears of the same mind that created 'Gates of Eden' and 'Mr. Tambourine Man' and all those other labyrinthine lyrics. He stands in (or should I say fearlessly withstands) a zone of verbal chaos that skirts word salad and turns up surprise juxtapositions, deep hidden meanings, and urgent paradoxes the way an eerily confident blackjack dealer might splay, shuffle, and deal the deck without ever looking at his hands."

I interviewed D. A. Pennebaker a half a dozen times during 2001-2012. Portions of our conversations were published in *Goldmine, Record Collector News, Treats!* magazines, cavehollywood.com, and in my 2006 book *Hollywood Shack Job: Rock Music In Film and on Your Screen.* An encounter with D.A. Pennebaker was always a delightful, revealing informative and spiritual process for me. Excerpts from our dialogues are below.

HK: What are your feelings about being given an Oscar? You told Annette Hinkle of *The Sag Harbor Express,* "It's a surprise. What I do, and now, what a large number of people do is make independent films - independent of whether they should or not. It's like home painting - you just do it. You're always surprised when you're included in Hollywood."

DP: It's a little complicated. It's like being given the champion pilot's award when you don't fly. I mean, I never thought the Oscars were a waste of time or anything. They helped a lot of industry and people who are actors and probably helped get a lot of films get seen that otherwise might have gone awry.

Although the process of distributing films is so huge. It's like aspirins or something. There must be thousands of theaters waiting to hear what Paramount has this week to give them. It's in place.

HK: You never moved to Hollywood, and for over 50 years you didn't make the predictable move into huge budget feature films. And now are honored by Hollywood with an Oscar.

DP: I never had the temptation. It was like I was an architect and somebody was saying, "We have a lot of need for water color pictures." And I'm saying, "But I build houses and I don't need work." I saw it as a totally difference of dimension for me.

HK: The Academy voters and the public at large missed your 1955-1965 world as a documentarian.

DP: The documentary, when I quit that life, was a harsh moment, because that was my salary. And I had a child by then, and I had to figure out that it wasn't gonna work for me, but I had to leave. So for the next 2 or 3 years Ricky (Leacock) and I made films that we couldn't distribute, but they were some of the most wonderful films.

HK: Here you are in the late 1950's and television really started to look like a potential option for your work.

DP: Ricky thought that television would be our marketplace. And the fact is, they didn't even want to answer the phone. They were busy creating their own kingdom. They didn't need outsiders. People who didn't walk the halls in the morning weren't part of them.

HK: What has happened in the last decade or two with more film festivals and more films schools. Why?

DP: I think it's like the rise of the electric train. I think nobody at the beginning of the century had any thought that a child would want an electric train. When Lionel or whoever invented it, when they came out with something that resembled the real world and in a very artistic way, it was really well done. The trains were not realistic exactly, but they were kind of beautifully crafted and all the scenery.

So a person could create a whole kind of thing just because they existed. And so everybody got one for Christmas. Well I think that the making of films by yourself, as opposed to going to a movie theater and seeing what somebody else has done . . . The idea of making your own is a contagious notion. It isn't just a home movie. You're getting an audience of people, who in a way pay to see how good you are. And it's a shootout.

It's like when people went to Revolver, Arkansas in the heyday of the cowboy to shoot it out with the local sheriff to see how good they were. You sort of ended up throwing silver dollars in the air and hitting them if you were any good. By shooting from the hip. In other words, it became a whole thing. A process that had its artistic and its spiritual aspects that people hadn't planned on. But there they were.

So I notice when I go to festivals every show is sold out. Why is this? Why are people so fascinated to see documentaries? Well, at first I thought they were getting a kind of news that they didn't get from theatrical films and that they certainly didn't get from television. Because television limited itself to the news that promoted them. But now I'm not so sure. I think it's become the electric train. And they want to see it. And they want to see it run. And it's different from the movies they pay to see and craftsmanship on Hollywood films.

I think it's more than just the news, but a lot of documentaries address the news and the problem I have with most of them, is the theater is lost. These films have that quality, a kind of news event that you're gonna find out about. But the theater is missing. And I must say I always think of my films when I'm doing them as plays. Because the playwright had the same problem we do. He had to get a lot of people on stage that had never been seen before. From the very beginning he had to give you an insight into what was going to happen, what the play was about, why you were there, what was important about it. That was done in different ways. Shaw was good at it.

HK: At film festivals and question and answer events, what are some of the almost-routine things film students and fans ask you? Are they careerists?

DP: I think a lot of students, because nobody knows what to teach, they don't know where to start. Well, I think that in the film world, where we go and some students gather, and want to hear some kind of wisdom and they are considering their own careers and how to begin them, they start off with questions taken from the various wisdom from Hollywood. Things like, "Don't cross the line." Whatever that means. And they're not sure whether there are any rules. And I tell them there are no written rules that I know of. I don't have any myself, you know. I wait and see what happens in the lens of the camera and then I kind of go with it if I can. And that leaves them wondering why they are in school. They can learn this at the drug store. So it's a funny thing.

I start with *Daybreak Express*, a silent film with Duke Ellington's music. Then I show them something with dialogue. It took us two or three years to get cameras so that we could do this. But when we could get dialogue in a film and the story is driven in what people say to each other. That's where you are going ahead of the fiction film. Which has to start with somebody making up a story and then everybody ironing it out and it can't change because the money is involved. And it doesn't open up a field of something that they can enter into and proudly in which their parents can applaud.

So you have a problem convincing people. But then you show them the films. And they then wonder what will happen and that's life. That's very vivid. The fact is that when you can produce something in front of you that kind of resembles life, like even as Picasso could in painting, it's something people really want. They need it in some way. It's like I needed those jazz records. My 78's. I need to hear some of that music because it was people jumping off a high board and not sure where they were gonna go.

HK: It seems you always knew it was about removal of ego as a director and cameraman or filmmaker.
DP: You know where I think it arose, I grew up in Chicago. And when I was there, Chicago was changing in a musical way that nobody understood. A lot of musicians from New Orleans, Kansas City, St. Louis were coming to Chicago because the money was there. The criminals owned all the clubs, and so they had the money. And talent always goes for the money. Sometimes they pretend they don't. but in the end they have to. They don't have any long range assistance. All they are lasts as long as people want to hear them, and they're gone.

HK: And you subsequently made many music films and documentaries. Why has music informed a lot of your work over the last half century?
DP: The fact is I learned about jazz from 78 rpm records, not hearing anybody play it. I never saw a live thing in Chicago in my whole life. But the record was interesting. It did a couple of things. It created a time limit. No matter how great your ideas were, they had to be contained. And containing ideas musically with artistic talent meant you had to shape it in some way that people would follow it. And you started slow or fast but you moved in an orbit and then you ended it. And some worked better than others. But when they worked the whole concept of condensing a story line and having it starting out with people who really weren't sure. You might have had some music written for people. But basically jazz musicians never paid much attention to it.

33

So what happened was you began something that you knew kind of where you wanted to get to. A quality, a ring, or a tune, and everybody worked on that and figured it while you were playing. The thing happened while it was being played. What you did when you heard the record you witnessed how that came out. And that was kind of exciting, the improvisational aspect as well.

HK: Tell me about the first time you screened *Dont Look Back* for Dylan.

DP: I didn't know what was going to happen. But I knew that room was full of people that I hated. I didn't know where they came from, or where they went. Two nights. At the end of the first evening, Dylan said, 'we're gonna do the same thing tomorrow.' It was a terrible screening anyway. It was out of sync, and I was really depressed. And then we were going to figure out how to change it, or whatever he was going to do. And then the next night, ya know - bang! 'It's fine. That's it.' He had an empty pad. So I thought well this guy is an amazing person, and I was really not only lucky to be able to film but to have his mind contemplating its release.

HK: Had Dylan viewed the *Dont Look Back* DVD?

DP: Yeah. We're partners. We deal with Jeff (Rosen) in his office all the time. But Dylan came over, and he looked at some footage on the DVD and said at one point, 'How did you get that great sound?' I said, "Well Bob, you're gonna be surprised at this. It's all mono.' 'Mono…I gotta tell the guys down at Sony about this…'

Originally when I made the film *Dont Look Back* I wanted to be sure it wasn't about music, that it was about Dylan.

What you see now that maybe it should have been more about music. And Neuwirth always thought that and cautioned me, 'Look out.' But in a way, Dylan was what everybody wanted to know about. And the music they could get on the records.

You had to see the music performed. The film took possession of me. I was in the zone for *Dont Look Back*. Maybe Dylan was in the zone.

I knew that once I got started, I just had to roll and not plan anything. I didn't try and be smart about anything. I never asked him a question. I didn't want to know anything. The whole thing was a walking tour, like walking up a mountain. Your feet take you there and when you get off the train you made sure you had a new roll of film there.

HK: *Dont Look Back* now contains bonus footage and complete "outtake" sequences that constitute an hour disc produced with your son Frazer.

DP: I started to look at the outtakes as 'evidence' of something new. As I looked at them I thought, 'those things look so great in the black and white you can put them upside down.' The fact is that the black and white looked kind of marvelous in its simplicity. The outtakes are like old girlfriends. And you have a kind of nice memory but when you see them they're grannies, ya know. It's hard to remember what it was that struck you about them at the time. A film that you do, like *Daybreak*, one of my earlier films, I see it now almost the way I see someone else's film. The uncut performances had an effect on me.

When I did *Dont Look Back* I was sure I knew what I was doing. I edited it in 2 or 3 weeks. It was like walking across the Peruvian Andes on a rope, and I had to move fast and not take time to think about it.

Well, when I looked at the stuff now, the complete songs, I realized first of all the things that worked really were the love songs. Not the protest songs. The songs when you hear 'em now complete, from beginning to end, what strikes me is the guy, at that time, the music was everything. The music accounted for everything he had to offer in a way.

HK: You offer in the DVD narrative that all films have a center. And *Dont Look Back* has a center. Does a film arrive and wind down?

DP: Yes! Absolutely. I never know when we are shooting but in editing I find it out later. Shooting is just summer camp. When I saw *Dont Look Back* I knew exactly what was the center and it changed the whole ending of the film.

HK: I was taken by the tension, anticipation of the crowds and fans and the hysteria around Dylan that you caught on film.

DP: I caught that in the audience.

HK: Haskell Wexler who in the late '60s directed *Medium Cool* told me you used modified portable Auricon camera equipment for *Dont Look Back,* and you let him borrow that camera for some of his earlier shoots.

DP: Yes, but on *Dont Look Back* the camera I had was the best one I made yet. I used Angenieux lenses. He was a Frenchman, and he's dead now. He invented the zoom lens. A marvelous guy. He had this lens for studio cameras where he had this long finder 'cause you had it on a tripod, right, and you had to stand by and look. And I told him 'that's not going to work for me.' And he said, 'why not?' And I showed him my camera on my shoulder and my eye was right there at the thing. And I told him what I wanted, and he said, "oh boy…That is really hard, and I can hardly wait.' And he made me one!

HK: What about film stock?
DP: I think I was using Tri-X and pushing it (increasing film speed). And I did it through Humphries in London 'cause they were a really good lab, and they did I think a pretty good job, and we wanted it right

**Dont Look Back DVD cover
(Courtesy of the Criterion Collection)**

away. I had no lights. We used available lights. The people I showed it to at United Artists wished I had used more lights. They saw it as a ratty, underexposed film, you see, because they weren't thinking that that was Dylan's film, that's what Dylan should make. They saw it in terms of Katherine Hepburn. So it lacked.

There was no myth or legend yet. It was so incredible. Dylan had such an amazing kind of mercurial sense that translated to people. And when I see these full songs I think, 'shit, I made the wrong film.' I mean, it really hit me like that. And I thought, 'No you can't just listen like that,' because a lot of something went into it and it worked.

HK: Any theory why *Dont Look Back* keeps finding new audiences.
DP: It kind of makes you feel like you did something right once. (laughs). It doesn't make me feel bad at all. It interests me that people have the same fascination with Dylan that a lot of people had without being able to quite understand it. I know how I feel about Byron. I think he's an important person in our culture and why everything is derived from what Byron set forth. Dylan I think in a hundred years will have some kind of same quality that people will look back and

say, 'Oh, that's where that came from.' So it interests me now that people see it in the movie that when it was made it was all a guess.

HK: After your 1965 black and white movie with Bob Dylan, *Dont Look Back*, in 1966 you worked with Dylan again on a color music movie that was commissioned for ABC-TV, *Stage '67*, that you initially titled *But You Know Something Is Happening*. Later Dylan edited that movie footage as *Eat The Document*. A few years ago half an hour of the footage was sequenced into Martin Scorsese's *No Direction Home*.

DP: After *Dont Look Back* Dylan said, 'I want you to shoot a film, and I'm going to direct it, and it will be my film. You have your film, and this will be mine.' That was the kind of handshake arrangement. We didn't have anything signed or no papers about it. We went off. I only knew how to film one way. I didn't change the way I filmed. And Dylan really didn't know how to direct and nor did I. It kind of stumbled along. We were moving around a lot. Sweden, France, England. It just wasn't a tour of English music halls.

And I think that Dylan got really intrigued by the kind of locales he was in and how they responded to him. And then John Lennon came in and we sort of got involved with John. At no time did I think I'm gonna capture this movie and do it myself. Although I could sort of see how to do it because it was different than *Dont Look Back*. Dylan was playing on stage with 4 or 5 musicians and having a great time doing it. I mean, it was so much more interesting than what he had been doing all by himself. And he kind of took to it. And I could see shooting the stage performances were really an important part of it. At one point I actually got out on stage with the band and he didn't know I was gonna be there and when he saw me he really cracked up, because it was such a funny idea that I was just like the band.

There was no difference in shooting Dylan in color than black and white. By then I was sort of interested in shooting color and I liked the fact you could make scenes. The contrast between one scene and another you could make much stronger. Whereas in black and white it went from black and white to black and white. But you could make sky blue turn into blue velvet. And that was sort of interesting but it did not affect the storyline.

HK: Then this footage sort of morphed later into *Eat The Document*.
DP: Well, you see, Dylan had the motorcycle accident. The thing was done for ABC-TV. And so Albert (Grossman) came and said,

'We gotta give them something. Can you guys cook up something?' So Bob Neuwirth and I cooked up the beginning of *But You Know Something Is Happening*. But then Dylan said he wanted to edit *Eat The Document*. And then he and Robbie (Robertson) kind of had a competition about doing that, which always soured Dylan on the film. And so that film got made but ABC didn't want any part of it.

So the film sat in limbo. And my film was in limbo. I wasn't trying to compete with Dylan at all. And I showed it to the critic in San Francisco, and he wrote a review of it, which was unexpected, and Albert took not kindly to it, because Dylan thought we were playing games with him. But I never had any intention of releasing that film and haven't. I kept it because I think we were on to something that was really interesting, and I don't think anybody else knew it and did anything with it at the time. I hated to see the film go down the toilet.

HK: Thankfully, portions of what you shot were utilized in *No Direction Home*.

DP: Yes. I turned it all over to Marty (Scorsese). That was the only way it was gonna get released. Someday my version will get released but it doesn't really matter. Because all the work was done on the first film, *Dont Look Back*. And that's what people remember. And the rest is just kind of, you know, throwing pictures on the sides of the pages of the book.

HK: What was the biggest change you noticed in Bob Dylan as an artist and songwriter when you filmed the 1966 European tour that is revealed in the cut of *Eat The Document*?

A: Well, I felt that he was really writing music sort of with Robbie (Robertson) and for Robbie. He was trying to show Robbie how to write music. There was something going on that drove him so that he would stay up all night. I filmed him endlessly where he'd write many songs during the night, and Robbie would play along. Robbie made him somehow do this. And on the first tour there was nobody doing that. Neuwirth never made him do that. He never felt competitive with Dylan.

HK: Jim Morrison spoke to you about doing a documentary. You were at a 1969 Doors appearance in Toronto where they shared the show with John Lennon and the Plastic Ono Band. But you didn't film the Doors.

DP: Morrison had come to me a couple of times, and he obviously was interested. He and Neuwirth came and showed me Jim's film. His student film. I was not impressed, but that didn't mean anything. And I was interested in anybody who was a poet and wanted to make films. That was interesting to me. I didn't look down like this was amateur. But the fact is that he was a boozer. And, you know, that's a hard thing to make a film about. My father was a boozer. You can't count on getting their real lives. You get something else. They put on a kind of a show. And that was a problem.

And I had the same problem with Janis (Joplin). The drugs. And I had nothing against drugs because I didn't know enough about them yet. I loved Janis and thought she was a fantastic person. And I always thought there was a film there and I shot a lot with her, but what she was doing was so hard for her it was hard for me to film her.

And Morrison was funded. He had some kind of money. And I had some concerns what he would look at in 20 years. When the Doors got to Toronto, they were all very puffy. They looked like chefs in a big restaurant. And I would have shot them, but we couldn't afford to stay for the two days. But I heard them and we couldn't afford the tracking. We paid for the track for Yoko and John and gave it to them to release as a record.

I shot Bo Diddley for *Sweet Toronto (Keep on Rockin').*

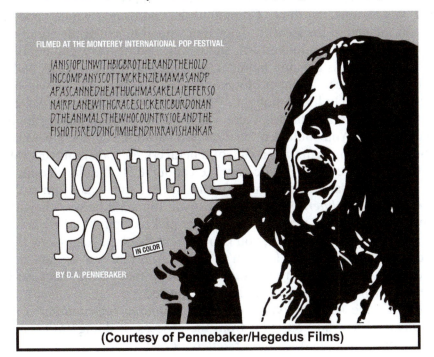

(Courtesy of Pennebaker/Hegedus Films)

39

HK: John and Yoko Ono performing in Toronto really impressed you. It's on DVD from Shout! Factory as *John Lennon and the Plastic Ono Band: Live in Toronto*. It's the one-day 12-hour festival held on September 13, 1969 at Varsity Stadium in Toronto. The debut of the Plastic Ono Band before Lennon officially resigned as a member of the Beatles. Yoko was not well-received at this event.

DP: It's an amazing thing. Coming at the end of that whole concert it was the end of the Beatles. They understood it, and at the end they fell silent. And John looked out, and it was kind of scary, and nobody was there. It was a funny moment. And they all left the stage, and I remember a piece of paper blowing across the stage, and slowly the audience came to life. I thought, "My God. This is a fantastic wake." Yoko was so crazy, but still, there was something so fascinating about what she did. You could see she did it with absolute conviction. What she was bringing to me was a kind of funeral cry for something that was lost. At the time I wasn't sure how I felt about it. But I did welcome it.

It was the same with (Jimi) Hendrix when I first heard him at the *1967 Monterey International Pop Festival*. I thought he was chewing gum on stage but it was actually his flat pick. I thought, 'This is not blues. This is bullshit.' But, you know, about the third song I saw that I didn't understand and I began to dig it. And that was an amazing moment. And that's why we shot every song that he did, because it kept growing in a way that we hadn't expected.

HK:. It's the 45th anniversary of the *Monterey International Pop Festival*. What did you learn from the process of doing *Dont Look Back* that you applied to doing *Monterey Pop*?

40

We've discussed over the years that for *Monterey Pop* you shied away from the use of interview footage. In *Goldmine* you mentioned, "Interviews didn't interest me, and I had access to do it. I didn't want to take the time. I wanted everybody to concentrate on music. Well remember: the guys I had filming for me there, except for Ricky (Leacock), he was the only other camera, they were all beginners. And I wanted them as I put them in pivotal positions 'cause they could be with the music. They served the music, and that was the thing. And I didn't want them to think about anything except getting film to match that music."

DP: I think of these films like *Monterey Pop* much more as if they were plays on a stage. And every play has to build to some sort of climax. Something it was all worth sitting there for. And that's how you decide what comes next. And there was no dialogue.

HK: With the recent retail releases of your catalog on DVD like *Monterey Pop* how do you feel about the DVD format, sometimes where you serve as a narrator to both original and newly re-mixed audio and film footage?

DP: I think it's added something quite interesting to our films. It's like listening to radio shows. It gives us a place to dump stuff, that's essentially valuable, but we don't know how to put it to film. So you feel, 'well, at least it's a drawer.' You can close it and think it's safe. The picture is better than video. We do a lot of work on these DVD's, especially on *Monterey Pop*. We went back to original sound, and re-mixed things with the 5.1 Dolby sound for the DVD player.

HK: Miramax Films released your *Only The Strong Survive*, a music documentary that you and Chris Hegedus directed with live performances and interviews filmed in 1999 and 2000 with 12 R&B artists.

DVD cover (Courtesy of Pennebaker/Hegedus Films)

Chris Hegedus and D.A. Pennebaker
(Photo courtesy of Pennebaker/Hegedus FIlms)

In my interview with Chris Hegedus she mentioned "it's a film of related events that tell a story. And in the initial editing stage it was a little challenging because it didn't have story arc, like *Startup.com* had, or *The War Room*. We had these pieces of performances. And when we started making the film we realized we had to add some archive footage of the performers for context, especially for younger people. There are people that I've met who have no idea what Motown is…"

DP: It's people like Sam Moore, Isaac Hayes, Mary Wilson, Wilson Pickett, Carla and Rufus Thomas, and Ann Peebles. These guys actually perform all the time. So they are doing songs from 25 years ago, and they're just as good. Somebody like Ann Peebles will make you cry she's so wonderful. When she does 'I Can't Stand The Rain,' it just knocks me crazy.

All this stuff is there, but you know that it's outside the mainstream, and there's a sadness about it all. Because basically it comes out of a religious conviction, it isn't like jazz. Well, they're all church and they're family. When they get together and they have a birthday, they're all in there and love each other, ya know. They're not competing for the only dollar in the house. There's something about it that is different from the jazz that I grew up in, and it's different than rock 'n' roll. It's something really wonderful.

Well, that's what is left for them. If we had all the money in the world, we could have arranged a big show for them at the Apollo Theater for them to do it, and we'd get the musicians, and the whole thing, and we didn't want to do that. We wanted it to be their gigs that they set up, with their musicians, and we sort of wanted to be there just like the audience. In the end it seemed more "righter" then trying to set it all up and do it like television.

We tried to find people who were coming into the New York area partially, and found groups that represented different aspects of soul music. Detroit, Chicago, Philadelphia, Stax…We had heard about this Luther Ingram benefit in Memphis and a lot of the Stax musicians came for that event. Mary Wilson was filmed during her 40th anniversary tour of the Supremes. The US film release also coincided with the reopening of the long-closed Stax Record studio in Memphis.

It does have an arc, but it's much more operatic. In seeing Carla and Rufus come together has such an operatic quality and to see Carla really belt that song out so beautifully. It's like suddenly you realize what she was all about. You know she knows music upside down and backwards.

Rufus…What a face. He has such a marvelous way of dealing with the instant, ya know. Everything is as funny as it is at that instance. That's amazing. He's like a 12 year old. I love that. I'd seen a picture of him before we did the film, and I thought, 'that's a great face to film!' And when we went to visit him at the radio station there he was. I couldn't take my camera off him. He was so wonderful just to look at. We had two cameras, which normally we don't, Nick Doob and I. But we started shooting Rufus on air the way we would shoot a narrative film, so we could cut quick dialogue, and it gave it a whole kind of style that I thought was radio-like.

HK: Writer Roger Friedman was your co-producer. Your early films were done with Ricky Leacock. Then you did your own thing. And for over the last 35 years you've teamed with Chris Hegedus.

DP: I've changed but you're never aware of your own changes too much. With Ricky, he was kind of a father figure but he was more than that. I knew that he had done these films, and I just felt very lucky to ride along with him. And I learned things from him. But they are things I would have learned along the way. I don't think it was a total teaching situation. But it was like we differed a lot in a kind of spiritual way. Ricky was always ready to accept defeat.

But the thing about Chris, who I've been partnering with for over 35 years, the moment she walked into my office looking for a job, this is gonna sound very unlikely, and this is a fact, we talked in a room across from my desk, and within 15 minutes I said, "This is what I've been looking for all of my life. Never let her leave this office." But we were almost in bankruptcy at that point and almost about to have an auction there. We didn't have any jobs and the woman who was working with me told her we didn't have any jobs. And I called Chris the next day. "Actually, we do have a job." And we didn't. And she came in and started working right way on *Town Bloody Hall*. And I knew that she and I are actually spiritually on the same course.

What she did on *Kings of Pastry*, the way she did it showed that she understood exactly what the film element was there. And I thought that was what I always knew she knew. It was in her. Everything she ever did with me. And the people that we filmed understood this too.

HK: *Ziggy Stardust and The Spiders from Mars* is now distributed on DVD and celebrating a 40th anniversary. In 1973 it was initially done by you for ABC-TV, Bowie's last concert in the UK as *Ziggy*.
DP: I was just amazed at how anybody could produce that kind of electricity. To me that was what art was about. Bowie and Dylan have a lot of characteristics in common. But for both David and Bob they both went into their heads from time to time and disappeared and I always assumed it was some sort of music room.

Dylan used to dress up and do funny things. He's kind of like David and I told Dylan once this and he was sort of anxious and said, "yeah…" I remember him on the phone. They were kind of alike, but they didn't seem alike at all, so it surprised me.

We saw one concert that night. I saw him once and I shot some stuff 'cause I wanted to see if we needed to lift the lighting or anything. And the lighting I could see was really crucial to this. We couldn't fake it. I shot some stuff and we took it down that night to a lab and they processed it and we looked at it and I made a couple of changes, like the blues were too strong and I went over it with the lighting person. And the next night we did the whole concert and there were only three of us. We had a skeletal crew and a Brit we hired with a camera way back in the rafters to get a broad shot, but we never actually used it.

RCA had supplied a real good 24-track machine. So we had good sound. It was just a question of getting in there. We have very few shots of anyone else in the band, other than his pal, (guitarist) Mick Ronson. David Bowie surprised us at every turn. And, boy, that was exciting to film. Because you had no idea what was coming next. I had put signs around the lobby, "Bring your camera with light bulbs and shoot all the film that you want."

The whole theater was a backup for him. They all sang backup for him. That was amazing. I had never heard that before. So I wanted that place to just be alive. You know, the girls singing along on "Moonage Day Dream." But the dressing room was where you see him just sitting there, so that in the beginning you use a long lens, that's why I use a zoom, and you can stand far away and the sound person can be close and you can really get on stage physically. So people know that he looks different from somebody else.

If you take these faces right you do portraits. But then, as the movie goes forward somewhere down the line there comes a point where you don't need to do that anymore so you go to wide angle. And with wide angle you usually don't have a finder 'cause you got to line up and pull the camera up and you start getting what is happening rather than picture to music. From then on everybody is going to recognize who's who and you don't have to worry about it, and that's the way the films go, most of them. There was a lot of kinetic energy around Bowie. He was like an orchestra leader.

HK: And during his *Ziggy* period, Bowie did a Jacques Brel song, "My Death" in the concert. He may have gotten the Brel songbook from Scott Walker before him, who used to do Brel tunes. That was my favorite piece in the *Ziggy* movie. I think "My Death" really informed the entire *Ziggy* studio album concept before he played it live. It's haunting and slow, and him with the guitar, a unique narrative story. And just the subject matter from Brel I know really hit Bowie strongly. I know very early on he was a big fan of Walker's work and cover tunes. He sang someone else's song and really made it his own.

DP: That's right. I was a fan of the *Ziggy* album and we used to play it all the time when I was mixing that film. We showed it in this little room where the sound was fantastic and that was the sexiest film you ever saw in your life.

"This incredible footage is really a piece of history in action because it shows that the most revolutionary thing about David Bowie was never his costumes, or even his vamping through the corridors of gender," suggests Daniel Weizmann.

"All that feels dated because it was always just his decoy, the Trojan Horse he rode in on. The real Bowie revolution was in the curious way he conveyed aloneness--the modern condition set to pop music.

"His peculiar distance from the audience, from his own material, and even from his own performing self in a way, is so dissimilar to everything else that was happening on stage at the time, it's like you're witnessing the birth of irony in real time. Yes, he's an actor, but he isn't just an actor. He's a man trapped in the zone between fully accepting the role and not accepting it at all.

"He started a whole new way to approach the thing, a 'new way to be' and it's right there on the screen."

In 1975 I interviewed David Bowie in Los Angeles at Television City at the CBS studios on Fairfax Ave and Beverly Blvd. when he taped the *Cher TV Show* for a story later published in the now defunct *Melody Maker.* Our brief conversation included comments on the recently completed filming of his feature-length *The Man Who Fell To Earth* movie. It was clearly obvious that David had already departed visually, musically and psychically from the self-imposed world of *Ziggy Stardust* character into his recent cinematic journey.

Ticket stub (Courtesy of Harvey Kubernik archives)

"The difference between film acting and stage acting is enormous. On stage you are in total control, whereas in a film the actors are instruments of the director. I think a stage performance is more of a ceremony and one plays the high priest, but in a film you are evoking a spirit within yourself. You feel a tremendous responsibility of having the power to bring something to life.

"For example, Major Tom in 'Space Oddity'."

Morgan Neville: Inside the Brill Building and *20 Feet From Stardom*

Filmmaker Morgan Neville was born in 1967 in Los Angeles, California and is a graduate of the University of Pennsylvania. He worked as a journalist in New York City and San Francisco and veered into film production in 1993. He founded Tremolo Productions in 1999.

Neville is an Academy Award, Grammy Award and Emmy Award-winning director known for his work as a cultural documentarian.

His heralded film, *20 Feet From Stardom* won, the 2014 Academy Award for Best Documentary as well as a Grammy Award for Best Music Film.

His documentary, *Best of Enemies*, on the debates between Gore Vidal and William F.

Morgan Neville, 2018
(Photo courtesy of Tremolo Productions)

Buckley, was shortlisted for the 2016 Academy Award and earned an Emmy Award.

For over twenty five years Neville has been directing, writing and producing films about music and cultural subjects, including *Troubadours; Search and Destroy,* and three Grammy-nominated films: *Respect Yourself: The Stax Records Story, Muddy Waters Can't Be Satisfied*, and *Johnny Cash's America.*

Won't You Be My Neighbor?, his 2018 documentary about television host Fred Rogers, premiered at the Sundance Film Festival and released by Focus Features in 2018, became one of the best reviewed and highest-grossing biographical documentaries of all time. It won the Independent Spirit Award for Best Documentary Feature.

Morgan has received critical praise for his catalog music titles on the Brill Building songwriters Brian Wilson, Burt Bacharach, Sam Phillips, Hank Williams, Pearl Jam, Yo-Yo Ma, Jack Clement, and Keith Richards.

Neville co-produced the Rolling Stones' 2012 documentary *Crossfire Hurricane*, and 2011's *The Union*, examining Elton John and Leon Russell.

In 2010, I served as Consulting Producer on Neville's singer-songwriter documentary, *Troubadours*, a retrospective study on Carole King, James Taylor and the Brill Building. (http://www.thetroubadoursmovie.com). The film was accepted at the 2011 Sundance Film Festival in the documentary category.

Now, in 2020, Neville is producing a documentary on celebrity chef, author, travel, and food documentarian Anthony Bourdain, who passed away in June, 2018.

James Taylor, Dec 13, 1969 (photo by Henry Diltz)

HK: In 1995 I went to the theatrical premiere of your *Shotgun Freeway: Drives Through Lost L.A.* The climate is sure different now for documentaries!

MN: When I first started, documentaries were the spinach of filmmaking. (laughs). They weren't cool and nobody wanted to pay for them. And even at the time when I was really starting, people really didn't want to do music documentaries. *American Masters* wasn't doing much. Leonard Bernstein was their big music documentary for the year. Look, I love Leonard Bernstein but it wasn't rock 'n' roll. And I did one of the first music documentaries for *A&E Biography.*

They didn't really want to do music, and I kept pushing them and saying, "These are great stories. Let's do them!"

So I ended up doing a lot for them: Leiber & Stoller, Burt Bacharach, the Brill Building, Brian Wilson and eventually Johnny Cash and Ray Charles. I did these things because I loved them. I was a music fanatic, and I figured out a way to legitimize my fanaticism by making documentaries. But the industry at the time really wasn't set up to make them. It could not be more different today.

Now documentaries are cool and people will go to a theater to see a documentary, which is incredible. I think part of it is that documentaries became better. And my real theory is that streaming services have streamed documentaries in a platform with dramas and comedies. A lot of people view documentaries now.

For years I heard people say "I love documentaries but I don't know where to find them." It's the accessibility that grew the audience for people who like documentaries and realized that documentaries can be every bit as good as any other kind of film if not better.

There's that whole kind of revolution that has happened in non-fiction, which is great. And then there's just the kind of maturing of the audience and the niche for music films.

HK: I know you've been doing documentaries for a few decades. What were a few of the influential music ones and the directors that were influential on you before embarking on your own career?

MN: There were some music films that were hugely impactful on me coming up, the music documentaries of D.A. Pennebaker, Murray Lerner, and Albert Maysles. Their films are legendary, and you had to see them or would view them at a midnight movie screening. Or you got a bootleg tape somewhere decades ago to watch them.

But they were hard to see. I love their films. I love *Monterey Pop* and *Gimme Shelter*. Those aren't the style of film I make but the person who was my biggest influence as a filmmaker was Peter Guralnick, the author and music writer. I was a huge fan of his. And I was also a big fan of writer Greil Marcus, but particularly Peter. And I think more as a historian like Peter. His *Sweet Soul Music* and *Lost Highways* influenced the kind of stories I wanted to tell, the forgotten stories of known and unknown music of the 20th century.

So in a way that was much more of an influence than any filmmakers, it came from writing about music but applicable to documentaries. The three least interesting things in writing music are sex, drugs and getting screwed over by your record label, because everybody tells

49

the same story. And I think about that all the time. And it's more about what differentiates the artists that you try and celebrate.

HK: Man, things have changed.
MN: Part of it as far as the new and wider appeal is that the gatekeepers grew and the people who loved this music and part of it is that the audience got older, they kind of realized that they'll show up and buy these kind of things. It wasn't just a teenage thing.

I think also, the music industry was making so much money for so long that to engage in what by and large was a money-losing proposition or a break-even proposition of making documentaries, just wasn't worth their time, or they didn't care.

A few decades ago they were funding large budget music videos. The catalog was the backwater of the labels. All they cared about were the new artists, and it wasn't about making documentaries.

Occasionally they would make one, like *Bring on the Night* because they were selling a new Sting album or whatever. There weren't many music documentaries that were getting theatrically released in the eighties. *The Decline and Fall of Western Civilization* and *X's The Unheard Music* had a big impression on me. They connected with me and somehow got made in that era.

HK: In that *X* film, where they moved the house, it's accompanied with a poem I produced with Exene reading "Percy Mayfield" from an album I did previously. I brought Exene into Gold Star Recording Studio employing their landmark echo chamber for that session.
MN: That's one of the pivotal scenes in that movie!

HK: I didn't get a screen credit. I guess that's punk rock… Talk to me about your pre-production process when prepping a film.
MN: For instance on *20 Feet From Stardom,* and I've done this on many films. *20 Feet* was an interesting one. I start by putting together a soundtrack. Like with Hank Williams, I put together a 35 song playlist that helped tell his story in his own words: an autobiography from song. And that became a kind of map on how to tell his story in film.

For *20 Feet,* from the day I started talking to my producer Gil Friesen about it. What do you think about backup singing in popular music, and off the top of my head I could only think about six songs as I was driving home that first day talking about it. By the very nature of backup you're not supposed to pay attention to their voices necessarily. You're not supposed to think about them. So that documentary was a process of re-training my ear to suddenly be listening to the background not the foreground. And I started collecting songs.

I assembled a couple of CD's worth of songs that I wanted to use. I ended up collecting hundreds of songs. And I started finding backup vocals in songs I knew very well but had never thought of in that context.

To this day I listen to songs differently because of making that film. Now I always notice backup vocals. So the process is sort of letting the music lead the way so that I can bathe in it and let it seep in, listen to the songs, the lyrics and the tone, and I can add more. There's part of it just like making a mix tape. It starts to send you in a certain direction I do in music films. And I find it really helpful.

One of my main points about music documentaries is that music films should be about music. Which is to say if you're making a film about somebody who made great music, let's actually hear and understand and feel that music. Let's not just play it in the background. Let's use the music to help tell the story as much as we possibly can.

The second thing is that it has to be about more than the music, which is music as the Trojan Horse to tell a deeper story. But let music be the material in which you build it.

**Morgan Neville directing the four-part series *Shangri-La*
(Photo courtesy of Tremelo Productions)**

HK: What is the secret of working with people and getting the best interview? Extracting information that informs the film?

MN: In one word: Listening. I listen very hard. What that means is when I'm talking to somebody I'm really not there with a list of questions. I'm there trying to have the deepest conversation that I can have with somebody and I'm really paying attention to what they are saying. And engaged and asking questions that come from those conversations. So, the interviews may not go the direction I want them to go but I'd rather have that happen than have me feel I have to hit a bunch of questions. The longer I do this to me it's more about listening hard.

HK: Let's discuss the editing phase on production work you've done.
MN: It's all about the editing. In a Hollywood film you'll write a script and shoot a movie. In documentaries you shoot a movie and then you write a script. So to me it's about the editing.

For *Troubadours* I had a history with Carole King because of the 2001 Brill Building documentary, *Hitmakers: The Teens Who Stole Pop Music*.

I'm a storyteller of course, but I'm interested in other storytellers. So I feel that part of my job is getting the most interesting people to share the most important thoughts and memories and then entrusting me to share those with the world. That's a pretty great job. But there is a sense of responsibility. I know when I put something to a film that this is how a person is going to be perceived in the popular consciousness.

And I know somebody like Carole King, people come up to her every day and tell her how important her music was. She might appreciate that, but it does not start a conversation. It ends a conversation. With my *Hitmakers: The Teens Who Stole Pop Music* it showed that kids had the opportunity to be creative. It was largely about teenagers being empowered to write songs for teenagers. Young people being given an opportunity to be as creative as they could possibly be.

There's a funny story regarding *Troubadours* you would appreciate. Lou Adler is sort of the "heavy" in that film. He opened the Roxy Theater after warring with Doug Weston of the Troubadour. And Lou wasn't particularly happy about that on screen.

In *20 Feet From Stardom* I wanted to interview him again and he was angry. And I was trying to tell Merry Clayton's story, and Lou had really been a champion and protector of Merry her whole career. And Lou said to me, "You didn't make me look very good in *Troubadours*." "Yea, but in that story you were the villain. In this one you're the hero." "OK." And he did the interview. *laughs.*

HK: I really dug your *Keith Richards: Under The Influence* film. What was the genesis of that collaboration?

MN: As to why Keith did the documentary, Jane Rose his manager called me and said "Keith is working on some music, and we're gonna have to do some kind of video. Will you come and interview Keith so we'll have some videotape to do something to promote the album." And I said, "Of course! I'd love to interview Keith."

So to do that I brought a hundred albums on vinyl that I had curated of songs by Muddy Waters, Little Walter, Hank Williams and Buck Owens. That was the first day of shooting. For the first 90 minutes or longer, two hours, I brought a turntable, some records, and "let's talk about records and play them." And Keith had such a good time he said, "Come back next week we'll do it again." He enjoyed that. It just snowballed from there.

As I've said before, it's not about forcing something to be something. But let it be what it wants to be. Listen. He's been asked a lot of questions about Mick his entire life. He doesn't get asked about Little Walter very often, you know. It was a chance for him to talk about things he wanted to talk about. And that opened him up. But it was really the listening that got him excited about it.

The interesting and specific thing about the Keith documentary, I felt like I had prepared for that interview for 25 years. I made films about country music, blues, soul and the Brill Building I felt that my interviews with Keith were decades of knowledge. It was the interview that I was preparing for my whole life, because it was my fandom of music. And I think the thing Keith and I could connect over is that we were both fans of this music. And in a way I feel like part of what that film is about is that rock stars could be fans and have their own rock stars. That they look up to somebody in the same way that somebody looks up to them. And I think that was a great way to approach those interviews. It's not what you're putting on them. It's about what you guys share in common.

HK: I love your *Respect Yourself: The Stax Records Story*.

MN: It has a link to the Brill Building documentary in the sense that Stax Records was about opening a studio in South Memphis and letting the kids in the neighborhood like David Porter, Isaac Hayes and Booker T. Jones come in and make music. The moment where somebody created a moment and situation where young people could come and do the best creative work they were capable of. They were challenged and they rose to that challenge. Just a great story of these people who ended up writing music that scored a popular culture for many years. But it's such an unlikely story.

HK: I learned so much about the backstory of Stax. The label never received media coverage and attention like Motown. I don't really mean to compare them. I worship both labels.

MN: I really think Stax is one of the rare stories where the music is as amazing as the story. Everything about Stax is a big story with big characters. And, it's about race in America the sixties and seventies. But the music is freaking good!

If I'm picking music I'll pick Stax over Motown any day. I started to learn about Stax through Peter Guralnick. Reading his stuff and becoming friends with him. I did a documentary with Peter about Sam Philips and Sun Records. Through Peter I got to know Robert Gordon. We did a Muddy Waters documentary and I started spending a lot of time in Memphis. And Stax was like the great untold story of popular music in the South to my mind. It had all the elements. It was like a Greek tragedy with an amazing soundtrack. It took a couple of years to get that film made.

HK: What do your documentaries reveal to you after viewing the finished results?

MN: The other thing oddly that I noticed about a lot of my music documentaries is that I tend to be more interested in songwriters and producers than I am in artists and performing artists. Part of that is that I'm a sucker for a creative process. Somebody who is great at what they do and is the thing understanding that the thing that gets me most excited. It's not about the great concert. What is the story behind the person who architected this song, this album or this movement, and those are the stories that I'm generally drawn towards.

HK: Now there's a constant demand for music documentaries: Netflix and Hulu, streaming library services, HBO, EPIX, Showtime, and YouTube, as well as the career retrospective or victory lap documentaries on recording artists in all genres. Plus the ever-emerging corporate sponsored film festivals that showcase premieres where distribution deals are made.

MN: Without a doubt, a lot of artists now view documentaries as like a capstone. Tell their story in a flattering way that kind of puts them into a context that helps sell catalog. In a way, my favorite documentaries are the ones that aren't actually about the artist.

20 Feet From Stardom, the great thing about that film was nobody had any agency in that film, including the backup singers. Normally when you make a film about a big famous band or artist they've got a music publisher, a record label, manager, and agent. Making a film about backup singers, there was nobody. Good or bad, it's a lot harder to get a film like that made. Because who is the audience for that? But I think the reward of it is that we made exactly the film we wanted to make. People were just happy we were telling the story.

The Brill Building film I made was like that. Lots of artists, but it was a tapestry of many artists, and none of them had any input whatsoever.

HK: Tell me about the current world for documentary filmmakers.
MN: Making documentaries today, it's gotten more expensive without a doubt. Record labels and other rights holders realized they could charge more money for these things. Catalog departments at record labels became profit centers. Suddenly, the rates went way up. Personally it's gotten easier. I just have a lot more experience, and I think I know how to get there faster. But also, if you've done enough work, the people know what you do, and you don't have to build so much time building trust. There's a kind of buy-in. At this point of my career, if someone wants to work with me, they have to give me my independence to make it. *laughs.*

HK: Do you have any theories about how and why there is an increase of music documentaries getting made? Is it the new platforms and venues for exhibition? What about trends and marketplace? I'm seeing records labels like Warner Music Group being one of the producers on documentaries, like 2020's *Laurel Canyon: A Place In Time.* I was a consultant on it. Polygram Entertainment/UMG just did the Go-Go's.
MN: Yes. It's also that era of music where music had the greatest cultural influence. It's not just that the music was good. It was that the music was defining a generation of people. I know that all sounds cliché, but politics, fashion, aesthetics, everything of that generation was defined by the music that never happened before or since.

I think music can be very popular and influential, but it was truly a symbiotic moment where the music was the very restitution of what was happening.

Trends. Record labels serving as producers on some music documentaries. The big labels, Warner Music Group, Sony Music, Universal Music, and BMG, all have very actively started pursuing actual music documentary production. Universal initiated the Amy Winehouse documentary, the Kurt Cobain documentary and the Velvet

Underground documentary Tom Hanks [and Playtone] is making right now. So now the labels are doing this stuff themselves so they can make real money. Music documentary content I think is going to be the future more than ever. I think it's a very mixed message. Good things can come out of that, and some very unhealthy things can come out of that.

HK: Let's speak about your 2018 documentary *Won't You Be My Neighbor* about television host Fred Rogers. You moved away a little bit from the music documentary.

MN: *Won't You Be My Neighbor* was not a music documentary but Fred Rogers had links to music. In a way it's a music documentary. He majored in composition in college. He wrote over 200 songs. There's a musicality to him that I also connected with. On the surface it wasn't a music film, but it was a vital component in the story telling.

HK: How has winning an Oscar impacted your career?

MN: It just helped me make the films I want to make. It has helped with funding. I think I used to spend 60 per cent of my time raising money. Now I spend four per cent of my time raising money. *laughs.* That has been the biggest impact. It certainly legitimizes you.

I always say I'm the same filmmaker after I won the Oscar as I was before. *laughs.* It's not that I became a better filmmaker because I won an Oscar. But if it makes people feel that way, fine. Let them feel that way, *laughs.* If it helps me get films made, then that's great.

RUMBLE:
The Indians Who Rocked the World

I'm blowing the shofar ram's horn for *RUMBLE: The Indians Who Rocked the World.* The dazzling feature documentary from Montreal, Canada-based Rezolution Pictures about the role of Native Americans in popular music history.

In *RUMBLE,* director and Rezolution co-founder Catherine Bainbridge and co-director and director of photography Alfonso Maiorana examine the journey of Native Americans on record and stage. They expose a critical and profound missing chapter, revealing how indigenous musicians helped influence culture.

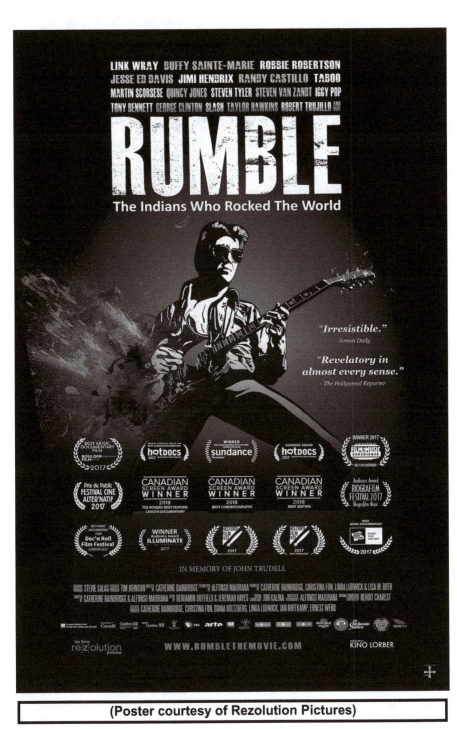

(Poster courtesy of Rezolution Pictures)

| **Catherine Bainbridge**
(Courtesy of Rezolution Pictures) | **Alfonso Maiorana**
(Courtesy of Rezolution Pictures) |

RUMBLE Executive Producers: Stevie Salas (Apache) Tim Johnson (Mohawk); Catherine Bainbridge; Christina Fon; Linda Ludwick; and Ernest Webb (Cree).

Producers: Christina Fon; Catherine Bainbridge; Lisa Ludwick; and Lisa M. Roth.

The on-screen participants in *RUMBLE* are a list of music artists, historians, family members, and experts who acknowledge Native musicians who helped shape the soundtracks of their lives: Buffy Sainte-Marie; Robbie Robertson; Martin Scorsese; Tony Bennett; Steven Tyler; Iggy Pop; Buddy Guy; Taj Mahal; Cyril Neville; John Trudell, Steven Van Zandt, Corey Harris, Jesse Ed Davis, Alvin Youngblood Hart; David Fricke; Guy Davis; Monk Boudreaux; Quincy Jones; Jackson Browne; Joy Harjo; as well as Pat Vegas (Redbone); Wayne Kramer (MC5); Slash (Guns 'N' Roses); Dan Auerbach (The Black Keys); Marky Ramone (The Ramones); Taylor Hawkins (Foo Fighters); Pura Fe Crescioni (Ulali); Rhiannon Giddens (Carolina Chocolate Drops); Mike Inez (Alice in Chains); George Clinton; Robert Trujillo (Metallica); and Taboo (Black Eyed Peas).

Native Americans Stevie Salas and Tim Johnson served as key consultants on the film as well as executive producers, and Christina Fon, was the lead executive producer/producer with Catherine Bainbridge, as Bainbridge and Neil Diamond previously helmed the Peabody award-winning Reel Injun about the representations of Native Americans in Hollywood movies.

Exec Producer Tim Johnson, Musician Marky Ramone, Exec Producer Stevie Salas (photo courtesy of Rezolution Pictures)

The press notes for *RUMBLE* offer additional information about the film. "Many artists and musical forms played a role in the creation of rock, but arguably no single piece of music was more influential than the 1958 instrumental "Rumble" by American Indian rock guitarist and singer/songwriter Link Wray.

"Rumble" was the first song to use distortion and feedback. It introduced the rock power chord — and was one of the very few instrumental singles to be banned from the radio for fear it would incite violence. *RUMBLE* explores how the Native American influence is an integral part of music history, despite attempts to ban, censor, and erase Indian culture in the United States. As *RUMBLE* reveals, the early pioneers of the blues had Native as well as African American roots, and one of the first and most influential jazz singers' voices was trained on Native American songs. As the folk rock era took hold in the 60s and 70s, Native Americans helped to define its evolution. Father of the Delta Blues Charley Patton, influential jazz singer Mildred Bailey, metaphysical guitar wizard Jimi Hendrix, and folk heroine Buffy Sainte-Marie are among the many music greats who have Native American heritage and have made their distinctive mark on music history.

Martin Scorsese (Photo courtesy of Rezolution Pictures)

"When recalling Link Wray's shivering guitar classic, 'Rumble,' Martin Scorsese marvels, "It is the sound of that guitar . . . that aggression."

For the most part, their Indian heritage was unknown. *RUMBLE* uses playful re-creations and little-known stories, alongside concert footage, archives and interviews. The stories of these iconic Native musicians are told by some of America's greatest music legends who knew them, played music with them, and were inspired by them: everyone from Buddy Guy, Quincy Jones, and Tony Bennett to Iggy Pop, Steven Tyler, and Stevie Van Zandt. *RUMBLE* shows how Indigenous music was part of the very fabric of American popular music from the beginning, but that the Native American contribution was left out of the story – until now."

RUMBLE earned a Sundance special jury award for "masterful storytelling," and multiple awards around the world. The movie had its US theatrical premiere at Film Forum in New York. I saw *RUMBLE* in West Los Angeles at the Landmark Nuart Theatre.

The film's title comes from the 1958 hit instrumental single "Rumble" by Link Ray & His Ray Men issued on Archie Blyer's Cadence label. Wray, born to a Shawnee mother in North Carolina, was a major guitar influence on Jeff Beck, Pete Townshend, Jimmy Page, and many others. In the documentary *It Might Get Loud*, Page describes hearing "Rumble" as a turning point in his own love of the guitar.

Link Wray 1970s (Photo by Bruce Steinway, courtesy of linkwray.com)

" 'Rumble' had the power to push me over the edge," stressed Iggy Pop.

"That was the rawest form of the kind of guitar that all of the guys that I listened to, that's where it started," confessed Slash of Guns 'N Roses, while Steven Van Zandt of Bruce Springsteen & the E Street Band recollected, "Here comes Link Wray with the theme song of juvenile delinquency...I'm not surprised it was banned."

Further testimony is supplied by the MC5's Wayne Kramer, "He was one of the first that really had a tone that pointed the way to the future."

"There might not be a Who, were there no Link Wray; there might not be a Jeff Beck Group, were there no Link Wray; there might not be a Led Zeppelin, if there were no Link Wray," summarized Taylor Hawkins of the Foo Fighters.

"Rumble" has since been heard in Quentin Tarantino's *Pulp Fiction* and in the surf documentary *Riding Giants,* directed by Stacy Peralta. It's also been used in the HBO television show *The Sopranos* and additional movies, including *Independence Day* and *Blow.*

"In *RUMBLE*, for the first time a film reveals a fascinating, and until now unknown, influence on the formation of rock and roll," explained Bainbridge and Maiorana in their Director's statement press notes.

"The music has become a part of who we are. We are so honoured to be able to tell this story about the influence of iconic Native American musicians speak of how these icons were an influence, you listen! Native American music – born of this land – was violently suppressed for many years as both American and Canadian governments outlawed Native ceremonies and rituals in a deliberate attempt to break the people.

"As a result, the music was forced underground and found its expression in alternative ways. It is important to note that the primary drivers in the creation of blues and jazz and therefore rock were African Americans, but Native Americans, like Europeans, also played a part.

"We feel that it is important for everyone, and especially Native youth who have so few pop culture role models, to have proof, through the icons we feature and the famous people that give our story credibility, that indigenous cultures were an integral part of the evolution of popular music. The truth that we want to expose in *RUMBLE* is that the attempted erasure of Native American people, their culture, and their music, didn't work. As Robbie Robertson said in one of our interviews with him, 'You wouldn't let me talk about it before, well now I'm going to talk real loud'."

Exec Producer Tim Johnson, Singer Tony Bennett, Producer-Director Catherine Bainbridge, and Exec Producer Stevie Salas (Photo courtesy of Rezolution Pictures)

"One can't help but notice the rhythms of—or the pulse that was here, that is here; been here. The feel of Native American is in a lot of rock 'n' roll," suggested George Clinton. "It's interesting how much the Native American element just filters through," offered Martin

Scorsese, while Joy Harjo, a Muscogee-Creek musician and poet added, "Our peoples were part of the origin story of blues and jazz and rock of American music, but we're left out of the story consistently from the beginning."

During *RUMBLE*, half-Jewish, half-Mohawk, Robbie Robertson, co-founder of The Band, reflected in an interview, "My real guitar lessons were at the Six Nations Indian Reserve in Ontario. All my cousins, uncles – everybody -- seemed like they could play an instrument. If you considered yourself a real rock 'n' roll guitar player, you had to learn 'Rumble.' It was raw and dirty, and had that rebellious spirit to it."

Steven Van Zandt Photo courtesy of Rezolution Pictures

The influence of the Native American has never been lost on musician/actor/producer, Steven Van Zandt, whose production company is named Renegade Nation. Van Zandt further cited the impact of Robertson and The Band, whose commercially successful roots-music groundbreaking sound emerged in 1968 after a 1966 world tour backing Bob Dylan and *1967 Basement Tapes* recording sessions with Dylan.

"The entire industry got right back to song writing, and Robbie Robertson, one of the great songwriters of all time, had effectuated that change by his own sensibility and The Band's sensibility."

A highlight of *RUMBLE* for me was seeing Coalinga, California-born Pat Vasquez, of Pat & Lolly Vegas fame. In the sixties, they were booked all over Hollywood at clubs like Gazzari's and the Haunted House and appearing on the '60s television series *Shindig!* They had the hippest wardrobe on the Sunset Strip and were patrons of the Beau Gentry menswear shop. In 1967, singer P.J. Proby had a Top 30 national hit single with "Niki Hokey," penned by the Vegas brothers with Jim Ford. In 1968. Jimi Hendrix, himself part Cherokee, Negro and Scot, told Pat and Lolly to form an all-Native American rock group. "Do the Indian thing, man."

Jimi used to go to Thee Experience club in Hollywood on Sunset Blvd. where Pat and Lolly jammed a lot. Hendrix loved playing with the Vegas brothers. One night they were on stage with Jimi, who announced, "Damn, you guys are hot! You've got to form a group. This is the group right here!"

They became Redbone, which is a Cajun term describing a mixed-race person. Pat and Lolly were of Mexican, Yaqui and Shoshone descent. Two other Native Americans joined them, Tony Bellamy and Pete DePoe. Redbone signed to Epic Records and had a hit single in 1974 with "Come and Get Your Love" followed by "We Were All Wounded at Wounded Knee" and "The Witch Queen of New Orleans."

"They couldn't believe it: here they are, these four Indians," marveled Pat, "with, you know, garb and moccasins and—and all the things that they've seen in films, actually playing rock!"

RUMBLE concludes with film footage of the ongoing Native American protests at the Dakota Access Pipeline site in North Dakota and a performance by Cree singer/songwriter and activist Buffy Sainte-Marie ("Bury My Heart at Wounded Knee"). Her core work has always focused on Native American social issues. Buffy's 1964 composition "Universal Soldier" was initially covered by Glen Campbell and Donovan.

The idea for *RUMBLE* was spurred by Canadian writer Brian Wright-McLeod's book *The Encyclopedia of Native American Music,* which is an anthology of Native musicians and included Stevie Salas (Apache), a renowned guitarist and music producer who has played with some of the most famous rock stars in the world. Stevie went on to collaborate with Tim Johnson (Mohawk), then Associate Director for Museum Programs at the National Museum of the American Indian, on the creation of an exhibit called *Up Where We Belong: Native Musicians in Popular Culture*, for the Smithsonian Institution.

Both the book and the exhibit inspired the film *RUMBLE: The Indians Who Rocked the World.*

Buffy Sainte-Marie Photo courtesy of Rezolution Pictures

James Cushing: "America — it's an Indian thing' (Allen Ginsberg, quoted in the film *Road Scholar* by Andre Codrescu).

"What didn't you do to bury me? But you forgot that I was a seed" (Greek poet Dinos Christianopolis, b. 1931).

"American popular music is a source of pride and joy; American genocide of the First Nations people is a source of shame and sorrow. *RUMBLE: The Indians Who Rocked the World* is the only document about the intersection of these powerful forces.

"Filled with strong interviews and shocking archival footage, *RUMBLE* restores American music's greater context. Its story is both tragic and life-affirming... like the real blues."

Celeste Goyer: "When I met Russell Means on the set of a movie filming in the mountains above Los Angeles in 1997, I had not yet read *Where White Men Fear to Tread*, his hair-raising autobiography. I had not yet been saddened and scandalized by the open hatred of many whites toward the Paiute-Shoshone in Bishop, California, where I lived for five years. Fear of the wild continues to drive racism and environmental destruction in this country and beyond. *RUMBLE: The Indians Who Rocked the World* arrives in wonderful contrast to that immensely damaging, limiting fear. Wildness has not only been always welcomed by rock and roll and other rhythm music, it was built on it. Thanks to the filmmakers for this essential contribution."

In 1964, I was introduced to the history and plight of Native Americans when Johnny Cash recorded *Bitter Tears: Ballads of the American Indian*, his Native Americans concept album. I then heard Cash do "The Ballad of Ira Hayes," written by folk musician and songwriter Peter La Farge, which detailed the life of Hayes, the Pima Indian and US Marine who is one of the servicemen captured in the iconic photo of the flag-raising on Iwo Jima.

Cash sent out personal letters and copies of his 45rpm recording of La Farge's "The Ballad of Ira Hayes" from *Bitter Tears*, after Johnny purchased a thousand of them from Columbia Records and mailed the entire batch to every radio station in the country. It eventually landed at number three on the *Billboard* Country Singles chart in 1964.

In February 1965, Cash performed "The Ballad of Ira Hayes" on a Los Angeles television program, *The Les Crane Show*.

Cash toured Wounded Knee, South Dakota with descendants of the survivors of the 1890 massacre, played songs from the LP at a benefit performance at Cemetery Hill for the tribe and helped the Sioux raise money for schools. This is four years before AIM, the *American Indian Movement* civil rights organization was founded in Minneapolis, Minnesota.

I became aware of Buffy Sainte-Marie when she was a guest on Johnny Cash's 1969-1971 ABC-TV show and sang Peter La Farge's "Custer." In 1985, I met her. I was living with a keyboardist who did European live shows with Buffy and played synthesizer on some film scores with her arranger/composer husband, Jack Nitzche. A few years earlier, Jack had seen Link Wray do a set in Hollywood at the Whisky a Go Go and raved at length about his show to me. In 1963 Nitzsche cut an instrumental version of "Rumble" that Jimmy Bowen produced for the Reprise label.

We all went out on a double date one evening to the Comedy Store in Hollywood, where Jack put together a band and the musicians performed for a Free Leonard Peltier benefit.

Buffy subsequently introduced me to her friend, Santee Dakota poet John Trudell, the political activist and poet, who in the '70s served as chairman of the American Indian Movement.

In 1986, I produced a spoken word event with Trudell and Jello Biafra of the Dead Kennedys at McCabe's Guitar Shop. The room was packed for this inspiring uncensored verbal platform of Indian and punk tongue. Later in '86 I presented a show with Trudell and Kiowa/ Comanche guitarist Jesse Ed Davis at Be Bop Records in Reseda. That century, I also met and interviewed musician, actor, author, and Indian rights activist, Russell Means, who played Chingachgook in Michael Mann's 1992 epic, *The Last of the Mohicans.*

In 2017, the John Trudell Archives, (a 501c3 charity) along with Inside Recordings just re-issued Trudell's AKA Grafitti Man in a partnership with Rhino Records, both digitally and on LP. The re-release is dedicated in honor of both John Trudell's life, along with his late musical partner, Jesse Ed Davis, who was the first person to put music to John's words.

Steven Tyler of Aerosmith also praised guitarist Jesse Ed Davis. "I particularly fell in love with Jesse Ed Davis, because he was with Taj Mahal and Taj's album is what spurred me to rock more that touched something inside me."

"In 1964, I got word that Mike Seeger, of the New Lost City Ramblers, was coming to the west coast for a rare solo tour," remembered multi-instrumentalist Chris Darrow.

"It was a chance to meet my idol and speak to him, face to face. Our bluegrass band, the Re-Organized Dry City Players, opened for him at the Meeting Place in Upland, and we had a wonderful night of music. Genius guitar player Clarence White, who would later join the Byrds, showed up with Buffy Sainte-Marie to see the show and brought a few of his band mates from the Kentucky Colonels with him. It was a night I will never forget. Buffy even gave me one of her tortoise shell flat picks!

"I first met Jesse Ed Davis in Claremont during 1966. John Ware had a band, and I had a band, the Floggs, and he needed a bass player for a gig at Pomona College. I sat in with John's group that day. John played guitar in those days, not drums, as he did later with Corvettes, Linda Ronstadt, Emmylou Harris and Mike Nesmith. He was raving about this guitar player from Oklahoma that was going to play with us. He and John Selk had been in a high school band together, where John had been the drummer. Levon Helm had been his teacher. We waited for a long time for this guy to arrive...minutes passed and then with less than 5 minutes till show time, this 1962 Chevy 4 Door drove up to the back door with throbbing mufflers. This Indian guy, with bangs, gets out of the car, wearing an 'RF' sweatshirt on with the sleeves cut off. Doesn't say a word, just goes behind the car and goes to the opposite side of the car and pulls a Telecaster out of the rear seat...with no case. He just walks up the steps, said hi to John, plugged into an amp already set up, and lo and behold, he was the best guitar player I had ever heard at the time.

"I first met Nik Venet in 1967 on Dick Clark's *American Bandstand,* while I was in the Dirt Band. He was the record producer for Linda Ronstadt, who was performing her new record on the show. Nik produced Linda's hit, 'Different Drum.' It was my first introduction to Linda, and I was deeply impressed both by her voice and her beauty.

"Nik and I were both interested in the Native American culture. My wife's uncle ran a trading post on the Navajo reservation in New Mexico, south of Farmington. Her family had been interested in American Indian art for years. We both collected rugs and ceramics as well as artifacts of the Native Americans.

"Later on, Nik got highly involved in the politics of the Native American Indian and worked to raise money for imprisoned Native American activist Leonard Peltier and was friendly with Russell Means. I played at a benefit at Doug Weston's Troubadour in West Hollywood to help raise money for Leonard. John York and I performed as a duet for another benefit at El Cholo.

"After the Troubadour show, Venet presented me with a surprise gift. There had been a beautiful Navajo rug on the stage that we all performed around.

"Nik picked up the rug and said, 'Here, I'd like you to have this, Chris. Both Russell Means and Leonard Peltier have wrapped themselves in this blanket.'

"I look at this rug every day and think of Nik," lamented Darrow. "He died of cancer in 1998."

Chris Darrow left us in 2020. A memorial was held in Claremont, California, where the blanket was displayed.

Insider Stories of the Evolution of the NBC *Elvis '68 Comeback Special*

Singer/actor Elvis Presley during 1967 was looking for a new spiritual and melodic road map. During this period, Elvis Presley had visited Self-Realization Fellowship center on Sunset Boulevard, near the Pacific Coast Highway in Southern California and devoured *Autobiography of a Yogi* from Paramahansa Yogananda.

The Capricorn seeker also had a friendship with Daya Mata of the SRF retreat in the Mt. Washington area in East Hollywood. Presley had read Aldous Huxley's *The Doors of Perception.*

Jerry Schilling is the author (with Chuck Crisafulli) of *Me and a Guy Named Elvis.* Jerry was a longtime insider/adviser and trusted Presley employee. In 2008 I interviewed Schilling.

(Courtesy of SOFA Entertainment)

"Elvis was a seeker," described Schilling. "He did go to the Bodhi Tree [spiritual book store in West Hollywood that opened in 1970]. A part of our group that did not like that. I was in the minority with Larry Geller. Elvis was open to show a spiritual and vulnerable side. He was into that. What I loved about it was that through his spiritual quest, I got to know the man even deeper. We would go to SRF in Pacific Palisades and Mt. Washington in East Hollywood many times.

"There were years when Elvis didn't get a hit record. It was hard for Elvis because he knew that it wasn't that he couldn't do it. It wasn't that there wasn't material out there. It was that he wasn't having access to it. He started listening to country music."

In Spring, 1967, Elvis wasn't making any personal appearances but he did allow his guitar to be displayed at the Popular Music Exhibit

69

in the special section of the US Pavilion, The American Spirit, at Expo 67, Montreal's Universal Exhibition, which was a world's fair held during April 27-October 29, 1967. That guitar is the instrument Elvis recorded "Heartbreak Hotel" with and was played at the time of his national television debut. Hundreds of teenagers welcomed the instrument upon arrival in Canada at the Montreal Airport. Presley's guitar shared the location with items of the Grateful Dead, Jefferson Airplane, Tiny Tim, the Tokens, the Supremes, Petula Clark, the Seekers, and Thelonious Monk.

"In December, 1967, Nancy Sinatra called and encouraged us to see her TV special, *Movin' With Nancy*," Schilling remembered. "We had a fine time watching her special. Elvis and Nancy did the movie *Speedway*, and I was his stand-in, and Nancy's cousin was her stand-in, Elvis started getting some calls from Frank Sinatra.

"Frank Sinatra really got who Elvis was at that point. I mean, he got it in 1960, and did the TV special when Elvis came back from the army. He got it musically. There became a real Presley and Sinatra bonding. I remember one time we were on tour and Frank got in touch with Elvis, 'Is there any way I can help out here?' Elvis appreciated the call."

It had been nearly six years since "Good Luck Charm" had topped the *Billboard* 100. Elvis hadn't been on the small screen since *The Frank Sinatra Timex Show* for ABC television, welcoming him back from the service in May 1960.

Presley's manager Col. Tom Parker negotiated a deal from NBC-TV's Tom Sarnoff. Colonel Parker was then introduced to television director, Steve Binder, who, with his partner, engineer/music producer Bones Howe, set Elvis off on a personal journey that bordered on a career resurrection.

Steve Binder is a Los Angeles native who left the University of Southern California just before graduating to apprentice under Steve Allen, whose pioneering variety show broadcast was a hothouse of innovation and imagination.

Binder, barely in his twenties, then took the helm of *Jazz Scene, USA* and later *Hullabaloo*, bringing live performances by musical masters to a network audience. Binder understood the unique requirements of lighting and blocking that showcased musicians in an optimal setting.

In October, 1964, Binder directed *The TAMI Show*, a seismic rock 'n' roll event hosted by Jan & Dean and starring James Brown, the

Rolling Stones, the Beach Boys, Chuck Berry, Lesley Gore, the Miracles, and Marvin Gaye, among many others.

In the coming decades, Binder would have a long and distinguished career in the television and film industry becoming an Emmy award winner for *Barry Manilow,* and a Golden Globe nominee for *Diana Ross in Central Park.* He has served on the Producers Guild of America Board of Directors and for many years was an adjunct professor at the University of Southern California Cinema and Television School.

In 1965 Bob Finkel of NBC had recruited Binder to direct their weekly pop music series, *Hullabaloo.* By 1967 TV specials featuring Leslie Uggams and Petula Clark solidified his reputation. Finkel, Colonel Parker, with the team of Binder and sonic wizard Bones Howe, collectively agreed that their Presley program would be a one-man show, no guest stars, and RCA Records would have a soundtrack album for retail outlets.

Engineer Dayton "Bones" Howe arrived to Los Angeles from Georgia in 1956, prompted by a suggestion from drummer Shelly Manne. Howe landed work at the mixing console at Radio Recorders, as tape recordist under engineer Thorne Nogar on some of the young Presley's breakthrough hits. Over the next decade and a half, Bones Howe became one of the most celebrated engineers in the music industry, generating a parade of big hit records from Jan & Dean, Johnny Rivers, and the Mamas and the Papas. Near the end of the sixties, Howe became a producer and regularly on the charts with the Association, Fifth Dimension, and the Turtles.

"The first time I saw Elvis was at the Florida Theater in Sarasota, when I was in high school. He was a young country singer. He performed between movies," Howe told me in a 2012 interview. "I first did some work with Elvis in late 1956 and early '57 in Hollywood at Radio Recorders.

"Elvis drove out from Tennessee in a stretch Cadillac, with DJ and Scotty with the gear in the backseat. They came out to record with Steve Sholes, the A&R guy who was responsible for signing them on to RCA Records. He brought them to Hollywood to record. RCA was doing all their recording in those days at Radio Recorders. Elvis and the guys stayed in Hollywood at the Roosevelt Hotel or the Plaza and later the Knickerbocker. I did some sessions with Thorne Nogar. He was very good to me and took me under his arm. I was a recordist, and he asked me to do some sessions with Elvis. Elvis could never get his name right so he called him Stoney.

71

"In Hollywood, I saw Elvis with his buddies. It was the first time anyone ever heard of block booking a studio for a month. We never had to tear it down. We could leave the studio at night. I worked on 'Love Me' and 'Old Shep.' I was around the session for 'Return to Sender.' Elvis never stopped moving in the studio. He recorded everything live. In those days you didn't separate people so everyone was in the same room. Direct to mono when we started. The two-track that we did on Elvis had his voice on one track and everybody else on the other track. When we started with Elvis, there was no stereo.

"He could sing a ballad. He could imitate anybody. Mention a singer and he would imitate them. Like Fats Domino. You would turn your back and you thought Fats was in the room," noted Howe.

"Elvis would come in with Hill & Range music publishers, and Elvis would record only their songs. They would show up with a box of acetate dubs and my job on those sessions, aside of running the tape machines, was that I had a turntable, which was hooked up to the playback system. I would take these dubs out one at a time and put them on a turntable and play it outside to him. Elvis would signal to me like running his finger across his throat if he didn't like the song and I would toss it to another box. Or he would pat the top of his head, meaning from the top again. 'Play it again.' And the guys would learn the song off the demo. There it all was for me. All in a nutshell: Demo, artist, song, record.

"The Colonel never came to the studio," added Bones. "Maybe once to get some papers signed. Elvis ran the session and Steve Sholes ran the clock. 'OK, Elvis. That's 2:14.' 'Sounded good in here. Want to listen?' Radio Recorders had the wonderful echo chamber in Studio B. A live chamber in those days. Not tape reverb. I watched Elvis become a huge star."

"I always was convinced that on those 1950s sessions after leaving Sun (before the Army, then all that soundtrack work in the 60s), Elvis basically 'produced' himself," marvels to this day King worshipper Gary Pig Gold. "An amazing feat for a young kid back then working for gigantic RCA, right?!! How he ever pulled that off and so successfully too, is still quite unbelievable."

"Elvis and I hit it off," beamed director Steve Binder in an interview we conducted in 2008. "I didn't feel like the awestruck audience to a super star—just another guy my age. And we hit it off as friends when we were working. He'd come to the office I shared with Bones on Sunset Boulevard every day. Everyone on the team was treated equally, and Elvis joined us in that spirit. He did not play star one day on the entire shoot. We all got to pick the music.

"My TV special before with Petula Clark and Harry Belafonte was done at the same location at NBC in Burbank. I used John Freschi and Bill Cole who were on staff there as lighting director and audio head, set designer Gene MacAvoy, musical director and composer Billy Goldenberg and worked with Bones Howe. By the time we got to Elvis we had a family.

"I told Elvis in no uncertain words I was not going to do 20 Christmas songs," mandated Binder. "Elvis told me he was scared to death of television. He told me he was only comfortable makin' records. He had been away from the public and was concerned they didn't want him back. I told him 'then why don't you make a record album and I'll put pictures to it.'"

Writers Chris Bearde and Allan Blye were hired to develop the show's script. The duo were veterans of *Rowan & Martin's Laugh-In* and *The Smothers Brothers Comedy Hour*.

Billy Goldenberg had worked with Binder on the television show *Hullabaloo*. "From the very first meeting I liked him," Goldenberg said in a 2008 phone conversation. "We had a great rapport. He always looked after me and was supportive. The most interesting thing to me once we started was the concept that developed.

"There was a movie soundtrack by Quincy Jones, *In Cold Blood*, probably the most interesting score I had ever heard at that point. It was a fusion of that kind of country redneck sound but at the same time something very classical underneath it all. Evil, sexual, and spooky, Elvis personified all of those things. And the music had to.

"This was like a film that had to be scored. The first thing I did was build a big medley around 'Guitar Man.' that was the test, actually. I went with that whole concept sequence—trying to make it as dirty and black and provocative and still being Elvis. We had the presence of those guitars that were very dark. His voice invited you into the arrangements. I wanted it all to be seductive, because Elvis was the ultimate seducer. A starting point was definitely the work of the bass guitar. Once I had that kind of bass thing going on and there was a certain kind of mambo riff with it. It also touched on some of the Beatles' darker stuff."

Keyboardist Don Randi in 1967 and '68 was working with Neil Young and Jack Nitzsche on recording sessions for Buffalo Springfield, and on *Forever Changes* with Love and the Monkees' *Head* soundtrack, when he got a telephone call from Billy Goldenberg.

"I had done some soundtrack things earlier in the sixties with Elvis," recalled Randi in our 2008 interview. "I worked on another Presley film, *Live a Little, Love a Little.* In 1962 Jack Nitzsche was the pianist in the lounge band in an Elvis' film *Girls! Girls! Girls!* Barney Kessel was on that soundtrack and others, and he played guitar earlier on 'Return to Sender' and 'Can't Help Falling in Love With You.'

Don Randi (photo by Henry Diltz)

"That night I got the Elvis call. I remember one thing, it was on a Saturday and we all were making a fortune, double scale, golden time, big time. I know this was a little different for Elvis working with us. Sometimes he sang live with us and sometimes he overdubbed. As a matter of fact, he sat down at the piano with me a few times for me to straighten out the part he had to sing on 'Jailhouse Rock.' We were on the incidental and interstitial music that was all over the soundtrack. He worked with us on the stuff. What's more important than hearing Elvis in headphones is that I got to hear him as a human being, having chats, going back and forth. He had a musicality to him.

"Look, Elvis has innate musical skills. He did not remind me of Brian Wilson or Frank Sinatra. They are all so different, which is a very interesting point. The individuality between those three people are from completely different places. They are all fantastic on their

74

own and rightly so, because they worked that hard creating what they do, and everybody is an individual there.

"I guess we were all taking Elvis into a different world. It was a completely different thing for him from the A band, or the Memphis band. Just having the Blossoms on the sessions. Elvis loved the Blossoms. He knew Darlene from her work with Ray Charles. Elvis was now playing with the Wrecking Crew, Hal Blaine, Tommy Tedesco, Mike Deasy, Tommy Morgan, Chuck Berghoffer, Frank De Vito, and vocal contractor BJ Baker.

"We cut 'A Little Less Conversation' with Al Casey, Hal Blaine, Larry Knechtel, the bass player, and me on piano.

"We all like to hear how our music is being used after we cut it," Don expressed to me. "On 'A Little Less Conversation' I might have made initially $160.00, a Local 47 contract. Over the years, with all the scales changing, and everything being re-done and re-mixed I've made close to ten grand in residuals.

"Let me tell you why. It's a very simple reason and most people don't have any clue. There were a number of people. It started with Phil Spector, then Brian Wilson, and caught on with everybody else, that when you hired us, there was a union contract. So, there was a Local 47 on a contract. And if that contract is there, they can trace it back to who was on the original track. Because of that, we get our residuals. Phil, Brian, and Jack made it possible, because if they could avoid it, they would. But these guys insisted on having these contracts. And because of this we all have residuals and I'm talking to you.

"It's nice at age 72 to get paid and hear these things again. Kim Fowley calls it 'mailbox money.' It's wonderful."

Hal Blaine had already played drums on Presley hits "Can't Help Falling in Love With You," "Return To Sender" and "Bossa Nova Baby."

"The *'68 Special* was a great time. Elvis was terrific and loved us all because a lot of us had worked with him before," reinforced Blaine. "I was on the soundtrack of *Blue Hawaii* and *Girls! Girls! Girls!* 'Hello. How are you doing?' He was relaxed but sweated a lot. I had to hand him a Kleenex when he was wearing that leather suit. Elvis was Elvis, and he was a phenomenon. And that's all there is to it.

"There was a song that we did, and he wanted to show that he had an operatic type voice, just a big voice. To me he was Elvis. That's all

75

there is to it. He was a one off. People who generally become famous are one off. He was also very handsome, and all the ladies were crazy about him. He was a decent guy. The Wrecking Crew could lock in with anybody. But with Elvis, you're gonna sit up a little straighter, maybe. I loved DJ Fontana. I hung with him a lot on the set."

"Elvis decided to literally move into NBC for the period when we were in production," reminisced Binder. "We cleaned out the Dean Martin dressing room off of stage 4.

"When we finished rehearsals, Elvis would start jamming with his friends around the baby grand piano and anybody who happened to be there or invited in started jamming with him. So they would just play acoustically, banging on chairs, piano tops, and Lance LeGault brought his tambourines in. It went on for hours and hours.

"I thought, 'this is like looking into a keyhole of something that only very few people get to see behind the scenes. I've got to get this on tape. I mean, this is better than what we are doing out there with all the dancers and singers, the production numbers. This is incredible; I am seeing the real Elvis now.'

Hal Blaine (Photo by Henry Diltz)

"I was barred from coming into the dressing room with any kind of equipment," disclosed Binder. "I started taking notes and brought my little tape recorder in and started recording what was going on. I kept it in my pocket so nobody knew what was going on. And then I started transferring the information I got onto paper. So I would remember what songs he sang and what he was talking about.

"Finally, I pestered the Colonel so much, he finally said, 'You can go on stage and re-create what you are seeing in here.'

"Then when it came time, I handed Elvis the paper with my notes, which he physically brought out to the stage, and referred to in one of his takes. Right before he went out, I got called into the dressing room.

'I changed my mind. I don't want to do this.' 'What do you mean you don't want to do this?' 'My mind is blank. Steve, I don't know what to sing and don't know what to say.' 'Elvis, just go out. This is not optional. I haven't asked you to do anything up to the point that you didn't want to do. Now I am asking you to go out there. I don't care if you just say hello or goodbye and come right back in five seconds. Just go out there.'

"Something happens when Elvis got to be in front of a live audience," indicated Jerry Schilling. "When Elvis plugs in with Scotty and DJ, I think it's fun. It's what got him into music. It's magical and not thought out. Steve put in Alan Fortas and Charlie Hodge. That just rounded out the whole thing. And Elvis added Lance [LeGault] to the show. He was a friend of ours."

"The best thing about the *'68 Special* is what Binder calls the 'Sit Down improv,'" LeGault mentioned to me in a 2008 interview. "Elvis had a sense of humor. When he says, 'My Boy, My Boy,' that means 'I'm tryin' to think of what the hell we're gonna do next.'

"Here we are in the middle of the stage, girls all around, Priscilla sitting in the stands. But we were not in the middle of a hurricane or microscope. You could have had an audience there or no audience there, or twice the audience, and it had no effect on what we were doing. I didn't notice them at all. You know, when you are on stage with your band, and you're playing whatever tunes you want to play, you are thinking about the running order of the tunes and the groove, and what you are doin' up there. You're not too interested in the audience. If you connect with the audience, you'll know it at the end of the song.

"Elvis was comfortable with us. See, he couldn't go to the cleaners or the car wash. And people think he didn't do anything. Hell man, we rode motorcycles on Sunday. I rode on the outside and he rode on the inside. He had a Harley. We took a lot of Sunday trips and played touch football on Saturdays when I worked Saturday nights."

A highlight of *Elvis Presley The '68 Comeback Special* was "Let Yourself Go," penned by the songwriters Joy Byers and Bob Johnston.
"I wrote 'Let Yourself Go' with Bob. Elvis did that for his ('68) TV special."
Byers told author Ken Sharp, in his book *Writing For The King*. "That was just a feel good, freedom song. After World War II, from

Kerouac and rockabilly onward, that's what it was all about. It was a burst of good feelings in the sixties. It was about freedom, feeling good, and being on the road."

"We were all there late one night in our production office in Hollywood and watched the Robert Kennedy assassination on the TV set," acknowledged writer Chris Bearde.

"We all sat around until 5:00 AM and Elvis told us his entire life story while playing the guitar and picked, not strummed, talkin' about 'Tiger Man,' and how guys would throw punches at him so they could say they hit Elvis. He just rambled on and we listened for all those hours. Part of the conversation went to his background in gospel singing and how he really was one of those white guys from the south who really understood not just his own rockabilly background but the music of the church."

"We were in our office on Sunset Boulevard rehearsing one evening and the television was on in Bones' office and Bobby Kennedy was assassinated," mused Binder. "And we stopped rehearsal and spent the entire night about both the JFK and Robert Kennedy assassination, and Martin Luther King before in April. Those are the kind of things that bond people…

"I was convinced we had to close the show with something powerful. Here we are with a black choreographer, Claude Thompson, a Puerto Rican choreographer, Jaime Rogers, the Blossoms, they are right behind Elvis on his side, and no one is saying anything. No one cares that we are mixing races," confirmed Binder.

"I went to Billy Goldenberg and Earle Brown and said 'Guys you've got to write an original song that says the inner dialogue that we are hearing and feeling about Elvis Presley in these past few months. We've got to make a statement that he makes. Color doesn't matter. Race doesn't matter. He accepts everybody. I need that song. Go home and write the greatest song you ever wrote.'

"The next morning Earle called and said 'Can Billy and I meet you at NBC an hour before Elvis comes in?' I drove out to Elvis' dressing room where he would dress and shower, and we had a little spinet piano in there and a baby grand in the main dressing room. So Billy sits down at the piano, and Earle and Billy now play 'If I Can Dream' for me. I got goose bumps the first time I heard it. 'You guys have done it. Congratulations. Fantastic. I'm gonna convince Elvis Presley to sing this song.'

"Earle Brown was a choral director on *The Carol Burnett Show* and in a music group, the Skylarks on RCA. I met Earle with Leslie Uggams. And I think 'If I Can Dream' was the song like a lot of people who write great one time first novels. I don't think Earle realized what he wrote, and having Elvis Presley perform it was the miracle of all miracles."

"They wanted to close the TV special with a song of peace, hope and brotherhood--a message song," Brown revealed to Ken Sharp in *Writing For The King*. "I wrote 'If I Can Dream" in my living room looking out the window at the garden with the sun coming in and thinking how much I meant it, how much I felt. I didn't even sit at the piano, it just came to me. It was a very inspired and pure song."

"Elvis walked in and was stunned by looking at all these musicians and singers," underlined Steve. "He came in his dark sunglasses and all of a sudden I was in the control room with Bones. Someone came in, probably Joe Esposito and said, 'Elvis wants to see you.' I went out, he had a very serious look on his face...Something is not right. He said, 'Come on outside with me.' We went on to Sunset Blvd. 'Steve, I've never sung with anything bigger than a rhythm section in my life. I never sang with an orchestra in a recording studio. You gotta promise me if I don't like what's playing here you're gonna send everybody home and just keep the rhythm section or I'm not going in there to sing.'

"And I had to promise him which I did. There was great trust to begin with. First of all, he had never heard anything Billy Goldenberg had done. So I promised him if he didn't like it I would send everybody home, the brass section and everybody and keep the rhythm section.

"We walked inside and Billy has a conductor's little stand, and he invited Elvis to come up and Billy gave the downbeat to the opening song 'Guitar Man' and it was total love at that point. Elvis couldn't get enough. And Bones was very instrumental. I heard Mike Deasy and Tommy Tedesco sitting around on a coffee break, having fun, and scratching their guitars into this incredible sound, and after the break I went over to Bones and said, 'I want that sound in the show.' And that became the signature of the titles, the scratching guitars.

"Not only were we not following the book as written, we were improvising in there all along the way in the recording sessions.

"The great night was when we were just recording a demo so he could learn the song to the track of 'If I Can Dream.'

79

"Realizing I had a shot with Elvis in really saying something, I felt strongly by Elvis singing 'peace and love' after all these 1968 assassinations it just seemed like the perfect song to say these words, And I think Elvis was a great deliverer of that message. Billy did the arrangement overnight and Elvis did five takes on the vocal. Colonel Parker did subsequently publish 'If I Can Dream' from the program.

"The special, and the music, shows you a God-given vocalist; he was a great guitar player and would always put himself down to others. He didn't even know how respected he was as a guitar player by his peers. That's all from growing up very humble in the South. I don't think Elvis himself realized how incredibly talented he was.

"The gospel segment we see and hear, and what I was amazed with was this was not shot and built in an editing room. It was all live, including the camera shots and the super impositions of the Blossoms on him. I was putting it all together and editing it all live in the cameras as we were going along. It's amazing how intimate those shots were and there are only 4 cameras. 'Guitar Man' and 'Trouble' was the hook for the whole show. The writers met with Elvis and their outline was trying to describe his entire life."

"When it was time to do the Presley pre-records this was the place, because he was gonna sing live," pondered Bones Howe. "With his hand taped to the microphone and complete with knee drops in front of the string section!

"He got all these violinists with their mouths hanging open. With some artists you can kind of plug in what the record is gonna sound like. But with Elvis, you sort of were relying on him to perform this piece. And he did. The soundtrack album version, not the DVD version, is the version that is the single. That's him singing live in the studio. I gave him a hand mike on a long cable. Because I knew he was not gonna stand in one place. He's gonna walk. 'I'm the engineer. Don't worry about it.'

"He loved being in the middle of a bunch of guys around him. They were like his audience. Not many takes. Not more than four or five. He heard it for the first time with the orchestra right then and there. He didn't wear headphones standing in the middle of the orchestra. He nailed 'If I Can Dream' when we did it on the show. He was a great performer.

"He sang 'Memories' live, but then I did a track, and he sang it afterwards. He wanted to sing it really, really softly. And we turned the lights out in the studio after the orchestra went home. With TV you have to have a track on everything. And I turned the lights off in the studio, and he just stood out in the studio and sang it all by himself in the dark, and we made two takes. And the second one is the one that is in the show."

"When I played Elvis the edited 60-minute version of the show in a projection room at NBC and at the first screening of the show we had a lot of the staff that did the show, the entourage in the room, it was packed," recollected Binder.

"When it was over Elvis told everybody to get out of the room and he wanted to see it again with just me in the room with him. Elvis said to me in that room, 'Steve, it's the greatest thing I've ever done in my life. I give you my word I will never sing a song I don't believe in.'"

"I didn't go to any of the NBC-TV '68 Special tapings," reflected Jerry Schilling. "My [then] wife Sandy went one afternoon with Priscilla, Pat Parry and Joe Esposito's wife Joanie. I saw the special the first time Elvis saw it before the world did. It was in a small conference room at NBC, a rough cut, Steve Binder put together for Elvis, myself, Joe, and Charlie Hodge. And I think Bones.

"So here I am in this conference room and after I saw the 60- minute cut I realized he still had it. I didn't miss it. I don't think Elvis realized yet how good the show was. He was a little pensive. I think he was a little bit nervous what the public's reaction would be. Imagine what is going on in his mind. It's one thing for his friends to say, 'Hey man, this is great.' It's one thing kind of rebelling against the Colonel. He's looking at himself. It was tense.

"Let's give Steve Binder a lot of credit. The show was a spiritual and career rebirth, and the money thing was incidental. It was always incidental to him. I don't think he had a sense of relief ,until it showed nationally and phone calls started coming in."

The Elvis '68 Comeback Special was telecast on December 3 at 9:00 PM. When the ratings were published on December 4, NBC reported that Elvis captured 42 per cent of the total viewing audience. It was the network's biggest rating victory for 1968 and the season's number one rated show.

In the December 4th story for *The Los Angeles Times,* Hal Humphrey bannered, "Elvis still generates considerable heat with his singing."

Robert Shelton in *The New York Times* wrote, "Rock Star's Explosive Blues Have Vintage Quality."

In early November, "If I Can Dream" was issued by RCA and by the end of the month it landed in the Top 40 and soon earned a number 12 slot on the singles chart in January of 1968. The soundtrack reached the 8th position on the album listings.

"I Can Dream' should have been the theme song of 1968," declared author and keyboardist Kenneth Kubernik. "It's right up there with 'A Change Is Gonna Come.' Sam Cooke and Presley in 1964 both RCA artists and both songs recorded on Sunset Boulevard.

Label copy acetate courtesy of Bob Say

"'If I Can Dream' reflects the nature of the Pentecostal church Elvis' mother belonged to. And Elvis grew up in this sense, and the whole idea of having these world shaking individual transforming experiences was part and parcel of Elvis' own upbringing in the world that he lived in. There was always this possibility of resurrection and re-invention. It was always a part of his religious upbringing.

"Whether he was conscious or not, when he starts to sing a song like 'If I Can Dream,' it doesn't sound like it was just selected by the producer of the show. It sounds like Elvis is dialing it in like Sam Cooke convinced us with 'A Change Is Gonna Come.' This is the revelation for me. And the fact that Billy Goldenberg made the arrangement bass instrument oriented makes it come out of the bass note, actually an organ note, which is again a church note. It was a freakish recording. I think they caught lighting in a bottle on this."

"After *The '68 Comeback Special*, Elvis was a happy person like he should have been," admitted Jerry Schilling. "He decided to put a band together and do a month at the International Hotel in Las Vegas. I became involved in what was happening around him, even though I wasn't working for him. Colonel Parker is never there for rehearsals or recordings at RCA studio in Hollywood. I watched a guy put a rock 'n' roll band together. That's what he does. He started by picking James Burton. That's where Elvis was a genius. That's where he was the most underrated producer in musical history, whether it was in the studio or putting the band together. Whether it was 'I hear voices here,' 'play this line here.' The guy was a great producer.

"Elvis pretty much picked and chose. He knew who James Burton was. He knew who Ronnie (Tutt) was. Ronnie was the guy who did what DJ had come in and done. He could accentuate Elvis' moves, but more importantly, when there were bigger name drummers in the audition, like Hal Blaine. I remember what Elvis told me and Joe. He would come over, and we both thought he was gonna go for Hal Blaine. It was the obvious choice. And he said, 'watch this guy' (Ronnie).' Elvis came over and he said, 'I need one guy on stage that has my temperament. Ronnie Tutt.' That's why Ronnie Tutt has the job.

"I saw Elvis open in Las Vegas," volunteered Lance LeGault. "*The '68 Special* influenced what he became in Las Vegas. Absolutely. I was there opening night directly in front of Elvis' center table. George Hamilton and a lot of actors were sitting down at those tables bending their neck."

"There was a special moment that I only heard about. And I was there the next night after the opening in Las Vegas," sighed Schilling, "where the Colonel and Elvis hugged because the Colonel knew Elvis had done it. Colonel had a tear in his eye. Colonel was a very human guy. He and I were dear friends."

"I went to Las Vegas to see Elvis and we went backstage to say hello," ventured Bones Howe. "We kibitzed a little about the *'68 Special* and stuff. We hung out a little. He said to me, just before he made 'In the Ghetto,' 'I got to tell you something. You've got the best feel for music of anybody I've ever worked with.' I said to him, 'Maybe we can make a record together sometime.' 'That would probably be a lot of fun.' 'Why don't you talk to the Colonel about it?' It never came about. But he went to Memphis and made all those great records."

83

My parents Marshall and Hilda went to see one of Presley's August 1969 shows at the International Hotel in Las Vegas and gave an enthusiastic review.

On November 14, 1970 I took three buses from West Hollywood to Inglewood to see Elvis Presley's debut at the Forum, his first concert in Southern California in 13 years. In 1968 I saw the Doors at the Forum, the Rolling Stones twice in 1969 at the same venue and now Elvis. It was a devoted crowd from another era. Hundreds of cameras clicked and flashed when Elvis emerged on stage. Elvis' voice sounded terrific as I sat in the colonnade section.

Upon my return that late evening, I discussed the one-hour Presley show with Rodney Bingenheimer at the Hollywood Ranch Market on Vine Street, over a slew of hot tater tots.

"I worshiped the *Elvis The '68 Comeback Special,* and he was back on the pop charts again," Bingenheimer enthused. "And, unlike a lot of people at the time, deejays, music reviewers, I never left the Elvis fan club. Around 1969, I went to the Presley band rehearsal with a local guy we called President Randy. It was at a rehearsal on Vine and Fountain. It was amazing watching Elvis rehearse. There were only a few people in the room. Elvis autographed the Elvis and Colonel Parker calendar for me.

"During 1969, when I was writing a column for *GO!,* I went to the Elvis press conference in Las Vegas when he was making his debut at the International. I know he played Las Vegas in the fifties on a bill with Liberace, but this was Elvis' return to performing after eight years. Grelun Landon, who was the head PR guy at RCA in Hollywood, totally took care of me. Nick Naff the PR guy from the Las Vegas International wanted me to cover the opening night as well.

"As a fan and reporter, I had a weekly music column in a national paper distributed in record stores, as FM radio was only a year or two old at the time. Over the years I was at many Elvis' openings and closings. After the first show and around a couple of parties, Colonel Parker told me that Elvis saw *GO!* and said, 'Get me a subscription to *GO!'*

"Elvis introduced me to Frank Sinatra. It was at Nancy Sinatra's party. Elvis was closing his engagement in Las Vegas and Nancy was opening the next night. Frank walks in the room while I'm talking to Elvis. 'Frank. This is Rodney.' I took a photo with Elvis, and it ran in *GO!* Magazine," he proudly attests.

In summer, 1970, Elvis Presley returned to Las Vegas for his headline engagement at the Hilton Hotel. "Memories" was included in the opening night set list. He was backed by his core band and the Sweet Inspirations under the direction of musical director Joe Guercio and his Orchestra. During October, Presley was back at the #1 position on the hit parade with the Mark James-penned cautionary tale "Suspicious Minds."

Portions of this text were published in periodicals *Goldmine* (2007) and *Record Collector News* (2008), my 2014 book, *Turn Up The Radio! Pop, Rock and Roll in Los Angeles 1956-1972,* cavehollywood. com website (2018), and *Ugly Things* magazine, (2018).

Brett Berns and Bob Sarles epic *BANG! The Bert Berns Story*
(Photo courtesy HCTN)

Virtually since its debut at the 2017 SXSW Film Festival, demand for a DVD version of *BANG! The Bert Berns Story* has been mounting. In the intervening time, the feature documentary has been screened at more than 50 international film festivals, including Boston Film Festival, where it won the Best Music Award, as well as Chicago's CIMMFest (Best Soundtrack), Seattle International, Athens International, US's Doc 'N Roll, Vancouver International Film Festival, Buffalo Film Festival, and the Mill Valley Film Festival, and was subsequently theatrically released in numerous major markets and digitally released thereafter. Along the way, it attained a 100% Fresh rating from *Rotten Tomatoes* and earned five (out of five) stars from *MOJO*.

At long last, a DVD of *BANG! The Bert Berns Story* was released in June 2018. It has an hour of outtake bonus footage incorporating Paul McCartney, Keith Richards, Andrew Loog Oldham, Ronald Isley, Ben E. King, Solomon Burke, Brenda Reid, Betty Harris, Mike Stollar, Charlie Thomas, the Strangeloves, Carmine "Wassel" DeNoia, Doug Morris, Brooks Arthur, Cassandra Berns, Don Drowty, Garry Sherman, and Joel Dorn.

It's "music meets the mob" in this biographical documentary about the life and career of Bert Berns narrated by Stevie Van Zandt and featuring Van Morrison, Paul McCartney, Keith Richards, Ben E. King, Solomon Burke, and many more. *BANG! The Bert Berns Story* tells the story of one of the most important songwriters, producers and label chiefs of the '60s whose hits include "Twist and Shout," "Hang On Sloopy," "Brown Eyed Girl," "Here Comes The Night" and "Piece Of My Heart." He helped launch the careers of Van Morrison and Neil Diamond and died tragically at the age of 38, before the decade was out. *BANG! The Bert Berns Story* was executive produced by Sid Ganis and produced by Michael B. Borofsky and Brooks Arthur.

Brett Berns (left) Bob Sarles (right) (Photos courtesy HCTN)

Brett Berns, Bert's son, co-directed with Bob Sarles who also edited the film. Sarles is an Emmy-nominated film and television editor and documentary filmmaker. He co-edited the Peabody Award winning documentary series *Moon Shot* and directed and edited *Sweet Blues: A Film About Mike Bloomfield; Fly Jefferson Airplane; John Lee Hooker: Come And See About Me; Feed Your Head: The Psychedelic Era* and *Soulsville*.

Brett Berns commented, "Because of the subject matter, there has been an understandable demand for a physical DVD of the film from fans of the music and collectors of my father's body of work. We're delighted to finally make it available now with a bounty of extra footage from many of the artists whose lives and music were touched by what he was able to accomplish in the short time he was given."

Until quite recently, Bert Berns had been relegated to obscurity, his very existence known only among the *cognoscenti* of hardcore record collectors and old school music industry veterans, but that has dramatically changed in recent years. The film is part of what *The New York Times* called "the Berns boomlet," which began in 2014 with the acclaimed Joel Selvin-authored biography *Here Comes The Night: The Dark Soul of Bert Berns and the Dirty Business of Rhythm & Blues* (Counterpoint Press) and the source of the film's narrative thread. The Broadway bound musical *Piece of My Heart – The Bert Berns Story* originally premiered Off-Broadway in 2014 in an extended run called "stunning" by *The Village Voice* and "gorgeously tuneful" by *The New York Times*.

Steven Van Zandt, the musician (Bruce Springsteen and the E-Street Band), actor (*The Sopranos*) and radio mogul (SiriusXM's *Little Steven's Underground Garage*) posthumously inducted Berns into the Rock and Roll Hall of Fame in 2016 and is, most appropriately, the film's narrator.

BANG! The Bert Berns Story chronicles the life of a musical genius who, over the course of a tragically brief career, managed to write and produce numerous groundbreaking hits on both sides of the Atlantic. Berns founded Bang, one of the most successful independent record labels of all time, the home of hits by Neil Diamond, the McCoys, the Strangeloves and Van Morrison. Shout Records, Bang's sister label, yielded hits for Freddie Scott, Erma Franklin and other R&B greats. Bert Berns is the only songwriter in history whose work has been recorded by the Beatles, Rolling Stones, Animals, Lulu and Led Zeppelin.

Legacy Recordings, catalog division of Sony Music Entertainment, issued *BANG! The Bert Berns Story Official Soundtrack* for the first time on vinyl as a two LP set in December 2018.

Eighteen selections offer an insight into the stellar musical catalog of Bert Berns (November 8, 1929-December 30, 1967) who was notable for having been a hit songwriter, wildly successful record producer and label chief whose work juxtaposed him not with only R&B greats but also pop artists, British Invasion acts and American rockers.

Inducted as a non-performer, Berns received the Ahmet Ertegun Lifetime Achievement Award in 2016 to the Rock and Roll Hall of Fame.

The LP includes "Piece of My Heart" - Erma Franklin; "Tell Him" - The Exciters; "Twist and Shout" – The Isley Brothers; "Cry Baby" - Garnet Mimms & The Enchanters; "Everybody Needs Somebody to Love" - Solomon Burke; "Here Comes The Night – Them; "Are You Lonely For Me Baby" - Freddie Scott; "Cry To Me" – Freddie Scott; "Brown Eyed Girl" – Van Morrison; "Am I Grooving You" - Freddie Scott; and "Piece of My Heart"– Big Brother & The Holding Company; – a cover of the Erma Franklin song featuring Janis Joplin's lead vocal.

The saga of Bert Berns is told in *BANG! The Bert Berns Story* documentary film that was launched worldwide on Apple Music and iTunes in 2017 where it immediately became the #1 documentary on the platform.

Bert Berns, unlike his music business contemporaries, was equally at home producing American soul artists in New York as he was working in London during the height of the British Invasion where his songs were covered by the Beatles, Animals, Them and the Rolling Stones.

"One of the side benefits of America opening its doors to our version of their music was we got to meet our heroes and villains," asserted Rock and Roll Hall of Fame inductee Andrew Loog Oldham. "Bert Berns was a hero."

One LP on the Bang label made a big impact on Staff Sergeant Roger Steffens in Vietnam, who had been shipped off to military service in May 1967, to Nam in November '67.

"Michael Herr's *Dispatches* understood better than anyone that it was a rock 'n' roll war," Steffens explained in *1967 A Complete Rock Music History of the Summer of Love.*

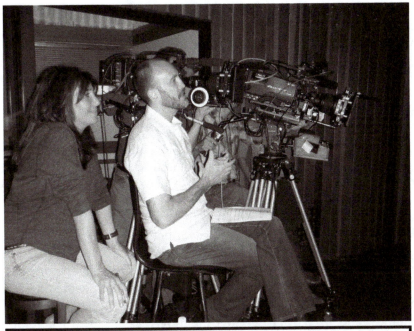

Brett's sister Cassandra looks on as Brett directs the action
(Photo courtesy of HCTN)

"Among the albums we heard in Vietnam that helped put our situation into perspective was Van Morrison's 1967 *Blowin' Your Mind,* produced by Bert Berns," reinforced Roger. "People primarily bought it because of 'Brown Eyed Girl.' But they weren't ready for 'T.B. Sheets.' Here was a real flat out rock 'n' roller, who had been in Them, suddenly making poetry. *Blowin' Your Mind* was the trailer for *Astral Weeks.*"

"I made *BANG! The Bert Berns Story* because this extraordinary untold story needed to be told by the people who worked alongside my father as he created his vast and unique body work," explained director Brett Berns, a graduate of the University of Virginia and veteran of the Israel Defense Forces Paratrooper Brigade.

"His death at a young age, combined with the neglect of powerful figures intent on burying his legacy, caused him to virtually disappear from the history of rock and roll. It thus became my life's ambition to champion my father.

"I was only two years old when my dad died in 1967. Knowing that his rheumatic heart would take his life, he would tell my mother, 'my children will know me through my music.' In tandem with my sister Cassandra, I set out to learn the meaning of this riddle and what we discovered was a revelation so great that it called for historical revision. For buried beneath the sands of time was a unique canon of music and a story greater than fiction.

"My greatest personal realization was that only through the telling of his dramatic life story would my father be recognized for his part in our musical history. He had been so utterly forgotten that only a multi-media barrage would make people take notice of this lost icon," reinforced Brett.

"I began interviewing subjects for the film nearly a decade ago. Being a first time filmmaker, I partnered with seasoned veterans and spared no expense on production. I personally conducted every interview and learned the fundamentals of editing. One door opened the next, and the greatest legends of rock and roll fell into the project along with a number of characters never before seen on film.

"It wasn't until world class editor and director Bob Sarles joined the project that the film truly took flight. A brilliant documentary filmmaker, Sarles reshaped the film, brought his best people on board to conduct B roll and re-creation shoots, orchestrated animations and graphics, and used Joel Selvin's biography as the bedrock for the film's narration. Stevie Van Zandt's narration brings the voice of Bert Berns into the film.

"What began as a passion project designed to introduce the world to Bert Berns has evolved into both an important historical document and an inspirational example of how to live life with courage and create art with passion, love and collaboration. With my father entering the Rock and Roll Hall of Fame in 2016, my greatest ambition is to share *BANG! The Bert Berns Story* with the world."

During May, 2018, I asked Brett Berns about the vinyl soundtrack of the documentary and the just released retail DVD product.

HK: Tell me about assembling the vinyl soundtrack to your documentary. I know there have been numerous collections of Bert's tunes, masters, and for music publishing usage, but how did you and your sister, Cassandra, choose these specific recordings for the soundtrack?

BB: Record industry legend (and *BANG!* star) Doug Morris produced the very first compilation of my father's work in 2002, *The Heart and Soul of Bert Berns*. ACE Records in the UK followed with three complete volumes of *The Bert Berns Story*. The *BANG!* soundtrack on double vinyl is a trophy for the film and all who took part in making it happen. Sony Legacy, who controls my father's Bang and Shout record labels, did a masterful job with the gatefold package. One of the film's principal producers, Michael Borofsky, produced the soundtrack. We came up with the track list together, aspiring to represent both the documentary and the larger body of work. The combination of classics and rare gems is an ideal counterpoint to the movie.

HK: As you embarked on this project, what was your initial goal?
BB: Bert Berns was one of the greatest record men of the twentieth century, but also the most obscure. Time and politics had buried his name. Thus the primary goal of the film was to raise awareness of the legacy, and propel my father's induction into the Rock and Roll Hall of Fame. My dad fathered three children during the last three years of his life, knowing he would not live to see us grow up, but believed we would get to know him through his music, and through a long journey of discovery, my siblings and I have made his dream come true.

The film is a pillar of this effort, along with Joel Selvin's epic biography *Here Comes The Night: The Dark Soul of Bert Berns and the Dirty Business of Rhythm & Blues* and the Broadway bound musical *Piece of My Heart: The Bert Berns Story*.

HK: And now after countless viewings at museums and movie theaters, along with critical acclaim, and the DVD being released, what new emotions and feelings emerged about your father and his influential catalog?
BB: I was struck by the reaction to the movie from audiences in the theater. With 50 international film festival screenings and a US theatrical release, the film made a deep impact on audiences as they laughed and cried together in the cinema. I think people fall in love with Bert Berns, and with his music and his story. The love for my dad expressed by my father's colleagues on screen is infectious. For me, personally, I've become closer to the father I never knew. His daring example has inspired me at every turn.

HK: Tell me about the bonus features. Did you always know that there was at least an extra hour of footage that could be incorporated into a DVD? Does the bonus footage add or further expand the saga? Or viewed as extra glimpses from them?
BB: It became clear early on that, following a decade of interviews, we had enough material to make two films. When my co-director and editor, Bob Sarles, came aboard the project, he structured the story mercilessly, cutting many of my favorite moments. When I would object, he would say 'DVD extras!'

The interview outtakes both expand on the story and provide additional revelations. Keith Richards riffs on 'the sensitivity and the toughness' of the songs. Ronald Isley and Paul McCartney tell the complete 'Twist and Shout' story. And the 10 minutes of my father's well-connected friend Carmine "Wassel" DeNoia is a short film in and of itself.

DVD cover courtesy of HCTN

HK: How 'bout a behind the music reflection about the film shoots of Keith Richards, Andrew Loog Oldham, Paul McCartney, Van Morrison, Cissy Houston, Brooks Arthur and Ronald Isley. They all seemed very receptive in general to talking about Bert's music and the impact on their repertoires. Van Morrison seemed to embrace Bert's short role in his musical career after somewhat distancing himself for many decades.

BB: I was admittedly terrified at having to sit opposite so many towering giants during the interviews, but the affection shown by my father's colleagues made it a joy each and every time. My dad's engineer, Brooks Arthur, was among the first to be interviewed, and joined me as a producer. Solomon Burke asked for a king's throne in his rider and delivered a sermon. Brenda Reid cried tears of joy throughout her interview. Cissy Houston reminisced about Bert and his collaborative spirit – she wrote (uncredited) many of the background vocal arrangements on those records.

Paul McCartney invited us into his home, shook everyone's hand on the set, and was so prepared that he basically interviewed himself. Andrew Loog Oldham gave a passionate, no holds barred interview, and helped bring Van Morrison and Keith Richards into the project.

We went to Belfast to interview Van, who was gracious and welcoming. Keith Richards was the very last interview. I'll never be able to properly express my gratitude to the stars of *BANG! The Bert Berns Story.*

Cassandra, Keith Richards, and Brett (Photo courtesy of HCTN)

93

HK: Has the movie and the soundtrack succeeded beyond your wildest expectations and brought attention to the music and life of Bert Berns? We also discover your colorful mother Ilene.

BB: The film has truly exceeded my every ambition. *BANG!* was the best reviewed documentary of the year. It inspired the Sony Legacy soundtrack. And it got my father into the Rock and Roll Hall of Fame. My mother – who was the most difficult interview to secure - is also immortalized in the film, and was able to see it on the big screen before her death last year. With DVD and international broadcast release this year, we look forward to sharing the movie with the widest possible audience.

HK: What were some of the key things you can say about collaborating with director Bob Sarles?

BB: Bob Sarles and his wife Christina Keating are brilliant documentary filmmakers – a team that brings two lifetimes of experience to a project. I had been conducting interviews for close to a decade, learned the basics of editing, and had a (very) rough cut of the film. It was Berns historian Joel Selvin who introduced me to Bob, who would spend a year reshaping the material into a movie. Bob is a storyteller who taught me narrative structure.

It was Bob's idea to include narration, and he used text straight out of Joel's book for the script, read fittingly and artfully by Stevie Van Zandt. We worked closely together, but I knew – like my father did with his artists – I should give Bob a free hand. For me it was a master class in filmmaking. Bob's contribution proved so transformative that he earned a co-director credit.

HK: Do you like the world of music documentaries after doing one? Do we need them for the real story? What advice would you give to producers and directors and estates involved in the undertaking?

BB: It's been said that we are living in the golden age of music documentaries. Music docs have taken the Oscar three times in the last six years.

Standing In The Shadows of Motown inspired me to make this film – I had even originally envisioned filming performances of the songs. But we had too much story to tell, and let the original masters serve as the score.

My advice to filmmakers is to let the truth guide you and leave the rough edges; be selective and don't try to tell the whole story; be true to your vision and don't take notes until you're finished; exercise patience and perseverance; and remember the difficult work begins when the film is finished. Find a great publicist (like Bob Merlis), promoter (like Elliot Kendall), sales agent (like Cargo Film) and benefactor.

Funding these projects is extremely difficult. We were fortunate to have Bert Berns as our angel investor, and still had to beg and borrow our way to the finish line. Film festivals are critical to building buzz, and proved key to our success with *BANG!*. And if the stars align, you'll distribute your film with Abramorama – leaders in independent documentary distribution.

Filmmaker Bob Sarles, co-director and editor of the film has his movies on permanent display at the Rock and Roll Hall of Fame in Cleveland, Ohio, Experience Music Project in Seattle Washington, and the Stax Museum of American Soul Music in Memphis, Tennessee. In 2017, I spoke with Bob Sarles about the acclaimed documentary.

Brett Berns and Bob Sarles (Photo courtesy of HCTN)

HK: Talk to me about editing. How do you weave the narrative tales with the music?

BS: I have directed and produced a ton of music related film and television content, but I also edit all of my own films, and continue to edit projects for others. It is the filmmaking craft that I have the most experience at, so I always look at a project from the editing standpoint. I have learned from decades of editing documentaries and television shows how to construct a compelling story out of the materials I have at my disposal.

In this case, and in much of the music related films I've made, the most important element in telling the story is the music of the era. The initial cut Brett was working on usually started with a song, but because Brett lacked the experience of an established editor, he would often let the song play until it ended or the story he was telling was completed. Sometimes I cut songs, sometimes to use a lyrical hook, whereas other times I used a musical break to score an emotional scene. Everything was done in service of the story we were trying to tell.

I look at the music first as score, and try and edit with the music to maximize its emotional impact on the story. Clearly, if you are telling the story of the recording of "Twist & Shout" you are going to use the appropriate version of that song in that part of the film. Brett, with his great knowledge of his father's output, was incredibly helpful in suggesting the lesser known songs in the Bert Berns canon for emotional hooks, even if that song may have been produced at another part of the timeline. Fortunately, we had a very deep well of amazing music to draw from.

In the few instances where we needed original music created for the film I turned to my old friend Barry Goldberg, the great organist from Electric Flag (currently in the band the Rides with Stephen Stills and Kenny Wayne Shepard), who has scored a lot of film and television, to compose and produce those interstitial music cues which integrated seamlessly with the needle-drop Bert Berns music cues that made up the majority of the film's soundtrack.

HK: What is the challenge of telling a story about someone who left the planet 50 years ago but the catalog continues to be utilized and heard?
BS: The single biggest challenge we had, and one that is rarely noted, is the fact that we did not have a single frame of film or video footage of Bert Berns himself. Any home movies of Bert were lost over the years. That was a tremendous handicap. But, by utilizing photos we had of Bert and augmenting them with other archival footage, we were able to disguise that fact. That the Berns kids controlled a good portion of the publishing made using Bert's music easier. Neil Diamond's decision to not participate in the film meant we had to work around not having his catalogue available to us.

In the end, that wasn't nearly the problem we originally thought it might be, as the film is the Bert Berns story, not the Neil Diamond story.

96

The easy part is that many of the songs used in the film's soundtrack are recognizable, and trigger an automatic emotional response in the audience. This is why these songs are still around. So many of them remain timeless.

Bert Berns and Jerry Wexler c. 1965   (Photo courtesy estate of Bert Berns)

HK: When you first began the venture, to now viewing the finished product, what were your initial impressions about Bert Berns, and what did he become to you after you completed the portrait?
BS: I initially thought of Bert Berns as a talented guy with an ear for great pop music. After immersing myself in the subject and the music I came to learn that he was a tremendously soulful guy and was responsible for helping to create some of the deepest soul music ever produced. He was a lot more than "Twist & Shout," "Tell Him" and "Hang On Sloopy." The sides he recorded with Solomon Burke, Betty Harris, Freddie Scott and Erma Franklin and so many others are simply sublime and right up there with the greatest soul records ever made.

Once Were Brothers:
Robbie Robertson and The Band

The Band on *The Ed Sullivan Show, November 2, 1969*
(Photo courtesy of SOFA Entertainment)

Once Were Brothers: Robbie Robertson and The Band, the feature documentary premiered September 5, 2019, as the Opening Night Gala Presentation for the 44th Toronto International Film Festival.

In February 2020 the New York City premiere was held at the Walter Reade Theater at Lincoln Center. It opened in Los Angeles at the ArcLight in Hollywood on February 21st, and went national on February 28th.

Inspired by Robertson's acclaimed 2016 autobiography, *Testimony*, director Daniel Roher's *Once Were Brothers* documentary explores Robertson's young life and the creation of The Band, one of the most influential groups in the history of popular music. The compelling film blends rare archival footage, photography, iconic songs, and interviews with many of Robertson's friends and collaborators, including Martin Scorsese, Bruce Springsteen, Eric Clapton, Van Morrison, Peter Gabriel, Taj Mahal, Dominique Robertson, and Ronnie Hawkins.

Once Were Brothers was made in conjunction with Imagine Documentaries, White Pine Pictures, Bell Media Studios, and Universal Music Canada's Shed Creative. The project is executive produced by Martin Scorsese; Imagine Entertainment chairmen Brian Grazer and Ron Howard; Justin Wilkes and Sara Bernstein for Imagine Documentaries; White Pines Pictures' president Peter Raymont, and COO Steve Ord; Bell Media president, Randy Lennox; Jared Levine; Michael Levine; Universal Music Canada president and CEO Jeffrey Remedios; and Shed Creative's managing director Dave Harris. The film is produced by Andrew Munger, Stephen Paniccia, Sam Sutherland, and Lana Belle Mauro.

In 2019, Magnolia Pictures acquired the worldwide rights.

In late January 2020, I was invited to the special screening with Robertson, Brian Grazer of CAA (Creative Artists Agency), Ron Howard and Imagine Documentaries hosted at the Ray Kurtzman Theater in Los Angeles. Rob Light, partner/managing director/head of music, Creative Artists, introduced the movie before Robbie Robertson, a 40 year client of CAA, offered some personal remarks and anecdotes about the movie. Among the attendees: Jonathan Taplin, Van Morrison, Jim Keltner and Cynthia Keltner, Michael Des Barres, Jimmy Iovine, John Scheele, Michael Ochs, Michael Simmons, Ken Sharp, and Robertson's manager Jared Levine, who initially suggested that Robbie hire Daniel Roher as the director. You'll be hearing a lot about Roher. There were plenty of unseen photos and archival footage. The editing was dazzling. There were many revelations on the screen.

The Magnolia Pictures production publicity materials detailed the backstory of the endeavor. Written over the course of five years without the aid of a ghostwriter, his 2016 memoir *Testimony* chronicled the period from his upbringing on the Six Nations Reserve in Ontario to his wild years touring with music giants Ronnie Hawkins and Bob Dylan to his role in the formation of one of the most revered and important groups of the 20th century: The Band.

"A lot of stories had mounted up over the years, and it reached a point where they were too heavy for me to carry around," Robertson says. "The only way I could get some relief was to set some of them free. Several authors had contacted me about writing my story over the years, but each time we'd hit a certain point where things just didn't ring true to me. It sounded like somebody else was trying to impersonate my voice, so I ended up writing every word of it myself."

After careful consideration, Robertson chose to option film rights to his book to the experienced Toronto-based film and television production company, White Pine Pictures. Co-founded and run by president and CEO Peter Raymont, White Pine has a 40-year track-record of producing Emmy Award-winning documentary feature films and TV dramas, including *Genius Within: The Inner Life of Glenn Gould* and the Sundance Award-winning *Shake Hands with the Devil.* "We were honored that Robbie put his trust in us," says Raymont. It was the beginning of a wonderful adventure.

Raymont and his documentary development executive, Andrew Munger, set about raising funds to produce the film, securing a partnership with Polygram Entertainment and Bell Media Studios.

Raymont and Munger also sought the best director for the film. Among others, they were approached by 24-year-old Daniel Roher, a passionate young Canadian filmmaker who had directed three short documentaries. Raymont and Munger were impressed with Roher's passion for the subject and his depth of knowledge of Roberson's music. "We were impressed with Daniel's passion, determination and extraordinary chutzpah" says Raymont, "Nothing was going to stop him." They introduced Roher to Robertson's manager, Jared Levine, who, in turn, introduced Roher to Robertson.

"Daniel had already made several documentaries that people felt were really good," says Robertson, "and when they asked him what he wanted to do next, he said he wanted to make a documentary from my book."

By his own admission, Roher's interest in developing the material became something of an obsession as time went on. "I told anyone who would listen that this was my dream project," he says. "The truth is, I would've begged, cried, or stolen to direct this movie."

Robertson, who was only 24 when he and Levon Helm, Rick Danko, Richard Manuel and Garth Hudson recorded their groundbreaking debut album *Music From Big Pink*, says he saw something of himself in Roher. "When I first started playing music I went against all the odds and broke down walls to make it work. I got that same feeling from Daniel. He knew he had to make this work."

**Robbie Robertson and Levon Helm, Woodstock, August, 1969
(Photo by Henry Diltz)**

Above all else, Roher reminded Robertson that his book's story was about a highly ambitious young man who bucks the odds to make his mark on the world. "Thankfully, my pitch resonated with him, because he said, 'Okay, kid, let's make trouble together.' That's when my life changed."

Roher spent months on a treasure hunt for photos, including Elliot Landy-shot Band images, film and video clips, and ephemera from The Band's past. "It almost felt like I was an archaeologist unearthing the documentary rather than writing it," Roher says.

In his director's statement supplied by Magnolia Pictures, Daniel Rother explained his relationship with the music of The Band and Robbie Robertson.

"The first time I heard The Band was through my parents, and I was instantly pulled toward their sound. Their incredible musicianship grabbed me; it seemed to come from a different place. The harmonies were rough and sweet. The music, timeless. I was hooked.

"The myth and legend behind the five men who made that music came into focus when I saw Martin Scorsese's film, *The Last Waltz,* as a teenager.

"When Robbie released his memoir, I devoured it. A wild musical journey built on a scattered upbringing in Toronto, on the Six Nations Reserve and in the living rooms of his underworld Yiddish relatives. I could see that this would make an extraordinary documentary, and making this film became my obsession. I wasn't the obvious choice, but I hoped that what I lacked in profile, I could make up for in my unbridled enthusiasm for Robbie's awe-inspiring story.

"Through sheer force of will, I wedged myself into the discussion. My maxim: 'I'll die before this film isn't great.' The producers at White Pine Pictures and Shed Creative Agency recognized my verve and zeal, and soon after I had the chance to meet with Robbie at his studio in L.A. I pitched him my vision, and promised I would work 25 hours a day, 8 days a week to make a documentary befitting of his mythic life."

Robertson's *Testimony* book and companion album deftly complemented one another to capture the time and place--the moment when rock 'n' roll became life, when legends like Buddy Holly and Bo Diddley criss-crossed the circuit of clubs and roadhouses from Texas to Toronto, when the Beatles, Jimi Hendrix, the Rolling Stones, and Andy Warhol moved through the same streets and hotel rooms. Robbie bumped into them all: Otis Redding, Marlon Brando, Charles Lloyd, the Crystals, Curtis Mayfield and the Impressions, Doc Pomus and Mort Shuman, Aaron Schroeder, Jerry Leiber and Mike Stoller, Morris Levy, Ahmet Ertegun and Jerry Wexler.

In a 2017 interview I conducted with Robbie Robertson for *Record Collector News* magazine we discussed *Testimony*.

HK: I learned a lot about your Brill Building visits with Ronnie Hawkins in the book.
RR: Things I really took away from all that was that Doc Pomus and Mort Shuman or Leiber and Stoller, or Otis Blackwell, was the obvious thing that they tapped into something that felt good. But it had to feel good. The song could be about anything, but it had to feel good. And I was like. "Wow…" I would see one of the guys sitting at the piano playing. "Let me think of something. What about this?" And they would start to play something. I was studying. I didn't know what the song was about but it felt good. So it was like coming in the back door of something, and when you start a thing if it doesn't feel good then stop it right now. "Ah ha. Now that's something."

Who would think, in their wildest imagination, that Tin Pan Alley was a real place? The Brill Building and then Donnie Kirshner's thing. All of it was actually a place you could go. And the doors were golden when you walked in. And inside there, in all those rooms were people who wrote songs and sent them out to the whole wide world.

I had such respect, and experienced a connection with these people. And I knew Doc and Mort all of their lives. Doc and Mort remained friends. And I recorded with John Hammond, Jr. on an album that Leiber and Stoller produced. I was friends with Jerry and Mike, so to say none of that rubbed off on me just wouldn't be true.

I wasn't the lead singer in The Band. I don't know if the Brill Building influence was ever that specific on arrangements and voices, but I tried to soak up as much as I possibly could from those incredible guys.

And it was a lot of stuff that I don't know that you can grasp it on the surface, but in seeing the way these guys could adapt to these different artists, and they could write something and then cast it... Or, someone could say, "We need this. We're coming to you," and they could write for that. I thought that was a special gift. I was doing that in The Band.

I thought my job in all this was to do what they were doing. My job was to say, "I'm going to write a song that Richard Manuel could sing the hell out of. I know what to do with his instrument." And so the answer is, in some subliminal way, absolutely yes.

And then, inside another door was Bob Dylan, who wasn't about that. It was about emotion and energy, but it was really about saying something. It wasn't about "These words could be anything." No. No. It was specific. So to me it was rebelling, in a beautiful way against this whole Brill Building thing.

The sound was really important to me, too. It still is. My first attraction to rock 'n' roll was as much the sound, as the song, and the song was the sound. So when I heard these early Sun and Chess Records, I thought, "What is going on here?" Before that, Les Paul and Mary Ford. This sound thing. Because records before that, you didn't think that much about the sound. It was a vocalist and some music in the background.

When rock 'n' roll came along, there were unique sounds coming from these different studios in Texas, Memphis and New Orleans. The sound of the records coming out of New Orleans that were engineered by studio owner, Cosimo Matassa. "What is going on there?" The sounds coming out of Chess Records in Chicago. I wondered "What kind of a room is that? What is this magic?"

Richard Manuel, Woodstock (1969 photo by Henry Diltz)

Rick Danko, Woodstock (1969 photo by Henry Diltz)

HK: Before officially being known as The Band for *Music From Big Pink*, the group recorded *The Basement Tapes* with Bob Dylan. Recordings of those sessions yielded some cover versions before they were officially released a couple of years ago.

RR: We did have the experience with Bob Dylan, and doing *The Basement Tapes* with songs that were supposed to be shared with other artists to record. It was because so many people recorded Bob's songs and we were hooked up together, you thought "Oh. That's part of it."

Garth Hudson, Woodstock (1969 photo by Henry Diltz)

And how that struck me. I didn't think about it in terms of writing the songs or making the records that other people would record. This was a very internal experience. An experience shared by the five of us in The Band. Something that we had assembled over time and pulled it all together and made this gumbo.

HK: I never knew that you were the guy who assembled the initial or original 14 song acetate demo that was serviced to music publishers. Then recording artists like Manfred Mann did "The Mighty Quinn" and Brian Auger, Julie Driscoll and the Trinity recorded "This Wheel's On Fire." I know Peter, Paul & Mary were first with "Too Much of Nothing."

RR: And when we were doing this without Bob, this was the germ that grew into the idea, and the beginning of *Music From Big Pink.* That was happening kind of in the back room too. So when we chose those songs to send out we were choosing what we liked. We were kidding around. I didn't realize Manfred Mann could do a really great job on "The Mighty Quinn." I didn't know that. But we were saying that "The Mighty Quinn" really had something to it. It was what felt right in putting that collection together.

HK: Who knew when I first heard *Music From Big Pink* that you guys logged years playing together long before *The Band* on LP.

RR: When we hooked up with Bob Dylan, it was made clear to Bob and to Albert [Grossman, Bob's manager]. "This is a whistle stop for us. We are on our own path. We'll do this in the meantime, but we're going to do our own thing. Right?"

When we recorded *Music From Big Pink,* Albert was astonished by the results of that record. And he so embraced it and made it his own and all that other stuff vanished. He was like "I knew it all along." It fit into his scenario.

Bob and The Band were so close to Albert. We had been through everything together. Like I say in the book, we were like war buddies. And we had

Bob Dylan, Inglewood Forum, 1974 (Photo by Brad Elterman)

105

gone to the edge together. And because we had done all that stuff and *The Basement Tapes,* and through all of this, still had no idea of what this was going to be when we did it. It was an unexpected, but welcome thrill.

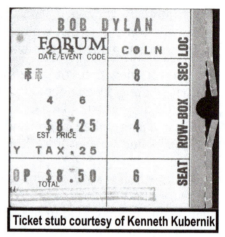

HK: *The Band* album was recorded inside Sammy Davis, Jr's pool house in the Hollywood Hills. In a way you started low-fi recording when a music group on

Ticket stub courtesy of Kenneth Kubernik

a major label moved into a home studio and did masters for albums not just recorded demos.

RR: That's where that Les Paul thing came back into the picture. Before *Big Pink*, I had had this dream of having a workshop, a place. A sanctuary where we could go into the privacy of our own world and do something and not be on somebody else's lawn. To really be in our own environment, left alone and away from studio union breaks, so all of these things played into it a little bit. We go into a studio and the guy is like "Well, it's almost 4:00 pm..." So all of these things are playing into it. even though the experience in the studio of recording *Music From Big Pink* was fabulous.

The producer John Simon was great, and the engineers were great at Phil Ramone's place, all of it, but the idea of having this private sanctuary that it would have its own sound...its own sound and its own flavor, became a passion.

We would be like Chess. We could have our own studio, and it would not sound like any of these other places. Going into somebody's environment and then saying, "you go over there. You sit here. And we're gonna use this kind of microphone on you." I thought that was what you did with somebody else. I felt like I'm was getting crumbs from someone else's table. Leftovers.

I was thankful for that period of time, though, because it was a period when (if artists wanted to something), an A&R guy like [Capitol Records engineer and staff producer] John Palladino, would let us go ahead. With us, he had nothing to do with the music. He was never there when we recorded. No intrusion.

When I said "We want to do this thing that started in the basement of *Big Pink*. We want to have the equipment with us in our own atmosphere, and record at whatever time the spirit moves us." We didn't want to be on someone else's clock. John was like "OK." We needed the equipment to come to us. And he had to kind of go along with it, you know. He went along with it, but he didn't understand it. We then did *Stage Fright* at the Woodstock Playhouse, we brought the equipment into that room. It's very common today.

When I went to Dublin, Ireland, to do some experimenting with U2 and they were recording in the living room of Adam [Clayton's] house, when I walked in, the producer Daniel Lanois, Edge and Bono said, "Does this feel familiar?" And I didn't quite understand what they meant. What they were saying was "You are the guys who started this whole thing."

HK: Last year Columbia Records and Legacy Recordings issued *Bob Dylan: The 1966 Live Recordings*, a 36 CD box of your joint 1966 concert tours of the US, UK, Europe and Australia. When we talked in 1976 about The Band reuniting with Dylan on the 1974 tour, you remarked "At least this past time we weren't booed," referring to nights on the Dylan/Hawks 1966 tour. I have a hard time comprehending Dylan and your group being booed on the world tour of 1966. What I remember about the 1974 shows I saw, everyone was totally digging the blend on stage.

RR: There was a thing that happened between Bob and The Band on stage that when we played together that we would just go into a certain gear automatically. It was like instinctual, like you smelled something in the air, you know, and it made you hungry. *laughs*. It was that instinctual. And the way we played music together was very much that way. And whether we were playing in 1966, or 1976, or when we did the tour together in 1974, we would go to a certain place where we just pulled the trigger.

It was like "just burn down the doors 'cause we're coming through." And it was a whole other place that we played, when we weren't playing with him. So it was like putting a flame and oil together, or something. I don't know.

When we did the Dylan and Band tour in '74, where we went and did a lot of the same things we did back in '66, it was like you weren't really there all along. It's interesting, and it's one of the things I talked about in my keynote speech that I made at the SXSW conference.

It's really a very interesting experiment to see, or go from something that people were so adamantly against in this music, and change nothing, except that the world revolved, and everybody came around and suddenly reacted with "This is brilliant." That was very interesting to see everything else change around you.

Well, we didn't change. *laughs.* I don't know that this has ever happened to anybody else. And it is a phenomenon. And that's why I feel bold enough to refer to it as a musical revolution. Because the world came around. We didn't. We didn't do anything that much different. *laughs.* We just went out there and hit it between the eyes. And now people have a completely different reaction to it. And I thought "It's kind of incredible that the world actually came to this place" you know. And I don't know who else has been through that.

In our *Record Collector News* magazine 2017 conversation Robbie and earlier for *Goldmine* magazine, we talked about the November 2016 Rhino Entertainment 40th Anniversary Editions of The Band's *The Last Waltz* in various CD, Blu-ray, and vinyl formats.

On Thanksgiving Day 1976, The Band took the stage for the very last time at the Winterland Theater in San Francisco, California. For the show, Rick Danko, Levon Helm, Garth Hudson, Richard Manuel, and Robbie Robertson were joined by an all-star group of music pioneers and recording artist friends, including Paul Butterfield, Eric Clapton, Neil Diamond, Bob Dylan, Ronnie Hawkins, Dr. John, Joni Mitchell, Van Morrison, Muddy Waters, and Neil Young, among others.

The roots of *The Last Waltz* began when Jonathan Taplin, executive producer of the film, who had been The Band's road manager for four years, and had produced Scorsese's breakout film *Mean Streets,* introduced Robertson to Scorsese, who had helped edit *Woodstock* and *Elvis On Tour.*

"I couldn't let the opportunity pass," Scorsese explained. "It was this crazy desire to get it on film, to be a part of it. The idea was to get the most complete coverage possible, so our 35mm cameras were scanning and zooming for the action," continued Scorsese. "When Bob Dylan shifts from 'Forever Young' to 'Baby Let Me Follow You Down,' the film truly documents Robertson, Helm, Hudson and Danko adjust and play on."

"I remember Marty saying," Robertson mentioned, 'This is something you never see. You're never in on this.'"

The Last Waltz became the first concert documentary to be shot in 35mm, and influenced future music documentaries. "We live so emotionally and powerfully through those moments," Scorsese felt. "The picture, for us, was so powerful. And it was bringing these emotions to us, creating the psychological atmosphere that I couldn't verbalize then. But it was pretty scary. As exciting and as fulfilling creatively as it was, it was extremely frightening."

Scorsese, with director of photography, Michael Chapman, and a team of seven cameramen, including Laszlo Kovacs and Vilmos Zsigmond, recorded the event that was produced by rock promoter Bill Graham. It was the same venue where they first debuted as The Band in April, 1969.

"There was something about this period from the '60s through the '70s, everybody had a pretty good run," Robertson offered "When you watch these things over and over again, and how stirring these performances were, you're almost seeing inside the whole era."

I was at *The Last Waltz* and seen briefly during "Don't Do it" in the movie. It was theatrically screened in April 1978 to critical acclaim. I went to the premiere in Hollywood at the Cinerama Dome theatre and found myself sitting near Liza Minelli and Martin Scorsese. *The Last Waltz* is still considered by many to be the greatest concert movie ever made. Muddy Waters' appearance was staggering.

Robbie marveled as well, "Because now, when I'm watching it, I'm also hearing it that way and the power of it. And you see this guy, [Muddy Waters], and I don't know what the Rolling Stones would have done, or if a lot of music would have ever existed, if it hadn't been for this guy. And you look at him, and you can see why.

"It is one of the high points for me in this. And just talking about pedal to the metal, and pulling the trigger, and he must have been about 65 or so, but he came out, and he was the daddy of the whole Delta blues scene for sure, but such a gentleman. He came out there with people who are so large and their own music, and held his own at 64, or 65, and didn't take a step backwards. There's a true master."

HK: Did you and The Band members have interaction with Dylan before the show regarding song selections?
RR: For sure. We all threw our thoughts into the hat and then we would try stuff, and if it felt right, then we just did it. It was one of those things like letting some higher power make the decision, because the proof was in the pudding. And "Let's play that song and see how it feels." We would then say, "that was fun. Let's do that." But Bob

109

wanted to do stuff that was connected with our origins together, which is why we did "Baby Let Me Follow You Down," which we played back then, and "I Don't Believe You (She Acts Like We Never Had Met)." And having a thread going back to 1965-1966, and because it felt real. One of the things I'm most excited about on the (new) *Last Waltz* is that we got to use "Hazel."

We were trying to find a connection, and not just do something that had nothing to do with anything. We wanted it to have some meaning, but nobody suggested "Hazel."

We were saying, "OK. Out of all of the songs we can do together what do you think we should do?" It was like we'll do some of the stuff from the 1965-1966 period. We'll do something from *Planet Waves* we had just recorded a couple years earlier. And in mixing it up we ran through a bunch of crazy ideas too.

Like Bob said, "We should do a Johnny Cash song." And he would start singing a Johnny song, and we all knew this was never gonna fly. But it would be fun to play it. We'd play through it and say. "Naw." But all of this stuff, it was really like throwing things up in the air and seeing where they would fall. But Bob said, "You know one song I think we should do is 'Hazel'." We were like "Really? OK. Let's do it." And we ran through it and it felt pretty good. "All right." But we knew we wanted to do "Forever Young," because it connected to the occasion with all the people there and this generation and all of this stuff like Dr. John singing "Such a Night."

We had to make sacrifices originally, obviously, in the movie, because it's a movie, and you have to edit a movie so it plays. But on the record we had a limited amount of space, too. And I was always taken by Bob's performance on "Hazel." I thought he did an amazing performance on it and poured such passion into this song.

This is the real thing in a setting of such respectful elegance and everything that when I was working on it I thought, "My God, I've known Van Morrison for all these years, I've seen him perform many, many times and I never saw him do what he did." Muddy Waters coming out there between all of these people and rock the very foundation of music in that whole place that night. This was like an outstanding experience. Sometimes I had to just catch myself not to be standing there with my mouth open."

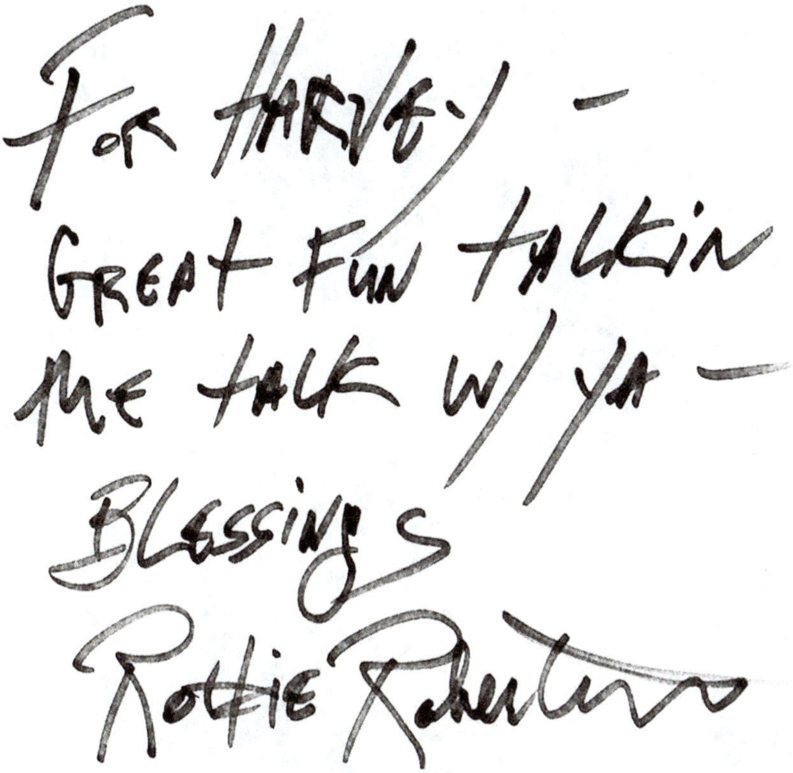
For Harvey –
Great fun talkin
the talk w/ ya –
Blessings
Robbie Robertson

(Note courtesy of Harvey Kubernik archives)

**Jimi Hendrix backstage at the Hollywood Bowl
(Photo by Henry Diltz)**

Writer/Director John Ridley's *Jimi: All Is By My Side* DVD

In 2014, for *Record Collector News* magazine, I interviewed writer/director John Ridley after his film, *Jimi: All Is By My Side*, debuted at the Toronto International Film Festival.

The movie stars, André Benjamin (*Idlewild, Smokin' Aces, The Great Gatsby*) as Jimi Hendrix. *Jimi: All Is By My Side* also stars Hayley Atwell (*Captain America: The First Avenger*), Imogen Poots (*28 Weeks Later*), Andrew Buckley (*Borgia*), and Ruth Negga (*World War Z*).

Guitarist/producer Waddy Wachtel, bassist Leland Sklar, and drummer Kenny Aronoff crafted the original musical score inspired by sounds similar to Hendrix's 1966-67 repertoire. The filmmaker's request for original Hendrix songs and recordings for licensing was denied by Experience Hendrix LLC, Hendrix's estate.

Ridley's movie covers a year in Jimi Hendrix's life from 1966-67, starting from when he was an unknown backup guitarist playing New York's Cheetah Club and following him through time playing in London's music scene up to his Monterey International Pop Festival triumph.

Before Jimi Hendrix played a note of music in England, songwriter and record producer Kim Fowley met Jimi the first day he arrived in England during 1966.

"In 1966, I was his neighbor in England at the Bayswater Hotel. In our first 45 minute meeting in the hotel lobby, Jimi was wearing a green suit. I was literally the first person he met when he got off the plane from New York. We talked music, and he said he wanted to play science-fiction rock 'roll. He mentioned a song 'Martian Love Machine' that was influenced by Ray Bradbury.

"Jimi liked the fact that I knew about the Spanish Castle venue in the Seattle area. I was the record promo man for 'Tall Cool One' by the Wailers from his neighborhood, since I was tall and cool, and I was a producer of L.A. based Richard Berry, who wrote 'Louie, Louie,' who wrote 'Half Love Will Travel' that were regional hits, and Jimi knew them. Jimi and I bonded in trivia over singer Gail Harris who had 'I Idolize You' on the Carlton label."

I asked multi-instrumentalist and blues advocate John Mayall about Hendrix who he first encountered in 1966.

"Jimi came to England, and a blues world which had been all my life, going back to Cyril Davies and Alexis Koerner, who started the British Blues boom. This attracted a lot of musicians who now had something new to inspire them. Blues had an audience in Britain. And [manager] Chas Chandler of the Animals who sort of discovered Jimi not doing very well in America and brought him over to England and that really positioned Jimi on an international scale.

"Jimi was very thrilled of course that people in Europe were blown away by his playing. He was really recognized for what he was. It was something he hadn't experienced in America. English and European audiences really put him on the map," reinforced Mayall.

"When Chas Chandler brought Jimi over to England everybody was totally impressed by his personality and his singing and his playing. I think it was a shot in the arm for all the British guitar players to have someone that they had never heard before. And it all started from there, really. It was important for Jimi to have had Chas Chandler who himself had reached great international regard playing with the Animals.

"When I saw Jimi Hendrix play with his group, you knew what he was doing was that music was the main thing, and the way that he played and the theatrics were all part of the way he played. People didn't really separate that from his body of work."

Writer and filmmaker, John Ridley, born in Milwaukee, Wisconsin, earned an Oscar for the Best Adapted Screenplay for his work on *12 Years a Slave*. Ridley is the author of seven published novels. He resides in Sherman Oaks, California.

HK: "A lot has happened in two years," as you said introducing the movie premiere in Hollywood at the ArcLight Cinema. What drew you to the saga of Jimi Hendrix to write and direct a portrayal of him covering a year in his life from 1966-1967?
JR: I've been very fortunate to be a writer in Hollywood for a good number of years. And it is one of those stories that in different forms people would either ask you to come in and pitch on or various versions to try and write it. To a degree they were serviceable ideas. Back in the day they tended to be the cradle-to-the grave kind of biopics that people were doing. For a long time that was the way stories were told. But I think audiences have matured, their expectations and tolerance for more depth of storytelling as opposed to greatest hits versions of the story has evolved.

And for me as someone who thought he was a Hendrix fan, when it got to the point that I really started to explore this particular year and these events and the rapidity that these events happened one after another. Meeting Chas Chandler, Noel Redding, Mitch Mitchell. Eric Clapton, playing for the Beatles, it really felt there was an emotional velocity to this story as well as an opportunity to look at some key relationships that a lot of people may not be aware of.

So, all of that to me together there just came a point where it was less about me trying to figure out a story and a story that was there that was really dictating the way it was told.

HK: What was it like being the screenwriter and director? Is it easier or harder as far as wearing both hats?
JR: It was unique because I think it was both of those things. I really believed I had a powerful script that was put together. And people were obviously attracted to it. But this time was my opportunity. I really wanted to come to it with a strong vision for these characters, a vision for their emotional drive and a vision in terms of the style of filmmaking. The language of cinema. I believe if I can do those things and keep the focus on all of them that there was a story here that people can relate to.

HK: So much has been written about the movie's lack of securing original Jimi Hendrix recordings but, even at his June 1967 Monterey International Pop Festival return to the States big moment, five of his nine numbers in his live set were cover versions. I found it refreshing in your movie to see Jimi's 1966 and '67 world where he was still doing covers and writing his first songs and not the constant usage of "Purple Haze" and "All Along the Watchtower." I'm on your side on this one.
JR: I do appreciate that. I think a lot of people appreciate that and the history of music and where it came from, whether it be Jimi or the Beatles and where they start somewhere and take these other songs and really make them their own. Jimi, more than anything, was an artist who could do that as well with "Hey Joe," and "All Along the Watchtower." People are gonna come to it and expect a greatest hits version of that and I get it, because those hits are hits for a reason.

But I do hope folks like yourself, who have a deeper, richer understanding of the whole process, will have an appreciation of songs that we were able to use in the film. "Mannish Boy" to "Hound Dog," "Wild Thing" to "Sgt. Pepper's Lonely Hearts Club Band." Not having a piece of music was not a limitation.

HK: You take us into the 1966 and early summer '67 world of Jimi in London. The people are really part of his orbit and not auxiliary friends.
JR: Honestly, I don't think the people around Jimi were auxiliary in any sense. These folks really informed the Jimi that we came to know. Whether it was Linda [Keith] meeting him and introducing him to Chas, who had a real understanding of both sides of the music business, having been a player, and at that point being a nascent manager and wanting to treat acts as people rather than dollar signs. Kathy [Etchingham] and the time they spent together, even going to the park and listening to the Salvation Army Band, Jimi being fascinated by the uniforms.

Ida, in this version, is a representation of depth, and the reason I call her Ida, yet they had not met at the time. But I thought it was very important to be additive with his girlfriend who had a real Afro-centric perspective on him and their relationship, and how it was different than with Linda and Kathy. So I think all of these individuals helped inform the Jimi we came to know.

Jimi at age 24, he had played with Ike & Tina Turner, the Isley Brothers, Little Richard and really hadn't found great success with them. So to speak, a little bit washed up and playing as a backing artist in a band. He probably could have gone on to be very successful but were it not for these key relationships we have the Jimi Hendrix we mostly identify with. It's hard to say.

So it was very important in this story to show these people as people, hopefully complicated people and try and delve into these relationships as possibly as I could. Honestly it remains these personal connections.

One of the things I always thought was the strength was the connectivity of these characters and the very quiet and thoughtful nature of someone like Jimi. To be able to take someone who so many of us revere 'cause of his outside personality on stage, and to be able to take quiet moments where people are just sitting in clubs and or in a room laying together. Sometimes some of these scenes are worth it for emotion, intent and they move together.

That to me to be able to feel that from the early stage of discovering the story and then watch the film playback time and time again and still feel that and be able to translate that from the inception of the idea to the words on the page to how we filmed it to the final edit, that to me is the most powerful thing.

HK: Do you write to music?

JR: Yes I do. Sometimes I like to write in a quiet space, but it can be distracting listening to music. Certainly the song that sent me on this journey was "Send My Love to Linda." [From a Record Plant session in summer 1970]. That was a song I listened to over and over again. Not just when I was writing but when I would go for a run and put it on my iPod and just play it over and over again.

Because I want to be reminded about the passion and the emotions I felt the first time I heard that song. A lot of times it's more when I'm out running or doing other things, driving a car because I'll start thinking about scenes and moments that I want to try and express. And it's a way to really keep me on point with the story.

HK: What did you learn as a screenwriter from *12 Years a Slave* that you applied to your Hendrix movie?

JR: Well, a couple of things. One thing I learned, in general, it's not about the words on the page. When you're a young writer, at least for me, you're in love with your own words because you're a writer. You got to write as much as possible.

That to me is, hopefully, where I've matured a little bit in about leaving words out and letting the moment play itself. And I think you see some of that in *12 Years a Slave* as well. In Solomon's memoir it is so nuanced, so rich, and rich in its environment there are places where it wasn't about the words, but hopefully, creating a scene that had its own power.

For me, again, I can only hope that it's a level of maturation as a writer to be confident in all aspects of both the material that I've been able to work as well as all the other artisans working on the film that it doesn't have to be all about words. And I certainly believe with the Hendrix film I found a way to express that.

HK: Tell me about working with André Benjamin

JR: I can't say enough about André, as a person an artist and his work ethic. This is someone who put in months, seven or eight months into the entire process from originally sitting down with me. He lives in Atlanta and came out to Los Angeles to work with me and talk about cinema, to talk about the kind of story we wanted to tell. He worked with a guitar and vocal coach and put himself on a diet. There was so much that he put into it as a performer as an artist, as an actor, building the chemistry between the two actresses, Imogen and Hayley, and that's really, to me, exceptionally important.

117

You can write what you think are terrific scenes. You can find interesting ways to hopefully direct those scenes, but if the actors don't have a certain chemistry, particularly in a film like this, which is so much about connectivity, you end up with a whole lot of nothing.

So for André Benjamin, who has afforded himself a place in life where he can do pretty much whatever he wants to choose to not openly be involved in this project but to really decide that he was going to be honorific in the approach to it that's pretty special. It really is. In that regard what he put into it was just phenomenal. I believe the movie works in general but I would say if it works at all it's because of André and the connection he has with Imogen, Hayley and Ruth as well.

The Jimi Hendrix Experience:
Live at Monterey DVD

For the first time ever, Experience Hendrix/Geffen/UMe will make available to consumers *The Jimi Hendrix Experience* at Monterey on DVD. The legendary US performance of Hendrix with drummer Mitch Mitchell and bassist Noel Redding at the *Monterey International Pop Festival* originates from June 18, 1967 in Monterey, California.

The awe-inspiring Hendrix item also has the two earliest known live unreleased *Jimi Hendrix Experience* repertoire numbers "Stone Free" and "Like A Rolling Stone" shot on February 25, 1967 at Chelmsford, England.

Bonus features are included in this new package. *A Second Look*, offers an interactive opportunity for the viewer to switch between multiple, never seen camera angles to glimpse several of the performances. In addition a new documentary, *American Landing*, incorporates unreleased interviews with Mitchell, Redding and Hendrix.

CD and vinyl configurations of the same title are also available on Experience Hendrix/Geffen/UMe, produced by Experience Hendrix CEO Janie Hendrix and author John McDermott.

"We have to be creative and conscious of how we put things out," Janie Hendrix explained to me in a 2007 *Record Collector*

News interview. "We're trying not to over saturate the market or make people feel like 'I already have this.' And, so we have a lot of wonderful fans from age 5 to 105. I've been at the cemetery and there are four-year old little girls singing Jimi's songs.

"I think *Monterey* from a historic standpoint is where Jimi really made his mark in the US and that was what he wanted to do at *Monterey*. What we wanted people to know was that there was the Pennebaker film that just shows a very small window of Jimi performing his little part, which is wonderful, but there was more history there that we wanted to tell.

"We met with (*Monterey* producer) Lou Adler, he thought it was a wonderful project, and he was all on board. Although it was our dream, we wanted the blessing of Lou as well. The vision came from Lou and John Phillips and that's what people need to recognize. Pennebaker is one of our partners.

"Once again we only have a limited amount of resources, and we're trying to educate the public. That's what we're all about, educating the public about Jimi and letting them know who he is and see behind the scenes and see a different side. My relationship with Jimi has evolved. Because as a child we think as a child and as an adult we think as an adult, and of course, I was blessed to see Jimi in concert 5 times. So there was kind of a thought that he was my big brother, my hero. I can tell you I wrote numerous papers on him in school. I admired him. And then as I grew older and listened to the lyrics and life happens… Jimi's music becomes the music behind the scenes. And his lyrics become more real as more life happens to me. And so, at this stage in my life, I'm 20 years older than when he was when he passed away, and I have 20 more years under my belt but his lyrics are definitely more profound, and I honestly wish I would have understood them when I was younger because it could have prevented a lot of problems. (laughs). But I do understand them now, and I think that we grow.

"With the *Monterey* CD and DVD items I think in any form of life when you remove one of your senses then the others get more acute. And, so not seeing him and just hearing him makes you rely more on your ears. And, hearing what he is doing and saying and the visual, although wonderful to watch, and the 'aha moments. That's how he did that.' When you take that away for me I concentrate on what he is saying and the different tones in his voice. If he is stressed during that time. What exactly was happening, like what you hear when he is in the middle of when he is trying to tune or get the band's attention.

"Listening just to the CD I don't have that visual and I don't see it, kind of putting myself in that arena. I can absolutely separate myself from administration and simply be a music lover. With the CD and DVD format, 5.1 mix and the new configurations I think technology has caught up to what Jimi visualized. I think when Jimi was creating the music, he was so far ahead of the time he was already hearing that in the way that we hear it now. I don't think we're quite there yet. He's there but we haven't got caught up, technology-wise. With the new *Monterey*, first of all, how do you lose with Jimi? It's not us. It's Jimi. And if people want to hear Jimi and want to get their hands on anything and everything that they can and they don't have, yes. So, really, we're just the facilitators. It's all about him and his music. It's his magic and everything what he was about as a musician and all we're doing is facilitating it," ventured Janie on the obvious spirituality and retail destiny of Jimi's legacy.

"I think the new *Monterey* is beyond my expectations. But, then I have to go, 'it's not about me anyways.' And it never was. We're just messengers. Mitch has been with Jimi the whole time. Noel came and went. And then there was Billy (Cox). Mitch was always there. I think out of the trio, and I'll take Billy out of it right now, between Mitch and Noel, Mitch was the closest to Jimi. Mitch got Jimi. He understood Jimi. There's a great admiration, and I think when Jimi died a large part of Mitch died. And for that I feel a strong connection with him. Like one year Mitch got me a bible from the 1800s. He's always been sweet, kind and considerate, and obviously I can see the personalities and how they got along. Jimi and Mitch. His personality is funny, and because he is British with some really British quirky things, but he's always right on the mark on what he says. And he'll say things in a way that are very profound but not in a mean spirit. Even if somebody is mean to him and has done things to him, like a lawsuit, or said things, he's still kind. And that is a similarity that he and Jimi have.

"Eddie Kramer is part of the vision. I think we couldn't have done what we've done without Eddie. And I think that Jimi chooses Eddie to work with him and being able to tell him what he wanted, and Eddie 'getting it' back then. In the studio we call Eddie the Professor or the Doctor because things will spark his memory. 'Jimi said this.' It's really like walking with somebody through time, you know. Being able to say he was there."

The Jimi Hendrix Experience at Monterey DVD was directed by Bob Smeaton, whose earlier directorial credits are *Festival Express, Jimi Hendrix: The Dick Cavett Show, Hendrix: Band of Gypsys* and *The Beatles Anthology.*

Mitch Mitchell and Hendrix scholar and Experience Hendrix's catalog development director John McDermott contribute extensive liner notes in a package that integrates a plethora of rare and previously unpublished photos of Hendrix, the band and memorabilia of the era.

Another revealing and groovy addition on the *Hendrix Monterey* DVD is *Music, Love and Flowers*, a fascinating inside tour at the legendary *Monterey Pop* festival with event producer and co-promoter Lou Adler.

"Besides the fact that the whole package is so well done and entertaining, it's an important document," Adler mentioned to me in a 2007 *Goldmine* interview. "Everyone is aware of this point what Jimi did at Monterey, and what it meant to his career. It shows you how he got there. It documents the feelings of the group coming to Monterey," Adler explained.

"You hear the group, and you hear from (then manager) Chas Chandler how this was an important moment of Jimi's career for a couple of reasons. One obviously, was the size and the attention of the festival, but also this was an American returning to America after being successful in England and parts of Europe. Coming home. It's his homecoming, and he pulls it off amazingly. It's one of those things you dream about. It's going up to bat, hitting the home run with the bases loaded, or throwing the touchdown pass to win the game. It's coming through after all of what you dream about. Jimi Hendrix dreaming about coming back to America."

"I remember Lou and (sound engineer) Wally Heider chasing after the wreckage Hendrix was creating on stage. They were both doing peaceful Betty Wright," mused Andrew Loog Oldham, who along with Paul McCartney simultaneously suggested to organizers Adler and Phillips to secure Hendrix for the festival. Oldham also steered the Who and Otis Redding to Adler for the happening at Monterey.

"There's some things about Monterey that I had never seen or hadn't remembered or I was a part of and had never seen the footage on," admitted Adler. "On the DVD documentary, there is a meeting we had at Monterey 10 hours before the festival is about to go. There are 20 people in the room including Derek Taylor, Ralph Gleason, Andrew

Loog Oldham, John Phillips, and Michelle Phillips discussing about what we're about to do. And there are still a couple of people in the room saying 'we're not ready!'

"The new DVD feature not only documents Jimi, but *American Landing* leads up to the festival appearance and has some really good English footage. There's footage in there that hasn't been anywhere before. 'Cause we've known the existence of the footage of our meeting in that room. But we could never find the sound the last 40 years. John McDermott found the sound and matched it up. It's terrific," praised Lou. "For me, it's a look at the preparation to the festival that has never been seen before. And the stories that you've heard about you've heard about Hendrix and Who thing (deciding who plays first), and they have Townshend close to that period, explaining what really happened. So, a lot of the stories in bits that have gone around are now documented."

The Jimi Hendrix Experience Live At Monterey has all available existing film footage of that monumental booking presented in its original sequence. Filmmaker D.A. Pennebaker's original.16mm footage has been transferred to high definition and produced in the original theatrical aspect ratio of 1.33:1.

In 2007, for cavehollywood.com, I discussed with director Pennebaker both Hendrix and his *Monterey Pop* documentary.

"Shooting *Monterey Pop* was the beginning of the fast color film. The 72-42 stock had just come out. I had shot a little bit the year before in 1966 with Dylan on *Eat The Document*. And up until then there was no fast color film. They had just brought it out. In effect, and the problem with the way we were filming was that we'd fill up a magazine and shoot it all. Then you'd fill it up again. So you never knew what you'd were gonna be into. So whatever it was, you wanted to process all the film at the same speed. And it is amazing how well it held up and how beautiful the color was.

"We shot everything," Pennebaker said to me in a separate 2001 *Goldmine* magazine interview about how he and his skeletal crew filmed Hendrix and Co. at the Monterey gig. "They had film for it. So, when Jim Desmond was shooting Hendrix at Monterey, we left almost all of his shot in. We had other terrific shots, I was right behind him, Nick Doob, we had great shots from every direction, but you don't need to cut necessarily, so I'm not big on cutting to enhance performance. I like to watch the person doing it handle it, kind of move it around and make it grow in front of you. That's what's interesting to me about performance."

One Hendrix selection, "Can You See Me," is available on the 2007 *Monterey* CD, but not spliced into the DVD, owing to the fact that Pennebaker and his team were reloading film during the song.

Acclaimed engineer/Hendrix confidant Eddie Kramer has mixed the DVD soundtrack in new 5.1 surround and 2.0 mixes from the original eight-track live recordings done at the fabled Monterey concert by remote engineer Wally Heider. Kramer along with John McDermott penned the terrific book *Hendrix Setting The Record Straight.* Chas Chandler, producer and manager of Hendrix endorsed their volume as "the best book I have ever read on Jimi Hendrix!"

"I think you have to look at the history of my relationship with Jimi, obviously a very intense four year period," Kramer told me in a *Record Collector News* 2007 dialogue. "I started with Jimi in January of 1967. I wasn't there for everything, unfortunately, but I was there for the majority in the sense of all the albums. The live recordings, for whatever reason, I was in the studio and always ended up mixing everything of Jimi that was recorded live, including *Band of Gypsys*. I can tell you quite categorically that Jimi was more than a little pissed off about some of the things that were going on with that. I think he was fascinated with the process or with any of the recording process whether it live or in the studio. His fascination and interest was very deep and very understanding of the process. We worked very closely together and when it came time to mix any live material we would sit together and work on it if we could," recalled Kramer.

"Monterey was a situation where it was a film first and foremost, and then I got my hands on it many years later. Which for me was a thrill, because I got to do the entire Monterey movie. (*The Complete Monterey Pop Festival/The Criterion Collection*). One of the advantages of modern technology is that you can fix things that you were not able to fix many years ago or rather it makes it much easier to do that.

"That was actually the first time I had seriously invested a lot of research into the digital world and how it could benefit me in the analog world in restoration work. We've used a program called Cedar that allows you to remove clicks, crackles and pops and was initially developed for the classical world. It was started for the classical guys to restore 78's and acetates when they had no other performances. It does a remarkable job of removing unwanted noise. And it's so sophisticated now that you can actually remove serious crackles, bangs and pops. And, I was a little dubious about using it at first but when we started working with it and we found this track on Otis Redding from Monterey.

"We couldn't use the drums because there was a huge crackle on the drums themselves. We put the program to work and my God it just removed all the noise and left the drums! Because of that fact we were able to use the one Otis track that had never been mixed correctly before. And just the whole thing sounded so much better when it came time for Jimi's stuff at Monterey, the same deal. The thing that was a serious bad noise that had nothing to do with the music I could get rid of without affecting the music. So that whole experience was a challenging one but an interesting one. But what was cool was to see all those 1967 tapes from Monterey all stacked up in the control room and you realize the enormity of the music that was just before you: the Mamas and the Papas, the Who, Jimi Hendrix, Ravi Shankar. We even restored some Ravi Shankar stuff that is unbelievable. He gave us a lesson on how to play a raga. It was just phenomenal," marveled Eddie.

"Now let's move on to the contemporary way we're looking at it with Hendrix. There's a lot that has to be said about the *Woodstock* movie that came out, which was restored to its full two hour length and also mixed to 5.1 and the same sort of principals are involved here. We're talking about 7 tracks, not 8 tracks, because, although *Monterey* was recorded on 8 tracks one inch, one of the tracks disappears because it's got a pulse tone on it for the film to lock up to. So, essentially you are working with 7 tracks and to try and make that sound as if you're at Monterey is really a challenge, because you weren't inside a hall. You were outside where the sound dissipates. And I had to electronically re-create some sort of rear sound reflection to make it feel as if the sound is not dissipating. And I think we've been fairly successful. And so those mixes that I did are now applied to this new edit which I think is lovely. Bob Smeaton and John McDermott did a great job in putting together that nice documentary," Kramer acknowledged.

"What it does is put the movie in perspective. Monterey is about that wonderful historical moment not only for Jimi Hendrix but also for Janis Joplin, essentially discovered there. My job is to find a tiny nugget of something and bring it out as much as I can. You are really digging for gold here, ya know. You're panning through the river trying to find a little piece of something to make it work with. And essentially that is what we've done. And to me that's the fun. It's like an archeological dig. The way I think of Monterey was that this was his premiere shot. He now is a returning hero, and the guy just tore it up. He knew this was his one opportunity to make a big splash, and he did. It is the most stunning performance. It is fantastic. It will live on. I can mix it without seeing the picture. However, when I see the picture, after I've mixed it, I'm usually mixing to picture, or if I haven't mixed to picture I'll mix or re-synch to what I've just done. And, inevitably, when I see the music synch up I see and hear things slightly differently. I might put an accent or push something dynamically that I would normally do in a straight audio mix. But it's very slight. It's not heavy handed. But it definitely helps to see the visual. There's no question. But it doesn't force my hand to make a stupid move and make it out of whack.

"With the DVD and 5.1 format now it's possible to put forward, and you can quote me, 'with testicular fortitude,' the correct sonic balance for Jimi, because at Monterey, previously, the bottom end was always missing. Now you can really bring that forward because of modern technology, and I've been able to combine the best of analog and the best of digital, and it works every time now. I'm always learning stuff about Jimi. Gosh. The backstage stuff. The behind the scenes stuff. The documentaries just fill in the gaps. 'Now I understand.' It's fascinating. Hendrix and his music, the songs, the lyrics, the playing, the sound, the sheer impact of him as an individual will last forever.

"At Monterey, I'm gonna suggest that he was in the mindset that he had to seriously kick everybody's butt. I think the mindset there was 'I am going to pull out every stop I have learned over the last 20 or 25 years.' Every show that he had ever played. Every show trick that he ever played. With the sweeping of the hand up and down the neck, between the legs, behind the back. All that stuff was absolutely executed with a fire, passion and urgency that comes across in the movie. You can tell that he is saying to the world. 'Look. I'm here. I'm Jimi Hendrix. And I'm gonna kick your ass. And you better take note of me. 'Cause this is the one performance that is going to just launch me into the American market.' And I think he just pulled it all out. I mean, look at the way he is dressed. Look at the way he is talking to the audience. He's so up and part of it.

"I think Noel (Redding) has been much maligned, putting aside his personality quirks. His playing and his understanding of what it took to support Jimi was remarkable. Mitch, being the ex-jazz drummer, was the perfect foil for Jimi. I don't think any other drummer kept up with him. One can make a case for Buddy Miles being the best fat back drummer which he was, and able to keep a tremendously steady beat, which he did, ridiculously, but Mitch was the little known genius, you know, who just sort of fiddled around the kit and did the most spectacular thing that would spark Jimi's imagination. And he was able to stay with Jimi and always land on the downbeat, even though he would do the most outrageous fills. You'd think 'there's no way in hell he's gonna land on 1.' But he did. We all know about the personality differences, and there were plenty. But musically, I think Noel is very underrated and I think he did a tremendous job. And, you hear it later on, like with *The Royal Albert Hall*, and stuff like that. Brilliant. To me it's an honor. I thank God that I'm able to still do this for his music and make it come alive. And, we've got tons of stuff left. Wait until you hear *The Royal Albert Hall*. It's just unbelievable," Kramer promised.

The Jimi Hendrix Experience Live At Monterey DVD track listing: "Killing Floor," "Foxy Lady," "Like A Rolling Stone," "Rock Me Baby," "Hey Joe," "The Wind Cries Mary," "Purple Haze," "Wild Thing."

The Jimi Hendrix Experience Live At Monterey CD and LP track listing: "Killing Floor," "Foxy Lady," "Like A Rolling Stone," "Rock Me Baby," "Hey Joe," "Can You See Me," "The Wind Cries Mary," "Purple Haze," "Wild Thing."

Monterey International Pop Festival veterans have their own unique bond to the Hendrix career-spawning recital. Pacific Coast life-altering memories from 40 years ago now support *Jimi Hendrix At Monterey* 2007 audio and visual gifts. I don't think many of us who witnessed Jimi, Mitch and Noel in a physical setting have ever been the same from that shared joint live experience.

Concert-goer Paul Body saw the future of rock 'n' roll immediately when Rolling Stone Brian Jones appeared in a haze and introduced *The Jimi Hendrix Experience.*

"Jimi, Mitch and Noel took the stage in their hippy finery. It seemed like they were wearing all of the colors of the rainbow. They jumped straight into Howlin' Wolf's 'Killing Floor' and all the while Jimi was playing guitar and smacking his gum. Super cool. They did some blues, like 'Catfish Blues' and B.B. King's 'Rock Me Baby.' Done at break neck speed. He did his English hits like 'Purple Haze' and 'Foxy Lady.' We were hearing a brand new thing. He was writing a whole new book. It was blues from Venus."

Then, there is a Kodak-like snapshot ongoing reminder of one still-startled Mamas & Papas member, Michelle Phillips, who still 40 years after seeing Jimi destroy equipment on the Monterey stage confesses, "I was so embarrassed and shocked. I had never seen anyone so sexually explicit on stage. I had never seen anybody treat their axe like that. We were always so careful about our instruments and when we traveled we had the guitars in the plane with us. And then to see him set fire to the guitar, and to slam it to bits on the stage was very upsetting to me. It was a form of expression that I was not prepared for," remembers the former John Marshall High School student.

Dr. James Cushing of Cal Poly San Luis Obispo in Central Coast California who formerly hosted *The Psychedelic Graveyard* radio program on KCPR-FM. He now has a shift on KEBF-FM in Morro Bay hosting *Miles Ahead*. Cushing commented in a 2007 *Goldmine* interview about Hendrix's Monterey performance, and revealed a telling aspect of Jimi's repertoire of June 18, 1967.

"It was 'A star is born,' 1967 style. Not showing how well you could fit in to the conventions of show business but showing how well you could wrestle those conventions of show business into an act of radical self-expression. The set was partially rhythm and blues hucklebuck and partially complete originally, and the blend of them combined with the audaciousness of the moment. He opened with 'Killing Floor.' There's a terrible poignancy to that because the last concert he ever played [Isle of Fehmarn Festival, Germany, Sept. 5, 1970] he also opened with 'Killing Floor.' So his first important show and his last show ever, he opened with a Howlin' Wolf classic that has the idea of death in the title. There's a tragic meaning to that opener that nobody could possibly have been aware of."

James presents another reason to re-discover Mitch Mitchell and Noel Redding as well on the 2007 *Monterey* endeavors. "Once again this specific *Monterey* disc and DVD shows that to have a guitarist who was all over the place, combined with a drummer, who is clearly seminally influenced by Elvin Jones is to have two extremely volatile things going on at once. The volatility of Mitch Mitchell, who is forgotten, underrated, nobody knows how terrific he was, that volatility gave the set the sense of going several different directions at once and the possibility of going in any number of other directions. What I like about Mitch's drumming is that he is always a little bit ahead of the beat and embellishes both the front and back of the beat in creative open ended ways. I like his solos. I think they have drama and structure. I'm glad on the new *Monterey* units Noel Redding's bass is a more audible than the initial *Monterey* LP and early tape configurations where it was poorly recorded and trebly."

Cushing also points to the riveting Hendrix version of Bob Dylan's "Like A Rolling Stone" in the *Monterey* song lineup. "With his rendition of 'Like a Rolling Stone,' Hendrix performs a similar kind of response to Michael Bloomfield in that song as he did to Hubert Sumlin in 'Killing Floor.' What

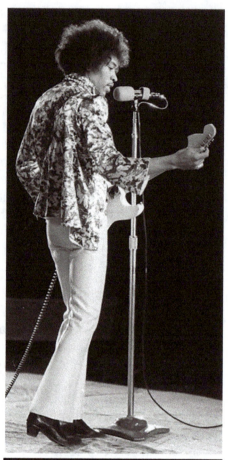

Jim Hendrix Experience at the Hollywood Bowl, August 1967 (Photo by Henry Diltz)

I also like about it is that he makes the song his own by not trying to copy the original aspects of 'Like a Rolling Stone.' 'Cause the original record of 'Like a Rolling Stone' is dominated by the two keyboards. And, so when you have a version of that song with no keyboards, you have a fundamentally different kind of thing.

"Minutes into his set at Monterey, Jimi Hendrix was no longer a complete unknown. Before the event he could walk around the Monterey fairgrounds pretty much unrecognized, after he got on stage, he couldn't do that. When you see the Hendrix set on screen on the DVD it becomes part of a larger drama of self-discovery and self-

128

assertion. But when you just hear it just as a piece of music on CD it becomes a radically, beautifully reconstruction of a song," instructed Dr. Cushing.

Two months after *Monterey* during August 1967, The Jimi Hendrix Experience was booked at the Hollywood Bowl. In June 1969 I finally saw the trio at *Newport '69* in Devonshire Downs music festival the weekend after I graduated Fairfax High School and just before enrolling at West Los Angeles College that July. For a brief moment I was "Stone Free."

Murray Lerner: The Godfather of Live Outdoor Music Cinema

Murray Lerner
(Photo courtesy of the Murray Lerner estate)

Oscar-winning filmmaker Murray Lerner died of kidney failure on September 2, 2017 in New York City at age 90. Lerner was born in Philadelphia, Pennsylvania on May 8, 1927, raised in New York City, and a graduate of Harvard University English major in 1948.

Murray Lerner's filmmaking career began from "industrial cinema." In 1980 he produced and directed the Academy-Award winning *From Mao To Mozart: Isaac Stern In China* about violin virtuoso Isaac Stern's 1979 goodwill tour of Red China.

Lerner's award-winning and trend-setting musical documentaries include Isaac Stern, Miles Davis, Bob Dylan, the Newport Folk Festival, the Moody Blues, Jimi Hendrix, the Doors, Jethro Tull, the Who and Leonard Cohen.

His documentary about Joni Mitchell, *Both Sides Now: Joni Mitchell Live at the Isle of Wight 1970* was released by Eagle Rock Entertainment in September 2017.

Also available in 2017 was the Criterion Collection director-approved special edition of *Festival Folk Music At Newport, 1963-1966.* It's a new reconstruction and remastering of the monaural soundtrack utilizing the original concert and field recordings and presented uncompressed on the Blu-ray DVD.

Festival incorporates *When We Played Newport*, a new program incorporating archival interviews with Lerner, music festival producer George Wein, Joan Baez, Judy Collins, Buffy Sainte-Marie, Pete Seeger, and Peter Yarrow. It houses *Editing Festival*, with Lerner, associate editor Alan Heim, and assistant editor Gordon Quinn.

There's also a selection of complete outtake performances, including Clarence Ashley, Horton Barker, Johnny Cash, John Lee Hooker, and Odetta. Package booklet text has an essay by critic Amanda Petrusich and artist bios by folk music expert Mary Katherine Aldin.

This Lerner Oscar-nominated film was the first of the theatrical documentaries on counter-culture music festivals, preceding both the *Monterey International Pop Festival* and *Woodstock.* Upon initial movie house release *Festival* garnered honors at every major international film festival, including Mannheim, San Francisco, Mar del Plata, and Venice.

I interviewed Murray Lerner in 2008, 2010 and 2014. My brother Kenneth and I hosted a question and answer session with Lerner in Hollywood at the *American Cinematheque Egyptian Theater* in August 2010 as part of Martin Lewis' *Mods and Rockers* film series. I cited Murray's landmark movie *Festival* in our 2017 book, *1967 A Complete Rock Music History of the Summer of Love.* Lerner is referenced in my 2014 book on Leonard Cohen, *Everybody Knows.*

In 2008 I talked to Murray by telephone about his *The Other Side Of The Mirror-Bob Dylan Live At The Newport Festival 1963-1965* DVD released by Columbia Records and Legacy Recordings. Jeff

Rosen serves as executive producer and filmed Lerner for a bonus feature interview contained in the package. Lerner's *Newport* DVD premiered at the 2007 New York Film Festival.

In 1967 Lerner's documentary *Festival*, lensed between 1963 and 1966 at the Newport Folk Festival, was theatrically released. The movie spotlighted performances by Pete Seeger, Bob Dylan, Buffy Sainte-Marie, Donovan, the Staples Singers, Judy Collins, Howlin' Wolf, Mississippi John Hurt, Peter, Paul & Mary, Johnny Cash, Son House, Mimi & Dick Farina, the Paul Butterfield Blues Band and Joan Baez.

We should collectively acknowledge that Murray Lerner is the Godfather of outdoor music cinema and a force that shaped a new film genre who was still active in the frame game at age 90. He is the person who stuck both his neck and camera out for rock 'n' roll and in the process forged alternative retail outlets and distribution for his products eventually inspiring film students, budding independent room workers, lawyers, and future moviemakers since 1967.

Producers and directors of music-driven documentary product and entertainment marketers hawking new media pop culture visual wares owe both psychic and fiscal debts to Lerner's trailblazing path for music product exhibition over the last half century. Murray Lerner taught at Yale and helped establish a film studies program.

I once showed *Festival* at San Diego State University in 1972. His office sent a copy to my dormitory room.

When watching and absorbing Murray's panoramic musical library of moving images and icons, it's quite obvious we always had a poetry head and storyteller for 50 years behind the camera.

Lerner's life and career trek is a hydra-headed distribution and marketing blend of Oscar Micheaux and Homer, four-walled by Samuel Z. Arkoff and Roger Corman.

His influential sound and vision work on Bob Dylan informed the obvious efforts of all rock 'n' reel film music documentarians who followed. like Andrew Solt and Malcolm Leo, who would produce and direct *This Is Elvis* and *Imagine: John Lennon*.

"Murray Lerner," remarked filmmaker Solt, "was a very interesting and important figure in visual music history!"

Lerner's 2014 *The Other Side Of The Mirror – Bob Dylan Live At The Newport Festival 1963-1965* is 83 minutes of filmed

Dylan, 70% available here for the first time. It opens a window into a critical epoch in American cultural history as reflected in the musical transformations of Dylan's watershed performances in 1963-1965 at the Newport Folk Festival.

The most extraordinary aspect is watching Lerner's work capture this unbelievable moment in time where the young artist shows up from nowhere, then projects his own voice, his stage presence, his ability to deliver his art, but watching the audience's reaction over the same period of time as if everyone was in complete lockstep. That Dylan's own personal growth mirrored the desire and the needs of an audience to have him there physically as well at the exact time.

Murray Lerner is sensitive to Dylan's personal magnetism, particularly that wonderful paradox of his assertive, even aggressive self-confidence combined with his physical presentation. Dylan on screen is a small delicate person, but would as soon blow you away as look at you. Dylan's uncanny abilities establish a compelling and distinctive vocal stylist.

The Other Side Of The Mirror has no sense of director Lerner asserting a point of view of what this DVD means. It just gives you what happened. This is all the existing footage edited together to be as coherent, as true to the moment as possible. Lerner takes our eyes into wordsmith Dylan's rabbit hole.

In 1995 Lerner distributed his long awaited *Message To Love: The Isle of Wight Festival* featuring the Who, Jimi Hendrix, Leonard Cohen, Moody Blues, Tiny Tim, the Doors, Taste, Free, Jethro Tull, and other acts.

In 2019, poet and deejay Dr. James Cushing described Lerner's documentary of Jimi's performance at this festival (released as a stand-alone DVD *Blue Wild Angel: Jimi Hendrix at the Isle of Wight* in 2002).

"It's almost shockingly intimate: we overhear Jimi, seconds before going on, reviewing how 'God Save the Queen' goes and who has the rights to the film and recording; we see an enormous range of emotions on his face, from bliss to fury, boredom to mirth, annoyance to pure absorption in the sounds coming out of those Marshall amplifiers. We enjoy the colorful, hand-made-looking clothes he and Mitch Mitchell are wearing, and we notice Mitchell being unusually kinetic behind his drum kit, ready to solo at any time.

132

"We notice the set list begins with an unusual three-song medley of 'God Save the Queen,' the 'Sgt. Pepper' theme, and then into 'Spanish Castle Magic.' He continues by introducing a song "written in 1847 but still has something": 'All Along the Watchtower.' Several songs would be unknown to any August 1970 audience — 'Freedom,' 'Dolly Dagger,' 'Ezy Ryder,' 'In From the Storm' — but he presents them confidently, without preamble.

"Both Cox and Mitchell in their interviews on the DVD stress that the 2:00 a.m. darkness, height of the stage, and size of the crowd (600,000?) worked against any tangible sense of audience, and we see that in the footage. Even though roadies trot back and forth occasionally, the three men seem so thoroughly left to themselves up there that at times we feel we're watching a filmed rehearsal rather than a concert document. This feeling is most prevalent during 'Red House,' which Jimi plays without a pick on a Gibson Flying-V instead of the usual Fender Stratocaster. The performance feels 'pure' in the sense of being unobserved — no self-consciousness is evident in his face or body.

"Was Jimi satisfied with the venue, or his performance? His spoken intro to 'God Save' ends, 'Stand up for your country and start singing! And if you don't, fuck you.' And his last words to the assembled: 'One of these days we'll get it together. Peace, love, and all that other good shit.' And he tosses his Strat onto the stage floor.

"Was he dissing the notoriously disorganized festival? Was he complaining about having to travel all the way from New York to England to play concerts when he most wanted to hole up in Electric Lady studios, recording away?

"My theory: he was building a protective verbal wall around his performance, asserting his independence from the judgment of an audience, emphasizing the unity of the trio's sound and the clarity of his compositions against the chaos of the surroundings."

"The cameraman must have been standing inches behind Jimi as he waited to go on at the Isle of Wight," suggests poet Celeste Goyer. "We overhear him as he discovers he has no guitar pick—we hear him taking this spare minute to have a brief conversation about rights to the live recording with touring manager Jerry Stickles. This fly-on-the-amp style of camera work is super intimate.

"As fans we want to get as close as possible, to peer into the soup cauldron, try and discern the ingredients. I felt this privilege watching from the back as Mitch Mitchell's psychedelic yellow tank top strap slips off his shoulder, and witnessing Jimi's split pants episode where he tells the guys to jam as he gets it fixed. Who knelt in front of Hendrix with a safety pin, I want to ask. I have safety concerns. It's wonderful to hear the way the band comes into and out of focus, with Jimi narrating their wanderings with his rumpled addresses to the audience, exactly the way a jazz combo patiently perseveres through cloudier bits before coming together into a groove.

"Somewhere I saw a snippet of footage where Jimi's lounging back on a couch, talking about his dream to get together a huge circle of musicians from around the world to jam and create a universal music that would erase all boundaries. This idealism places him in a long tradition of musicians working toward a functional concept of music: John and Alice Coltrane, Woody Guthrie, Anthony Braxton, John Lennon, Sun Ra, Pete Seeger and many more.

"Beethoven and the others of the European Romantic movement in the late 19th and early 20th centuries believed in the transformative power of art to unite people and lift them up, in contrast to what they saw as the alienating effects of increasing materialism and the advances of mechanistic science. And here's William Blake: 'The Imagination is not a State/ it is the Human Existence Itself!'

"This thread leads from Wagner and Goethe to Karlheinz Stockhausen, whose invention of intuitive music was designed to create holes in consciousness, through which divine inspiration could enter.

"*Amazing Grace*, the Aretha Franklin documentary, wonderfully demonstrates the transformative function of music to bring love and community to vivid life in a place where it would be easy to despair. Think of Jimi Hendrix, part Cherokee, part black American. Does a past get any more rubbed out than that? He didn't just imagine or pray for a better future, he actively sought to bring it about with his music."

Harvey Kubernik and Murray Lerner interview

HK: Can you cite the influence of any documentary filmmakers on your work?
ML: I wasn't influenced by any filmmakers, maybe Bert Stern and *Jazz On A Summer's Day*, also shot at Newport in the late 50s, largely because of his use of telephoto lenses, which I fell in love with.

HK: Is there any sort of general philosophy that guides you in preparation of a documentary film subject?

ML: I tend to make documentary films after thinking about it and researching it and having a concept in mind and finding iconic images that resonate with that concept. That's the way I work. When it came to *Festival,* when I started to go up there and look, I went up for the Newport festival, I was a folk music fanatic.

Before then, I did some industrial films, an underwater feature, *Secrets Of The Reef.* It actually played in theaters successfully, at least in one theater, the Baronet, and then Jacques Cousteau came along with *The Silent World,* and that was the end of our distribution. *laughs.* We didn't have any people in our movie. Ours was anthropomorphism, and it was a negative word. I had done a number of industrial films with sophisticated photography and editing before I did *Festival.*

HK: This 2014 *Newport* Dylan DVD is a different sort of film, in a sense, from what you usually direct.

ML: We decided on no narration, no pundit interviews, no interviews with Dylan. Nothing except the experience of seeing him...That to me is exciting. Just the clear experience gives you everything you need. I felt that when I screened the music of *The Other Side Of The Mirror,* because he is touted metaphorically as the mirror of his generation, and I thought no, he's beyond that. He always takes the generation beyond that, and he's like on the other side of the mirror, but I also felt the wondrous quality of his imagination took us like Alice to a new world on the other side of the mirror. I felt to break that would be bad.

Dylan's songs and his ideas were so powerful that my thesis, or premise, was that once I got you involved in him and you were also seeing a change in his imagination going in his music that you wouldn't want to leave it. Either I pulled you into it or I didn't. If you weren't pulled into his music and took this journey with him then you're not going to like the film. Nothing you say is gonna make you like it more.

HK: Was it by decision that you chose to shoot *Festival* and *The Other Side Of The Mirror – Bob Dylan Live At The Newport Folk Festival* in black and white?

ML: I had a choice for black and white over color, and it was a major decision in the face of a lot of negativity. First of all, I thought at that time you could really get good color in the original, but you couldn't get good color duplicates. That the prints, which is, after all, that was going to be what you were going to show, and also the contrasts were too great, and the blacks wouldn't have any detail in it. As a matter of fact, I was a fanatic about that, and I earlier had done an industrial film, which became a big hit in that industry, *Unseen Journey*, and I couldn't stand the idea of Kodachrome prints, so I actually talked the people into paying to me to go to Technicolor, and do three strip prints. And it worked. It was beautiful and I shot it in 35mm to begin with. But the 16 mm prints were also great, so I was really into thinking about those things in a way.

HK: How did you get the initial Newport job that resulted in 1967's theatrical release of *Festival* and later utilized in your 2007 *Dylan at Newport* DVD item?

ML: Through debt and through cajoling people to help. *laughs.* There weren't a lot of obstacles to shoot *Festival.* Once it got

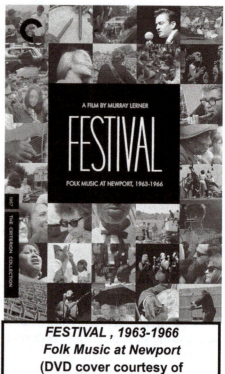

FESTIVAL , 1963-1966
Folk Music at Newport
(DVD cover courtesy of
the Criterion Collection)

rolling then the obstacles were different people associated with the festival who had their own favorites to make a film. I had to overcome that. Anyway, I was determined to get it initially released theatrically. I knew there was where the workshops and live performances were interesting and cinematic. And, music was always my passion for the soundtrack of a film. For the form of a film, when I did *Festival,* it was the form of the film should also be musical, and it should be like experiencing a piece of music in addition to being about music. It seemed to work.

At the *Venice Film Festival* people in a 1,000 seat theater really got up and applauded. I was alone. I was brought up to think that things should be well exposed, in focus, and you can hear the sound. I had no encounters with Dylan except through Howard Alk. He was great, a marvelous human being. You had to stand up to him with a powerful personality. So, every time I told him to change something, a storm would come over the room that we were in. But I stuck to my ground, and that's why he needed a director like me. If you look at the editing of *Festival* you will see how sophisticated it is. He'd carry over the tiny sound from one thing to another. It was a three picture two sound movieola and we spent most of our time repairing the film.

Howard called me up and said 'why don't we edit this in *Woodstock?*' and I said, 'No!' Because I would have a lot of powerful voices around me. 'How 'bout Martha's Vineyard?' It was edited for two summers at Martha's Vineyard, then he saw a film I did about Yale, finish that.

I had to deal with Albert Grossman for clearances. It took a while to convince Al, who was not a control freak. Not the slightest influence in the editing. As time went on, each artist was different. Dylan was a buddy of Howard Alk. Howard had their ear and was a friend of Dylan, and had known Grossman from Chicago.

The concept was that, going beyond the entertainment value of the music that was the music being used was a crucible for creation of a counter-culture and a message. The prize I got at Venice was not only for a form of entertainment but a means of an expression of youth. That's what I wanted to do and look for stuff that helped me do that. So, when I did an interview, I had that in mind. Like in the new *Newport* DVD, and in *Festival* I interview Joan Baez in the car. She did a good one because she discusses what the kids ask. Joan could make fun of Bob on stage because they were close. I think they thought of themselves, and the crowd did as well as the king and queen of Newport. The movie I really wanted to make was about all the tension backstage from the other performers and managers. *laughs.*

HK: *Festival* was always well received when it played at universities and the midnight movie screenings.

ML: It had more festival showings than any other. San Francisco, Argentina, In Italy Federico Fellini, the director, gave me his phone number, but I never called him. I always admired him. I was rather shy at the time. At Venice, it sounds crazy, but there were a lot of big wigs there, Pasolini, Antonioni. My film was the most popular of the festival. It was a hit. *Festival* was not just about Dylan. They loved Baez and the rest of it. The whole crowd at Venice got up and danced in the aisles, it was amazing. It was thrilling. It's always been available for schools and screenings and before a *Festival* DVD, it was on videotape. I was determined not to let it die through mail order and schools. We never made any money. I was a terrible self-promoter and this was before DVD and cable TV.

HK: In *Festival,* and once again in the *Newport* DVD, the live footage of "Maggie's Farm" was so powerful and jolting to see in a theater originally, and now on DVD. And Dylan with some members of the Paul Butterfield Blues Band for this effort is always being confrontational. With the camera, daring it to love him, he is being confrontational with the audience.

ML: I knew the Butterfield band and had done some industrial film with some of their music. On stage, Paul came alive. He's not performing with Dylan together in the 1965 set because Paul mentioned something like it wasn't right to have two stars on stage at the same time. I interviewed Mike Bloomfield in *Festival* talking about (Paul) Butterfield. I wanted to show in the movie that this was a movement for white kids and white people to get into the blues. Bloomfield and Butterfield were iconic figures in my mind.

HK: You understood Dylan moving into electric rock 'n' roll from an acoustic setting.

ML: I felt that electricity was needed to distribute the music in a wide basis, radio and television. Then, once it happened, the hunger for the feeling that electricity gave people listening to it was more than volume. I think electric music gets into your body, and enters into your nerves quite deeply, and almost puts you into a trance. It's hypnotic. I've always felt this, and this was the feeling I had when I watched Bob. And I was excited by it. I not only appreciated the changes, I loved it! I really was mesmerized and hypnotized by "Maggie's Farm" on many levels. As I was filming it, I knew it was a gateway to a new culture in the form based on the older culture, and I thought this was it. I was mesmerized by electric music, by Paul Butterfield earlier in the thing, and Howlin' Wolf played with a band. But what Dylan did, the electricity got into your bones. I was both in the pit and on the stage.

In the DVD, we didn't use "Phantom Engineer (It Takes A Lot To Laugh A Train To Cry)," because I didn't think it was up to the standard of "Maggie's Farm" and "Like a Rolling Stone," to be honest with you. "Stone" is too big a climax to extend it with something not as good.

I knew it was going to be a major breakthrough. It was a mixture of booing, applause and bewilderment. I was intensely involved in the filming so I didn't pay much attention to what the audience was doing. I was hypnotized in a way by the electric music and had to get the shot. And, the interesting thing about "Maggie's Farm" which was a breakthrough musically, but the lyrics were expressing the same kind of idea that he wasn't gonna be a conformist. And in a way, "Maggie's

Farm" was a symbol for America working. We're all working on "Maggie's Farm."

HK: What impressed you the most about Dylan as a poet?

ML: The words just fell on his music. I knew that when I saw him walk in a room at a party around 1962 for Cynthia Gooding. He came in and pulled out his guitar, played a few songs about New York, packed it up and split. He intrigued me. At Harvard University I majored in English and my main interest was modern American poetry. T.S. Eliot and Ezra Pound and their technique of two opposite symbols creating a third idea. Two different images, the unexpected juxtaposition of two different images for the third idea. Which guided me into filmmaking.

HK: What is the genesis of your new *Newport* DVD?

ML: Jeff Rosen loved *Festival* ever since it came out and we became friends. He directed and filmed the interview with me in the *Newport* DVD. He loved my Miles Davis' film. How we got to the Dylan thing? Someone who shall remain nameless, an attorney I was dealing with in L.A. about the *Isle Of Wight*, saw some papers, turned out to be a Dylan freak, played the guitar. I showed him a copy of my work print from 1973, '74, a draft edit, and told him not to ever show it to anyone because Dylan would be annoyed if it ever came out bootlegged.

Then, years later, Jeff Rosen called me up and said, "We'd like to buy your Dylan footage." "What do you mean?" "I have a copy of this thing you did." I was annoyed. *laughs*. But it turned out to be good. Jeff had a long range view of what turned out to be *No Direction Home*. I have some footage in *No Direction Home* which he twisted my arm to buy. *laughs*. So, I said OK, and he made a few good suggestions, but it had to be released after *No Direction Home*. I was at time in conflict licensing things from my work. Absolutely. Always in conflict. *laughs*. What did happen, when I revisited it, I saw I had a real film there. not just a series of shots, but in chronological order. Once the New York Film Festival took it, I knew I had a film.

HK: Your *Message To Love* music documentary shot in 1970, finally released commercially in 1995, included the Who's cover of Mose Allison's 'Young Man's Blues' and Townshend's 'Naked Eye'. The DVD also birthed a retail relationship with the band that exists at the moment with the release of the Who's *Amazing Journey* 2007 documentary that you've co-produced and co-directed. But, there was a 20-year period, before the Betamax and VHS-formats, the growth of home video market, and the DVD as a viable format where we could

139

not find your catalogue and music documentary products, largely because the market had not been developed yet to distribute.

Man, talk about being early on the scene. *Message To Love* emerged as a joint venture with Castle Communications and BBC in association with Initial Film and Television.

ML: *laughs*. The thing that got me re-introduced, known again, was my *Isle of Wight* feature that took a long time to get made. Dylan had played at the 1969 Isle of Wight festival, not at *Woodstock* that same summer. Bert Block was the agent got him to go. Bert was sort of acting as Dylan's manager at the time, not Albert Grossman. The Foulk brothers were looking for a performer, a headliner for my film. Block was a great fan of my Newport film. And he called, "Would you like to rent us the Newport film to show at the Isle of Wight?" I responded and suggested, "Why not make another film?" "OK" That was part of it. And, actually, they did license my film, and if you watch my film once in a while there are two big projectors sitting there. *laughs*.

What happened at that festival was you couldn't show a film because there was chaos. I did get a check. In those days the English currency regulations were such you weren't allowed to send money abroad except under certain conditions. I decided to shoot *Isle of Wight* in color and duplications of color were OK.

I predicted what would happen. Conceptually, I thought the counter-culture, having followed it, was being co-opted commercially, kids were getting angry and I knew there would be tremendous tension and anger. I knew it was brewing, and one of the people interested in it was in England. I got an English crew of about 9, after I did it, and Howard [Alk] helped me edit a little initially, a demo reel, but then he moved to the west coast to live on Dylan's property editing *Renaldo & Clara*. It was really exciting. Everyone loved it but wouldn't back it.

They didn't think the music would sell, they didn't think the political aspect would sell. But I knew the Who, Jethro Tull, Miles Davis, the Doors were potent performers on stage and on camera. Absolutely. And, there was a feeling "Oh well. These are older acts," which I never agreed. These are the people who control this media.

Looking at the Who through a lens was incredible. We all felt it was almost a religious experience. You've seen my Who film from the Isle of Wight. That was really incredible. And the crowd was with it, and of course, except for me, the crew was British, and they knew their music quite well. I had a great chief camera man, Nic Knowland, an incredible find, another one like Howard Alk. He did a lot with the counter-culture. And Jethro Tull leapt off the screen with 'My Sunday Feeling'. I finally got to put their full set out from the Isle of Wight a couple of years ago. I interviewed Ian Anderson 30 years later, a land squire, still a musician. I've done a number of interviews, like with Ian, and the people who played with Miles Davis at Isle of Wight, 30 years later.

The *Message To Love* festival film documentary was both a harder and easier sale. I got the financing from Jeff Kempton who followed the production many years from Castle to Eagle Vision. BBC put up half the money with Initial Films for BBC to do it. They didn't bother me at all. It took a lot of money on my part to keep showing this demo reel of the Isle of Wight. *laughs*.

I remember Haskell Wexler, a friend of mine, he said, "I'll tell you what. I'll talk to you, but you've got to promise never to mention the Isle of Wight again. *laughs*." That was then. It really was an interesting journey. It ended up being the last filmed live performance of the Doors.

In the 2007 Who documentary, I conducted the new interviews with everyone. Pete Townshend is not only bright, but perceptive, and he's thought a lot about issues that I've thought a lot about, the meaning of rock 'n' roll. Anyone who thinks about it has to think, "Why is this so powerful?" "Why do millions of people respond to it all over the world?" And then the bigger question I ask people I want to make a film about is "what is music?" That really throws people when I ask them that. Why is it so powerful? And Townshend realizes that the audience is part of the music. At least that's the way he plays and they play. He doesn't speak the way you want him to. I mean he can throw you! (laughs).

HK: *Leonard Cohen: Live at the Isle of Wight–1970*. Now out as a full-length DVD. How did your Cohen and Isle of Wight film happen?
ML: From the Newport festivals on, I decided I wanted to show something behind the scenes in the music business. Not just the festival, because I saw the festivals were not quite as loving and peaceful as it seemed. Every night there would be big meetings at Newport until two or three in the morning arguing about who was gonna be next and the order of the lineup, all of that. And you never saw that, and I was startled. How many blacks, how many Appalachian singers, this and that? So I decided I would like to turn the cameras the other way

141

at some point. And then when I saw *Woodstock*, I decided I had to because I thought it was phony, so that made me determined to do it.

And then by chance really, when (Bob) Dylan was breaking up with (Albert) Grossman, and Bert Block, who became an agent for (Kris) Kristofferson, at the Isle of Wight festival, he came to me. He had been Grossman's partner and now was with Jerry Perenchio's Chartwell Artists. He liked my movie *Festival!* He said these promoters from England came to America and asked him to get the performers for the 1970 Isle of Wight, an island off Southern England. They wanted to run and screen *Festival!*

So I said fine, 'But I'd really like to make a film." OK. That started me down this path. And they did make a deal with me to license *Festival!* They even rented two projectors and in the Tiny Tim scene you can see them. They had rented the projectors but the guys in charge fled, they were really afraid of staying in the festival grounds 'cause they were worrying about the atmosphere. They refused to work it. So they gave me a check for licensing. That was the first one. It was organized by Ronnie, Ray and Bill Foulk, and Rikki Farr *compère* (the host), did the stage introductions.

I decided to do a film and the promoters, I got them in touch with ABC Films at the time, and they decided it wasn't a good enough deal. So then we started to negotiate and talk. Everyone wanted to do this film and they were willing to do it with me. And I organized an English crew. And I had one person from staff, a guy who had been my assistant on a lot of shoots.

I had a loose outline between the idealism of the music and the commercialism of the music business.

I shot color for the *Cohen and the Isle of Wight* performers. It was high-speed Ektachrome reversal. And I'm glad I did it because the color lasts a lot better in reversal. The camera people I had were with their own cameras for the most part but they used Arriflexes, and a new camera, the main camera man used an Aaton, a kind of avant garde camera at the time.

HK: *The Isle of Wight* footage and the Cohen section you seem to capture close ups and focus on the dramatic aspect of faces, Cohen, some band members, female background singers are terrific.
ML: Yes. I always use very long lenses as an adjunct to my photography. I believe in the long shot because I would like the thing to feel musical and not jumpy. I think film is visual music. And it should be, and I

believe in editing that way. You can have moments where you are doing quick montage. Most of the time you need to relax.

I like really long shots and before anyone ever did it I used 2,000 mm lenses and for crowd shots, moving in slow motion on Broadway, a lot of unusual stuff. I love people coming towards the camera and coming into close up. And then I got a 600 mm lens for my 16 mm camera, played around with it during Sonny Terry and Brownie McGee at Newport. Real close ups.

HK: What was the one thing you learned from your Newport Films which you applied to the *Isle of Wight* shoot?

ML: First of all, on the technical side, I learned and made sure everyone examined and knew their equipment well enough to be sharp to be on a very literal level. Sharp when they were close in and wide angle. Very often when you go to a wide angle it can lose focus. So I had them check their cameras for that problem and fix it. And, going from there, I had to call them all together and explain what I don't like. I don't like, and some of them did it anyway, I don't like fast pans, fast zooms.

I said, "If you are panning over to a musician that is playing but you don't see because he comes in after the musician is on, go slow." You'll hear the person, and it will be more dramatic than if you swish the camera or zoom in. That is one of the big things. And, I said "Close Up! Close Up!" I don't mind looking into the lights for effect. A bunch of stuff I directed them to do. I took special shots, positions. Like with the Doors, I took the shots from behind looking into the lights. The idea is to be musical in the movements and try and move with the music.

When I showed some films a few years ago in Hollywood at the Egyptian Theater, *The Who at the Isle of Wight*, Andrew Loog Oldham was there and commented, "You were part of the band." That's what you gotta do.

I personally have a technique where I practice the choreography of the camera. Every day for about an hour before I shot, having an assistant stand by, and I would focus, zoom and figure out how big the moves had to be to get the result I wanted, so I could do it myself. And I practiced all of that. And I kind of instilled that sense of the choreography of the camera being part of the concert. For the most part, in the planning stages, I picked positions to shoot. And I gaev them assignments, "You concentrate on the close ups; and you concentrate on something else."

HK: At the August 31, 1970 Isle of Wight music festival the crowd had its own agenda, metastasizing into a frantic and hectic situation, crushing the gates and fences at this seaside community. They numbered 600,000 and Cohen was at the epicenter of the event which now had fire and smoke encroaching structures and equipment. Cohen and some band members had taken Mandrax. And they followed a very late set by Jimi Hendrix finally taking the stage at two o'clock in the morning. My brother Kenneth Kubernik described the scene remarkably well after viewing your 2009 *Leonard Cohen Live at the Isle of Wight-1970* DVD.

"The punters, restless in the aftermath of Jimi Hendrix's incendiary performance, were instantly tamed by this unkempt, unprepossessing gentleman, adorned in pajama bottoms (he'd been having a nap backstage and barely answered the bell to perform). As poised as Caesar before his legions, Cohen took command of his 'Army' – his group's nickname – and held the half million attendees in thrall. Documentarian Murray Lerner captured it all on film. The resulting 2009 DVD – *Leonard Cohen Live at the Isle of Wight–1970* – demonstrated his gift for conjuring magic out of mayhem. The oft-derided listless baritone voice, the plodding rhythms and the deathly pallor of the lyrics conspired to produce a hypnotic calm."

ML: I first heard Cohen as a literary character, a poet. And then in the late sixties a couple of his records on the radio. I heard his debut LP.

He came out acoustic and walked out electric. I felt hypnotized. I felt his poetry was that way. I was really into poetry and that is what excited me about him. To put music to poetry was like hypnotic to me.

When he told the audience before a number, how his father would take him to the circus as a child. He didn't like circuses, but he liked when a man would stand up and asking everyone to light a match so they could see each other in the darkness. "Can I ask of you to light a match so I can see where you all are?"

But when he sang the lyrics of the songs they took over, and he had 'em in the palm of his hand. Even removing myself from being the director, how this guy could walk out and do this in front of 600,000 people? It was remarkable. It was mesmerizing. And the banter was very much in tune with the spirit of the festival. And, more particularly what he said, you know. "We're still a weak nation, and we need land. It will be our land one day." It was almost biblical.

When he did "Suzanne," he said, "Maybe this is good music to make love to." He's very smart. He's very shrewd. The other thing he was able to do, the talking, I think the audience was able to listen to

144

him. They heard him and felt he was echoing something they felt. The audience and I were mesmerized. It was incredible and captivating. That night, Leonard was on some sort of mission. His band was called the Army.

My film shows the roles of the background singers. Sure, Ray Charles and Raylettes, and the Cohen singers had beautiful skin. They were a balance to him up there, and the fact I was jealous of the guy that this guy was able to get all these women. *laughs*. And he's up there very late at night, the morning, unshaven. The music is great.

The Isle of Wight journey was worth it. That was the most exciting event I've ever been to. 'Cause it was so all-encompassing and new. In terms of the possibility of the crowd killing us and always living on the edge of that precipice.

And I was always thinking, in relationship to the performers, "What's my role in what they are singing about? How do I fit into that?" I change with each one as I am watching them. Like with the Moody Blues, I liked their music. It was different and interesting, and like Leonard Cohen; it had an undercurrent of mysticism to it.

I thought the *Isle of Wight 1970* and the Cohen footage had touched the deep chord of people. I realized how deep it was, and I was startled how prophetic it was. I was proud and excited at what I had done.

At Isle of Wight, Leonard was much different than Miles, Jimi, the Doors and the Who. Because the talking on stage was very insightful of him, you know. He must have understood that by talking and speaking to them, it gave him, or put him in touch or gave him a kind of camaraderie with the crowd that no one else tried to do. Maybe he felt he needed it and he may have.

Leonard also had that fabulous guy, the producer who was in his band, Bob Johnston. I had quite a time over decades later getting him to be interviewed for the DVD.

HK: All performers have a common thread of some kind or they wouldn't perform.
ML: Leonard, on stage and in film, is different than Bob Dylan.

HK: Can you compare and contrast them?
ML: If I can. Dylan depends on music in a way that Cohen doesn't, I think. It stands on its own more than Dylan does, I think. Dylan is brilliant. I trust in a sense whatever he says. He actually likes to tour

and he likes the involvement with the crowd. You never know what he really thinks. He loves teasing people.

HK: Your Bob Dylan and Miles Davis films are time capsules. Dylan at Newport before he went electric was like Dorothy in *The Wizard of Oz* before the road became color. Before it was post-War America, where nothing had sorted itself out yet, by the time Dylan went electric, everything changes. Between 1963-1964 people started screaming for him. The electric set demonstrates paramountly that Dylan was his own man. That he was not going to wait for anyone.

It reminds me of the famous line by Miles Davis, that my brother Ken told me, when someone came up to Miles and said "I've grown up with your music, and now that you're playing this electric stuff I just don't get it." And, Miles looked at him and said, "What do you want me to do? Wait for you?" That's what great artists do by definition. They're not being held back by their audience.

ML: In my Miles Davis film, I thought the change in Miles Davis was very similar to the change in Bob Dylan and the hostility that he encountered as for them going electric. Because of Dylan, and I read a lot about Miles going electric, it took a lot of courage on his part to go electric. That music at the *Isle of Wight* was cinematic, like Dylan earlier at *Newport*. Dylan was at the absolute height of the involvement and charisma. Absolutely. Of course he has words and Miles doesn't. It's a big difference for me. *Shooting Miles,* I knew I had an important moment, especially in a rock music setting. That's the point, again.

HK: You and D.A. Pennebaker have witnessed and participated in the rock and music documentary world for well over 60 years. Have you done panel discussions with Pennebaker in front of university film students?

I've been attending some of these events. Unlike the sixties and seventies, most of the students and wannabee filmmakers now in the audience at the question and answer session want to know about royalty points on the back end of film deal and not about film stock, lenses or concepts to creating a story.

ML: The best one of those was at the Santa Fe, New Mexico Film Festival, a documentary panel. Pennebaker was there. (Ricky) Leacock was there. I was there. It was a seminar-type thing, where people would question us afterwards, you know. It was all about "how do you get the money?" Not about creative stuff, but financial. One kid said to Pennebaker, "How do you get the money to finance a film?" And without missing a beat he said, "Marry a rich woman."

Curtis Hanson and *Wonder Boys*

In 1998, Curtis Hanson was nominated for Best Director for *L.A. Confidential*, starring Kevin Spacey, Russell Crowe, and Guy Pearce. He didn't win the Oscar for directing, but Kim Basinger took home an Oscar for Best Actrress in a Supporting Role, and Curtis Hanson and Brian Helgeland both went home with Academy Awards for Best Writing, Screenplay Based on Material Previously Produced or Published.

Fast forward to Paramount's 2000 release of *Wonder Boys*, directed by Curtis Hanson, starring Michael Douglas, Toby Maguire, Frances McDormand, Katie Holmes, Rip Torn, Richard Thomas and Robert Downey, Jr., and featuring music from some of the world's most popular and acclaimed singer/songwriters including John Lennon, Bob Dylan, Van Morrison, Neil Young and Leonard Cohen.

In late 2000, Columbia Records released the soundtrack album to *Wonder Boys,* and Dylan's song, "Things Have Changed" was nominated for a Best Original Song Academy Award.

In the Awards Show, Dylan and his band played the song on a satellite feed from Australia where they were touring. Ultimately, "Things Have Changed" received the Oscar for Best Original Song, and in his acceptance speech, Dylan thanked Hanson a couple of times, as well as Columbia Records, and the Academy voters who acknowledged "a song that doesn't pussyfoot around or turn a blind eye to human nature," before signing off by wishing all the viewers "peace, tranquility and goodwill."

Hanson and music supervisor Carol Fenelon hand-picked the songs included in the film and soundtrack album, and Hanson himself wrote the liner notes. As he explained in the promotional literature of the music from the motion picture, "Many of these recordings were chosen before we began the first day of filming. I played several of the songs before and during the shooting of certain scenes, so the actors would understand the texture the music would eventually add to the completed movie. In *Wonder Boys*, the songs are very much part of the storytelling process."

Oscar winner Michael Douglas stars as Grady Tripp, the one-time wonder boy of the literary world who still hasn't completed his long-awaited follow-up novel. Toby Maguire (*The Ice Storm*) portrays a gifted writing student that teacher Grady takes under his shaky wing. Frances McDormand plays his mistress. *Wonder Boys* also marks the motion picture debut of jazz musician Richard Knox. His group, the Dirty Dozen Brass Band, had been playing around the world for over two decades. Jane Adams who received critical notices for her breakthrough film performance in *Happiness* is in the flick as well.

I had previously interviewed Curtis Hanson for *HITS* magazine about the music he selected for *L.A. Confidential*. In March 2000, he invited me to his office in Westwood, California to talk about *Wonder Boys*. Our conversation focused primarily on the just issued soundtrack album. Curtis was very receptive to outlining the reasons and song choices that constitute *Wonder Boys*. He is very passionate about all sorts of music.

The *Wonder Boys* soundtrack is filled with influential singer/songwriters. It brings attention to some overlooked artists like Tim Hardin and Tom Rush, features four Dylan songs and recordings from Van Morrison, Leonard Cohen, Neil Young, Buffalo Springfield and John Lennon, among others. I dug the movie, even paid a second time to see it again. Under a wall photo of Sam Fuller, which Hanson himself took decades ago, we went over the artists and tunes placed in *Wonder Boys*.

HK: In the mid-'60s through the latter part of the '60s you did a stint as a movie reviewer/entertainment writer for the school newspaper at Cal State Los Angeles. It's pretty obvious that you saw some early music club dates of Tom Rush and Tim Hardin, who both have songs in *Wonder Boys*.

CH: When I was 18, I went to Cal State L.A., over on the other side of town, pretended to be a journalism major, became the movie critic for the college paper, and then turned that into entertainment editor. They gave me a page a week. So then I was at The Ash Grove, the Troubadour, Shelley's Manne-Hole, The Light House, McCabe's. That's when I was seeing people like Tim Hardin and Tom Rush. And seeing them free (laughs). I was also a fan of (early) FM radio in Los Angeles, and of course, the movies. Movies are music, and music is movies. That's the thing I've always resented about 99% of the music videos is that they impose images on songs that, once you've seen 'em, you have to try and get them out of your mind. It prevents you from dealing directly with the artist who wrote the songs. And the artists we've been talking about were all amazing visualists. I'd rather let the words of Leonard Cohen take me where they take me. Tim Hardin I've been a fan of since day one. The album *Tim Hardin 2* was an album that I wore out a couple of copies of back when it was new.

At that time in my life, albums were really important in the way movies were important, and it didn't have to do with success. It was like the movie, *Jules and Jim*. It was not a big box office success, but everyone that you knew who loved movies saw it and talked about it. And *Tim Hardin 2* with that photo of him in a little house in West Hollywood was just a great, great album. His "Reason to Believe" was on the wish list because we were dealing with a story that is about fiction, redemption, reinforcement. And, by the way, Tim Hardin is a tragic wonder boy. Tim Hardin was so talented, but because of the combination of his bad luck and bad drugs, people forgot he wrote these amazing songs and had a wonderful voice that spoke his own words so well.

HK: What is the genesis of the movie project?
CH: It began for me when Michael Douglas sent me the script. I read it and really responded to the characters. I read it again and got together with Michael the next day to talk about the character, to see if he'd be prepared to go all the way in playing this character. And we had a very quick meeting of the minds, and at the end of that meeting,. we said "Let's do this together."

HK: Had you read the Michael Chabon book?
CH: No. The next thing that I did was read the book. Then I met with Steve Kloves, who

Tim Hardin, Woodstock, August 15, 1969
(Photo by Henry Diltz)

149

had written the adaptation, and talked with him about what I thought could still be done with it. And again, had a great meeting of the minds, just like with Michael, and we were off and running. We all liked it for the same reasons, which made it much easier.

HK: When you received the script, were there inherent music or song cues, or did the script spark music selections and tunes for potential soundtrack inclusion?

CH: There were many music references in the book. But they were very different. In the book, Grady Tripp, Michael Douglas' character, was into jazz, which is obviously appealing and perfectly valid. And Steve Kloves was a jazz fan, who had carried that over into the screenplay. And actually was very specific about it. When reading the screenplay, that was what I first reacted to. I'm a jazz fan, too. It felt extremely comfortable. But very early on, in discussions with Carol Fenelon, my music supervisor, we started thinking why not let Grady Tripp be someone, given that he is a novelist, who responds to the singer/songwriters, the poets of his generation?

HK: What is the movie about?

CH: *Wonder Boys* is a coming-of-age story, but a coming-of-age story about a guy who's 50. Grady's still finding his way and struggling to figure things out. All the characters are disparate and yet similar in certain ways. They're all mucking around trying to figure out their lives just like we all are. I responded to the fact that even though their struggle is a serious one, they made me laugh as they lurched along their way.

HK: When you read this script did you immediately start making notes in the margin and blocking out scenes that would eventually integrate music and tunes?

CH: The first thing was to get an overall concept, then become specific with the scenes. That's what's different with the music in this picture, let us say from the music in *L.A. Confidential*, which started by being scene specific. Each song in *L.A. Confidential*, from my point of view, could only be in the scene that it's in. But the music, other than being accurate to the period, ranges from the jazz of Chet Baker to the pop vocal of Kay Starr, with Jackie Gleason in between. In *Wonder Boys*, we wanted to have a more cohesive concept for the music.

HK: Regarding the actors and their relationship with the music and songs utilized in the film, was Michael Douglas or any member of your cast impacted by music or the songs in the environment?

CH: No, not really, but Michael's persona was factored in. If Michael did not have the presence he has, it would not feel right for him to be into this music. The connection had to feel true. And Michael was aware of the direction we were going because I told him about it, and as Carol and I zeroed in on the songs that we felt were going to be keepers, I played them on the set when we shot the scenes. As we drove around Pittsburgh, doing some of the driving shots, I was in the back seat with the camera operator and I would flip on my cassette player, and for instance we would hear the Buffalo Springfield song ("A Child's Claim To Fame"). It was one of the first songs Carol submitted to me.

HK: I've done a couple of interviews with director/writer, Paul Thomas Anderson for *Boogie Nights* and *Magnolia*. He mentioned he picked the songs for his films months in advance, and really avoided hassles and a lot of potential heart-breaking situations like songs falling in the cracks. When did you really start to zero in on the songs that would be in *Wonder Boys* and the companion soundtrack?

CH: I love that you bring up Paul, because Paul is a director who really loves music and also loves using music as part of the story-telling. The first movie where I was able to use songs effectively as part of the storytelling process was *Bad Influence*. Prior to that,

Richie Furay, Buffalo Springfield
(Photo by Henry Diltz, 1966)

I lost a lot of battles over music. Unfortunately, with songs, score and the casting of actors, everybody feels their opinions are as valid as yours, even though, done right, the selection of the actors and the music is as important a part of the storytelling process as any line of dialogue in the script. For this movie, Carol and I came up with the singer/songwriter concept in pre-production and then went from there.

First, we came up with our wish list of artists, all poets and all former *Wonder Boys*. There are certain artists who meant a great deal to me back in my formative years. Like Tim Hardin and Tom Rush, people that are not well-known today, but were important artists to me back in that time when Grady was in his early writing years. Once we had this list, Carol spent months delving into their catalogues to find songs that expressed the themes we wanted to address.

HK: Have there ever been times over the years, and decades, where you said to yourself, "If I ever make a movie, or can put songs in a movie, I want to have so-and-so's music used?"
CH: That was the case with Lee Wiley on *L.A. Confidential*. She was somebody I loved for years and who was relatively unknown, a great jazz singer, the first in fact to record the so-called "songbooks." Also, I've had a decades-long dream of working with Bob Dylan.

HK: We've talked about the fact you've been a fan of Bob Dylan's music his entire career, and you attended a 1963 Hollywood Bowl concert where he played with Joan Baez. In addition, the movie *Pat Garrett and Billy The Kid* is one of your favorites. Talk to me about that film and Dylan's music in the movie. And Dylan's participation in *Wonder Boys* marks the first time since 1973's *Pat Garrett and Billy The Kid* that he has been instrumentally involved in a film's musical bed. I also know you are an admirer of the film's director, Sam Peckinpah.
CH: I vividly remember seeing the movie the first time right here in Westwood. I then saw it several more times. It was butchered but it was still great. And Dylan's music was such a knockout. That score cue when Pat Garrett is walking toward that house where he will eventually shoot Billy The Kid is just beautiful. It's a stunning piece of music. And of course, "Knockin' On Heaven's Door" and "Billy's Theme."

It's funny, each movie that I've made when I've gone on location, I've always taken that soundtrack album with me. I'll take a dozen things I enjoy listening to, but I always include that album because to play it in my car driving toward location at certain times, is like tonic. "They don't want you to be so free" expresses the feeling that you get when you fight and lose, and yet persevere and try to win the more important battles yet to come. It brings back Peckinpah's struggles. I've always carried that with me. It's an important part of my musical identity.

HK: The *Wonder Boys* soundtrack includes a new Dylan song, "Things Have Changed," the first new recording from Bob Dylan since his 1997 Grammy-winning album *Time Out Of Mind*, which is utilized in the film as both the main and end-title theme, and was composed by Dylan especially for the film. You also chose three other Dylan songs for inclusion in the film's score, including "Buckets of Rain," from *Blood On The Tracks,* "Shooting Star" from *Oh Mercy* and "Not Dark Yet" from *Time Out Of Mind*. You also directed a video of "Things Have Changed," featuring both Bob Dylan and Michael Douglas. Take me through the steps. Run down the journey of Dylan's participation in *Wonder Boys*. Did he have multiple songs in the initial wish list?

CH: It started with "Not Dark Yet." Dylan is the quintessential

Bob Dylan
(Photo by Jimmy Steinfeldt © 2009)

wonder boy. Bob Dylan, more than almost any wonder boy excels at reinventing himself decade after decade, challenging his fans and their expectations and keeping himself vital, which is what the theme of the movie is. I was in Pittsburgh scouting locations for *Wonder Boys,* and Carol sent me a cassette with "Not Dark Yet" on it. I knew the song and I knew the album, but hadn't heard it lately. Early on, I had talked to Carol about where songs would go in the movie, and we came up with a menu of scenes. One of the key musical moments was the scene where Grady and Crabtree bring James Leer back to Grady's house. It's a series of shots of Grady walking around in his own house and going through the journey of looking at his life. I had "Not Dark Yet" in mind before shooting that sequence and was able to plan the shots around the lyrics and music of the song. It's all of a piece.

HK: How was "Shooting Star" considered?

CH: If you were to put Dylan aside and say, "What is the perfect visual metaphor for a wonder boy?" the answer would be a shooting star. Dylan's great song was an obvious choice.

HK: I know it's rare to do anything you want to do, and especially in the world of music and the politics on soundtrack albums. What a cool trip -- kick-starting your soundtrack with some old and new Dylan tunes.

CH: Harvey, it's the payoff. Unlike Grady, who was paralyzed by the success of his first novel, by the time I got some success, it liberated me. The commercial success of *The Hand That Rocks the Cradle* and *The River Wild* allowed me to make *L.A. Confidential*, and to make it the way I wanted to make it. And then it was the success that movie was fortunate to enjoy that gave me the leverage to do *Wonder Boys* the way I wanted to do it. It's as simple as that.

HK: How did the title track come together?

CH: It came together this way. Carol had lunch with Jeff Rosen, Dylan's (music) manager in New York, and talked about the possibility of using one or two of Bob's songs in the movie. I learned from that meeting that Bob had been a fan of *L.A. Confidential*. This was very early on. I was already in Pittsburgh. And then months went by, and Carol nurtured the relationship and began discussing the possibility of a new main title song. Not long after I started editing, she arranged for Bob to come by my editing room in Santa Monica. I had never met him before. We skipped through the movie. I showed him about an hour and a half of rough cut footage and he responded immediately to the visuals of the movie, the performances, the way it felt. We talked about the themes and visual metaphors in the film. I went over bits of the plot with him so it made more sense, because there were a lot of characters to follow.

He asked questions about the tempo and feel of the music I wanted. He then went away and went on tour with Paul Simon, and he called me from the road a couple of times, and we talked a little more. Then we eventually heard he was actually putting some words down on paper. A few weeks later I get a little FedEx package with a CD in it. Carol came over, I knew it was coming, and we closed the door and popped it into my CD player and played this song. The themes and metaphors of the film, the nuances of the character, were all there, restated with Bob Dylan's unique imagery and poetry. And we looked at each other and played it again and again *grins*. "Things Have Changed" is a compelling song that brilliantly captures the spirit of the movie's central character, Grady Tripp. It's been a long wait since *Pat Garrett,* but it was definitely worth it.

HK: Then you directed the video, actually there are two versions.
CH: In the video we wanted to humorously convey that "Things Have Changed," a first-person song, is Grady's song, and that Bob and Grady Tripp are alter-egos. The goal was to make him interact with all of the characters of the film by intercutting the new footage of Bob with footage shot for the film. We wanted him to become part of Grady's world.

HK: What do you like about the track and video?
CH: The wisdom and the wit. The most gratifying aspect of the video is that it really shows the wit of Bob Dylan which is there in the lyrics anyway for those who get it. And it was fun to show his witty persona. It is so enjoyable to see people watching that video for the first time and see them laughing with Bob Dylan.

Neil Young in the Barn, July, 1971 (Photo by Henry Diltz)

HK: The placement of Neil Young's "Old Man" in the movie is also subject-specific and logical, but did you also want to insert a Neil Young as solo performer, linking him to another song, Buffalo

Springfield's "A Child's Claim To Fame," which chronologically showcased an earlier part of his recording collaboration career?

CH: I liked the *Wonder Boys* themes and imagery in the Buffalo Springfield song. We thought, "Wouldn't it be great to show our musical wonder boys at different stages of their careers?" Hence, "Old Man," after "A Child's Claim to Fame" and the new Dylan along with the early Dylan. With this thought in our minds, I was struck by how appropriate it was that "Things Have Changed" seemed to be a combination of the old Dylan and the new Dylan. Some of the lyrics seemed from the *Highway 61 Revisited* period or *Blonde On Blonde* period, but the tone of it is the mature, reflective tone of his most recent work. So we tried to do that with the music in general.

HK: Does that apply to the use of Neil Young's "Old Man," which I assume has never been in a movie soundtrack?

CH: The use of "Old Man" was a situation where you go, "Is this too right?" But it just felt so good. Neil Young is an artist I've also connected with over the decades. And, like Bob Dylan, he has always succeeded in protecting his art and remaining vital.

HK: You also include "No Regrets" by Tom Rush, a song that he wrote.

CH: He also has a terrific voice and a unique quality. And here's this one great song for our movie, "No Regrets," which so beautifully reveals Grady Tripp's conflict.

HK: Did some of the actors learn or remember the impact or inclusion of certain songs you played them on the set or eventually ended up on the soundtrack?

CH: Katie Holmes (Hannah Green) was quite taken with the music in her dancing scenes at the Hi Hat club.

HK: You tossed some hot R&B at her with songs from Jr. Walker & The All Stars ("Shoot Your Shot"), Little Willie John ("Need Your Love So Bad") and Clarence Carter's "Slip Away."

CH: First she was dancing to Jr. Walker and then to Little Willie John in the arms of Michael Douglas, playing a big scene with him. That song she told me will always be a personal favorite of hers. Little Willie John will be in the Katie Holmes library from here on out.

HK: I know you go all the way back to Leonard Cohen's *Songs Of Leonard Cohen*.

CH: His first album. The art work, the woman in flames. I've been a fan since his debut.

HK: His "Waiting For The Miracle" from an early '90s CD, *The Future*, appears in your movie and CD collection.

CH: [*starts to quote early Leonard Cohen song lyrics.*] But "Waiting For The Miracle" expresses where Grady's character is heading during the party scene in which it plays. It's the turnaround. Grady is not going to be waiting anymore, he's gonna do something. The miracle is gonna happen.

Leonard Cohen   (Photo by Henry Diltz)

HK: From this conversation I am even more aware how much music means to you, and it's apparent in some of your earlier films, you didn't have total control in selecting and placing songs and sounds in those movies.

CH: Harvey, *L.A. Confidential* and *Wonder Boys* are the most personal movies I've ever made. And as I mentioned before, I had a little bit of leverage, and was able to follow through with all the details. Sometimes you get music shoved down your throat. *Bad Influence* was a happy experience musically. Carol did a great job on that one as well.

HK: Van Morrison's "Philosopher's Stone" is on this compilation and screen.

CH: I've been a fan since *Moondance*. For me, that album is one of the great albums. Every song. As an artist, he was a key one on our wish list. "Philosopher's Stone" was the one that uncannily captured the wintry imagery of Grady on the road, searching for the answers, and trying to turn lead into gold.

HK: O.K. Here we are. All of us are hearing songs to visuals that you have applied. Do the songs become bigger when augmented by a visual?

CH: The music changes the visuals for better or for worse in a very marked way. Sometimes the visuals will change the music but the music always makes the visuals feel different. And sometimes in an unexpected way, certain things don't feel right, or it feels better without it. And when the marriage is a happy one, it's magical because both things feel better as a result. I don't mean to imply that any of these songs are improved by the movie, but they become part of something in a felicitous way.

HK: Was there ever a time during this movie where you had some serious review of the music, or even became receptive to bringing in some newer artists or new school doing some old school versions? It would probably be pretty lame, and it wasn't gonna happen on *Wonder Boys*, was it?

CH: No. It would have violated the whole point, polluted it totally. I was urged to do that on *L.A. Confidential* for all the obvious reasons. It wasn't what I wanted to do. Not that that can't be done and done well under the right circumstances.

HK: I didn't want to hear a fusion guy next to Kay Starr.

CH: Or instead of. That's the point. That's what I was urged to do. Have the old songs be redone by new artists. But, in this situation, who knows more about being a Wonder Boy than Neil Young, Van Morrison, John Lennon, and Bob Dylan? Whether the audience thinks about it or not, they feel that. There are also certain situations like "Old Man," where we are using the song as score played very up-front. Other times they are used as source, played more in the background of the mix, but they are there for reasons that were considered important. I wanted the audience to be able to hear them. There are also times where the song is played, and the characters talk over the lyrics, and if a word is lost here and there, it's O.K. In the overall style of the movie, the hope was that the picture would have a kind of loose feel to it in terms of the way dialogue is delivered, and in terms of the

158

way dialogue is heard. It's a very specifically scripted movie, but we wanted the audience to feel that it wasn't that way.

HK: John Lennon's "Watching the Wheels" shows up on *Wonder Boys*.
CH: It was selected to reflect where Grady ends up. It's saying in another way what Dylan says, "I used to care." It's a key song in the movie and on the album.

HK: Christopher Young did the music and score for *Wonder Boys*. I realize his score doesn't drench the movie, but he links key scenes and provides some instrumental work that brings characters to other characters like glue.
CH: Before we hired Chris, we had already selected all of the songs. They were our musical foundation. We then set about trying to find someone to create a score to compliment the songs we were using. We wanted the composer to do something that would feel part of the same musical world. We found Christopher Young, and the mission that we were in a sense giving him was to express the personality, the emotional personality of Grady, number one, and, specifically, the growth of the relationship between Grady and Sara (Frances McDormand).

By changing the instrumentation of Sara's theme each time it recurs in the film, until at the end we finally hear a female voice coming into Grady's musical world, we were able to help the audience feel Grady's growing commitment to Sara. We wanted the score to be an expression of Grady's evolution. There's not a lot of score in the movie, 27 minutes or something like that, but we wanted the score to set the overall tone of whimsy. There are a lot of scenes in this movie that an audience could interpret either way until it becomes more clear what is going on. The first score cue is when Grady exits that class, gets in his car, and lights up a joint. We always call that cue "Grady in denial." The music is kinda bouncy, 'cause Grady is in total denial and looking on the bright side.

HK: Can we further talk about Carol Fenelon's role in producing the album soundtrack with you?
CH: Carol's contribution was invaluable. First, starting with the movie, we put together our wish list of artists. The idea was to have the voices of these wonder boy auteurs of the music world reveal Grady's voice as a writer and his struggles as a man. I sent Carol videotapes of the dailies as we were shooting and she began combing through hundreds of songs in search of the ones with lyrics that were reflective

of the characters, imagery and themes of the movie and music that would reflect the tempo and tone of the scenes we had targeted. Every week or so, she would send me a tape with her recommendations.

After production was finished, and throughout the post-production process, the song selection process continued. We knew we had songs we were committed to using at that point, but as the movie began taking shape and the scenes evolved during editing, we had to change some of our earlier selections and move some of our committed choices to other scenes. Carol would come by the editing room and we'd play songs against the cut footage. None of the songs were truly locked until the end of the final mix. But with a few of the songs, it would have taken a bomb to dislodge them. Carol also supervised the editing of the tracks and actively participated in the temp dubs and the final mix. Once we locked into our song selections, she sequenced the album and worked with Sony on the mastering.

HK: Does it help to have someone else involved regarding the songs?
CH: Yes. A director working with a music supervisor is not that different from a director working with any of the other department heads. The goal is to communicate what you want the movie to be and then let your collaborator help you be true to your intent. With the music, there was also a secondary goal of putting together a CD that would create an overall listening experience that was representative of the movie.

HK: What movie that you've ever seen has been the most successful at merging music with celluloid?
CH: *Rear Window*. I'm partially kidding. *Rear Window* has no score. The only music in that movie is the music that comes from the apartments in that world (Alfred) Hitchcock creates for us: the music that the piano player is writing, the music that is coming from a radio. It's all organic to that location. Despite that example, I've always loved movie music, scores. The great movie scores beautifully compliment the images they accompany. Songs are often badly used in movies. I single out Cameron Crowe and Paul Thomas Anderson as guys who love music and use songs effectively in their films.

Just after my interview with Curtis, we sat together at a Bob Dylan show in Los Angeles at the El Rey Theater on Wilshire Blvd. where I was introduced to Roger Steffens in the lobby. Jack Nicholson walked by, shook my hand, and grinned, "Hello kid!" Jack saw Dylan at the

160

Hollywood Bowl in 1965. I first met Nicholson in 1967, when my mother Hilda worked for Raybert Productions, who produced *The Monkees* television series. She typed some of the weekly TV scripts and did stenography. Jack co-wrote the Monkees' movie, *Head,* with Bob Rafelson and was around the office in Hollywood at Gower Gulch inside the Columbia studio.

Since my last conversation with Hanson, Curtis directed *8 Mile,* the film debut of Eminem, that earned him an Oscar for his *Loose Yourself.*

Shortly before Curtis Hanson's death at age 71 in 2016 of natural causes at his Hollywood Hills Home I encountered him one afternoon in Hollywood at Musso & Frank Grill. I was with Dr. James Cushing. Curtis asked us to join him at the counter.

We three film buffs devoured our delicious meals and walked across Hollywood Blvd to the Egyptian Theatre for the premiere of a documentary, *Charles Beaumont: The Short Life of Twilight Zone's Magic Man.* There was a Q and A. which preceded a book signing afterwards. On hand were Norman Corwin, Marc Zicree, George Clayton Johnson, Bill Nolan and Earl Hammer Jr.

From All Over The World: *The T.A.M.I. Show* and *The Big T.N.T. Show*

Fans of classic rock and soul rejoiced when the legendary concert, Steve Binder-directed film, *T.A.M.I. Show,* made its DVD debut on Shout! Factory in 2009.

Now that landmark film made its Blu-ray debut, along with its long-lost—and much requested—follow-up, *The Big TNT Show,* directed by Larry Peerce, on December 2, 2016, as part of the 2-disc Blu-ray set, *T.A.M.I. Show / The Big T.N.T. Show Collector's Edition,* from Shout! Factory. *The Big T.N.T. Show* was also released as a stand alone DVD on the same day.

The package contains all the bonus features from the *T.A.M.I. Show* DVD, plus new interviews with *The Big T.N.T. Show* performers Petula Clark, Henry Diltz and John Sebastian. The product is mastered from a High-Definition transfer.

The Big T.N.T. Show was filmed in Hollywood on Sunset Blvd. on November 29, 1965 and stars some of the biggest acts of the day, including the Byrds, in their original line-up of Gene Clark, David Crosby, Chris Hillman, Michael Clarke, and Roger McGuinn, who perform two # 1 hits, "Mr. Tambourine Man" and "Turn! Turn! Turn! ("To Everything There Is A Season.")

One of the most heralded rock events ever captured on film, the 1964 concert known as *T.A.M.I. Show* [Teenage Awards Music International] presented a lineup like no other. The Rolling Stones, James Brown, the Beach Boys, Marvin Gaye, the Miracles, the Supremes, Chuck Berry, Lesley Gore and other acts one after another, rehearsed and recorded over two days and nights on October 29 and 30 on Pico Blvd. before taking the stage at the Santa Monica Civic Auditorium. David Winters and Toni Basil served as choreographers. Marshall Berle, Howard Wolf, John Landis and David Cassidy were in the audience.

Steve Binder, Marvin Gaye and Leon Russell
(Photo courtesy of Steve Binder)

The Byrds
(Photo by Jim Dickson, courtesy of the Henry Diltz archives)

I was across the street with my surfer pal Peter Piper during one afternoon at the Con Surf Board shop and too busy buying paraffin wax for my skateboard to even realize what was happening inside that venue.

Aside from the five rock groups, all the performers were backed by a band assembled by musical director Jack Nitzsche. Including Hal Blaine, Glen Campbell, Tommy Tedesco, Don Peake, Barney Kessel, and Leon Russell, along with Fanita James, Jean King, and Darlene Love, billed as the Blossoms, provided backing vocals.

Director Steve Binder, a native of Los Angeles, departed the University of Southern California just before graduating to apprentice under host Steve Allen, who pioneered a variety show.

Binder, barely in his twenties, then took on *Jazz Scene USA,* bringing live performances by musical masters to a network audience. Binder understood the unique requirements of lighting and blocking for musicians in an optimal setting. Once *The T.A.M.I. Show* was screened in Britain and the United States theatrically in 1965, the flick informed every subsequent rock concert feature film. [It had a very brief December 1964 exclusive run in Los Angeles area movie houses].

"Going back to *Steve Allen* and *Hullabaloo,* I was collecting people all the way through my career that I wanted to have in my team and work together with," Binder explained to me in a 2008 interview. "And in those days, technically, union-wise, unless you had a union card you weren't supposed to participate. I learned together the difference between making records and television audio. It was a perfect marriage. Even in lighting I would bring in rock 'n' roll guys who did concerts with guys bred on television and movies. All of a sudden they were learning about the contemporary music business."

Binder would go on to direct many music TV specials, including the seismic *Elvis: The '68 Comeback Special.*

"I met the Stones in '64," Jack Nitzsche told me in a 1988 interview. "Andrew Loog Oldham called me up. He and the group had met Phil Spector, and Andrew and the Stones wanted to meet me. Brian Jones was in a three piece suit and tie. It was at RCA studios, and I was working with Edna Wright, Darlene Love's sister.

"A little later, the Stones started working at RCA.

"I got them into *The T.A.M.I. Show.* I put the band together and did all the arrangements. I was the musical director. I had told the producer, Bill Sargent, the Stones were going to be big. I felt the Stones could close the show.

164

"Bill said 'James Brown is going to close the show.' We all stood at the side of the stage watching James Brown do his act. People were standing and screaming for James. (Legend has it that James told the Stones, 'you'll never be able to follow this.')

"Then the Stones came out and all the girls started crying. It was a whole new emotion! In a stunningly monochromatic case of Life imitating Art imitating Pop and Soul, *The TAMI Show* is the living, beating, in-the-flesh reincarnation of all those cavalcades of stars Alan Freed would assemble during the closing reels of most each and every Fifties B-flick beginning with the word 'Rock," is how music journalist Gary Pig Gold described the legendary sight and sound collaboration in 2005. "Indeed, in *TAMI* we can still see Gerry Marsden in a guitar duet to the death with none other than Chuck Berry, Mick Jagger wisely conceding to take on the blue-flaming Butane James Brown, the Barbarians' five-fingered drummer practically inventing Garage Rock, Marvin Gaye hitch-hiking after Diana Ross' supreme eyeful, and to top it all – to HOST it all, no less – those Clown Princes of Surf 'n' Roll themselves, Jan and Dean!

"Steve Binder recorded absolute history with this screaming little film; even the briefest glance towards Dennis Wilson's moptop during 'Surfin' USA' will tell you why.

In 2004, I interviewed Andrew Loog Oldham, the manager/producer and publicist for the Rolling Stones, and I asked him about *The T.A.M.I. Show* in my 2006 book, *Hollywood Shack Job Rock Music In Film and On Your Screen.*

"Why it works for me is the fear and loathing in Santa Monica There you go. Come on man, it's a magic moment.

"Seeing the Motown acts was terrific. Seeing Jack Nitzsche and Dave Hassinger. It was the film within the film. 'Isn't it nice to be in this business? Everyone is working together for one thing. The Beach Boys' shirts were horrendous. Isn't it nice we're all here?' The Stones were becoming successful, and getting good, and wait a minute, we gotta follow James Brown?

"Bill Sargent did *The T.A.M.I Show* and the black and Electronovision *Harlow* with actress Carol Linley."

In the early sixties, engineer Sargent with Joseph E. Bluth developed an electronic camera system with better resolution than traditional television cameras known as Electronovision technology. Bluth

165

served as technical director on the Los Angeles television station KTTV 1950-1951 TV series, *The Buster Keaton Show.*

In a 2001 interview I had with Bill Wyman, I asked about *The T.A.M.I. Show* and the stage presence of the Rolling Stones.

"The band was great live always. Always. The Stones were a better live band than any other band at that time. I'm not saying they were the greatest songwriters or the greatest recording artists, but they were the best live band wherever you went. They could go up on stage and blow everybody away no matter who they were.

"As long as me and Charlie could get it together, then the rest of the band could do what they'd like, and it worked. And that's what happened in the studio, and that's what happened live. Me and Charlie were really always on the ball, always straight, always together and had it down."

In 2001, I spoke with dancer Toni Basil, who helped choreograph *The T.A.M.I. Show* with David Winters.

"I said to myself 'How can anybody follow James Brown?' Anyway, Jack [Nitzsche] pointed this out to me, and I later heard as well, that Andrew Loog Oldham was so smart that he staged a massive equipment breakdown as well as suggesting some camera angles. I just knew that Andrew was saying that the Stones' equipment broke down and they had to wait for stage set up. We knew some time would pass after James Brown's performance.

"So, finally, maybe the tune was 'It's All Over Now,' where there is a big cymbal crash in the opening of the song, and Mick had a tambourine in his hand, and I wanna tell you simultaneously with that crash in the music, Mick jumped up in the air, and as he jumped up in the air, Brian Jones turned his back to the audience, which was the first rebellious piece of theater I had ever seen in my entire life.

"I come from vaudeville. My parents were in vaudeville, on stage shows. You never turned your back to the audience. So, Mick was jumping in the air, Brian had his back to the audience, and Mick hit the ground in a crouch. Not one person ever remembered James Brown again. And neither did I.

"Mick's moves were fantastic. What is this? What is he doing, ya know? As a trained dancer and even as a Go Go dancer and a street dancer, I had never seen such moves in my life. I mean, what they really were post-modern and right on the beat.

166

"It doesn't matter what physically you're doing, as long as you're grabbing the beat. But Mick was doing physical moves that no one had ever seen before. In the same way James Brown was doing physical moves that no one had ever seen before. And Brian [Jones] had his back to the audience for a lot of the set. He was a rebellious comet and hardly turned around which made it extremely powerful. It helped this rebellious theater. It really did.

"If Brian would have faced front, it would be great, and Mick would have been great, but there was a theatrical ambience that Brian brought because he turned his back. And the Stones didn't take a bow, which I thought was shocking. I mean, even James Brown came on and took a bow.

"Elvis Presley, James Brown and Mick Jagger had some similarities regarding dance. They moved exactly to the beat. They understood the back beat. And James of course, understood it from a gospel sense. But Mick, even though his moves were very abstract, and they were almost like where white boys do that can't dance to the beat, but the difference with Mick is, he did dance to the beat.

"What Elvis, James and Mick had in common was that they were nailing the beat. They were all physically dancing to the beat. They weren't like guys who came before them like Frank Sinatra, or those people who would move to the lyric. Their movements came about from the story. Their movements didn't come about the story. Their movements came because of the music.

"One more thing about *The TAMI Show*. When Smokey Robinson and the Miracles earlier did 'Mickey's Monkey,' I lost my mind. That was really something. And Jack Nitzsche was brilliant. He was the one who called the shots of what order people went on. And man, he didn't make a mistake. How did he know he could put the Stones on after James Brown? To this day I didn't know how he had the balls to do that, and how he had an idea that it could be pulled off like it was."

Musician Michael Rummans and his sister Jeanne were at *The TAMI Show*, courtesy of their father, Larry, a local boxing promoter, who got tickets for them and "all access" backstage passes. Rummans would eventually be in the Sloths, who are still active, and had a stint in the Hollywood Stars.

"I had no idea what was in store," Rummans told me in 2020. "I was 15 years old and already into the Rolling Stones and had their first LP.

"James Brown blew my mind. A force of energy I had never seen. I was backstage, with my sister and father, who had a gregarious personality. He came up to James Brown, told him that I was interested in getting into music and did he have any advice for me. James said, 'the most important thing is to stay original and never copy anybody.'

"My sister got a comb that Brian Jones used. Eventually the Stones went on stage. They were great! When they started to play it seemed Mick Jagger was a bit intimidated by James Brown, you know, doing leg wiggles. But they got into their own groove and rocked."

Originally billed as a companion piece to *The T.A.M.I. Show* after that event's success, *The Big T.N.T. Show* holds up as an essential time capsule from its day.

David McCallum, a rising star appearing in the new TV series *The Man from U.N.C.L.E.*, was tapped to emcee. Footage also includes shots of the Hollywood haunts Chateau Marmont, Ben Frank's coffee shop, and hot spot, The Trip nightclub.

Don Randi was the musical director for *The Big T.N.T. Show* that Phil Spector produced and Larry Peerce directed, who would eventually helm the feature movie *Goodbye Columbus*.

The Big T.N.T. Show set location at the Moulin Rouge was where portions of the Ross Hunter-produced and Douglas Sirk directed *Imitation Of Life* motion picture starring Lana Turner, Sandra Dee, Susan Kohner, Juanita Moore and John Gavin, were lensed.

Many girls in my Los Angeles junior high school homeroom class were invited to the affair while the boys were encouraged not to attend.

One afternoon in 1976 at Phil Spector's mansion in Beverly Hills, while doing an interview with him for *Melody Maker*, I asked Phil about his monumental and liberating catalog and music he produced in live settings as exemplified in *The Big T.N.T. Show.*

"I always thought I knew what the kids wanted to hear. They were frustrated, uptight. I would say no different from me when I was in school. I had a rebellious attitude. I was for the underdog. I was concerned that they were as misunderstood as I was."

During *The Big T.N.T. Show*, Ray Charles gives a rousing performance of "What'd I Say" and "Let the Good Times Roll." A sultry performance by the Ronettes on "Be My Baby" is met with impassioned screams from the audience; the Lovin' Spoonful perform their Top 10 hits "Do You Believe in Magic?" and "You Didn't Have to Be So Nice"; and Bo Diddley delights the crowd with "Bo Diddley" and "Hey, Bo Diddley."

To close the show, the Ike & Tina Turner Revue give an electrifying recital, spotlighting "I Think It's Going to Work Out Fine" and "A Fool in Love."

**Ike and Tina Turner at the Hollywood Bowl
(Photo by Henry Diltz)**

Also on the stage that evening was Petula Clark, performing her No. 1 hit "Downtown"; Roger Miller, playing his biggest hit, "King of the Road"; Donovan, opening his set with Buffy Sainte-Marie's "Universal Soldier"; and the reigning queen of folk, Joan Baez, reflecting the continuing popularity of the genre as the Vietnam War escalated. Phil Spector also played piano for Joan Baez's rendition of the Righteous Brothers' "You've Lost That Lovin' Feelin'."

Donovan would remain in Hollywood after the taping, and soon record "The Trip" and "Season of the Witch" at the Columbia studios on Sunset Blvd. later sequenced into his *Sunshine Superman* album.

Performing to the side of the stage in between acts, but not seen in *The Big T.N.T. Show* film, was the Modern Folk Quartet. Made up of songwriter/producer Chip Douglas, Lovin' Spoonful member Jerry Yester, rock photographer Henry Diltz, and songwriter/musician Cyrus Faryar, with session player "Fast" Eddie Hoh on drums, the band closed the evening with the show's Harry Nilsson-composed theme song "This Could Be The Night."

Frank Zappa, Sky Saxon, Mary Hughes, Rodney Bingenheimer, Joey Paige, Johnny Legend and Ron and Russell Mael [later of Sparks] are shown on screen in *The Big T.N.T. Show* audience.

Donovan
(Photo by Henry Diltz)

"I went to the taping. There was an open-door policy," volunteered Bingenheimer, now a deejay with Sirius/XM. "I might have gotten tickets at Wallichs Music City on Sunset and Vine. Phil Spector was around. Backstage, there was food, and all the cool bands from the Sunset Strip were there. This was the event of the sixties in the Moulin Rouge with its revolving stage.

"I spent some time with David McCallum. We talked about music. His father was a classical musician in England. I was introduced to Donovan. And I sat in the middle of the audience when he sang on a stool. It was cosmic!

"The Ronettes were amazing. I loved Ray Charles. To this day, his LP, *Ray Charles Sings Country and Western* is one of my favorites," he enthused.

"We were watching this mind-blowing show in color but we knew the movie from it was going to be in black and white. What was really nice about the whole thing, and what Hollywood was like during 1965-1967, was that many of the acts at the show hung out in the lobby and talked to fans and signed every autograph. It was incredible.

"Man, I have been waiting a long time for this official retail release."

"We did *The Big T.N.T. Show* with Phil," offered Don Randi in a 2008 interview I conducted with him. "And, on all our dates, we all

170

could read, except maybe a few of the guys who were brought in as players and specialists. All the guys could always read chord charts. That's for sure. I had Barney Kessel on *The Big T.N.T. Show.*

"My guys in the studio could play live anywhere," stressed Randi. "They were capable musicians. *The Big T.N.T. Show* was fantastic because of Phil. And he gave me the opportunity, 'cause otherwise I could have taken another date. But when Phil calls, he was 'first call' for me. If I were going to do something else many times I would move things around to accommodate him.

"You've got to remember that most of the guys that were in 'Phil's band' especially were all jazz players, and rock 'n' roll was a living for them. And a lot of them didn't like it as much as I did. I have to be very frank about it. I always liked the rock 'n' roll part of it. I thought it was great fun and sometimes very musically interesting. Not all the time; 80 per cent of the time. We got to do some things on rock 'n' roll dates we could not do in jazz and studio settings. It's an interesting concept, but those guys were very capable. They were the best musicians and still are the best musicians," Randi boasted.

Randi's principal stagehand was Robert Marchese, a record producer, who later won a Grammy for producing the first live Richard Pryor comedy album from The Troubadour. Marchese had previously engineered some sessions for Spector.

At the taping, Marchese observed a conversation between Spector and Ray Charles.

"Don Randi got me the gig as his assistant," recalled Marchese. "I was setting up the stage and working with the orchestra in the pit.

"The arranger/producer, Arif Mardin, was there and gave me a copy of the Otis Redding album, *Otis Blue*. I saw Joe Adams, who was a well-known radio DJ in L.A. (The Mayor Of Melody) and an actor (*Carmen Jones*, among other credits).

"He was also Ray's right hand man. I told Joe I wanted to shake hands with Ray Charles. He said 'sure.' I said hello to Ray, and then he motioned to Joe and me to take him to 'meet' Phil Spector, who was overseeing the whole ball game. The Byrds were setting up. Ray says to Phil, 'Are you Mr. Phil Spector?' 'Yes.' 'Are you the Boy Genius?' 'Yes.' 'Are you the inventor of the Wall Of Sound?' 'Yes.' 'Are you the guy who had over 20 hit singles in a row?' 'Yes.' 'Then Mr. Spector, how come there's no toilet paper in the bathroom'?'"

"The then King-Of-All-Media-in-waiting, Phil Spector, not only fully launches action with the ultra Modern Folk Quartet's 'This

Could Be The Night'–setting composer Harry Nilsson's career on its way in the process," underscores writer and archivist Gary Pig Gold, "not at all coincidentally – but stuck all the way round to produce the *T.N.T.* to boot; glimpse his ivories right beside righteous Joan Baez f'rinstance.

"Uncle Phil also graciously allowed Ronnie to front her fabulous Ronettes ...while keeping both ears keyed onto Ike and especially Tina Turner too, you can bet.

"Meanwhile, a still freshly-flying Byrds were counseled backstage by no less than Roger Miller to stick to their countrypolitan guns, Petula Clark can be seen serenading Sky Saxon (as a somewhat dejected Frank Zappa sulks elsewhere within the Moulin Rouge), and ingenious-as-ever, Ray Charles adds full frug to his American International Ingredients for Soul. Dump into the gloriously mono mix Donovan, Diddley, Illya Kuryakin and a positively scene-stealing– thanks to Canucklehead-in-residence Zal Yanovsky, naturally– Lovin' Spoonful and, lighting its stick and letting off one brash bang indeed, *The Big T.N.T. Show* in many ways somehow even managed to one-up its big *T.A.M.I.* brother!"

The Lovin' Spoonful
(Photo by Henry Diltz)

172

The Story of *Ready Steady Go!*

On March 20, 2020, BBC Four, the UK television channel, premiered a music documentary of the iconic and influential music show of the sixties: *The Story of Ready Steady Go!,* the landmark British series, a music and dance programme, broadcast every Friday night. that debuted August 9, 1963 with a final taping December 23, 1966.

"On Friday nights in England in the 60s you didn't do anything until you'd checked out the music, the dances and the fashions on *Ready Steady Go!,* beamed live from a London studio," stressed author and music journalist, Richard Williams, in a 2020 email.

"You could see the Stones, the Beatles, the Yardbirds, Lulu, Donovan, Them, Sandie Shaw, the Who or the Animals playing to an audience as cool as they were. Jimi Hendrix and the Beach Boys made their first British TV appearances on *RSG!*. Visiting American soul singers were treated like gods. One entire show was devoted to James Brown, another to Motown artists: the Miracles, the Supremes, Stevie Wonder and Martha and the Vandellas, introduced by Dusty Springfield. The show had the greatest slogan: 'The weekend starts here!' And it truly did."

"I was a dancer on the Beat Room, which was on BBC2 in 1964," music business veteran Kim Fowley boasted in a 2006 conversation. "In 1965, I appeared and sang on *Ready Steady Go!* Otis Redding being booked on *Ready Steady Go!* in September 1966 was a seismic event for the UK and must-see TV."

"Otis developed an English audience slowly. It began to mushroom with, funny enough, a song that was not a hit for him in the US, his cover of the Temptations' 'My Girl,' a massive hit in the UK taken off the *Otis Blue* album. It pre-dated that 1966 tour he did over there. That created the beginnings of a market," underscored Canadian author and York University Prof. Rob Bowman.

"When Otis played there in fall of 1966 the word of mouth on those gigs was extraordinary, and of course he was given a whole show on *Ready Steady Go!* It wasn't just two songs on *Ready Steady Go!* He did that whole hour devoted to him, with Chris Farlowe and Eric Burdon.

173

"The impact of that in furthering, if you will, the gospel of Otis Redding among an English audience that was already prone to looking at America for black culture. Going back to trad jazz, the blues revival, the mod fascination with soul music and eventually mainstream Britain's fascination with soul music. It's just a logical extension of that. The Northern soul thing happened a little bit later."

For writer, author and musician, David N. Pepperell, just the mere existence of any available *Ready Steady Go!* footage was cinematic therapy. "The deliciousness of Cathy McGowan - 'oooh super!' - the cheekiness of the early Beatles, the moodiness of the Stones, the pitch black of Them, the eternally gorgeous Dusty - such a bright and cheery scene in the 60s, such an antidote to the misery of Now, in so many ways. *RSG!* could have been called 'Viva' because it was so full of life, so brimming with joy and pregnant with a belief that the future could only be fabulous. Anyone who was there will shed a tear for those fantastic times when girls were impossibly beautiful, boys were dandies incarnate and the music took us all to a place where only happiness reigns.

"How could a time exist when the Beatles, Stones, Kinks, Dusty, Cilla, Searchers, Gerry, Cathy McGowan and Donovan were all in one place? This brilliant documentary shows they all were and because of *RSG!* they always will be.

"We didn't get *RSG!* here in Australia except for a few clips shown on local shows which was a great tragedy and a loss to our cultural development. Luckily these two documentaries redress that a little and give us a look into that magic time in London when everything was happening."

For many years, Dave Clark from the Dave Clark Five who purchased the rights to the programme in the eighties was restrictive and very protective about licensing footage, which might be a reason, why an essential figure, Cathy McGowan, who served as a presenter, doesn't appear in this documentary.

In 2018, the BMG company secured all the ancillary rights from Clark. *Ready, Steady, Go! The Weekend Starts Here: The Definitive Story of the Show That Changed Pop TV* book on the subject by music writer and historian Andy Neill to be published later this year by BMG Books.

"While undertaking the considerable research involved, I really got a sense of how the show became an important part of the switched-on British teenager's life, particularly in its peak years 1964 and '65,"

174

emphasized Andy Neill in a July 2020 missive to me.

"*RSG!* made the performer and the audience equal participants, removing the real or imagined barrier between them. The fact that the show wasn't tied to any stringent formula like *TOTP* made it that much more adventurous, particularly when *RSG!* went all-live in 1965 and moved out of central London to the larger Studio One in Wembley with Michael Lindsay-Hogg as director." Director Michael Lindsay-Hogg helmed many Rolling Stones' promotional video clips after 1966: "She's a Rainbow," "2000 Light Years From Home," "Child of the Moon," and "Jumpin' Jack Flash," as well as the Beatles' "Paperback Writer," "Rain," "Hey Jude" and "Revolution."

Like visionary director/producer Jack Good before him, both studied at Oxford. Michael Lindsay-Hogg viewed and lensed rock 'n' roll as a dramatic subject. Michael's first job, at age 16, was serving as an apprentice for John Houseman's repertory theatre company in Stratford, Connecticut.

"I started out as a child actor and fell in love with the theater," Michael Linsay-Hogg told me in a 2019 interview. "The first jobs I had were in Shakespeare on stage. And that's how it started, and I tried very much to bring some of those elements to *Ready, Steady Go!*"

RSG! was conceived by Elkan Allan, then head of Rediffusion TV. Vicki Wickham assembled the talent and dancers and served as one of the producers. Allan hired Frances Hitching as producer. Bill Turner directed the first shows, and a line of

Director Michael Lindsay-Hogg
© 2019 Photo by Jimmy Steinfeldt

175

directors followed including Robert Fleming, Rollo Gamble, Daphne Shadwell, Michael Lindsay-Hogg, and Peter Croft.

RSG! beamed live from Stuio 9, in the basement studio in A-R's headquarters in Kingsway, London, and from 1964 was aired nation ally over most of the ITV network. It gave a platform to some of the most successful recording artists of the sixties: the Who, Otis Redding, the Animals, Gene Pitney, the Zombies, Sandie Shaw, the Beatles, Burt Bacharach, the Stones, the Temptations, Donovan, Marvin Gaye, the Kinks, James Brown, the Fortunes and the Walker Brothers.

"*RSG!* was a black and white program," reinforced Michael Lindsay-Hogg. "A lot of the great comedies and dramas from the forties and fifties were in black and white. In England we had no color.

"I had no worries from the people above me. Elkan Allen was the creator and always encouraged me to go further. Very helpful. And I think people were stunned by the comparative substance of the rock 'n' roll that was on television," Lindsay-Hogg asserted.

"1963 was a revolution. It was the kids who had been children in World War II. The world was opening up for them. They could have long hair if they wanted too. And it was the discovery of the pill for pregnancy. And so a whole nation was open for young people and freedom. There was long hair, the pill and music. The paper was ready to be lit and the match came," ventured Lindsay-Hogg, who along with John Lennon, Andrew Loog Oldham, Vicki Wickham, Mick Jagger and other bold Brits embodied the confidence of a new London.

"There were new managers in rock 'n' roll and around *Ready Steady Go!* Don Arden, Andrew Loog Oldham, and Kit Lambert and Chris Stamp had been assistant stage managers, or involved in acting."

In my 2004 book, *Hollywood Shack Job: Rock Music In Film and on Your Screen.* Andrew Loog Oldham recalled, "*RSG!* represented the time when we were in the business we wanted to be in and the *RSG!* Green Room, on a Friday night, was the meeting place of all those similarly blessed. Vicki Wickham booked the show from late 1963 to December 1967. Michael Lindsay-Hogg directed it, and tried new techniques like stop action and freeze frame while the band was on camera.

"Safe to say I still communicate with both of them so that tells you the lot. You were dealing with nice people. None of the people had an agenda. On the show, the visuals propelled the music."

In 2016 Andrew further elaborated, "For one it was obvious that 'this thing of ours' was not going to disappear. We had come in following the Twist, Davy Crockett, skiffle, and trad jazz. Skiffle and trad jazz had been very important; they had been the BBC and the Establishment's last chance to control the key to what music we got to hear. You had during 1957-1958, *The Six-Five Special*; hosted by Pete Murray (God bless him!) and Jo Douglas which invited us all to deck up in jeans and sweaters and be really daring with our shirt collars turned up.

"There were villains, there was mayhem, action, and if we had not had Pirate radio I might not have had a hit with Marianne Faithfull's 'As Tears Go By.' The BBC would not touch it, they said Marianne could not sing. Mind you, that's what they'd said about Mick Jagger a year earlier when the Rolling Stones failed their BBC live audition. They said 'The singer cannot sing.' The BBC was the enemy, a limp-wristed arm of the government, trying to keep kids on a rationed musical diet of trad jazz and skiffle."

"On *RSG!* Andrew had some ideas about lighting and shots," offered Lindsay-Hogg. "One evening at the Ad Lib club I met up with Andrew, and we agreed to debut a couple of new songs he was hyped about, including 'Satisfaction.'

"When the Stones did 'Paint It Black,' we put camera effects on Mick's face and made it darker and darker," Lindsay-Hogg emphasized. "We were broadcasting live. It felt dangerous and primitive.

"The cameraman, Bruce Gowers, later did the great video of Queen's 'Bohemian Rhapsody,' which was a very calculated video.

"With *RSG!* it was about as much about the technique as the performer. In the early *RSG!* stages, I was always thinking about the performer and somehow marrying the technique to them. If the performer was Mick Jagger and John Lennon you don't want to get in the way too much. Mick is a very bright person, and he always has been," observed Lindsay-Hogg. "And Mick, when he was a younger man, was as keen to know what was going on in the world. He read a lot. Or at least he said he did. And was into movies, and Andrew was very much interested in movies and presentation.

"He had been trying to figure out how to make a movie with the Rolling Stones, which Mick and Keith were interested in. Because in those days, even though rock 'n' roll was coming to mean what it came to mean, movies were still sort of the art form going back to comedies. So Andrew was always trying to find a book or a script.

And Mick went on to act in *Performance* and *Ned Kelly*.

"*RSG!* went off the air in 1966, when the video was music promotion for the record to be out. 1967 was a difficult year for the Rolling Stones. The set-up drug arrest in Redlands. Touring was becoming a headache.

"And so did we know what was gonna happen to rock 'n' roll in the sense that we know that it was ultimately going to blast through the roof? We thought it would.

"When I worked with the Beatles and the Rolling Stones, they were really the first videos which tried to take the form a little further. Like the Beatles playing out in the fields. Following me was a long line of very interesting visual attempts with music."

The heroic efforts of *RSG!* in 1965 ushering in soul/R&B music to the UK should also be hailed. Two programs were exclusively devoted to *The Sound of Motown*. Vicki Wickham coordinated the televised tributes, and an enthusiastic Dusty Springfield hosted the shows. Tamla Motown label recording artists Martha and the Vandellas, the Supremes, the Temptations, Stevie Wonder, the Miracles, and bandleader/conductor Earl Van Dyke. During 1964 Marvin Gaye had previously been on *RSG!*

The relationship forged and cemented between the UK EMI Records distributed Tamla Motown Records products and touring artists were never lost on label founder Berry Gordy, Jr.

In 1995. I interviewed Gordy inside his Bel-Air California mansion for *HITS* magazine when he was promoting his autobiography *To Be Loved*. We discussed the love affair the UK has always had with his catalog and the pivotal support of Dave Godin, founder and secretary of the Tamla Motown Appreciation Society, and Clive Stone, along with the crucial TV spots on *RSG!*

"As far as the UK is concerned, it is very, very special to me. I think, more popular there than we were in our own country, you know, for a long time, it seemed. I think the appreciation was different," volunteered Gordy. "They were not blasé about our music early on. Way back, the pirate ships and all that stuff, they discovered the sound, and they were always very important to me when I'd go over there.

"They were just together. I loved their creativity with what they did with our album covers and how they just did it. And when we first went over there with the fan clubs, and the signs and stuff that they had for us. So the UK has always been special for Tamla-Motown.

And when *The Beatles Second Album* had three of our songs ("Money, (That's What I Want)," "You've Really Got A Hold On Me,"

178

and "Please Mr. Postman"), it just indicated to us that they obviously had been listening to our music, and they were aware of it, enjoying it and loving it.

"Tears of a Clown" by Smokey Robinson and the Miracles went to number one in England, I believe, and we hadn't even released it here, or something like that (laughs). They were on top of everything.

"It's always been very important to me. England, the Continent, Europe, a very loyal audience but a very deep-feeling people. They certainly are not fickle in their musical tastes. Fans are fans and they are great. I wanted them. The book has been published in England, and I was very concerned that there are those people out there that I talk about in the first chapter."

In November of 1974 for *Melody Maker,* I interviewed Bobby Rogers, a member of the famed Miracles, and Tamla Motown fixture since their inception in 1958, when he joined up with his sister Claudette, Ronnie White, Pete Moore, and William Smokey Robinson.

Smokey Robinson and the Miracles
(Photo courtesy SOFA Entertainment)

"I really loved touring with the English groups, back in 1963 and 1964," marveled Rogers in our conversation at a Hollywood recording studio. "We used to tour with the Rolling Stones and people like Georgie Fame. During the breaks from touring, a lot of the groups would ask questions about certain songs on our albums. I remember when we filmed *The T.A.M.I. Show* in '64. Mick Jagger would ask me about what I'd thought of the album *James Brown Live At The Apollo*, which was his favourite LP. One time on a tour he mentioned that he'd like to record a Marvin Gaye song for the next album by the Stones. A month later, 'Hitch Hike' was being played all over Detroit radio.

"Man, those early tours were a trip. Endless hours of bus rides and all these skinny English dudes asking us about the Tamla-Motown sound. I never realized how important or influential we were on groups like the Beatles and Stones. He said his name was George and he was in a group named the Beatles. We used to party with all the groups, and have become good friends. You know, music travels in sort of a cycle. The early days were beautiful. We dug all the people we played with. Back in 1965 my favourite song was 'Get Off My Cloud'."

Andrew Loog Oldham on *Charlie is my Darling*

The long-awaited official release from ABKCO Films of *The Rolling Stones Charlie is my Darling – Ireland 1965*, the cinematic debut of the band has arrived. This 2012 cut of the film features newly discovered, never-before-seen or heard performances.

The ABKCO company has set Tuesday, November 6th as the commercial release date for *The Rolling Stones Charlie is my Darling – Ireland 1965*, the director's cut, the producer's cut and this new 2012 version will be available on DVD, Blu-ray and as part of a Super Deluxe Box Set.

The 1965 version of *Charlie is my Darling* was produced by Stones' 1963-1967 manager/record producer and music publisher, Andrew Loog Oldham. He enlisted director Peter Whitehead to travel with the group and film them as "(I Can't Get No) Satisfaction" rocketed the band to the pinnacle of the US and UK charts.

Whitehead, who would later capture "swinging London" in *Tonite Let's All Make Love in London*, crafted a 35-minute version of the film (director's cut) that would surface, from time to time over the years, usually seen with grainy visuals and out of phase music.

Andrew Loog Oldham
(Courtesy of Andrew Loog Oldham)

Later, Oldham put together a 50-minute producer's cut that was first seen in the 1980s. As noted, both the director's and producer's cut are part of the DVD, Blu-ray and *Super Deluxe Charlie is my Darling* release.

The Rolling Stones Charlie is my Darling – Ireland 1965 was shot on a quick weekend tour of Ireland just weeks after "(I Can't Get No) Satisfaction" hit # 1 on the charts and became the international anthem for an entire generation. *Charlie is my Darling* is an intimate, behind-the-scenes diary of life on the road with the young Rolling Stones featuring the first professionally filmed concert performances of the band's long and storied touring career, documenting the early frenzy of their fans and the riots their live performances incited.

Producer Robin Klein and director Mick Gochanaur developed the new 65 minute version after researching and locating additional film footage shot by Whitehead and uncovering a source of first generation audio recordings of the band's concert performances.

Both individual Blu-ray and DVD editions of the package mirror the discs featured in the *Super Deluxe Box* comprising the 2012 version, the director's cut and the producer's cut. Simultaneously, there will also be a digital-only release of the 2012 edition of *The Rolling Stones Charlie is my Darling – Ireland 1965*.

During 2012, for *Record Collector News* magazine, Andrew Loog Oldham talked to me about his film.

"Sean Kenny, the maverick Irish stage and set designer, who worked closely with Lionel Bart on many of Bart's musicals like *Oliver!*, was the resident art director at the Mermaid Theatre. Sean recommended the director Peter Whitehead to me. Whitehead had done this film *Wholly Communion* on beat poets at the Royal Albert Hall. Sean had heard about it, I had not. I offered Peter two grand and said 'Can you start on Friday?' He could. He did. Peter spoke from the upper ranks, and his demanding questions carried weight.

"Then I spent more than a few grand more because I had to make it look like a film. The credits and slow motion stuff and mixing the soundtrack with Glyn Johns.

"It never received a theatrical showing. The director screened it in Germany. You know, there were none of the places where everybody was hungry for average product. I'm not saying this is average product, you know what I mean. The BBC, if they had been interested, which they wouldn't be, because the Rolling Stones were still *persona non grata*, even in 1965, on that level, you might have been able to get 500 pounds for it, or something like that. They weren't going to devote an hour of prime time," underlined Andrew.

"I have always embraced and enjoyed the world of black and white film because it ages better. Can you imagine how pasty they might look if it was in color? There's also my love for French and German cinema.

"The reason I did *Charlie is my Darling* was as a demo to see did the camera love the Stones, which one it favored and their speaking voices. We were getting all sorts of offers. We'd been pursuing *A Clockwork Orange*. I'd meet Anthony Burgess much later when I was after his *The Wanting Seed*. We were also pursuing *Only Lovers Left Alive*. We met [director] Nicholas Ray, who had done *Rebel Without a Cause*. After the meeting Mick said, 'Don't ever put me through that again…' I did not.

"It was filmed in Ireland, and there was an expression, 'Charlie is my Darling or he is my darling' with the Irish accent. Also because Charlie Watts was the most photogenic and had the most interesting speaking voice, apart from Brian. It's a much more valuable document now because of when and how it was filmed and what they were up to. The size of life, so to speak. But it was a valuable document for me because it let me know that the Rolling Stones should not make a film in which they were actors as opposed to musicians.

andrew loog oldham presents a peter whitehead film

THE ROLLING STONES

Charlie is my Darling

IRELAND 1965

(DVD Cover courtesy of M.f.h./ABKCO)

"The film was done as an audition to see which one of the Rolling Stones the camera actually loved off stage. We knew who the focus was on stage. The concept was to see who was telegenic off stage. Like an MGM screen test or how studio heads would view talent at RKO. Who could handle a lead part, and Charlie Watts was the lead.

"I, in my dreams, thought a director like Jean-Pierre Melville would call to cast Charlie in a role since Alain Delon and Charles Bronson can't make this flick. 'Could Charlie do it?' That's why, you know, the combination of the fact that we were everybody's darling. Everyone then in show business was called darling. And I called it *Charlie is my Darling*. Because he was just wonderful. It was him that the camera loved. Ironically, Harvey, is it not the same camera that loved Ringo? There you go."

In my 2006 book, *Hollywood Shack Job: Rock Music In Film and On Your Screen,* Oldham commented on *Charlie is my Darling*.

"I showed *Charlie is my Darling* in 2004 at film festivals in Scotland and Ireland. It was an interesting learning curve. It really accentuated the dividing line between the two parts of the sixties. The natural black and white, speed propelled burst of innocence versus the 'been there, got that' slightly jaded cinemascope and color wide screen, wide hatted, bigger shaded affair that was the kandy-koloured, acid-enhanced, royal affair that became rock pomp. *Charlie* captures the end of the innocence and is quite darling and sweet for just that.

"And Peter did our video, 'Have You Seen Your Mother, Baby, Standing in the Shadow?' live at The Royal Albert Hall. It's an extension of having to be involved with *Charlie is my Darling*.

"I was at the time, starting Immediate Records, dressing up in a suit. I was Stephen Boyd in *The Oscar*, with the De Voss collar. Videos were a way of keeping the Stones focused and commercial. You do have to create work for the act. And sometimes you deserve to be filmed.

"Whitehead also directed the Rolling Stones music video in 1967 for 'We Love You.'

"I have often shown a print of this movie for charitable events earlier this century. Things in Vancouver, Glasgow, Ireland and for film festivals. The film was never meant to go out, even though I had to tell the director that we were going to put it out to get him to feel good about the whole thing."

Painstaking work was done on restoring the footage to come up with the new film that offers a coherent narrative and gives the viewer unprecedented access to the Rolling Stones' original line-up – Mick Jagger, Keith Richards, Charlie Watts, Brian Jones and Bill Wyman –on stage live and captured, literally, in trains, planes and automobiles as well as backstage and in smoky hotel rooms where they candidly discuss their future. Never-before-seen footage of the band's early songwriting process is also included as motel rooms host impromptu songwriting sessions and familiar classics are heard in their infancy as riff and lyric are united.

The Rolling Stones Charlie is my Darling – Ireland 1965 Super *Deluxe Box Set* includes both DVD and Blu-ray discs that incorporate the new 2012 version of the film as well as the director's cut and producer's cut, plus significant unseen additional performance and other footage shot in Dublin and Belfast in September of 1965, bonus content, two audio CDs, one of which is the film's soundtrack album and the other a compilation of 13 live recordings the band made over the course of their 1965 UK tour. A 10" vinyl record of the live material is also part of the package, as well as a replica poster heralding the September 4, 1965 date they played in Belfast.

"Back in those prehistoric pre-YouTube, even pre-Internet days, with both Beta and VHS still a glimmer on the NTSC horizon, seeking, then viewing actual moving images of the music makers who moved us most could pose quite the challenge," recalls budding multi-media maven Gary Pig Gold. "In my particular case, it meant commuting by train and two buses to the local community college, masquerading as a Visual Arts student therein, commandeering the lone Sony U-matic playback machine, and repeatedly viewing gems such as the posthumous *Elvis in Concert* and London Weekend Television's monumental *All You Need Is Love: The Story of Popular Music* series. The 'Hail! Hail! Rock 'n' Roll' episode's Jerry Lee Lewis footage especially.

"There was also the burgeoning midnight movie phenom; back-alley guerrilla screenings featuring crinkly 16mm spools of vintage Alan Freed and beach-movie romps . . . if, that is, you knew where and when the projectors took action. It was at one such late-Seventies soirée, sandwiched between *Magical Mystery Tour* and the Monkees' *Head* that I first encountered the barely-an-hour wonder which was, and enhanced plus expanded today on DVD and Blu-ray remains *Charlie Is My Darling*.

"The unflappable-as-always Mr. Watts naturally endures, a near half-century past the fact, the indisputable darling of this harrowing Stones Irish tour document. Sounding as blasting and shattering as always, thanks in no small part to the audio wizardry of original recordist Glyn Johns, this film sails far above and beyond the anti-Beatle ethos of Andrew Loog's original Stones-view to rival even D.A. Pennebaker's concurrent *Dont Look Back* as *the* true, bluesy, monochromatic document of The Road circa '65. Indeed, Mick, Keith, Brian, Bill, and even Charlie may have never beaten the Dave Clark Five's *Catch Us If You Can* to the darker cinematic side of those once

Swinging 60s, but one minute spent alongside Jagger/Richard(s) in some gosh-forsaken post-show bedsit as they birth 'Sittin' on a Fence' alone makes this film an absolute Required View."

Michael Lindsay-Hogg: Backstage at *The Rolling Stones Rock and Roll Circus*

ABKCO Films in spring 2019 announced an expanded edition of *The Rolling Stones Rock and Roll Circus*, showcasing the original line up of the Rolling Stones -- Mick Jagger, Keith Richards, Brian Jones, Charlie Watts, Bill Wyman (with Nicky Hopkins and Rocky Dijon)--who serve as both the show's hosts and featured attraction.

For the first time in front of a live audience, the Rolling Stones do six of their classics ("Jumpin' Jack Flash," "Parachute Woman," "No Expectations," "You Can't Always Get What You Want," "Sympathy For The Devil" and "Salt of The Earth.")

This movie marks the first musical context in which John Lennon performed before an audience outside the Beatles. A mirthful conversation between Jagger and Lennon captures these two at a pivotal creative point in time. *Circus* is the only time Tony Iommi (Black Sabbath) played with Jethro Tull and the last time Brian Jones would perform with the Rolling Stones in front of an audience.

Brian Jones 1969 (Photo by Henry Diltz)

186

The program includes the long-awaited performances by the Who, Jethro Tull, Taj Mahal, Marianne Faithfull, Yoko Ono as well as The Dirty Mac a 'supergroup' before the term had even been coined. The band was comprised of Eric Clapton (lead guitar), Keith Richards (bass), Mitch Mitchell of The Jimi Hendrix Experience (bass) and John Lennon on guitar and vocals.

Michael Lindsay-Hogg, the acclaimed music video director who guided the landmark *Ready Steady Go!* music and dance television series during 1963-1966, filmed the Rolling Stones and their guests in Britain at a big top venue in Wembley. The shoot happened in 1968 on the 11th and 12th of December. The crowd was comprised of the Rolling Stones fan club members, *New Musical Express* contest winners and a few American Hells Angels.

Envisioned as a BBC special, the project was shelved, but in the intervening 28 years it was regarded as "The Holy Grail" of rock films until it finally saw the light of release in 1996 through ABKCO Films.

Critic/historian David Dalton reflected on the event in a 1996 article in *The Independent*: "*The Rock and Roll Circus* captures the delirious optimism of an era. Depending on your point of view, it was either the high point in the history of the cosmos, or a period of mass hallucination, or both. But call it what you will, for a brief moment it seemed that rock 'n' roll would inherit the earth."

"It was an incredible shoot, I think, 36 hours or something," stated Keith Richards. "I remember not remembering everything towards the end... but it was fun... we went through two audiences... wore one out... it was great!"

It will be the first concert film to be presented in both Dolby Vision and Dolby Atmos sound. The film's 4K restoration was sourced from the 35mm internegative and, for the first time, presented in wide screen format (16:9 for home and 1:85 for theatrical showings, supervised by original cinematographer Tony Richmond).

Richmond is the veteran cinematographer whose feature film credits include *The Kids Are Alright* featuring the Who, *The Man Who Fell To Earth* starring David Bowie, and Jean-Luc Godard's *Sympathy For The Devil*, a restored version ABKCO Films release.

Director Michael Lindsay-Hogg is the pioneering music video director behind the Beatles' *Let It Be* feature film and many of the Rolling Stones' seminal video clips. During the course of his career, he has directed specials for Simon and Garfunkel, Neil Young, Paul Simon and the Who.

Michael Lindsay-Hogg is also the author of the 2011 autobiography *Luck and Circumstance: A Coming of Age in Hollywood, New York and Points Beyond.*

"In 1966 I had done earlier videos of the Beatles' 'Rain,' and 'Paperback Rider." And Mick knew that. And it always was between the Beatles and the Rolling Stones," admitted Lindsay-Hogg.

"The music video had been around. There were earlier attempts. Scopitone. [A jukebox 16 mm film]. The first Scopitone ones were made in French. Lip-sync to a pre-recorded track. Used to be seen in bars or in diners with French acts [Serge Gainsbourg, Johnny Hallyday] miming to rock 'n' roll videos.

"There was Dick Clark's *American Bandstand.* I used to watch it in the fifties, Jack Good, the wonderful producer and director of *Shindig*!

"Mick was always thinking of the next step. 'Because we can.' That is to say 'we're strong enough and powerful enough like the Beatles are. And this is the way to get our song out to most of the plug shows who were gonna play it. Because they want the Rolling Stones.' What do we do? How can we do it?' And I asked what song they had. 'Jumpin' Jack Flash.' 'OK. Let's hear it.'

"And we went out on a Saturday, and we did it and then another version of it. And Brian Jones went over to the makeup table and started messing around with makeup and I said to Keith 'Go over there.' And, after a while they got into it.

"Makeup made a difference. It had a different quality to the first one. In fact, we went with the second one. They liked it a lot, and that helped to my ongoing life with the Rolling Stones.

"I don't know what Mick was like as a student, and I know he got into LSE but he's smart and he never wanted to be not able to keep up with the conversation about the arts, politics or anything.

"And so did we know what was gonna happen to rock 'n' roll in the sense that we know that it was ultimately going to blast through the roof? We thought it would. Let's see what can happen with visual presentation of rock and roll. Which as you know ended up on MTV and generation 2. But when we were doing 'Child of the Moon,' Mick and I talked about it," acknowledged Michael.

"Mick was open to anything that would take it a step further for them. And then we got there. He was miming. And I said, 'Let's try this and not mime. Let's just create a little scenario.'

"As for *Rock and Roll Circus,* I had this idea that I really didn't want to do a regular performance clip, because we had done that thing before. And I thought it would be interesting if we could put the Rolling Stones in a location which was not a rock 'n' roll location. And maybe add a couple of ingredients like three others characters. It was to be done in an unconventional carnival circus-like setting. I drew up a circle on a piece of paper."

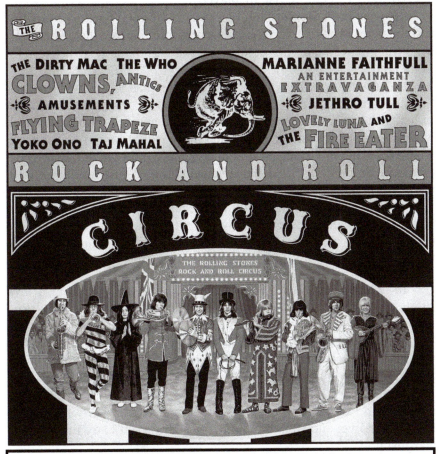

The Rolling Stones Rock and Roll Circus DVD Cover
(Courtesy of M.f.h./ABKCO)

"Michael Lindsay-Hogg . . . is a very creative guy," added Mick Jagger. "We came up with this idea and the whole idea, obviously, is to make it a mixture of different music acts and circus acts, taking it out of the normal and making it slightly surreal . . . mixing the two up. And also we wanted as many different kinds of music as possible. So that's why we thought about who would be the best kind of supporting acts."

One of the highlights of *The Rolling Stones Rock and Roll Circus* is Marianne Faithfull singing "Something Better," a Barry Mann and Gerry Goffin tune, arranged by Jack Nitzsche and produced by Mick Jagger. Charlie Watts introduces Faithfull on screen.

I asked Lindsay-Hogg about Marianne's sequence in the film and his sweeping directorial pan displayed.

"It goes back to the song," he stated. "It goes back to Marianne and the years when she and Mick were going out together. She was a beautiful girl with a lovely figure. And she was the only girl except for Yoko Ono.

"Marianne appeared, and I thought 'this has to be about her and the camera work.' A one of a kind beauty. And the way Tony Richmond lit her with her hair on her face. She was a beautiful young woman. It was partly celebrating her. And, then there is that long musical break where the camera circles around and 'what would we cut away too?' And so I thought 'let's do the unusual thing of just holding on her when she is not singing. Just move the camera around.

"I also wanted contrast with her because there were a lot of men on the show. Everyone on the show, except for Yoko, were guys. At the time there weren't a lot of women in the rock 'n' roll world yet. There was wonderful Dusty Springfield, but mainly guys."

In a July 28, 2014 interview with Robert Ayers in *Rural Intelligence*, Michael Lindsay-Hogg reflected about *Rock and Roll Circus*.

"I still have a very soft spot for it. It has a poignancy to it. When you're 28 you can't imagine you'll ever be 70, not can you imagine that some of the participants in the movie will soon be dead-in Brian Jones' case in only five months, in Keith Moon's in less than ten years, and in John Lennon's in twelve years-because everybody seemed so incredibly alive, and so in the moment. There wasn't any future, there was just now."

The 50th Anniversary edition of *Rock and Roll Circus* was produced by ABKCO's Robin Klein and Mick Gochanour, the

GRAMMY® award winning team behind *Sam Cooke: Legend* and *The Rolling Stones Charlie Is My Darling – Ireland 1965.*

Gochanour noted, "Watching it in widescreen is like seeing a whole new film at times with amazing intimacy and detail."

Greg Penny, a celebrated immersive audio consultant reiterated "Dolby Atmos provides the listener with the most comprehensive experience that exists today. The objective was to give the listener the most realistic, immersive *Rock and Roll Circus* to date. It's as if you were in that tent with the Rolling Stones, The Who, Taj Mahal, John Lennon, Jethro Tull and Marianne Faithfull, and you were part of the audience there fifty years ago."

It can be said that what Dolby Atmos does for sound, Dolby Vision does for visuals. Dolby Vision is an advanced HDR technology that delivers enhanced contrast, detail and dimensionality to the screen by empowering every pixel with a much broader range of color and brightness. Both of these technologies have never before been applied to a concert film simultaneously, making *The Rolling Stones Rock and Roll Circus* a first of its kind.

I asked Michael about the DVD format, the inclusion of bonus tracks and/or implementation of director commentary added to the initial retail configurations and products we coveted and collected the last half century. Did he ever feel an audio dialogue track dilutes and lessens the mystique of his innovative work?

"That's a real good question. As for DVD, bonus tracks, and interview sessions as long the questions are intelligent. And if the person has done a little research. I do it mainly because it was at the beginning when certain ideas and techniques which completely taken hold of the culture where it was a formative kind of birth period. There really hadn't been done before except for Scopitone and some studios in America, but not very well done.

"When I worked with the Beatles and the Rolling Stones, they were really the first videos which tried to take the form a little further. Like the Beatles playing out in the fields. Following me was a long line of very interesting visual attempts with music."

On August 27, 2021 the Walt Disney Studios will distribute acclaimed filmmaker Peter Jackson's previously announced *The Beatles: Get Back* documentary. The film will showcase the warmth, camaraderie and humor of the making of the legendary band's studio album, *Let It Be,* and their final live concert as a group, the rooftop performance on London's Savile Row.

Although the original *Let It Be* film, directed by Michael Lindsay-Hogg, and the accompanying album were filmed and recorded in January 1969, they were not released until May 1970, three weeks after the Beatles had officially broken up. The response to the film at the time by audiences and critics alike was strongly associated with that announcement. During the 15-month gap between the filming of *Let It Be* and its launch, the Beatles recorded and released their final studio album, *Abbey Road,* which came out in September 1969.

Shot on 16mm and blown up to 35mm, the 80-minute *Let It Be* movie was built around the three weeks of filming, including an edited version of the rooftop concert. The GRAMMY®-winning *Let It Be* album topped the charts in the US and the UK

The new documentary brings to light much more of the band's intimate recording sessions for *Let It Be* and their entire 42-minute performance on the rooftop of Apple's Savile Row London office. Shot on January 30, 1969, the Beatles' surprise rooftop concert marked the band's first live performance in over two years and their final live set together. The footage captures interactions between the band members, reactions from fans and employees from nearby businesses, and comical attempts to stop the concert by two young London policemen responding to noise complaints.

A fully restored version of the original Michael Lindsay-Hogg *Let It Be* film will be made available at a later date.

Albert Maysles on the Maysles Brothers
The Rolling Stones: Gimme Shelter

The Rolling Stones in 1969 had become a critically and commercially dominant force, composed and recorded their eighth long player (tenth for the U.S.) amidst both geopolitical and personal turmoil.

In June of 1969, during the peak of the Vietnam War and the era's social upheaval, the group was in the process of recording eight Jagger/Richards-penned tunes and one cover ("Love In Vain" from the canon of bluesman Robert Johnson) when they made the difficult decision to part ways with founding member Brian Jones who was found dead in his swimming pool the following month.

Jones had already been replaced by 20-year-old guitar prodigy Mick Taylor formerly of John Mayall's Bluesbreakers. *Let It Bleed* stands as the only Rolling Stones full-length that contains contributions from both members; Jones played autoharp on "You Got the Silver" and congas on "Midnight Rambler," while Taylor laid down slide guitar on "Country Honk" and guitar tracks, along with Richards, on "Live With Me."

The Rolling Stones 1969 US tour was, in current parlance, a "game-changer," stressed Ken Kubernik, author and a contributor to *Variety* magazine.

"The Stones had been off the road since April, 1967, a European jaunt that trafficked in scream-splattered thirty minute sets, triggered by Brian Jones' Carnaby Street flash and Jagger's poncey posterings. (Interestingly, a tape from the Paris concert reveals the Stones jamming ferociously on 'Goin' Home,' with Jones wailing on harp like a man possessed-which, of course, he was. It's a tantalyzing coda to a version of the Stones growing bolder with Brian on board, which, alas, would never come to fruition.)

**Keith Richards, October 20, 1969
(Photo by Henry Diltz)**

"The autumn of '69 promised much more than a great new Stones album (the Navarrone heights of *Let It Bleed*) and a return to the concert stage; in the intervening years Cream and Hendrix had dramatically raised the bar in terms of sonic substance (amps, PA's, listening audiences) and, more crucially, the level of pure musicianship. The pastiche of pop songcraft and rock 'n' roll rhythms were quickly becoming passe.

"A new genre was emerging - rock. To that end, the addition of John Mayall's Bluesbreakers' guitarist, Mick Taylor, whose fluid, legato lines suggested the sensibility of a tenor saxophonist, added a vibrant filigree to the Stones impertinent attitude and rhythmic punch. If for no other reason, the reissue of *Get Yer Ya Yas Out* should remind discerning listeners that Taylor's contributions - the nuanced phrasing, tonal control and magisterial command of the bar slide - elevated the Stones' performances into a more visceral, captivating experience.

"Taylor stood stoically apart from the onstage rabble, a cipher to Jagger's prowling and parrying Leo the lion. Yet it was Taylor's exquisite soloing, like a surgical swipe from a paring knife, which seemed to both subvert and legitimize the sinister undercurrent of the music's *mise en scene*. Listening anew, one is compelled to ask, 'How could anyone look so Angelic and sound so treacherously sensual?'

"The Mick Taylor era begins here."

The second of four Rolling Stones albums made with producer Jimmy Miller (Traffic, Blind Faith), *Let It Bleed* perfectly captures the ominous spirit of the times with "Gimme Shelter," the opening track.

Keith Richards came up with the song's hook while witnessing people scramble for shelter during a storm; it evolved to a much darker direction with background singer Merry Clayton's cries of "rape" and "murder" on the choruses of the finished recording.

Mick Jagger, during a September 10, 1970 interview on Danish radio, ruminated about the creation of the tune.

" 'Gimme Shelter' is just about the fact that it doesn't matter how safe you are or think you are safe, something could always happen to you at that very minute or that minute later that could either destroy you or change you in some way. So it means that just because you are safe and secure in your house doesn't mean that you really are safe."

Before vocalist Merry Clayton's spine-tingling haunting vocals were added to those of Mick Jagger's on "Gimme Shelter," Merry had already shared a microphone with Bobby Darin, Pearl Bailey, and was

194

a member of both the Blossoms and Ray Charles' Raelettes. During her studio career she has sung backup on records with Elvis Presley, Joe Cocker, Phil Ochs, Burt Bacharach and Carole King. Clayton also starred in director Morgan Neville's Academy Award-winning Best Documentary Feature *20 Feet From Stardom* released in 2013.

By October 1969, the Stones had already prepared the basic rhythm track for "Gimme Shelter" with producer Jimmy Miller and engineer Glyn Johns in England at Olympic Studios. Jagger, Richards, Miller and Johns in late October relocated to Elektra Studios in Los Angeles with engineer Bruce Botnick, who had previously worked on albums with Love and the Doors.

"First of all, Glyn Johns did all of the recording," Botnick underlined to me in a 2009 interview. "I facilitated and worked as a second engineer to get him through the night. Glyn did a great job. And he was under a lot of pressure with them. The first playback of 'Gimme Shelter' was incredible...On the *Let It Bleed* album I made suggestions and brought in the country music fiddle player Byron Berline for 'Country Honk.'"

"Gimme Shelter" songwriters Mick and Keith, Miller along with longtime associate multi-instrumentalist Jack Nitzsche huddled during their October 18th -27th Southern California studio visit just before the Stones embarked on their US tour in November '69.

Nitzsche was an omnipresent figure and key Stones' collaborator on over a half a dozen of their previous LP's. Jack was a major contributor to *Aftermath* and *Between the Buttons* albums. His keyboard and percussion efforts are evident on "Satisfaction," "Let's Spend the Night Together," "Yesterday's Papers," and "Sister Morphine."

"Later I was in London doing the music for *Performance*," Nitzsche reminisced to me in a 2000 interview. "I thought 'Memo From Turner' had a clever lyric. I felt Mick was going in another direction from the band. The apartment they got me was right around the corner where Keith was living with Anita (Pallenberg). Then they began *Let It Bleed*. I arranged the choir on 'You Can't Always Get What You Want'."

Nitzsche and engineer Andy Johns worked with Jimmy Miller, the gifted producer and percussionist.

"Jimmy was an extremely talented man. His main gift I think was his ability to get grooves, which for a band like the Stones is very important," summarized Johns. "He was quite influential then and came up with all sorts of lovely ideas for them. In fact, that's him playing the cowbell at the beginning of 'Honky Tonk Woman.' He sets it up.

"Nicky Hopkins added so much to the band. He was extremely rhythmic. When people think of Nicky, they think of his right hand. But he would make the groove happen sometimes."

Initially, Mick, Keith, Jimmy and Jack had intended to utilize singer Bonnie Bramlett of the well-respected and admired Delaney & Bonnie for the role Clayton eventually filled. Bonnie had practiced with them at the studio but by the time of the "Gimme Shelter" session had worn out her voice. There were also alleged reports that Bramlett's husband, Delaney, had business concerns about her contract since the duo were inked to Elektra Records. He met the Stones in 1965 on the set of the television series *Shindig!*

Nitzsche then suggested Clayton to augment the hypnotic and weaving guitar efforts of Keith, who sang on the recording as well, along with the propulsive drum work of Charlie Watts, pianist Nicky Hopkins, Bill Wyman on bass, percussionist Miller, and Jagger's harmonica playing.

"Jack phoned me at home from the studio in the Los Angeles area one night where I lived with my husband, Curtis Amy," remembered Merry Clayton in a 2008 telephone interview we did. (Amy was a legendary jazz musician himself, known for his classic album with Dupree Bolton, *Katanga!*).

"Jack called, and Curtis told him I was just about ready to go to sleep. See, I was pregnant," disclosed Merry, "but Jack insisted that he had to talk to me about this Stones' session immediately as I was about to go to sleep. Curtis then woke me up. Jack was on the line. 'Merry, I really need you to do this part. There is no other singer who can do this. Please.'

"I always loved Jack, like Lou Adler, he always took a chance on me. I worked with Jack on the *Performance* soundtrack he did, and I had worked with Jack earlier on a record he did with Neil Young in 1968 or '69. 'OK...' I was really tired that night, but I got up, put on my coat, got in the car with Curtis and we drove up La Cienega Blvd. to Hollywood later that evening where the studio was located."

Arriving with her hair in curlers, Clayton was warmly greeted by Keith Richards, and then checked out Mick Jagger in the flesh. "'Man, I thought you was a man, but you nothing but a skinny little boy!'

"They played me the song and asked if I could put a little somethin' on it...I said, 'stop the song and tell me what all this stuff meant' before I went any further. 'It's just a shout or shot away' was something in the lyrics. I said, 'I'm gonna put my vocal on it, and I'm gonna leave. 'Cause this is a real high part and I will be wettin' myself if I sing any higher!' 'Cause my stomach was a little bit heavy...

"So, we went in and did it. Matter of fact, I did it three times. I didn't do an overdub. Mick's vocal was already on it when I heard it and I recall he did a bit of touching up after I left, but they got what they wanted," concluded Clayton.

"'It was so nice meeting you

Mick Jagger at the Forum 1969 (Photo by Henry Diltz)

guys.' 'Oh Merry you sound incredible. We just love you. We're gonna work with you...' I was walkin' out the door as they were talkin'. 'OK. Love you guys, too! See you some other time...'

"And I got in the car with my husband who took me right home, and I went right upstairs to bed. And that was the 'Gimme Shelter' session."

Just before her vocals were added on the track, Merry, no rookie in the music business, had politely voiced concerns about payment procedure and credits. Very swiftly the Stones' legal team generated an agreement requesting her signature. "Next thing I knew, lawyers had talked, and everything was cool. And, it was a go on the record."

Brian Jones wasn't on "Gimme Shelter" but had been in attendance when the initial "Gimme Shelter" session was done in England at Olympic.

I remember when KMET-FM in Los Angeles first spun "Gimme Shelter" from an acetate dub they acquired just before *Let it Bleed* shipped to rack jobbers. I discovered Merry Clayton's voice coupled

197

with Jagger's lead. I was stunned. Clayton is both sonic witness and participant in this dark doomsday audio warning.

"In a way, maybe when you write songs without even knowing it, you're kinda saying, 'Can I do this live?' And so in a way you add that in," Keith Richards detailed to me in a 1997 interview around a Rolling Stones' concert in San Diego, California.

"You don't know if it's gonna work, but I guess what you keep in the back of your mind is, 'We're making a record here; what happens if they all like it and we gotta play it live?' So, in a way, maybe in the back of the mind that sets up the song to be playable on stage."

"Gimme Shelter" was debuted on the Rolling Stones '69 United States tour. I then really heard the number performed at their two November Southern California concerts in Inglewood at the Fabulous Forum that I attended as a teenager, which made an indelible impression. And still does. The first show started on November 8th at 11:45 pm and the second one spilled into November 9th ending at 5:15 am. My fellow Forum concert attendee Paul Body is a drummer and writer. We were in that huge room alone, but together. He emailed me earlier this decade.

"It was a cold November night in 1969. It was way past 12 in the morning and the first show was still going on. Man, the Stones made you wait. It was their first tour and they were way past the British Invasion, they were way past that whole English mop top thing. This was 1969, and they were the STONES. They were the World's Greatest Rock and Roll Band. We had to wait until 2 in the morning to see if they lived up to that moniker. First things first, missed the opener Terry Reid, I can't remember why. Maybe we were eating at the House of Pancakes across from the Forum. Anyway, we did get to see B. B. King do his thing. It was a slick chitlin' circuit set. Remember this was just before 'The Thrill Is Gone.'

"I remember that his band, Sonny and the Unusuals, had these shiny jackets on, and they were swaying to the grooves. They were super pros, and they made us forget the hours that we had spent waiting. We went to the school of blues that early morning at the Forum. Of course, he did 'Sweet 16' and he made 'Lucille' sting and bite.

"It was even later by the time the Ike and Tina Turner Revue came on complete with funky dancing Ikettes and super sexy Tina.

She wasn't a lady from the canyon or anything like that. She was the sexiest thing on Prairie Avenue. This wasn't bobby soxer or going to prom music. This was music for and about the midnight handicap. I couldn't keep my eyes off the stage. I had seen them a few months earlier at the Rose Palace in Pasadena but they were a lot more sweaty opening for the Stones. By the time the Stones came on, it was real late. This was their second show of the night and from the opening riff of "Jumpin' Jack Flash" they were cooking the gator, they were lean, clean, and oh so bluesy.

"You have to remember this must have been about four in morning. When they did 'Carol,' I thought the Forum was going to lift off. They sounded like a locomotive pulling into Barstow. They weren't jiving. When they played 'Love In Vain,' they turned into a Memphis Soul song. 6/8 with feeling.

"Mick Taylor's two lead breaks just about brought tears to my eyes. It was the closest thing to Rock and Roll Heaven. I just wanted to slow dance with my date, Foxy Roxy. In reality 'Little Queenie' should have been Foxy Roxy's theme song because that song seemed to have been written about her. She truly did look like a model off the cover of a magazine.

"Well, they were the World's Greatest Rock And Roll Band, and they rocked the Forum in the wee hours of Sunday morning. We got home, and the newspapers were all over the dewy lawns, Foxy Roxy's makeup had run from tears of happiness and somewhere with the blood of B.B. King and the sweat of the Ike and Tina Turner Revue, the Stones must have been patting themselves on their backs because they had picked up that torch.

"I always dug the '69 version of 'Under my Thumb' because it has bits and pieces of everything that are the Stones. It was the one song that they were doing at that time that still retained that mop top 60's feeling.

"I seemed to remember at the Forum that they did 'Prodigal Son' and 'You Gotta Move' one right after another. Those songs sounded real nice at 4 in the morning. Since I had never heard 'Little Queenie' by Chuck Berry, I asked one of my buddies the name of the song and he said it was called 'Johnny B. Sweetly.' Hey it sounded right to me. I had really cool seats right on the floor and by the end of the show, Foxy Roxy and I were right up front and we could see the sweat.

"I remember pounding my fists on the stage. I never thought that I would get that close to a Rolling Stone. 'Satisfaction' no longer

199

sounded like 1965 or '66 for that matter, it sounded like 1969. It was a bit more menacing just like '69 was. They were the coolest bar band' and they turned the Forum into the world's biggest juke joint. I was so inspired that a few hours later I was playing drums in my first band, the first song we played....'JUMPIN' JACK FLASH'."

There would be no story about the Rolling Stones' 1969 US trek without Ronnie Schneider who solely managed their tour finances during 1966-1969. An ABKCO veteran and the nephew of entertainment accountant Allen Klein, Schneider graduated with a Business Administration degree from the University of Miami.

Ronnie Schnieder had a very personal, appreciated and important role with the band 1965-1970. He established new business models regarding performance fees, merchandising and ancillary rights that were copied by a plethora of acts setting the stage for larger arena and stadium show box office revenues.

It was Schneider acting on behalf of the Rolling Stones in 1969 who hired the Maysles brothers to film the Stones working out the deal with Madison Square Garden officials so they could chronicle their November New York dates. He is the executive producer of *Gimme Shelter* and author of *The Rolling Stones, The Beatles and Me.*

Rolling Stones in Los Angeles, 1969
(Photo by Henry Diltz)

HK: Let's discuss their '69 US tour.

RS: The Stones dictated everything. They wanted the art seen. It was the perfect storm. They got a guaranteed 65 percent of what I got out of the gate from gross box office as opposed to a flat fee. It was a percentage deal with a 50 per cent advance.

They were at the peak of their powers. And, I could watch every part of the show and it was great. During the 1969 tour, I could catch Ike & Tina Turner with the Ikettes. I loved them. I had tons of interactions. Tina Turner was always funny. Tina was a flirt. (laughs). She would roll her eyes and wore a see-thru top.

I liked Ike Turner a lot. He was incredible. There was a big potential money shakedown scene that might have gone down at the Oakland Coliseum 1969 show. And Ike said if there was a problem with me handling and delivering the money he'd take care of it. And showed me he was packing a big Colt .45.

I loved B.B. King. I chatted with him on the 1969 tour, and he was so appreciative of the slot he had on the Stones' tour.

Even when I left ABKCO in 1969, Mick Jagger, who I now saw taking over the finances and the money, called and asked me to do their 1970 European tour. I didn't say yes immediately until it was discussed with my uncle Allen. I did the tour. And the rule that I set for the European tour were no people backstage."

The 1970 documentary film, *Gimme Shelter* that was directed by Albert and David Maysles and Charlotte Zwerin, which chronicled the Stones' '69 American tour derived its name from the song. A live version played as an end title theme over the credits.

Two of America's foremost non-fiction filmmakers, Albert Maysles (1926-2015) and his brother David (1932-1987) are recognized as pioneers of "direct cinema," the distinctly American version of French "cinema verité." It is a method in documentary where events are recorded that couple naturalistic techniques without pre-planned set-ups or agenda.

The Maysles team were the first to capture the Beatles first US visit chronicling the remarkable two weeks in February 1964 that began America's still-enduring love affair with the group in their *Here's what's happening baby-The Beatles!*

The duo caught the two-week hysterical reaction to the Beatles that was the real-life inspiration for the subsequent Beatles movie *A Hard Day's Night.*

David and Albert were granted all-area access to the lads from Liverpool who had just conquered America with "I Want To Hold Your Hand" sitting at No. 1 in the US charts. Manic moments as the Beatles arrived to America on Pan Am Flight 101 to New York are woven around frenzied fans. In their revealing film, the Maysles Brothers shadow the band in dressing rooms, hotels, press conferences, outdoor photo sessions, as they travel from New York to Washington, D.C., and Miami. It is an intimate portrait of a musical band pulling America through the despair of a slain President a few months earlier in November 1963 that in the process established the benchmark for rock 'n' roll cinematography.

The Maysles 1964 footage is now incorporated into a more recent DVD, *The Beatles The First US Visit.*

Albert was made a Guggenheim Fellow in 1965. Their next three films became cult classics. *Salesman* (1968), *Gimme Shelter* (1970) is the dazzling portrait of the Rolling Stones on their American tour, which captured a killing at the notorious concert at Altamont.

In 2009, Maysles revisited the Rolling Stones once again with the film, *Get Yer Ya's Out!* the band's performance in New York at Madison Square Garden in November 1969. It was included in the *Get Yer Ya-Ya's Out! 40th anniversary Stones deluxe edition* from ABKCO which included a bonus DVD of their full-length performances of five previously unreleased Stones songs presented in 5.1 surround sound.

This DVD incorporates a sequence with Jagger, Charlie Watts, and Jack the donkey during the cover shoot for the *Ya-Ya's* album and newly displayed footage of Keith Richard, Jimi Hendrix and Jerry Garcia.

After the Rolling Stones 1969 tour's planned conclusion, the band organized one more performance on Saturday, December 6th, for a free show that featured the Flying Burrito Brothers, Santana, Jefferson Airplane, Crosby, Stills, Nash & Young and the Grateful Dead (who chose not to perform) in a free thank you concert acknowledging their successful 1969 US tour that has always been reported as the disastrous Altamont Free concert.

Earlier this century I interviewed Albert Maysles for *Treats!* magazine.

HK: Let's talk about your *Gimme Shelter* film.

AM: We got a phone call one day from Haskell Wexler who said the Rolling Stones were in town in Los Angeles, and they were about to go on a nationwide tour. And they were going to be in New York the next day at the Plaza Hotel. "Maybe you should look them up." Again, in this particular case, neither one of us knew their music. But we trusted Haskell. "These guys must be interesting."

So we knocked on their door at the Plaza Hotel, and we started talking to them. "Well, we're going to be performing the next evening in Baltimore, you are most welcome to attend." We went to the show. "Yeah. These guys are good." And we followed it up by making a deal with them. And we then filmed them at Madison Square Garden. They paid us a small amount to get going. I think it was $14,000.00.

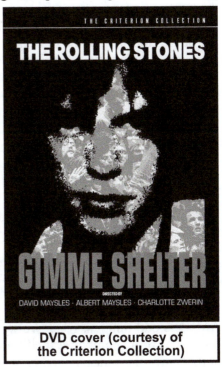

DVD cover (courtesy of the Criterion Collection)

We did have several cameras. I think there were four of us. That was different. The camera people were people we knew already. They knew my style so everything was consistent from one camera to another. And that worked out beautifully.

I don't know how to put it into words to describe Jagger on stage. You just have to see the footage. Regarding their live show. It's interesting. You put the camera in the hands of one person and it's so cold. And another person, it's hot. You get the hot cells from what you see on the screen. What is so startling to me is that so many reviewers think that the camera work is just great. When it is so cold that I would dismiss it. But the lighting is right and the angles are right. This, that and the other.

We joined after the tour began and a moment in American history. Mick Jagger was very invested during the process of the movie without in any way trying to control it. That was important. He never said, "Oh, you need to get this. And you need to get that. Do this." And we had a lot more cameras at Altamont. That was unusual.

HK: Talk to me about being at Altamont and filming it.

AM: It was interesting the way the press handled it. There was a very good reviewer in *The New York Times*, Vincent Canby, in the middle of his review he said "The Maysles must have said, 'A-ha!' when they saw that they had captured the killing on film in the editing room. But the title of his piece, which the editor ascribed to it was "Making Murder Pay."

In fact, it was wrong both ways. We weren't doing it just to make the money. Secondly, it wasn't a murder. No one was able to prove the motivation, whatever that was behind. I was on the stage just behind the Stones for most of the filming. I could see them and the immediate audience. A side view where my brother with another cameraman was luckily on a truck to the side of the stage out of my view, and maybe out of the view of the Stones, but in view of the killing.

It's interesting, very early on, just before the concert began, I had myself placed just down below, filming the audience in exactly the same spot where the killing took place. So I'm there, and I'm filming and the guy just below me with his child gets up and he says, "If you don't leave this place right here, right now, I'll kill you." He may have thought that I was gonna drop the camera on his son. I don't know what his explanation was. Fortunately, my brother was at the right place and I was at the best place to get the Stones themselves.

HK: After principal filming and you are in the editing stages, the movie sort of becomes a documentary about a documentary, or at least moments where band Jagger and Charlie Watts are commenting about a work in progress.

AM: The odd thing is, when we were filming them. Mick said at one point, "At some point after the film was shot they'd like to take a look at it." It was their idea. And then when Charlotte (Zwerin) was editing it, she said, "let's call them up on that and let's film them watching. It would be just great." It was their idea and her idea, and it worked beautifully of course. For example, when I was shooting the Stones listening to the playback of "Wild Horses," my brother whispered in my ear, "Take a look at Keith's boots," and I shot the clothing.

And then when we showed Mick the film he didn't say, 'Eliminate this." But he was taken by the horror of the events, and he couldn't give us the release. So we waited six months. We never talked it over with Mick. But my brother happened to meet the producer and director of *Performance*, Donald Cammell on one occasion. And David told him that we had some problems in getting a release. So Donald said,

"Let me take a look at it." So he saw the film and said, "Don't worry. I'll take care of it." And that's it. That is how we got the OK.

HK: Did the 1970 premiere and the first screenings of *Gimme Shelter* support or help your subsequent long-form documentary work? You and your brother were respected filmmakers before *Gimme Shelter*.
AM: We'd already triumphed with the theatrical showing of *Salesman*. And this wasn't a brand new experience. But to see *Gimme Shelter* on that big screen with full audiences is also equal to the actual moments you spend in filming it. In fact, when I see a film of mine, even from 20, 30 or 40 years ago, and I'm watching and still in the process of shooting it. (laughs)."

Dr. James Cushing of the Cal Poly San Luis Obispo English and Literature Department, who hosted a weekly Friday radio program on the station KEBF (97.3-FM) The Rock in Morro Bay in Central Coast California, theorized about Altamont.
"1968 was a heavy political year — King and Kennedy being killed, the Democratic party collapsing in Chicago, Nixon winning the election, the war dragging on and on and on, and the sense that the counterculture was failing in its attempt to build a new America.
"1969 was Nixon's first full year as President and the ugliness at Altamont expressed a hopelessness that seems now connected with Nixon's cynical self-serving narcissism.
"The ancient ritual of Dionysus involved the ritual stabbing of a goat, who was understood to function as a stand-in for the God (who must die to be reborn) and an offering to him. Rock festivals are already Dionysian events, but Altamont got a little too authentically ancient for the modern conscience: an actual African-American man named Meredith Hunter was stabbed to death, in front of a Dionysian band whose rise to fame had involved loving attention to and respectful appropriation of the music of African-American men. It's an awful irony."

Tony Funches was a friend of mine from West Los Angeles College in Culver City, who in November 1969 was head of Rolling Stones' security and served as Mick Jagger's bodyguard.
In the summer of 1969 to 1971 I had a job at the school library around a full schedule of classes. I also received a student deferment. The first semester it opened we were taught in bungalows. We laughed that in some ways it was a high school with ash trays.

It was during September of '69 that I first made an acquaintance with Tony, Vietnam veteran, boxer and karate black belt holder, who soon became our student body president.

For some reason I didn't see Funches on campus again during last quarter 1969 and the entire year of 1970. I never knew why.

Needless to say, when I first saw the West Coast premiere of the movie *Gimme Shelter* in Hollywood with fellow WLAC classmate Bob Sherman, we immediately looked at each other when Tony Funches suddenly appeared on screen at their Muscle Shoals recording studio session during a playback of "Wild Horses" and later protecting Mick Jagger around the group's airstream trailer in the chaos of Altamont.

We both marveled, "Hey! Isn't that Tony Funches from school?"

I am grateful and thankful to report that in 2015, before his death in 2017, I re-connected with Tony at the former residence of Jim Morrison in Laurel Canyon. Funches was Morrison's confident and bodyguard in 1970-1971.

Home owner Matt King, and Rob Hill, two friends and fans of the Doors had encountered Tony at a hotel bar in Denver, Colorado, and when my name was mentioned in conversation, Funches quickly demanded my phone number.

When we eventually rendezvoused, Tony was carrying a copy of my *Canyon of Dreams The Magic and Music of Laurel Canyon* and wanted me to autograph it. He greeted me comically with "who would have thought the only white guy in the remedial English course at a junior college would end up writing these books?"

Tony Funches didn't really do interviews about the Rolling Stones, has rarely talked on record, but he graciously consented to an interview.

Tony discussed the Stones, Altamont, December '69, and provided several new and revealing insights into his October-December 1969 life and world with the rock 'n' roll band.

HK: Reminisce about that '69 Rolling Stones/Ike and Tina Turner/ B.B. King US tour.
TF: I was with Mick and Keith when all the overdubbing and mixing were going down on the track "Gimme Shelter" at Elektra Studios on La Cienega and then also at Sunset Sound.

HK: You were in other US recording studios with the Stones, including sessions in Alabama in Muscle Shoals. You watched them cut "Wild Horses" "Brown Sugar" and "You Got to Move."
TF: It was really fabulous. First things first, I had to make sure I had my gig covered, which was really pretty easy. Because it's easy

don't mean you don't do it. You do it anyway and make sure you do it well. That being said, I sat around in the studio, often at the console, twiddling my thumbs a lot 'cause I didn't play an instrument. How many people can you stuff in one little studio? Ben Sidran was next door to me in the motel. I spent some time hanging out with Ben, and other than that, sometimes I was bored to tears in the studio. They were spending most of the time jaw jacking and runnin' off at the mouth.

Every once in a while they would get around to recording a few bars of the song. So it was difficult to get the continuity going, but when they really get on to slappin' the track together and splicing up all the different tracks and bits and pieces, you could get into groove and romp and stomp and say hey, "Hey. This is kick-ass stuff here."

But again, I fully understood that is what they do, which wasn't my gig, something apart from them, so I didn't get those things mixed up.

B.B. was a gentleman. Wonderful cat. I was aware of his manners, his professionalism, how kind he was to everybody. Not arrogant or rude. Gracious, polite, well spoken.

The Stones are tied to the musical legacy of L.A. Modern and Kent Records. Ike and Tina along with B.B. King had been on both of those record labels.

HK: You had already been in Vietnam and in jungle wars, seeing friends of yours shot in a river.

TF: The world of personal security was a new world for me. Absolutely. I didn't see it that way. I still saw myself as a Vietnam vet, a student body president at WLAC, getting a degree, and the expectations of the family, and these other folks just paying me dough to do this, that and the other was laughable. At first I thought it was a joke. They can't be serious.

HK: We were both at the Rolling Stones' 1969 tour at the Forum in Inglewood, California after they did a debut show in Colorado. I stood in line for many hours to buy tickets. You were on the side of the stage that night. I suspect it was not lost on you that the band you are working for, and the only security person and minder, were seeing the group at an 18,000 seat arena, literally a mile or two from where you grew up.

TF: I would go in the limo with the band to all the shows. Sam Cutler said, "You're going with us." "Why? What for?" "Because I told you." "OK. Whatever." Yes, the place was close to home, and at that time, I lived in the jungle, off of Coliseum and La Cienega where Fedco was. Walking distance, well no, but very close.

I was mostly thinking about good weed, and good dough to stash and pay bills, you know. Remember: I was always waiting for the Veterans Administration to send me my checks as a V.A. student.

HK: Ike Turner. I think his legacy has been swept under the musical carpet, owing largely to the movie about Tina Turner. On stage he ran a tight ship and the band cooked. Why does extra-curricular stuff away from the recording studio and live shows completely wipe out his pioneering musical efforts, and he's primarily known as a bad guy?
TF: He led that band every night. Absolutely. A consummate professional. Ike had been in the business before I was born. He was part of the St. Louis and Chuck Berry rhythm and blues community, as opposed to Chicago and L.A. He wound up in L.A. Anna Mae Bullock was from Nut Bush, Tennessee. Ike had his initial success as an arranger. And here they are, in View Park, the Baldwin Hills area, on the whole tour.

HK: I only met B.B. King once. Saw him many times. I know what the impact of that US '69 tour did for the careers of King and Ike & Tina. In 1966, Ike & Tina did a UK tour opening for the Stones and the Yardbirds. What was Tina like backstage? I never saw a woman work a live show performing in high heel shoes with the dancers. It was dazzling. And the music propelling the action smoked. I had dinner with her once at Chasen's in the mid-seventies while doing our interview for *Melody Maker* when the music business really didn't give a damn about her.
TF: Backstage, Tina was busy. Don't mess with that woman. Leave her alone and stay out of her way. Yes, she was gorgeous, but any woman who has that much energy and commands a room the way she can, give her space and peace. Stay out of her way. "Yes ma'am." Besides, Ike had a straight razor and a derringer on him at all times. (laughs). I ain't ready to die over this woman.

HK: I know that B.B. King being booked on the '69 tour and especially his spot at the two L.A. shows in front of record label executives was a career-altering opportunity. I wrote in one of my books "On that cosmic night in 1969, King played in front of music reviewers, rack jobbers, deejays, guitarists, booking agents, and paying folks who had never heard, let alone seen, him in action. It was a moment in which he knew that, by the following Christmas, his next half a century of dates and live bookings were going to be taken care of."

208

TF: B.B. was a gentleman. Gracious, polite, and well spoken. And it wasn't phony. You can spot phony at fifty yards. Wonderful cat. I was really jazzed meeting him and traveling with him. I had the chance to tell my mom, my aunts and uncles that I met B.B. King. I knew it would blow their socks off. They got all "wow wow wow."

Because I'm a Motown generation kind of thing. But I go back to the early fifties with B.B. King when I was age five. Upon meeting him I was aware of his manners, his professionalism, how kind he was to everybody. Not arrogant or rude.

HK: He got started before the media was totally obsessed with celebrities. I know Jimi Hendrix and Janis Joplin came to the New York dates at Madison Square Garden.

TF: At Madison Square, Leonard Bernstein came to a show. All the glitterati of Manhattan, besides Hendrix and Janis. Everybody was bowing and I'm putting up with it 'cause it ain't on me. It's up to Mick who tells [tour manager] Ronnie Schneider, who then tells Sam Cutler where to start and stop. When it finally came time to clear the dressing room to get on stage, Sam would give me the look, and I'd just say, "Everybody out!"

HK: As you look back at the Altamont situation, give me an observation. The movie shows some aspects of the ill-fated free concert. I know it was a zoo and an insane disaster waiting to happen. You had already been in Vietnam. Maybe that is one of the reasons you survived.

TF: You are not reading too much into it, but the insanity of violence doesn't change whether it's Vietnam, Altamont or the inner-city. Rural or urban. It doesn't make any difference. Bullies and events will kill other human beings for no reason. Yes, did it happen at Altamont? Yes. It happened in the whole neighborhood.

HK: But I remember you from college, a serious student, a Vietnam veteran, student body president who knew about planning and execution. You were way older than us teenagers as you went to school on the G.I. Bill.

TF: I knew about chaos. I told 'em. I saw it comin' way, way far in advance. I told a couple of people, and they said, "That's not what we pay you for." I was lookin out. "Do what we pay you for and it will be fine." "OK."

HK: You were very busy on that December 6, 1969 day. I still think the Stones did a nice gesture to try and mount a free concert. Locations changed, not enough time to do pre-production, some other groups didn't play. More homework was required.

TF: 20/20 hindsight, and God bless everybody that tried, but I don't think anybody in the exalted positions of those calling the shots, the shot callers or deal makers, that put that thing together, of which there were quite a few, there was nobody ultimately in charge, until the Stones took charge at the last minute. So it lacked the necessary structure to have a person make the final decisions far enough in advance to make it happen.

It depended too much on the spontaneity of the Aquarius age as opposed to Machiavellian logistics planning far out in front. Which should have had both, but it didn't. It was an utter fiasco, and at the time everybody's egos got in the way of common sense.

And when it blew up into a Class A mess, it was because of interference and sabotage from other quarters. Nixon's plumbers were suspected of having a hand in it. So it was a constructed perfect storm. If alchemists got together and put together a perfect storm of their devising, then it was Altamont. You can't single out one party. Several were involved in it.

Sam Cutler has been unfairly portrayed. Absolutely. Sam was not in the least bit responsible for Altamont. But somebody had to fall on the sword.

And it fell to Sam, which he did fall ahead and fall on the sword. But by no stretch of the imagination was that fiasco his responsibility. The old saying is "success has many fathers but the fiasco is a lonely bastard."

HK: In the *Gimme Shelter* movie, I noticed you had a splint cast on one of your arms, from punching out a Hell's Angel. You fractured your forearm. I heard you went to the medical tent and prepared your own cast setting.

TF: Yes, that's true. A fractured arm is Boy Scout's stuff.

Tony Funches with the Stones at Altamont, 1969 (Snapshot by Ron Lando)

HK: Footage shows you hovering around the helicopter that left Altamont with band members. But you did not get into the copter. There were a lot of people and luggage in that air transport vehicle.

TF: In the late afternoon we were choppering out a lot of the bands who were either there or very anxious, including Crosby, Stills, Nash and Young. I was flashing on Vietnam, and I don't like choppers for that reason, but the helicopter is overloaded, and I'm afraid the thing is gonna go out of balance and decapitate two three hundred people.

"The movie does not do justice. The format of the medium is a two hour documentary, a B-movie, *50 Foot Woman From Mars*. If there was really a story from a musicologist or anthropological viewpoint, it would have to be a mini-series comprising six to eight hours so you could introduce and develop enough of the characters that affected the story so that the total context is explained and people can understand that. And then the various characters become secondary to the overall story which is the context that could be illustrated or portrayed or mapped out over a period of time in that great six to eight hours. But are you gonna tell a complete story in two hours? No way. So it is what it is. So what they tried to say in two hours was not complete at all.

"I don't carry the hassles of Altamont or the tour of 1969. When I hear the Stones on the radio I just smile and keep it to myself.

It's like the tune "Stolen Moments" by Oliver Nelson. It mostly has to do with quiet introspection. This is my giggle. I'll keep it to myself. Let me be outside. There's no problem."

When I learned Tony had passed on, I felt compelled to contact music journalist and esteemed author Stanley Booth and asked him to reflect on Tony.

Booth penned three books essential for any music library: *Dance with the Devil: The Rolling Stones and Their Times, Rhythm Oil: A Journey Through the Music of the American South* and *Keith: Standing in the Shadows*.

"I was with the Rolling Stones when I met Tony Funches," emailed Booth. "Steve Stills and some of his crowd had a house somewhere in the vast and mysterious Hollywood Hills, and the Stones had rented it, among other places, for a few days before starting their 1969 United States tour. The first time I was at that house with the Stones, Tony greeted the car we were in at the front gate. He was, as ever, cool, pleasant, quiet, strong, competent. (Also big, black and handsome.) I liked him right away and in the years since have never stopped liking

211

him. Tony is one of Nature's Noblemen. My life has been enriched by his friendship. Tony will not be forgotten."

"Altamont was dark and dreary from dawn until dark; the sun never came out," music memorabilia collector Ron Lando emphasized in a 2016 email. "The crowd was extremely restless all day with lots of beer and pot making its way throughout the entire venue. By the time the Stones hit the stage. The unified crowd became somber. And it was all downhill from that point on."

Contrary to popular belief, many people who went to Altamont that afternoon and evening had a good time and left with a sense of wonder and delight. Take into consideration actor/poet Harry E. Northup, who was at this infamous gig.

Northup has made a living for over 30 years, appearing in 37 films, including *Mean Streets, Taxi Driver, Over the Edge* (starring role), and *The Silence of the Lambs*. Northup is that rare American actor who is also an accomplished poet with 10 books of poetry published. The latest one is *When Bodies Again Recline*, published by Cahuenga Press.

He emailed me, "I was working as a waiter at the Old World Restaurant on the Sunset Strip. My first wife, Rita, and I had arrived in Los Angeles, from New York City on March 5, 1968. That day we got an apartment in Santa Monica and that night, I got a job as a waiter at the Old World. I came to L.A. to work in the movies. I worked at night and auditioned for movie and TV roles in the day. We hung out at the beach and went to every rock 'n roll concert that we could at the Santa Monica Civic Auditorium, Hollywood Palladium and Venice Beach.

"Rita and I and our 10-month-old son, Dylan, drove to San Francisco on the 5th of December, 1969, in our blue and white Volkswagon van. It had a bed in the back. We slept in it in the Haight. The morning of the 6th, we ate at Brother Juniper's. I remember seeing a black man, sitting next to us, with a cross cut into the top of his head -- and then we drove to Altamont. It was slow going when we got near the Speedway. We parked on the side of the road and walked a long way. We took turns carrying Dylan.

"At the concert, we met five long-haired surfer guys and three girls we knew from Santa Monica. It was a gray day. It seemed like half a million people were there.

"We had driven up Pacific Coast Highway many times from Santa Monica to see the Grateful Dead, Jefferson Airplane, Janis Joplin, and

212

**Mick Jagger before the show, Altamont, 1969
(Snapshot by Ron Lando)**

the Paul Butterfield Blues Band, among others, in Golden Gate Park and other venues, but had never been at a gathering this large.

"Most of the time, we stayed on the perimeter and danced. My wife loved the Stones. She pranced and pointed and sang like Mick. She had seen the Beatles at Shea Stadium years before. (Harvey Keitel, who was my fellow student in Frank Corsaro's Method acting class in Manhattan, had introduced her to me at the one party that I had given in New York City in the five years that I lived there, from 1963-1968. He also introduced me to Martin Scorsese, who hired me to play The Rapist in his first feature, *Who's That Knocking At My Door* in 1968. Marty hired me to act in his first six features and first TV show. Bette Midler, by the way, sang Bob Dylan's 'A Hard Rain's Gonna Fall' at that same party.)

"We shared joints, people gave us food: fruit, juices, sandwiches. Our surfer friends danced, held Dylan. Once, I snaked my way down to the left side of the stage just as the Stones sang, 'Jumpin' Jack Flash.' It was electric. I saw a young woman, who kept trying to climb up onto the stage, and at each attempt, a Hells Angel, who wore a wolf's head kicked her in the face. She must have been a masochist, because she kept going back for more. I headed back to our group. We danced and had a wonderful time. The Stones and Santana were tremendous. We felt renewed.

"It was a long slow journey back to our VW. It wasn't until we were driving south on the 5 Freeway that we heard, on the radio, about the killing at Altamont.

"In 1970, I saw *Gimme Shelter*, by the Maysles Brothers, which showed the violence in all its vividness. In 1968, I had seen the Mayles Brothers' film, *Salesman*.

"To most audiences the film reflected an American consciousness and lifestyle more of the 1950s than of the Summer of Love, hippies, LSD, radical politics, and headlines and buttons proclaiming 'God is Dead,' wrote the film scholar, Vincent Lo Brutto. *Salesman* was about "selling Bibles door to door," quite the opposite of *Gimme Shelter*.

"In 1973, I played the Vietnam vet who destroys his own homecoming in Scorsese's first masterpiece, *Mean Streets*. Scorsese utilized 'Jumpin' Jack Flash' on the soundtrack for Johnny Boy's (De Niro's) entrance into the bar."

Allan Slutsky and director Paul Justman: *Standing in the Shadows of Motown,* with the Funk Brothers, Mary Wilson, Ed Sullivan and Andrew Solt

The ongoing appreciation and critical response to the Motown legacy this century has to be traced to Allan Slutsky's award-winning book and Paul Justman-directed feature length documentary of the same name, *Standing in the Shadows of Motown,* which illustrates the story of the legendary Funk Brothers, the Motown session musicians who fused the backbeat and soul into the countless hits of Motown Records.

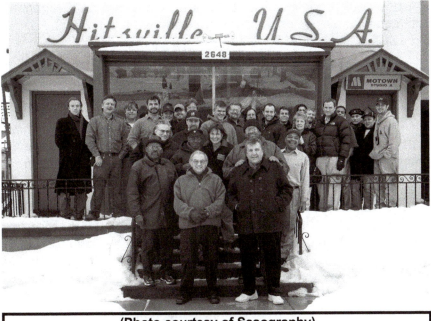

(Photo courtesy of Sasography)

In the movie, the Funk Brothers perform new live versions of several Motown hit songs backing up Chaka Khan, Montell Jordan, Gerald Levert, Joan Osborne, Ben Harper and Meshell Ndegeocello.

Narrated by actor Andre Braugher, the film, initially released in November 2002, tells the tale of the surviving Funk Brothers by combining reminiscences, archival footage, exclusive interviews, re-enactments and brand new performances by the reunited Funk Brothers. Shot on location in Detroit, the Funk Brother's recordings were filmed in Studio A at Motown's famed Hitsville.

"I am extremely proud of this movie," said Sandy Passman, the producer of the film. "The music is so rich and meaningful to me personally and to millions just like me. The 1960s were a turbulent time. The country was tearing itself apart, and for people who grew up on this music it just speaks volumes. If I never make another movie, my name will be on this for all time. I'm happy to have spent the years working on it. I get very emotional about it and all that we went through. But when I see it on-screen and hear the music I can't tell you how thrilled I am."

The soundtrack of these recordings has been issued on Hip-O Records/UMG Distribution. In February 2003 it earned a Grammy in the Best Soundtrack Album category.

Artisian Entertainment distributed the movie in the US and Lightning Entertainment outside of North America brought it to theaters. A DVD through Artisian is now available.

In May, 2004, Hip-O Records/Universal Music issued a Deluxe Edition of the acclaimed 2002 two-CD album set of *Standing in the Shadows of Motown*. Disc One is the previously issued soundtrack from the documentary, plus three bonus tracks heard in the film. There's a Disc Two *In The Snakepit presents Naked Instrumental Remixes* of 16 original hit tracks from the Motown vault. There's even a bonus vocal-and-instrumental track of "You're My Everything" from the Temptations with Funk Brothers bassist James Jamerson.

The core foundation Funk Brothers were: Joe Hunter, Johnny Griffith, and Earl Van Dyke on keyboards, Robert White, Joe Messina, and Eddie Willis on guitar, James Jamerson and Bob Babbitt on bass, Jack Ashford on percussion and vibraphone, Eddie "Bongo" Brown on congas, Benny Benjamin, Richard "Pistol" Allen, and Uriel Jones on drums. Paul Riser, a Motown producer, who currently works with Lauryn Hill and Stevie Wonder once remarked, "As individuals they were great musicians, as a unit they were the best."

Slutsky's 1989 book, *Standing in the Shadows of Motown: The Life and Music of Legendary Bassist James Jamerson*, winner of the first Rolling Stone/Ralph J. Gleason award for music book of the year, provided the film's initial inspiration.

Earlier this century, I went to meet and talk to the surviving members of the Funk Brothers, who were in Hollywood at the Knitting Factory venue for select promotions and media-events around *Standing in the Shadows of Motown*, along with the Slutsky and Justman team.

"It started as just another book," Slutsky told me in an interview. "Working on another project, I had to transcribe some of James Jamerson's Motown bass lines. Like everybody else I had never really thought about the musicians of Motown, I was listening to the singers, be it Marvin Gaye, Diana Ross or Stevie Wonder. You take it as a whole because it's so familiar.

"I went to visit Jamerson's widow in Detroit, just to talk about royalties for a transcription book, and she took me around to visit some of the other guys. Their stories were so riveting. I realized there was more there than just a bunch of notes. And from there the project kept building-first the book and now the film."

The genesis of the movie might have been started with the Jamerson project, but Slutsky also cites the death of Funk Brothers' guitarist Robert White.

"There were various kicks in the butt along the way that made me ratchet it up to another level. Robert's death was one of them. Earl Van Dyke's death was one of them. The fact that toward the end I started to see the window close because a couple of the guys are in their seventies, a couple in the sixties. And, when Earl died, and Robert died, I really felt I had let them down. Of course I hadn't. I got 30,000 hours in this thing, but being Jewish, I have terminal guilt. It just killed me when they died, and I just refused to give up, and not have their story documented for all time. We knew we had the greatest story of the sixties.

"When we were doing the research," he continued, "we talked to a lot of record labels if they had interest. What was the point of having the Funk Brothers playing with the original Motown stars? You can buy that album in the store right now. There was nothing new about it. We picked the songs and the artists. This is like spreading the gospel. The young urban audience does not know about the Funk Brothers.

"They need to know. The rock audience does not know about the Funk Brothers. They need to know. We had a lot of masters we were trying to serve in the recruitment of the stars. Joan Osborne was with us ten years ago. Joan was into this thing for ten years. We didn't even have a deal yet, and wanted an artist to put their name on the line so I could go to somebody, 'if you give us the money.' And nobody would do it, but Joan did when I pitched her.

"I walked around for 11 years a very angry man. I couldn't deal with the level of disrespect. Here I had a diamond in my hand, and when we would pitch it, people would look at me like I was bringing them a sack of garbage. It got me angry, but kept me going. And I did not want to let these bastards win.

"After the success of *The Buena Vista Social Club*, that helped, because now we had a category. 'It's like this…' After seven years *Buena Vista* comes out, 'Oh, you mean like *Buena Vista*?'

"The Motown sound is two things: the songs and the grooves. The songs had an instantly accessible sound and such strong hooks that as soon as you heard one, you remembered the whole melody. But the music of Motown also makes you want to get up and dance. And what is that? The grooves. And that's the Funk Brothers. There have been soul aficiandos waiting for this for decades," declared Slutsky.

217

Over the years. Slutsky would be joined by veteran music video and documentary director Paul Justman (J. Geils Band, Diana Ross, the Doors, James Brown, the Neville Brothers), who was co-editor on Robert Frank's infamous portrait of the Rolling Stones' 1972 tour of America.

"To me it is such an important American story," documentary director Paul Justman underscored in an interview. "Turn on your radio and you hear Motown. Walk through an airport or go shopping, you hear Motown. It's everywhere. But you don't think of the guys playing it. To me there's only one story like it. It's a unique set of circumstances that brought their music to the world and yet left them unknown. And once I met the guys I felt a real emotional bond to them."

It was the passing of Funk Brother Robert White, guitarist on such classic songs as "My Girl" and "You Can't Hurry Love" which in some way was the final push to get this movie to the finish line.

"I don't like to look at it this way, but time was running out," Justman admitted. "After Robert White died, I said to myself, I thought it was over. We had been at it for seven years. I'll go up to Detroit and film with just a MINIDV camera if I have to. I just decided to do it no matter what. I wanted to do something for them. I had a hundred versions of the story with Allan.

"When Allan brought it to me, I realized these guys had played on the soundtrack of my life. And I didn't know who they were. And that idea for a director is mind blowing. So I knew there was a movie there. As we got to know the guys, we got more and more determined to make the film. Robert White lived in L.A. so I got to know Robert well. The footage in the film is footage that I had shot in order to make a little piece to try and sell the film. It was a 'pitch piece' done in the studio. On the DVD there is more stuff from him talking about Stevie Wonder."

Director Justman has done a masterful job of weaving all the visual source tapes and audio clips into *Standing in the Shadows of Motown*. I asked him about the challenges of combining so many different technical formats and archive elements into the film.

"I had come from an editing background, and had worked on the Stones' thing with Robert Frank who shot it in 35mm, 16mm and super 8, which had just come out in 1972. So that was a film of a lot of textures. When you put the film together you have to come up with a kind of vocabulary, so the film doesn't look like one big mess. So if you look at the film there are places where it's all black and white, and then in the re-creations that we did, because we had no footage of these guys when they were young, and it was important to see them as young guys when they were funny. We wanted to give a flavor.

"With the new live concert sequences, it was impossible, due to scheduling, to get all the artists on stage at once. So we did one artist a day. The casting people put out the word on the radio and in newspaper ads and

**Joan Osborne
(Photo courtesy of Sasography)**

crowds would come to that particular day. We cut two songs a day, with some multiple takes. The Stones' movie had a lot more money for the performances, and many more cameras. I thought a lot about these songs because they had to be changing focus all the time. We had six cameras for concerts. My idea, because I'm an editor, every camera had to film a full performance. In other words, the camera was not the drum camera. There was not a vocal camera. Every camera from their angle had to film an entire performance, because I didn't have that much film. And I said if you don't feel it in there, we would rehearse, and if you don't feel it in the lens, and I don't see it in the monitor, I'm not gonna use it. So take chances. Things can go out of focus. It's OK. I'm not going to jump down your throat for mistakes. What's gonna bother me is if I'm not excited about this footage. We don't have a lot of money for lights. We don't have a lot of money for film. But what we have are great cameramen and the vision of how this was gonna be. I had a crane. So I knew what I wanted and the cameramen had balls."

In 2020 I asked Justman via email to reflect back on *Standing in the Shadows of Motown* and what he learned from Swiss photographer and documentary filmmaker Robert Frank that he has applied to his own work.

"What I learned from Robert Frank... Everything. It's so I learned, not how to do it, but what you go for. Of course, with Motown I had a different mission. I had more of a story to tell, than moments to capture—to literally tell the ten year old kid (the audience in my mind)

219

a story about some musicians who should never be forgotten. The 'moments to capture' in *Standing in the Shadows of Motown* were the performances, and in those I wanted to present the musicians as the royalty they were. No one had ever heard of the Funk Brothers. You didn't have to do that for the Stones.

"It was an emotional journey for me. I got to know Robert White, the guitar player on 'My Girl,' and did some filming of him with a little video camera in my studio. He was doing construction, cement work, around Los Angeles. He died four years before we got the film funded—a heart attack. So my mission was to do those musicians justice—a movie about people I got close to over ten years trying to get it going. They were wonderful people to film—charming, funny, brilliant, handsome, enlightened— totally sure of themselves and of what they contributed to the world of music.

Director Paul Justman
(Photo courtesy of Sasography)

"So in everything I've done I've used what I learned from Robert [Frank], of course. Robert and I had a great time putting the film together—every day we laughed a lot. What I learned—everything."

Maybe not the tight-knit recording unit they once were, the Funk Brothers have stayed in touch throughout the years. Benny Benjamin

220

(died 1968), Eddie Brown (died 1983), James Jamerson (died 1983), Earl Van Dyke (died 1992), Robert White (died 1994), and Pistol Allen (died 2002), but he is, thankfully, a recent participant in the documentary.

Johnny Griffith, who died the night the movie premiered in Detroit, a month after I interviewed him, played shows in Las Vegas before his passing.

The rest are still going strong. Joe Messina, besides owning a successful chain of car washes in the Detroit area, has become a virtuoso of the chromatic harmonica. Bob Babbitt is an in-demand session player in Nashville. Jack Ashford and Eddie Willis are semi-retired, but still play the occasional club date.

Joe Hunter (keyboards): From Jackson, Tennessee, he was playing with Hank Ballard and the Midnighters when he joined Gordy's fledging operation in 1958. This is the guy who was instrumental in recruiting many of the players who would define the Motown Sound. That's him on "Heat Wave," "Hitchhike," and "Come Get These Memories."

"Well, Berry had come on one of my gigs and told me what he was all about," remembered Hunter. "He wanted to start a record company, and he also mentioned that really wasn't his goal. He wanted to make some motion pictures. But he had to do that record business first. I met him at a nightclub I was working at. I had been working with Hank Ballard and the Midnighters, and one of the guys quit, so I quit when he quit, because he gave me the job. And he had told Berry about me and Berry came on my job. He bought me a drink and asked me if I had time to talk. And I had time to talk to him because he was very interesting. He's a very charming individual. He was very convincing also. He could convince you that we would all make a lot of money, but he didn't tell me it wasn't until I would be 100 years old. (laughs). I love him, because if it hadn't been for him, I wouldn't be here today.

"Our first rehearsals were at Claudette's house, the person Smokey Robinson married. I knew 99 per cent it was going to be successful, but the 1 per cent came when James Jamerson came, 'cause we had another bass player who played on the first hit, Professor Joe Williams. He spoke three languages. Our first tune was with Marv Johnson via United Artists. People from my high school called me at the time 'cause they heard it on the radio. It was a hit. 'Hey, introduce me to Mr. Gordy!' That's what I did. And that's my story."

Before he split, I cornered Hunter and ask about the song "Heat Wave?"

"Well, it meant a whole lot to me for the simple reason that the morning we went in for the session, Brian Holland had a little chord sheet, and asked me 'what kind of beat goes with this?' I walked to the piano and ran down the chords, and I said I would put a 'Charleston Beat' to it. One of the beats they had way back in the 1920s. So, that's what I did on the piano. That's why it was so interesting when I really heard it when it came out, and it had a groove.

"Me and Marvin Gaye had played with a fellow named Jimmy Reed when he came to Detroit, at a lounge. So I told him, 'when you do your next gig I'm gonna put some stuff in the game.' That's when we did 'Pride and Joy.' One of my favorites, really, because it allowed me to steal Wes Montgomery's introduction and do what I wanted to do."

Eddie Willis (guitarist) hails from Mississippi. He was a part of many of the early Motown hits. His imaginative rhythm playing and flourished fills were a vital component of the "funk" in the Funk Brothers sound. His distinctive sound can be heard on "I Was Made to Love Her" and "The Way You Do The Things You Do." Even after he left Motown, he did years touring with the Four Tops. "Levi Stubbs is a beautiful, beautiful person. I worked with him for 15 years on the road," he volunteered. "If you need anything, ask Levi.

"I'm so grateful the people in the press are really supporting this film and getting the word out who we are. The "I Was Made to Love Her" session, that's me on the lead guitar, was a thrill. I knew at the time within a couple of weeks I would hear it on the radio. It jumped out of the AM car radio. I could not wait for that song to come out."

I mentioned to percussionist Jack Ashford that I felt the *Standing in the Shadows of Motown* movie did bring all of us into the physical world of the actual recording studio at Motown. Still photos and grainy black and white film clips did illustrate the logistics and the sonic sound geography of the music making. We did get a sense of how the Funk Brothers recorded the basic tracks on these monumental recordings.

"Yes, you get a glimpse of that in the movie, but how we recorded in the day you can't capture that," disclosed Ashford. "It was all unique. How many times can you cut horns sittin' seven feet away from the rhythm section? Man, it was unreal! But the closeness of it made it right. It was uniquely right. We cut some stuff man where we could

222

throw spitballs across and hit the horn players on the head! It was so small, and you had a big nine foot grand piano sittin' up in there. The closeness made us feel one another. You could feel the percussion from the horns blastin' across the room from you! It was beautiful. One thing is, you can't duplicate it. When you went in the Studio A, you got a different kind of feel. It's a different feeling when you go into a bigger studio. The sound is gonna have a slight delay when you listen to Jamerson across the room. But when you're close together like that, man, you can feel the sweat of these guys, the anticipation. It's just different."

Joe Messina, hometown of Detroit, guitarist on "I Can't Help Myself," "Your Precious Love," and "Dancing In The Street," was a jazz musician in his teens, and by his mid-20s he was playing on the nationally televised *The Soupy Sales Show,* alongside such guests as Miles Davis and Charlie Parker. He was with the label until operations were moved to Los Angeles in 1972.

"Playing on the *Soupy Sales* TV show was a thrill," Messina beamed. "I don't know if my work on that show and with the jazz artists who came on it influenced my Motown work, but it seemed to make that music a little easier to play, after playing jazz. I backed Miles Davis and Charlie Parker on *The Soupy Sales Show*, but they were limited to six minutes. Those guys can't play six minutes. They need like an hour. Or longer." (The only existing film footage of the Max Roach and Clifford Brown group originates from a *Sales'* broadcast). Did he know he was playing on a monster smash when he cut "Dancing In The Street?" "No. *laughs.* Never expected it. That's one of the nice things," he added. "The beat was a little different, and everybody automatically started to dance to it.

"Paul Riser was my favorite arranger at the label. His arrangements were very interesting, and at the end, our charts were like little scores. He was very detail-oriented. He could write whatever he said, whereas in the earlier days, they would hum the stuff to you, and you would have to remember what was hummed to you.

"In jazz, I got to solo all the time. With Motown it was a little restricted, telling you what to do. I played mainly Telecaster. I converted a Telecaster body with a Jazzmaster neck. Because it was smoother. One of a kind.

"My favorite vocalist was Marvin Gaye. We never associated. We did our tracks, and then he'd overdub. Marvin was a drummer and it made it a little bit different. Levi (Stubbs) was my guy as well. H-D-H

223

would come in with a chord sheet and say 'Run this down.' And we put our little things in there and they would keep it. That was their arrangement. We didn't know we were donating like that *laughs*."

Tom Scott, Jack Ashford, Uriel Jones, Joe Messina, Marcus Begrave, and Johnny Griffith. Jack, Uriel, Joe and Johnny are all Funk Brothers. The special session players were Tom on saxophone and Marcus on trumpet (Photo courtesy of Sasography)

Perhaps one of the overlooked ingredients in the Motown musical brew was that keyboardist Johnny Griffith was one of the few classically trained musicians to walk through the doors of Motown. The other Detroit-born Funk Brother, Griffith, toured as an accompanist with Sarah Vaughn, Dinah Washington, Aretha Franklin and Lou Rawls. His technical playing was the perfect compliment to the aggressive gutbucket style of Earl Van Dyke, and together they would swap off between the organ and piano. Among his greatest performances were "Stop In The Name Of Love," "Wonderful One," Marvin Gaye's version of "I Heard It Through The Grapevine" and the organ and shotgun effects on Junior Walker and the All-Stars' "Shotgun."

"I had done a version of 'Grapevine' with Gladys Knight first," Johnny recalled, a few weeks before his recent death. "And that one was good. But when I did it with Marvin, it was better. It seemed to flow easier, rhythmically. It was quite interesting. Gladys was great also, and I can't take anything away from her. But with Marvin, it was a totally different approach on the same song."

What did you learn as an accompanist to singers that you applied to your work on the Motown sessions?

"The flexibility of the chords, the sound itself. I never heard them sing. When I played with Sarah or Dinah, I was there on the scene. And you accompany. With Motown you just play 'cause you never knew who was going to sing it. So you never knew how they were gonna sing it, but they more or less adjusted their voice to the sound to the way I played it. Which was just the opposite. Sometimes they would put someone's name on the track, and when you heard it by another singer or group, you'd say' 'What the hell happened to so and so?'
"We had Earl Van Dyke, too. He was a powerful player. And he did a lot of piano work. In the earlier days I did all the piano before Earl came in. I was the utility man."

I asked Griffith about drummers Benny Benjamin and Richard "Pistol" Allen.

"When they played Motown, their styles were similar. But jazz-wise they were completely different. Pistol was a jazz drummer originally, and then he made the adjustment, so he could blend with Benny and play together. They were compatible and in agreement when they played together. The two drummers…That was very unusual because I had never worked with two drummers playing basically the same thing that sounded like one drummer. The same with the guitars. We'd have two or three guitars down there, and it sounded like one guitar.
"And if there was an advantage about us cutting without the singers, it was that they then had a choice of who would sing that song. They'd try an artist. If it didn't work, they'd try another. They were looking for the right combination. The one who got the record was the one who could fit the format. Like I've said before, we put the tracks down and built the basement on the first floor. And what you do with the rest of your house is up to you. What you put on the top, the bottom, strings...
"And, we never petitioned for musician credits. When it started, it was all singles. We didn't make albums. That came later. And they sold more singles than any other company."

And the songs? "It was an assembly line. We used to call it the factory. I remember when Norman Whitfield first joined Motown and he was making $30.00 a week. He would be our Burt Bacharach in a couple of years," he marveled.

225

Marvin Gaye (December 28, 1968)
(Photo by Henry Diltz)

Griffith also did some moonlighting around his non-Motown recording dates. As a keyboard player he appeared on Jackie Wilson's "Lonely Teardrops" and "(Your Love Keeps Lifting Me) Higher and Higher," the Chi-lites "Have You Seen Her?" and the Capitols "Cool Jerk."

In February of 1976, I interviewed Temptation David Ruffin in Hollywood for a profile in the now defunct *Melody Maker*.

"The Temptations were individuals who happened to sing together," stated Ruffin. "I never regretted any of the songs we did and even the choreography on stage has been widely copied. I liked the dancin' part of that group. Then you couldn't just stand there and sing. The audience was moving, and you just reflected what was goin' on. If anything, I'd like my association with the Temptations to be remembered as that we gave something. We helped young artists get in a position."

"And let's not forget that great American soundtrack-The Sound of Young America, Jobete Music," record producer and author Andrew Loog Oldham reminded me in a 2004 phone conversation. "You can still hear it every day…in Motown music and recently the U2 single 'Vertigo,' sure sounds like 'You Keep Me Hanging On' to me."

Musical history now illustrates how vital television exposure was for Motown and the label's recording artists. None were more essential than a booking on *The Ed Sullivan Show.*

"The relationship between Berry Gordy's Motown label and *The Ed Sullivan Show* made music and television history," stressed filmmaker Andrew Solt of SOFA Entertainment, owners of *The Ed Sullivan Show* library.

"Soon after the Supremes' debut on *Sullivan* (December 1964), it was clear that showcasing the latest Motown releases on CBS on Sunday nights (35 million viewers was average) until 1971 was a way to expose the record company's newest hits and boost the show's ratings. *Sullivan* introduced nearly all the Motown acts, including the Supremes, the Temptations, Stevie Wonder, the Four Tops, Smokey Robinson and the Miracles, Marvin Gaye, Gladys Knight and the Pips, and the Jackson 5."

Universal Music Enterprises (UMe) and SOFA Entertainment released *Motown Gold from The Ed Sullivan Show* (2 DVDs), and, in celebration of The Temptations and Supremes 50th Anniversary, *The Best of The Temptations on The Ed Sullivan Show* (1 DVD) and *The Best of The Supremes on The Ed Sullivan Show* (1 DVD). All three collections released on September 13, 2011 are packed with classic Motown performances from *The Ed Sullivan Show*, taped live between 1964 and 1971, and are fully restored with never before released footage.

Motown performances on *Sullivan* were followed by a Monday morning spike, and it was a perfect formula for mutual success. Berry

Gordy's dynamic sound aimed to appeal to America's white teenagers and with *The Ed Sullivan Show* stage as the entry point for his incredible roster of talent, this show business marriage remained rock solid until the show went off the air. Ed Sullivan and his producer, Bob Precht, were especially proud of the history these two iconic American institutions forged together.

Andrew and Josh Solt, whose company, SOFA Entertainment, owns *The Ed Sullivan Show* library made the following statement in 2011 about their Motown collection.

"We are so pleased that after working on this project for many years, the definitive *Motown on Ed Sullivan* collection is now available to millions of fans who love the Motown sound. *The Sullivan Show* featured more Motown artists than any other television show, and now these timeless live performances can finally be enjoyed by fans of what many believe is the greatest music of the 60's. A considerable amount of work has gone into making sure the sound and picture quality on the discs is optimal. We hope people will be dancing in the streets and in their living rooms when they play the *Motown on Ed Sullivan* DVD collection."

Andrew Solt's other credits include the 1979 TV special *Heroes Of Rock And Roll* and 1988 feature documentary *Imagine: John Lennon* as well as the 1991 Warner Brothers theatrical feature film *This is Elvis*, to the 1995 TV documentary series *The History Of Rock 'N' Roll* and 2006 home video *Elvis: The Ed Sullivan Shows*. SOFA Entertainment has produced approximately 400 programs for television and home video.

"Sullivan knew how to give a show that was for every generation that might be watching," emphasized Andrew during a September 2011 phone interview. "If you look back the show was such a launching pad for such great important iconic moments. Whether it's Elvis or Bo Diddley.

"When the Beatles stepped onto Ed Sullivan's New York stage on Sunday, February 9, 1964, to make their American TV debut, 86% of all TVs on at that hour—73 million Americans—were tuned in. It was the most watched program in history to that point and remains one of the most watched programs of all time. To some, it will always be remembered by his introduction: 'Here they are—the Beatles!' "

"For us, being on *The Ed Sullivan Show* was so much more than record sales," hailed Mary Wilson of the Supremes during my 2003 and 2016 interviews with her.

The Supremes on *The Ed Sullivan Show*
(Photo courtesy of SOFA Entertainment)

"It wasn't about promoting us. It was about that we had grown up watching *The Ed Sullivan Show*. We had grown up watching shows where you didn't see a lot of black people starring on those shows. For us, we were like every other family in America who spent hours watching *Ed Sullivan*. So for us, being on the show was such a great honor. Because we were there to see the world changing. To see America changing. We were excited! We're on *The Ed Sullivan Show*.

"We came from a time when a whole family of all different colors didn't sit around watching black people on television. *The Dick Clark [Caravan of Stars]* tours were before us, and there were segregated hotels.

"For us, that is what it was all about. We were part of that change. We were part of helping America to see black people, black women, being proud, beautiful and successful. It wasn't just us, many people before us. But they didn't have the television to expose them to that wide range of people as we did at the time when we came. We were lucky. And we stood on a lot of shoulders. But we were there when the doors opened.

"The other thing was that we were seen in color after our initial appearances were in black and white. Recently, my granddaughter was watching a DVD collection of the Supremes. And she said to me, 'Grandma! What happened to the color?' 'Cause she has never seen a black and white TV!"

I asked Mary if fans and the record buying public have a greater appreciation of the musicians now. Several members of the Funk Brothers told me that the issue of musician credits really wasn't a major concern since the first era of the Motown label was singles oriented, not an album-driven company.

The Temptations on *The Ed Sullivan Show*
(Photo courtesy of SOFA Entertainment)

"That's what people should have been doin' all the time," she felt. "The problem is that I think people took the music for granted. Because the musicians didn't have the big publicity machinery back in those days. Only the upfront artists were the ones who were pushed. So, therefore the media and no one else paid attention to the music, even though you did, but it was sort of subliminally. And that's a shame. Because of what goes into the peoples' home is a total sound, not just the voices. But no one put a face to the music. They put a face to the voices, and a name to the voices, but they just sort of took the musicians along with that. So you have this faceless music, but it was the music that made you move."

"That was a shame, but it was never intentional. And that's why now, people are able to finally put a face to that music, and the musicians can be appreciated as individuals. Because I understand, because I was a background singer, but I don't think I was a background singer, but that's how the publicity was presented. So we kind of became faceless Supremes."

The Temptations helped Ed Sullivan celebrate his birthday on the air!
(Photo courtesy of SOFA Entertainment)

"And yes, when the label first started, it was about singles, not albums, and there weren't musician credits on singles. It wasn't until Marvin Gaye's *What's Goin' On* that there were album credits for the musicians. So, they fall into a category where they were appreciated, but not given their dues, the total respect. These are breathing people, and this film is doing a lot to help.

"In the earlier days we actually recorded with the musicians, do the vocals a couple of times. For years we recorded right there with the musicians. The magic for me was lost after we became really famous because then the tracks were laid down and we would come in and do it without seeing the musicians. The magic was when we recorded with the musicians. That was the beauty," she praised.

"Now everyone is asking me about the musicians," Wilson merrily confessed. "From my perspective, we always knew and felt that. The public now can appreciate them as individuals. We always appreciated them that way. We as artists had to look out for ourselves, and we had our PR pushing us. The musicians didn't have PR companies pushing them then. See the difference? Thank God now they can get their final due, which they totally deserve. I want to be really clear about this: No one really intentionally didn't talk about the guys. It wasn't that, it's just the way the business was. The artists out front," she reiterated.

"One thing I remember Berry said that had something to do with it. 'This is the sound of young America. There is no time on it. I want to make this music where everyone in the world can listen to it and enjoy it. We're singing from our guts. I want to make music that everyone around the world can enjoy.' And that's what he did. How, I don't know...

"I have to give credit to Berry for putting us with Holland, Dozier and Holland. Because previously, we were the 'No Hit' Supremes for a long time. Berry said, 'I can see that you are really serious, so I'm gonna put you with my top writing team, H-D-H.' So it was their music, their direction, I was active behind the group, behind the scenes, people don't know that. On TV, Diane would jump out in front, and that wasn't really the way we ran it. Which is fine.

"When they brought us 'Where Did Our Love Go?' I told Eddie (Holland), all three of us said, "I don't like that record.' I went to Eddie, 'We need a hit here.' 'Mary,' he said, 'trust me. You girls are gonna have a hit.' That changed my life.

"It proves that as a kid you knew you had fallen into heaven. So now, not only do you know it, but the world knows it too. That feeling... Like Florence said, 'we really were fantastic. All of us.'

"I love and adore all the groups on Motown, and listen to them all the time. When I hear Levi Stubbs' voice...It's just magic. Levi is one of the best singers in the world. And always has been. I admire him because he stayed with his group (the Four Tops). A lot of lead singers didn't, and so then they were singled out. That is what happened to our group as well. Our songs from 1964, '65 and '66 were heard in1967.

232

Berry Gordy and the A&R department knew what was happening," reminisced Ms. Wilson.

"And we didn't have to think about that. But we were happy for it. And as a group, it took us into areas we wanted to go, which is great. I loved to tour.

Levi Stubbs with photographer Brad Elterman
(Photo courtesy of Brad Elterman)

"I'm just so fortunate to have known so many brilliant people. However, just to talk about Holland-Dozier-Holland was such a wonderful experience for our growth and journey. They took us through the times that were going on in the world. Each time they would bring us to another level. The records show this. We did 'You Can't Hurry Love' and 'You Keep Me Hanging On.' That's why we had wanted them in the beginning. We had to grow into that."

In 1994, I interviewed Berry Gordy, Jr. for *HITS* magazine. We discussed the heralded Holland, Dozier and Holland production and songwriting team.

"H-D-H was phenomenal. They came up with hit after hit. They started a thing. They had a lock on the Supremes and they took them, and did stuff on Marvin. H-D-H was absolutely brilliant. The three of them were different and they all complemented each other.

"Eddie (Holland) did mostly vocals, Brian (Holland), I thought was the most talented, creative person. He was my protégé for many years. I thought Lamont (Dozier) was also a good writer, and he was good on backgrounds and this and that and so forth. But Brian would do something like he would play and sing and create something and all he would give 'em was, like, 'I Can't Help Myself' 'Sugar Pie, Honey Bunch,' and pass it on. So they had their own assembly line. And they were tremendous."

"After we no longer had H-D-H there was a period where we didn't have anyone," Mary lamented. "That to me was the worst period musically. So we got with Frank Wilson who was just brilliant," enthused Mary. "What was great about him is that now it was more a West Coast. It wasn't Detroit. We did everything pretty much on the West Coast, even though we still recorded in Detroit.

Lamont Dozier (the D in H-D-H)
(Photo by Brad Elterman)

"And I'm also very proud of the songs the Supremes did later after Diane left that we did with producer Frank Wilson like 'Nathan Jones,' 'Stoned Love' and 'Up The Ladder To The Roof.'

"Frank brought a different feel. There's a wah-wah pedal on 'Up The Ladder To The Roof,' a more seventies soulful kind of feel. And after we no longer had Diane. Berry Gordy was very helpful in bringing Jean Terrell, who I just adored. And she was the best replacement for Diane, not that anyone could ever replace Diane.

"For me, the only group was the three of us. Me, Flo and Diane. The seventies was a seventies group. And Frank was able to capture who we were at that point with Jean Terrell. He was just a brilliant producer.

"We had a whole other concept when we moved out to the West Coast. We did our sessions in Los Angeles. Hollywood. The Motown studio," Mary recollected.

I asked Mary about now hearing a Motown song and is it a difficult moment for her with so many of her Motown performing friends who have passed on. "Yes," she sighed. "I always get that…When I hear them…For us, we were a family, so for us, the loss is greater than it is for you guys, for the fans…Because it's like losing our brothers and sisters. There's a huge sadness. Their contribution continues…

"I saw Eddie Kendricks' face flash across the screen recently when I was watching TV, which I don't do too often, and I almost cried. I felt the tears well up in my eyes. It's always there. Everyone of us at Motown feels the same way."

The Supremes at the Hollywood Bowl (April 29, 1967)
(Photo by Henry Diltz)

Dreams to Remember: The Legacy of Otis Redding

Reelin' In The Years Productions and Stax Records (a division of Concord Music Group) in 2007 issued *Dreams To Remember: The Legacy of Otis Redding* on DVD, acknowledging the 40th anniversary of Otis Redding's death to celebrate his life, and the 50th anniversary of Stax Records.

Collected for the first time on this 90-minute DVD are 16 classic full-length performances by one of our greatest singers and performers of all time. Interspersed

(Cover courtesy of Reelin' in the Years Productions)

between the selections are more than 40 minutes of exclusive new interviews documenting Otis' life and career.

Dreams To Remember: The Legacy of Otis Redding had its theatrical debut in September 2007 in Hollywood, California at the Egyptian Theater as part of the annual *Mods & Rockers* film festival produced by Martin Lewis for the American Cinematheque.

In a short chat I had at the venue with Zelma Redding, Otis' widow who was in attendance, Mrs. Redding said she was delighted with the DVD and big screen broadcast of it shown to a rabid bunch of Otis and Stax Records fans.

"Otis has always been bigger in England than the US based on the respect and the amount of licensing requests we get for commercials. It took me many years to be convinced to allow this film to be made, and I'm very happy."

The DVD interviews paint a portrait of Otis as singer, artist, songwriter, an open tuning guitarist and family man. The Otis Redding journey begins with memories of his first amateur talent contests and concludes with the touching recollections of the final days leading up to his tragic US plane crash on December 10, 1967.

Issued with the full cooperation of his estate, this is the first official DVD anthology of classic archival Otis Redding television appearances. The impressive compilation was produced by David Peck, Rob Bowman and Phillip Galloway for Reelin' In The Years Productions, a leading California-based television and film archive in conjunction with Universal Music Group. Zelma Redding serves as executive producer.

The DVD houses stories about Otis writing songs, recording at Stax and performing on stage (including the historic 1967 Monterey International Pop Festival.) *Dreams To Remember: The Legacy of Otis Redding* incorporates a wealth of staggering performances filmed throughout America and Europe.

On the DVD, Otis sings one of his earliest hits, "Pain In My Heart" and progressing through his enduring Stax/Volt recording career, including complete and intact performances of "I Can't Turn You Loose," "I've Been Loving You Too Long," "(I Can't Get No) Satisfaction" and a plethora of others. There's a December, 1965 "Pain In My Heart" television performance culled from Dick Clark's *Where The Action Is* and "Just One More Day" from another Redding TV appearance the same day on *Hollywood A Go-Go*. In the case of lip-sync performances, the original Stax master recordings have been used, replacing the original TV broadcast audio.

Dreams To Remember: The Legacy of Otis Redding has a 24-page booklet with an extensive essay by Rob Bowman, author of *Soulsville U.S.A.: The Story Of Stax Records*. The bonus section features interviews conducted by Bowman with Stax veterans Steve

237

Cropper and Wayne Jackson. Jim Stewart, founder of the Stax label is also interviewed. In addition, the package integrates a photo gallery with never-before-seen images from the Redding family's personal archives and a recently discovered radio interview recorded in London in 1966. Also, commissioned and created exclusively for the DVD, is a new video for "(Sittin' On) The Dock Of The Bay" (a song that wasn't completed until after Otis' death).

Three seismic numbers from the monumental 1967 Stax/Volt tour of Europe and England are housed in this "must own" collection. "I've been Loving You Too Long (To Stop Now)" and "Satisfaction" from London, 1967, and "My Girl" from a live TV show taping in Oslo, Norway.

Stax legend Steve Cropper has his own reflections on the memorable Stax/Volt tour of Europe and England. Calling from Tennessee, Cropper informed me in 2007 that the '67 trek "changed the musicians and the executive end.

"Most of the guys in the band never played in front of 100 people in a nightclub, except Wayne Jackson and "Duck" Dunn, because of our success with 'Last Night'," Cropper mentioned during an interview published in *Goldmine* magazine.

"We were treated with more like royalty and respect in England. It was amazing. Like the Beatles! When we'd finish a show there would be hundreds of people wanting to touch us, grabbing a piece of hair, wanting an autograph, hundreds of people trying to touch us. They used to have to line bodyguards up so we could get from the stage to the bus. We'd never seen that before. That was something that just was unheard of, especially in the States.

"All of a sudden it changed everybody's egos. And things started happening, and all of a sudden, the whole aura around Stax started changing because everybody all of a sudden wanted to be an individual. They didn't want to work as a team anymore, and I was fighting for the team. I fought for that team big time. To me it was like the greatest basketball team that ever came together. When they went into the studio together magic things happened. And they won. And winning was to have a hit record. A hit single on the charts."

Wayne Jackson additionally has fond memories of the 1967 Stax/Volt tour. In an interview from Tennessee, Wayne explained during 2007, "Initially it was going to be Otis and his guys who went on the road with him. It was Jerry Wexler who said, 'No. They want to hear the sound of Stax.' The UK audience knew it as the Stax/Volt band. The Mar-Keys and Booker T. and the M.G.'s that made up the band. They loved Otis Redding like we all loved Otis Redding, but the band at Stax was the diving board he jumped off of. You can tell the horn sound. Me, Andrew Love and Floyd Newman sound a certain way. All those records had that in common. All those records had Steve Cropper's guitar, Al Jackson's drums, Duck Dunn's bass and Booker's organ. Those things are very distinctive, and that made up Stax sounds. And that's where Otis came from. So Jerry Wexler was really hip to say that," Jackson remarked.

"Stevie Winwood told me personally that it changed his life that night. Rod Stewart. He was foaming at the mouth when I got the horn section in for *Atlantic Crossing*. Before that we did *Smiler*. I recently heard *Smiler*. Boy, we were some excited folks. I mean me and Andrew were like 31, 32, so anyway we were in England again and recording with a rock star. It was so exciting. He was in love with all of us. Peter Gabriel. I went up to Bath. He saw Otis in Brixton (at the Ram Jam club). I did the arranging on 'Sledgehammer.' (The song was written as a tribute to Redding.)

"I just feel absolute joy and thrilled when I watch the DVD and my luck was that good and God was that good to me to put me into that situation as an 18 year old. I was there the whole time and thrilled the whole time. I loved Otis, and he loved me. We were big friends. 'Cause we all liked to laugh, and we were all young, and the testosterone levels were out of this world. That's what you heard in that music. Al Jackson was a joy to watch. He was the most fun drummer I ever was around. He was just the best drummer you ever heard, and the best drummer you ever saw. He was a great musician.

"Musicians are not in competition. No one in that band was in competition. We were one thing. We were there to support and glorify Otis Redding. And we did that. And it shows on screen. We were there to respect glorify and hold the singer up to glory. Whether it be Otis, Eddie Floyd or Sam and Dave. We did that. That was our job and we loved it and did it good. Everybody in that band had his position. Like Duck Dunn. Have you ever seen anybody work that hard on bass? It makes my hands cramp up," howled Wayne.

"Looking at the Otis DVD when I see that how strong I was. I made very few mistakes in that show as a lead trumpet player," Jackson continued. "The guy you hear the most is me and I was terrified a lot of the time, but also having a lot of fun. I was strong and 26 years old. Playing on the 1967 Stax/Vault tour, I didn't alter anything. I just tried to hang on. 'Cause the tempos were higher. Jim Stewart told Otis in England, 'we're recording this Otis, so we need to get into the groove of Stax.' And Otis said, 'This is my show and I'm gonna leave these people out of breath.' And that's what he did. He ignored Jim completely.

"It was his way to keep the fire under their feet. I don't think he had more confidence. I don't think he could have had anymore confidence if he tried. He was just an exuberant, wonderful guy. He brought all of that to the stage with him.

"Sam and Dave tried to cut him every night. They tried to blow him out of the water, but they never did. They were as strong as nine acres of garlic, but Otis was ten acres of garlic!"

For producer/writer Bowman, the DVD is a logical extension of work he began over two decades ago documenting in a variety of media the wonderful music and the incredible musicians that made up Stax Records.

Bowman has overseen and written liner notes for 75 Stax and soul reissues, (several Band re-releases as well), authored the book, *Soulsville U.S.A.: The Story Of Stax Records,* and was involved in a 1994 French/German documentary of the Stax label back in 1994. Co-producing this Otis Redding DVD is obviously a continuation of all his groundwork Stax expeditions.

I asked Bowman in a telephone call to Canada, why does Otis have such a commanding presence on stage?

"He really leaps out of film for the same reasons that anybody who got a chance to see him was simply mesmerized by the experience. And perhaps we take that even further even for those who didn't get a chance to see him and heard those records there is a kinetic, dynamic energy to this man. Whether you're just hearing it orally or you get the oral and visual experience. Seeing him on the big (and small) screen is pretty amazing.

"I know a lot of people who saw those shows in the UK who have recounted various experiences. One of the first things was a shock that Booker T. and the M.G.'s wasn't an all black band. They heard these sounds. They were intimately connected to these sounds and had never had a chance to experience it live in this way.

"It's arguable that the one 1967 tour, the Stax/Volt Revue, was the most important soul music tour ever. Because you gotta remember that they were only playing to 1,500 and 2,000 seat houses, so the reaction was intense, rabid, maniacal. Lots of people in those audiences were musicians and the hipper people around that scene, like the Rolling Stones and Beatles, and a lot of musicians who weren't as famous yet, like Peter Garbriel, who talks about that show as transforming his very life. And also the tastemakers in their local neighborhood, or writers from *Blues and Soul*."

A live 45RPM version of "Shake" from the Stax/Volt tour of Europe was released in May 1967 This new Otis DVD corrals Otis' galvanizing version of "Shake" from the seminal June 1967 Monterey International Pop Festival. that really propelled Otics Redding to global attention. My brother Kenneth and I concur, and we wrote the book, *A Perfect Haze: An Illustrated History of the Monterey International Pop Festival* published in 2012.

It was Rolling Stones' manager/record producer and omnipresent musical tastemaker, Andrew Loog Oldham, who initially called (manager) Phil Walden to secure Otis for the Monterey booking.

In 1967 Redding was voted number one male vocalist over Elvis Presley in the annual *Melody Maker* reader's poll awards. Andrew Loog Oldham suggested to Monterey festival producer, Lou Adler, that Otis play the non-profit charity Monterey event. Walden then in turn dialed Atlantic's Jerry Wexler to see if the festival was kosher. Wexler also explained to him what the logic of it would be, and Walden wisely then took Wexler's advice that Otis should do the gig for free.

In 2007 Andrew Loog Oldham emailed me from Bogota, Colombia.

"When Otis came on stage, you forgot about the logistics. We knew we were taking one small step forward for mankind. Phil Walden, his manager, was in heaven. He knew he'd just graduated from buses to planes. Phil Walden was one of the greatest managers of his time. His enthusiasm, his pure chicanery, his belief, his service to Otis was an example to the game."

Then, there is Monterey festival attendee Paul Body who is still recovering from witnessing Otis with Booker T. and the M.G.'s at that poptastic gathering.

241

"The cool air was rolling in as they were playing and I felt like a million bucks. Booker T. and the M.G.'s came on and did a few numbers and then Otis Redding joined them and took the night. He brought Memphis to Monterey. He turned the festival grounds into a sweaty juke joint on a foggy night. I was standing up on someone's car that was outside and we danced on the roof. Otis looked like a king dressed in an electric green Soul suit. He came on like a hurricane singing Sam Cooke's 'Shake' at breakneck speed. It was a real electric moment. He looked like a damn fullback up there. He was as magnificent as a mountain. It looked like nothing could stop him. He could rock but when it came to that slow burn Southern style, no one was better. He was giving the love crowd a lesson in slow dancing.

"He ended with 'Try A Little Tenderness' turning it inside out and making it scream for mercy. He slowed it down to a simmer, started off some mournful horns, Booker T.'s organ and his voice. Al Jackson came in with light rim shots that sounded like raindrops from heaven in the foggy night. Then Cropper came in with some tasty rhythm chops, then Al started beating out the groove, pushing it and they took it home. I had never seen anything like it."

Henry Diltz, who was the official Monterey photographer, gave me another perspective during 2007 on Redding's Bay area '67 exhibition.

"Being a rock photographer you get the best seat because you are in front of the front row. I remember nothing was between me and Otis. The warmest most wonderful music and so different than the rest. A different flavor of music. It came from a whole other place, not these things, bands that emerged out of folk music. I just basked in this amazing sound. Warm and tender delicious tension. The feel of his voice. The edge of it."

In a 2007 conversation with Al Kooper for *MOJO* magazine, the multi-instrumentalist then serving as assistant stage manager of the festival, quipped, "I watched Otis Redding disarm the audience. And, he had one of the greatest bands in the history of rock 'n' roll behind him. I'd seen Al Jackson before. He was like the Charlie Watts of black music."

The D. A. Pennebaker-directed *Monterey Pop* documentary followed in 1969 which helped unthaw his frozen legacy. I attended the world premiere of the movie at the Fine Arts Theater in Beverly Hills.

242

"Otis Redding was stunning," D.A. Pennebaker enthused to me in a 2006 interview.

"It's a great film, almost a perfect film. He had a pretty good band, I was editing, or re-editing the section of his for *Monterey Pop* in late '67 and changed the film a little bit when he went into the lake and I remember that's when I got into all that stuff of doing things with the lights. And I know at the time I felt, 'Gee. What am I doing? This is crazy.' But I left it that way because I felt so bad that he kind of died on us, and that made me sad. So it was the only thing I could do to mark that was to edit that way."

"I couldn't wait to see Otis Redding at Monterey," exclaimed documentarian Andrew Solt [*This Is Elvis* and *Imagine: John Lennon*] in 2017. "He was one of the acts that I knew I couldn't miss. I loved his voice, his albums and his enormous on-vinyl passion.

"Otis came out dressed in a shiny suit, his collar open and absolutely blew us away. He was as dynamic in person as anyone I had ever seen live. He owned the stage, and the crowd was in awe. His enjoyment at singing at this early pop festival was palpable.

"Otis's tragic death later in the same year depressed me to no end. What a horrific, massive loss. That voice stilled? Couldn't be!

"When we did *Heroes of Rock 'n Roll* in 1979, [a two-hour music documentary which debuted on network ABC television channel 7] we came across Otis's final performance on *Upbeat* before that dreaded flight. He had appeared in the tight quarters of a small local TV station in Cleveland. We made sure Otis was included in rock's pantheon. He continues to hold a revered place in our history. He always will."

Steve Cropper recalled in another long distance chat, "Everything Otis touched he made it his own, like Sam Cooke's 'Shake.' All of those things, you listen to them, and it's sort of like a great actor, like if Gene Hackman takes a part, or if James Stewart takes a part, they become that character. And at the time you watched it, you became part of them. You know what I'm saying? You don't think about somebody else doing it."

Wayne Jackson has some revealing thoughts on Otis Redding's set at the Monterey International Pop Festival. "We were in a hotel room rehearsing for Monterey, and the question of tempos came up, because tempos had been an important question in Europe. Al (Jackson) said in Europe 'they were pretty darned fast.' And that was all up to Otis. 'I want to keep them up and jumpin'. I want to keep them up there and hook 'em.' And he knew the songs were better for a live crowd fast because they would jump. Boogie a little harder. The Stax thing was a dance groove, and it's not fast. At *Monterey,* when we were done, they kind of forgot about Jefferson Airplane. And Otis was the man. He really knocked them over. That was a mind changer," Jackson beamed.

Steve Cropper has a whole other slant and overview on Redding's well–chronicled Monterey star turn.

"The way I recall it, they took us over to the festival in a school bus, we could hear the music and heard a concert going in that afternoon. Now, we didn't play until that night, but they took us over early, 'cause some of the guys wanted to hear some of the other artists. And, the Association was on stage as we pulled up, and I will never forget that. And here's a connection, and I always loved their records on the radio, the influence of the Association in 1966, '67, that the bridge on 'Sittin' On The Dock Of The Bay' that I wrote with Otis was inspired by my like for their music.

"Hearing them was a little thing, but that was the inspiration for it, because we knew we had a hit, and we wanted to make it pop. To me the Association loved R&B but they were a pop group. You know what I'm saying? So that's sort of the way I was trying to go with that. Of course, with Otis singing it became an Otis song. He got the idea when he was staying at a houseboat later when he was workin' the Fillmore West.

"At Monterey, that audience sat out through the rain to see us, or wait to see Otis Redding, and that's the first time I ever experienced that. And they were more curious than anything else. Because they heard who Otis was.

"Otis had found his audience, and Monterey helped him cross over to a wider white pop market. They already knew how big he was in Europe, and Europe was not an ethnic rhythm and blues audience. It was more general. He was big in France, and he was big in England. And he was big, and Phil Walden and Atlantic knew that, and they wanted that same kind of recognition over here, and they were finding it very difficult to get pop radio play. No problem getting R&B play whatsoever. So we knew what we wanted to do.

"Without question," he reiterated, "the Stax/Volt tour of England and Europe itself changed everybody's life. The musicians and the executives, and Phil Walden, Otis's manager, his whole perception of 'I'm gonna make Otis Redding the biggest star on the planet.' When you saw Otis perform with the band on his records, he knew 'we got something special goin' on here. We've got to preserve this.' He saw a whole different vision."

Steve Cropper provided additional observations on his group and the men behind the sound of Redding.

"Al Jackson, Booker, Duck and I grew up playing nightclubs in Memphis. Wayne Jackson grew up that way. Playing live, like at Monterey, if a vocalist is not there, I'm playing vocal parts. When a vocalist is there I back off and play rhythm and fills" The Otis DVD underscores the energy and musicality of the Otis and Booker T. and the M.G.'s super-charged unit.

"There's no need for me to be bragging on myself, and I don't do that and it's not an ego thing, and all that. I don't think there ever was or ever will be a band that had the magnetism that Booker T. and the M.G.'s had. Whether they back somebody or played on their own in our high school days and upbringing. We had that band mentality thing 'cause we worked as a unit. Because if some guy wants to go out there and ego on stage, he's gonna blow it for everybody else. We learned to play as a unit in the studio. We were there not for ourselves ,but for the artist we were playing behind. In the studio when I was writing songs and starting to record them, I always saw it in my head as a finished product. I knew where to go with it."

The final two performances contained in *Dreams To Remember: The Legacy of Otis Redding* are "Try A Little Tenderness" and "Respect," taped at a local Cleveland television show *Upbeat*. An appearance less than 24 hours before Otis and all but two members of his band, the Bar-Kays, perished in a plane crash into Lake Monona three miles from his intended destination of Madison, Wisconsin on December 10, 1967. Singers Johnnie Taylor and Joe Simon were among the pallbearers at Redding's funeral in Macon City, Georgia. Booker T. played organ to the grieving congregation and Jerry Wexler provided the eulogy.

On the 2007 DVD there is Rob Bowman's information-packed interviews with Wayne Jackson and Steve Cropper, always telling, factual, anecdotal and humorous. I quizzed Bowman over the telephone asking why these two Southern gents are so passionate and personable on camera?

"It's partially because they are great players like all of them, but Wayne and Steve have a gift you will to be able to talk about, moments in the studio or on stage. They are able to talk about individuals, the way they approach music making. They have a gift for memory, and for stories and a gift for the sort of language that animates that stuff. They are incredible interviewees. They both have dynamic personalities. It's partially memories, personality.

"Neither Duck Dunn nor Booker T. (Jones) are the extraverts that Wayne and Steve are. And especially in Wayne's case, he's a poet. He has a gift for images, metaphors that are so evocative and so gorgeous, that very few people have, musicians or non-musicians. Steve has a great memory and a very good interview, but Wayne is the poet of the two of them. I love Cropper. Steve has been a cornerstone of so much of my work because his memory is so precise, and he's willing to go deep.

"The Steve and Otis relationship was the most intimate of any of the relationships Otis had at Stax. But Steve, quite quickly, developed an intense bond with Otis, and it had to do with pragmatics. Steve was the guy who ran the studio. Steve was the guy that Jim Stewart assigned to write with Otis. And because of that, they spent an inordinate amount of time outside of that studio hanging out together in hotel rooms, private homes, working on songs, of course, eating, drinking and shooting the shit.

"Zelma Redding talked about being in Memphis, and it isn't in the film. Otis would go down the street and Steve would be at his side. She described it as where Otis was Steve was going to be. That's how much he was into Otis Redding as a person and a musician as well. An intense deep-seated relationship that was, of course, born out in all these great songs. Wayne's relationship was not, I guess, as intense, but equally full of love and especially given Otis' unique abilities and horn arrangements and the impact that had at Stax," Bowman fortifed.

In 2007, Wayne Jackson cited the sense of destiny that imbued the sound of Stax wax.

"Duck Dunn and I are both left-handed, born on the same day in the same hospital. It was a real spiritual and astrological happening at Stax. Andrew Love is three days older than me, and he and David Porter were born the same day. Booker is a musical genius. Otis always brought a great contribution to all the sessions he was on. He was educated. Steve Cropper invented a style of guitar where the little guitar parts were singular. He played licks that became part of the song. The horns were part of the song. Without us they would not have been the same.

246

"Otis used a guitar to write songs and would use open key. So he could just bar it put a bar on his finger and play up the scale and chords. He could easily write with it. When I was with Otis, he was on another energy track. Otis was like a 16-year old boy with a hard on all the time. Because all he could think about was writing a song and getting into a studio. That was his life. Zelma and those kids and the farm and his music in that order I think. But outside of the farm, he didn't think of nothing but his career. Otis did an amazing body of work in the six years he was recording," emphasized Jackson.

Available in DVD, *The Stax/Volt Revue Live In Norway 1967,* widely bootlegged in truncated and poor condition for years, this first time 75-minute concert, re-transferred from the original master tapes that had been resting in the television vaults for the last 40 years, is now on sale. The producers also discovered an additional lost reel with an extra 20 minutes of previously unseen performances from the same concert. This footage had been edited out and forgotten for the last four decades, but now the missing songs have been restored, making this DVD the longest and most complete visual record of the legendary 1967 Stax/Volt tour.

Highly recommended are the potent full-length performances, including five songs by Otis Redding, and a blistering four song mini-concert recital by Sam and Dave. The DVD also spotlights Booker T. and the M.G.'s, Arthur Conley, Eddie Floyd and the Mar-Keys. Issued with the full cooperation of the artists or their estates, this DVD captures the Stax/Volt Revue on an amazing night during one of most landmark and important concert tours of the last five decades.

The Stax/Volt Revue Live In Norway 1967 includes Otis Redding's versions of "Shake," "Satisfaction," the only known filmed concert performance of "Fa-Fa-Fa-Fa-Fa (Sad Song)"

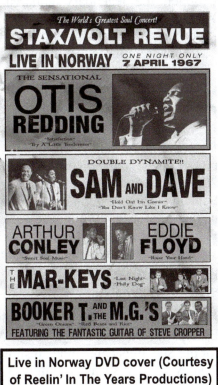

Live in Norway DVD cover (Courtesy of Reelin' In The Years Productions)

247

and a six minute version of "Try A Little Tenderness" in which he returns for four encores. Sam and Dave show why they were nicknamed "Double Dynamite," with powerful performances of "Hold On! I'm Comin'," and "When Something Is Wrong With My Baby." Plus, there's a riveting version of "You Don't Know Like I Know." The DVD has Booker T. and the M.G.'s scorching rendition of "Green Onions," Arthur Conley's definitive version of his big chart hit "Sweet Soul Music," the Mar-Keys glowing version of their top-five hit "Last Night."

Then there's Eddie Floyd's stellar "Raise Your Hand" a song Bruce Springsteen & The E Street Band performed in the late 1970s, introduced into their live set then by Miami Steve Van Zandt.

Finally, the bonus features section includes an additional rendition of "Green Onions," culled also from that vibrant Norway TV program that provides an interesting contrast, demonstrating how unique each performance could be.

The bonus featurettes incorporated are with Jim Stewart, Steve Cropper, the legendary guitarist for Booker T. and the M.G.'s, Wayne Jackson from the Mar-Keys/Memphis Horns, and Sam Moore (Sam and Dave) along with Stax historian Rob Bowman, providing additional reminiscences about this game-changing tour.

Bowman wrote the informative and educational 24-page booklet on this concert, thankfully captured on film.

"About 50 or 55 minutes of *Live In Norway* has been bootlegged for years. Poor quality, of course, and the new DVD is right off the master tapes, so the quality is inordinately superior. We found an extra 20 minutes, upon David Peck's urging, an extra Otis song, an extra Sam and Dave song, an extra Arthur Conley performance that none of us had ever seen. 20 minutes were filed under a tape, the Atlantic All Stars. And the reason the tape was filed that way was because on the show posters it was Otis Redding and the Atlantic All Stars, because over there Atlantic was still distributing Stax. And, the name Stax didn't have any particular meaning in Norway," explained Bowman.

The April 7, 1967 artifact reminds us again of the versatility of Booker T. and the M.G.'s, and why the Mar-Keys provided the glue for the Stax music machine. It showcases the promise of young Arthur Conley, who Otis was grooming, as well as displaying how expressive

248

a vocalist Eddie Floyd truly was. The DVD contains the scripture of songwriters Isaac Hayes and David Porter, delivered by Sam and Dave to the excited Stax fans.

I've said it before: This Otis Redding treasure is what *Twilight Zone* screenwriter Richard Matheson meant describing compelling programs on fifties and sixties TV screens as examples of "the powerful chilling charismatic effect of black and white film."

The Stax/Volt Revue Live In Norway 1967 is specifically what Matheson suggested.

The Doors: Live at the Bowl '68 DVD
The Doors: Live at the Isle of Wight DVD

The Doors at the Hollywood Bowl, July 5,1968

A Doors live 1968 concert from the Hollywood Bowl was just released on DVD, Blu-Ray, and Digital Video from Eagle Rock Entertainment. A CD, Digital Audio, and double LP from the event was issued from Rhino. The performance has been restored from original camera negatives and remixed and mastered using original multi-track tapes.

This Doors concert is considered to be the band's finest documentation on film. The group's engineer Bruce Botnick has done a masterful job in this new restoration and an upgrade from previous video, DVD and laserdisc formats that have documented this sonic experience.

"You can hear it as if you were at the Hollywood Bowl, on stage with us," states Ray Manzarek, who was joined at the legendary venue with John Densmore, Robby Krieger and Jim Morrison.

The Doors at the Hollywood Bowl, July 5, 1968
(Photo by Henry Diltz)

"The Doors radiated a sexual heat that evoked ancient blood rituals," suggests Dr. James Cushing, Professor of English and Literature at Cal Poly San Luis Obispo, and a deejay on KEBF-FM.

"Morrison's poetry formed one part of a larger theatre-music-performance that climaxed when tragic heroism blossomed up out of his intimate Freudian night-garden. The Doors' first two records almost captured that dark bloom, and they retain great power to disturb us with their shadowy images of private life palpably heightened to the realm of myth. When the band performed, they also had a jazz flexibility in their set lists. The 1967 Matrix Club repertoire and their Hollywood Bowl summer '68 concert are examples of that."

LIVE AT THE BOWL '68 includes three previously unreleased tracks from the performance. Technical issues with the recording of "Hello, I Love You," "The WASP (Texas Radio And The Big Beat)," and "Spanish Caravan" prevented them from being released in the past. Now, through meticulous restoration of the audio, all three are implemented, marking the first time the concert has been available in its entirety.

The DVD, Blu-Ray and digital video each feature a 16x9 high-definition digital transfer with both a stereo and 5.1 audio soundtrack as well as over an hour of bonus material. Integrated in the additional content are *Echoes From The Bowl*, The Doors' route to the Hollywood Bowl; *You Had To Be There*, memories of the Doors' performance at the Bowl; *Reworking The Doors*, an in-depth look at how the film was restored; and three bonus performances: "Wild Child" from *The Smothers Brothers Comedy Hour* in 1968, "Light My Fire" from *The Jonathan Winters Show* in December 1967 and a version of Van Morrison's "Gloria" with specially created visuals.

Geoff Kempin, executive producer for Eagle Rock reiterated. "The Doors were one of *the* most incredible live bands ever – we wanted to apply the top technology so that everyone can fully appreciate the phenomenon of the Doors captured at their height on 5 July 1968."

LIVE AT THE BOWL '68

Track Listing

1. Show Start/Intro
2. "When The Music's Over"
3. "Alabama Song (Whisky Bar)"
4. "Back Door Man"
5. "Five To One"
6. "Back Door Man" (Reprise)
7. "The WASP (Texas Radio And The Big Beat)"
8. "Hello, I Love You"
9. "Moonlight Drive"
10. "Horse Latitudes"
11. "A Little Game"
12. "The Hill Dwellers"
13. "Spanish Caravan"
14. Hey, What Would You Guys Like To Hear?
15. "Wake Up!"
16. Light My Fire (Segue)
17. "Light My Fire"
18. "The Unknown Soldier"
19. The End (Segue)
20. "The End"

"As far as the Hollywood Bowl, it was amazing to be asked to play the Bowl," offers Robby Krieger. "Growing up in Los Angeles and playing the Bowl must be like playing baseball in New York and playing Yankee stadium. We were really psyched! So much so that we actually rehearsed! [First time ever just for a gig], and we decided to capture the whole thing on film [and 8 track tape]. Normally, we would just wing it at gigs...We might discuss what to start with, two or three songs and then just go with the flow.

"Looking back," adds Krieger, "the rehearsal may have been a mistake. I think it may have made things a bit unspontaneous, not a good thing when the Doors were supposed to be so wild and free, never knowing what might happen next . . . Also the fact that Jim was peaking on acid was not in line with such a tightly controlled show. Check out the Granada film, *Doors are Open* . . . That was more of a spontaneous Doors show . . . Luckily, the footage from the Bowl looks great and we fixed up the missing songs, so we now have the complete show."

My friend journalist Kirk Silsbee was at this event. I asked him to reflect on seeing the Doors at this famous venue.

"Doors at the Bowl. The warmth of the July day had burned off and the evening had taken on the moist chill familiar to Hollywood Bowl audiences. It was the biggest and most important booking to date for L.A.'s favorite band, and the restless crowd was expectant. The openers, Steppenwolf and the Chambers Brothers, had revved up the crowd with their hits. But the Doors were not a hit record band. The experimentation and arrangement that they unspooled throughout their set was musical psychodrama.

It's received wisdom that Morrison was acid-tripping that night, and he threw the tempos off for the rest of the band. And a real arrogance surfaced, as the singer burped in the mic, let a couple of the vamps run too long, and tried to manipulate the light man. It kept the audience off-balance—with just enough new material to command attention. Coupled with the off-road spoken word sojourns, the crowd was spellbound, wondering what would come next. But after the most esoteric recitation, the Doors instantly pulled the audience's wheels back on the road with "Light My Fire." And Jim Morrison, with the wind of the Hollywood Bowl in his sails, couldn't resist shouting 'Fuck!' repeatedly in the song. Having made it to the biggest stage in SoCal, he had to be the bad little boy in leather pants."

252

"If Morrison ingested LSD that night, suggests Ray Manzarek "it didn't affect his performance at all. If anything, it deepened it and broadened the performance.

"We played the Hollywood Bowl. We had made it. We had come all the way. We were a success, and 'Light My Fire' was the number one record in America during the '67 Summer of Love. It was an L.A. show. And the Doors were playing the Hollywood Bowl, where Igor Stravinsky has conducted. Where Aaron Copeland had conducted. Where Carmen Dragon had conducted. The Doors were now playing it. It was one of the high points of our career.

"The Doors employed a five-camera film crew to shoot their set. I will say that Jim's performance was very intense. He was very stationary and [gave] a very intense

**Jim Morrison at the Hollywood Bowl
(Photo by Henry Diltz)**

performance. He only really gets to cut loose at the end of the show where we play 'The End.' He let it all hang out. He was doing the Shaman's Dance. You saw Jim Morrison possessed and became the Shaman in 'The End.' The last ten minutes of that show were visually intense, an insane performance. The first hour was deep and dark. Very passionate. A lot of restrained passion from Jim Morrison and the band. We played great but were bummed out because we couldn't play at 210 decibels."

"In '79, on a rare broadcast series called *Album Greats*, Ray Manzarek told L.A. radio station KLOS-FM that 'Once you see where you stand in relation to eternity, making pop songs for AM radio seems a little inconsequential,'" underpinned writer and UCLA graduate, Daniel Weizmann. "The proof of his seriousness is in this footage.

"The Doors at the Hollywood Bowl went down only 35 months after the Beatles August '65 appearance but it represents a complete passage from innocence to experience. That the Dionysian Princes of Experience also happened to be local dudes just makes it that much more thrilling. I mean, who drove them home after the show? Did they hitch a ride after they recaptured the High Temple of Electric Sound? Or did they get into their own cars and reenter the river of motel neon, traffic, and the throbbing AM radio with its songs about lollipops and peppermints?

"Hollywood psychedelia was always a strange Janus-faced animal--part freak out, part show biz, part burlesque, part teenybopper a go go--but even by these anti-standards the Doors stood apart...from their peers, their audience, even from each other as they jammed choppy organ jazz and broken poetry in the shadows. They weren't folkies. They weren't loveniks. They weren't even blues fanatics, not really.

"Onstage at the Hollywood Bowl, with all the power in the world to move the crowd, they refused to play a single trope of "the performing artist," not even good will. At one point, Jim asks them for requests half-heartedly, then ignores them, and chides 'No--you do something,' as if the pop star game is wearing on him. Then they burrow down into the swirling music and reach for pitch darkness, precisely where another performer would hog the spotlight--they literally beg to cut the lights. They were ready for eternity."

In August of 2014, at the *American Cinematheque* in Hollywood, I programmed, with John Hagelston and Grant Moniger, a series *Turn Up The Radio: L.A. Rock On Film* co-sponsored by Amoeba Music and Santa Monica Press, celebrating the intersection of music and media in the City of Angels with several evenings devoted to L.A. rock icons on film. One evening *Live At The Bowl '68* was shown on the big silver screen at the legendary Egyptian Theatre to a packed room of enthralled viewers. More than one attendee came up to me in the lobby afterwards sharing their experiences at the UCLA Film School with fellow students Ray Manzarek and Jim Morrison.

The Doors: Live at the Isle of Wight 1970

The historic last concert ever filmed of the Doors is now available for the first time in late February 2018 when Eagle Rock Entertainment proudly presents *The Doors: Live at the Isle of Wight 1970* on DVD+CD, Blu-ray+CD and Digital Video.

254

The last known unseen performance of the Doors in existence, *The Doors: Live at the Isle of Wight 1970* has been completely recut and remixed, from the original film footage. Fully approved by the Doors, this previously unreleased concert was meticulously restored via the latest 21st century technology, color correcting and visually upgrading the original footage.

The entire concert, which is now presented in 5.1 Dolby Digital sound, was mixed from the original multi-track audio by longtime Doors engineer / mixer / co-producer Bruce Botnick. Fans may have caught a glimpse of this performance in the Murray Lerner-directed 1997 Isle of Wight film *Message To Love,* however this DVD presents the Doors' set with the full-length songs in maximum visual and sound quality.

The scene is August 1970... Front man Jim Morrison's ongoing obscenity trial, from an incident a year prior in Miami, weighs heavily on the band. "The Last Great Festival" is taking place in England, which boasted a venerable who's who of 1970's top acts: Jimi Hendrix, the Who, Leonard Cohen, Miles Davis, Joni Mitchell, Joan Baez, and more.... The band touches down on the Isle of Wight. The show must go on.

The Doors: Live at the Isle of Wight 1970 captures and showcases the essence of this poignant performance, as well as offering a snapshot of the era, with footage of fans (over 600,000 in attendance) tearing down barriers and crashing the gates to gain access to the event.

The Doors hit the stage at 2:00 a.m. on August 30, 1970, delivering a set that further proved the musical power that marked them as a beacon of the Summer of Love. In this 84-minute DVD, Morrison, organist Ray Manzarek, guitarist Robby Krieger, and drummer John Densmore traverse such staples as "Roadhouse Blues", "Break On Through (To The Other Side)", and "Light My Fire". Illuminated by a mere red spotlight (the band wasn't informed that they needed to bring their own lighting equipment) gave the show an eerie crimson hue, almost echoing the figurative weight of the trial.

"Our set was subdued but very intense," Ray Manzarek later stated. "We played with a controlled fury, and Jim was in fine vocal form. He sang for all he was worth, but moved nary a muscle. Dionysus had been shackled."

The DVD is completed with bonus featurette *This Is The End,* 17-minutes of interviews conducted by the film's original director,

Academy Award-winning Murray Lerner, with Krieger, Densmore, and Doors' manager at the time, Bill Siddons. Additional archival interview footage with Manzarek from 2002 is also included in the featurette.

I saw the Doors perform in concert at the Forum in Inglewood, California in 1968, and first met and interviewed Ray Manzarek in 1974 at Mercury Records on Hollywood Boulevard. Manzarek penned the introduction to my 2009 book, *Canyon of Dreams: The Magic and the Music of Laurel Canyon*. My 2014 book, *Turn Up The Radio! Rock, Pop and Roll in Los Angeles 1956-1972*, is dedicated to Ray.

In 2010 we discussed the Doors relationship to film and television. Ray revealed the impact a film class had on him while attending the UCLA School of Film with director Josef von Sternberg (*The Blue*

(Courtesy Kirk Silsbee Archives)

Angel, Morocco, Shanghai Express). Von Sternberg eventually applauded Manzarek's student film *Evergreen*. The director's influence informed the way Manzarek and Morrison would eventually wed cinema and music that's inherent in their audio and celluloid work.

"He's the guy who really kind of gave a real sense of darkness to the Doors, not that we wouldn't have been there anyway," Ray explained. "But having von Sternberg and seeing the deep psychology of his movies, and the pace at which he paced his films, really influenced Doors' songs and Doors' music. The film school is always there.

"Our song structure was based on the cinema. Loud. Soft. Gentle. Violent. A Doors' song is again, aural, and aural cinema. We always tried to make pictures in your mind. Your mind's ear. You hear pictures with the music itself.

256

Doors co-founder Ray Manzarek December 20, 1969 (Photo by Henry Diltz)

"Film school guys founded the Doors. When we made the music, each song had to have a dramatic structure. Each song, whether it was two and a half minutes or an epic like 'The End' or 'When The Music's Over,' you had to have dramatic peaks and valleys. And that's the sense of drama within the Doors' songs which comes right from the theatre."

In 2007, I interviewed John Densmore. I asked him about aspects of theater and film in the Doors' concert settings and recordings displayed again in *The Doors: Live at the Isle of Wight 1970.*

"I wasn't thinking cinematic, but certainly Ray and Jim coming out of the UCLA Film School were cinematic dudes. That's for sure. I mean, I hear the world. Filmmakers see it," observed John.

"In live performances, I had to work harder on the tempo because Ray's left hand was the bass. And when he took a solo he'd get excited and speed up. 'Hold it back. Hold it back.' But, without a separate guy doing bass line runs and grooves there are holes. 'OK. I'm going in.' Sometimes I didn't do anything. That was my territory between the beats.

"Let me tell you, at the Rock and Roll Hall of Fame induction, (Bruce) Springsteen came up to me and said, 'I like your drumming. It's so quiet, and then you drop a bomb.' Thank you, Boss."

In 2013, I interviewed director Murray Lerner about the Doors as well as his unique and influential camera work in this last concert footage captured on the Doors.

"I've tried to put out the Doors' [1970 Isle of Wight] full set," Lerner told me in a 2013 interview. "It was dark but that was the mood. And the darkness is interesting, I think. (Jim) Morrison said to me, 'you can film but you're not gonna get an image. But we're not gonna change our lighting.' 'I'll get an image.' I did.

"I met and knew (Jim) Morrison earlier at the Atlanta Film Festival. I was showing *Festival!* It won an award and they had a film they

John Densmore and Harvey Kubernik (Photo by Heather Harris, 1996)

had made played. We talked at the party afterwards, we had both won awards, but they were bullshit awards. Mine was for the best music. What does that mean? At the party and I really gave it to the organizer out loud a hard time, told him what I felt about him, and they came up to me and said, 'We agree with you.' I got friendly and tried to help them distribute their *[Feast of Friends]* film."

Tony Funches was my 1969 West Los Angeles College pal, who in 1970 became the Doors' head of security and Morrison's bodyguard.

"As I remember it, Isle of Wight gig was difficult," Tony mentioned in our 2014 conversation.

"Late at night, delays, cold weather, 2:00 a.m. and they were not using their P.A. system. They used the [Grateful] Dead's P.A. So they had a hard time getting the sound right on the monitors and stuff, and they soldiered on through. It was pretty miserable in terms of personal comfort. Not that they wanted to be pampered or anything. It was just dreadful conditions.

"I was on the stage. When the Doors are on stage Uncle Tony was there. [Bill] Siddons had one side of the stage, and I had the other. They did the gig. Isle of Wight security was really up to the task and there wasn't really much concern about nitwits come flying out of the audience. Miles Davis stretched out backstage during the set and we all talked later.

"Jim had the artistic bent that allowed him, given his rebelliousness and the idiom he was expressing himself through, to do that improvisation in live performances or on records. He did that in his artistic expressions because that capability was resident within his personality. While at the same time he drew comfort in knowing that others had been doing similar things as with Cab Calloway doing scat singing with the Zoot suit or Bobby Darin when he did 'Mack the Knife.'

"So he knew of those things but he did not do them as they did but he was aware others had improvised similarly, and since they had, he figured, 'I'm gonna give it a try. But I can't do what they do.' So he did what he did according to what made him tick which made it separate but not equal. But separate."

I also connected with former *Sounds* magazine journalist Sandy Robertson. He was at the 1970 Isle of Wight festival.

"I date my transition to real rock music from my purchase of the sublime *Morrison Hotel* by the Doors, and my subsequent solo trip all the way from Scotland to the Isle of Wight Festival to see them live, age 17," Robertson emailed me in August 2017.

"I had a glamorous older cousin named Linda Gamble (later a music and movie publicist) and she seemed the height of sophistication to me because she took a chance on *Love* and *The Doors* when no one else I knew had their records.

"None of my buddies cared about Jim Morrison and company, so I fetched up alone amid crowds of 1970 hippies in scorching summer weather with not even a blanket to my name. I saw the Who, John Sebastian, Kris Kristofferson (who was booed for 'Blame It On The Stones' by irony-free dolts), and Tiny Tim, who sang 'There'll Always Be An England' to the delight of the mob because he wasn't being ironic at all.

"Night and cold descended and the Doors didn't appear until the early hours of the morning - Morrison a distant, gleaming blue-black leather figure, his feral growl on 'Break On Through' introduced by Ray Manzarek's sparkling, icy electric piano. As Kim Fowley rightly has it, in many ways they were like a jazz group, John Densmore's drum flourishes and Robby Krieger's nimble guitar being just as capable of entrancing the ears as kicking ass.

"The critical consensus seems to be that this was not one of their great shows, Jim having his fragile eggshell mind on legal troubles looming, and indeed, looking at footage of 'Ship Of Fools,' Morrison seems like he can hardly be bothered to get the lyrics out.

"Nevertheless, at 17 I came to worship, not to deconstruct, and it was only with age I realized how tough it can be for bands to play the same songs every night while trying to deliver an hour of magic.

"Salvation from the cold was at hand in the form of a cute young girl who let me snuggle under her sleeping bag, alas however under the watchful eye of her glowering bro, so there was no chance of romance.

"I left pre-Hendrix as a certain thuggishness was in the air. I arrived home with some dreadful flu-type virus. Never mind - I had seen the Doors open. To this day, when some kid is playing a Doors album in a record store and I mention I'm so old I actually saw Jim Morrison onstage, it's great to feel the excitement bridge the generations to that mystical place where people down there like to get it on, get it on."

Denny Tedesco's *The Wrecking Crew*

"Everyone was a hundred chaps, and some of them were delightful." - Andrew Loog Oldham

The Wrecking Crew music documentary, directed by Denny Tedesco, is now theatrically released in 2015 from Magnolia Pictures in the US. A two DVD package is in retail outlets.

A companion book **to** Tedesco's film was published

(Cover graphic courtesy of Denny Tedesco)

by Wrecking Crew LLC. *Sound Explosion! Inside L.A.'s Studio Factory with the Wrecking Crew* by Ken Sharp art design by Mark London and John Sellards.

A four-CD soundtrack album was issued in fall 2015 from Rock Beat Records.

The Wrecking Crew tells the story of the unsung musicians in the Hollywood area that provided the backbeat, the bottom and the swinging melody that drove many number one hits of the 1960s.

The film examines their music-making regional studio work in Hollywood, with some emphasis on the 1950-1983 world of the RCA, United Western, Radio Recorders, Sunset Sound, Columbia, Gold Star and Capitol studios. It's a fun and moving tribute from Denny Tedesco to his guitarist father Tommy and to the music, the times and to the secret star-making machine who would be known as "The Wrecking Crew." Denny Tedesco and his dedicated team interviewed: Al Casey, Al Jardine, Bill Pitman, Bones Howe, Brian Wilson, Carmie Tedesco, Carol Kaye, Cher, Chuck Berghofer, Dave Gold, Dick Clark, Don Randi, Earl Palmer, Gary Lewis, Glen Campbell, Hal Blaine, Herb Alpert, Jimmy Webb, Joe Osborn, Julius Wechter, Larry Levine, Leon Russell, Lou Adler, Lew McCreary, Micky Dolenz, Nancy Sinatra, Peter Tork, Plas Johnson, Roger McGuinn, Snuff Garrett, Stan Ross, and Tommy Tedesco.

Joe Osborn (Photo by Henry Diltz)

Tedesco grew up in Los Angeles and is an alumnus of Loyola Marymount University. He started his film career as a set decorator on feature films such as *Eating Raoul*. Denny then traveled the world as a lighting technician and location producer for IMAX films. From the shark infested waters of Australia, to an exploding Volcano of Mt. Pinatubo (Philippines), and to the plains of Africa, he has filmed under the most challenging conditions. Denny has produced promos, videos and commercials for various companies and networks. In 2000, he produced the Academy Awards 'opening' with Billy Crystal and also the music video for the Elton John song, 'I Want Love,' directed by artist Sam Taylor Wood and starring Robert Downey Jr.

"I started this project in 1995 when my father, Tommy was diagnosed with terminal cancer," wrote Denny on his official Wrecking Crew website.

"I guess it was a way of me dealing with what was going in our lives and at the same time wanting to let the world know about what impact he and his friends made in musical history. I was so determined at first to actually say so in the interviews, 'please say 'Tommy' instead of your dad.' I really wanted to keep myself out of the picture but in the end, I came around and embraced it.

"The hard part was telling the story of the 'Wrecking Crew' and at the same time telling my father's story. Finally a friend mentioned to me that you really couldn't tell one and not the other, so you might as well literally acknowledge it. Once we did that, it was easier and felt right.

"You have to realize, these guys and Carol Kaye, the only woman, were at the top of their game at the right place and at the right time. They really don't have much to complain about. My dad was thrilled to be able to

Denny Tedesco photo courtesy Denny Tedesco

make a living at guitar. To make a living at an instrument puts you in a small minority. But to record as many hits as they did, they were even part of a smaller minority.

"So when years pass by and you still have your chops as a musician and you're wondering why no one is calling, I think it takes its toll. Everyone has it in every career. Sometimes you last longer than others, and some take it better than others. My father always said he was like a baseball player. You have your time in the minors, you make it to the majors and then you slowly move on out while the new guys come in. That's how he broke in. It's part of the cycle."

Bassist Chuck Berghofer formerly worked with Shelley Manne and Pete Jolly. He's featured on Nancy Sinatra's signature tune "These

Boots Are Made For Walkin'" and heard on the *Elvis '68 Comeback Special.*

"Tommy Tedesco had the most common sense of anyone I ever met. Musically he could read and play anything. But he had the greatest attitude. He taught us all how to handle this stuff."

"We created a lot of music that became renewable copyrights just by what we played." Mike Melvoin told journalist, Kirk Silsbee earlier this century.

"Sometimes they'd put a lead sheet in front of you that just had a few basic chords, and we brought that stuff to life and made music out of it. Many times, people booked sessions, and they didn't have the faintest idea of what they wanted. The L.A. studios had the reputation of being able to interpret and create any kind of music and sounds that you wanted.

"We were so frustrated doing the 'Good Vibrations' tracks because Brian (Wilson) was feeling his way along and didn't always know what he wanted. What you'd worked all day to get down the day before could all be wiped out if he decided he didn't like it, and you'd start all over. We used to finish up every day and head for the bar because we were so worked up from the intensity of the experience. But he's really a genius, man."

I've been continually writing about the Wrecking Crew and the Gold Star principals for 48 years in articles long before it was fashionable. When they first were booked into the studios around Hollywood, they really weren't referred to as the Wrecking Crew. They were members of American Federation of Musicians, Local 47. Arranger/producer and songwriter, Jack Nitzsche, came to Los Angeles from Michigan in 1957 after seeing an ad in *Downbeat* magazine for the Westlake School of Music. In a 1988 interview I conducted with Nitzsche for *Goldmine* magazine, he commented on the individual Wrecking Crew members he hired for many years.

"I had met Don Randi, one of the piano players a long time ago. He was a pianist at a jazz club on La Cienega. He was cool. He looked like a beatnik. His hair was right. He had the attitude. He didn't smile when he played.

"Hal Blaine. I liked his work, but sometimes felt he overplayed. That's just the way he plays, a lot of fills. As it turned out, Phil and the people loved the breaks Hal took, especially at the end of the tunes, the fades. Hal had a big kit. I liked the fills. Earl Palmer was the other drummer on the records. He's the best. Like a rock, a real good New Orleans drummer. Harold Battiste, Mac Rebennack. New Orleans guys were on the dates, so you had a good mixture of jazz guys, West Coast studio cats and New Orleans players.

"Leon Russell. I met him with Jackie DeShannon; she introduced me. Leon at the time, was playing piano in a bar in Covina. He was an innovative piano player. He was good. I heard him on a Jackie DeShannon record. In those days it was real hard to find rock 'n' roll piano players who didn't play too much. Leon talked the same language. During the Spector sessions, a lot of the time we had two or three piano players going at once. I played piano as well. Phil knew the way he wanted the keyboards played. It wasn't much of a problem who played. Leon was there for the solos and the fancy stuff, rolling pianos. The pianos would interlock and things would sound cohesive. I knew Leon would emerge as a band leader.

"I knew all the horn players. Steve Douglas on tenor, Jay Migliori on baritone, other horn players as well. I had met Steven through Lester Sill. We were friends for a long time. Phil had an idea about horns. It started on 'He's A Rebel.' Phil sure knew what he wanted. He had all the basses covered.

"Percussion. Well, Sonny Bono. I love Sonny. He helped me get into the business. Julius Wechter later of the Baja Marimba Band, was on a lot of the dates. Frank Kapp was on a lot of sessions. He was a jazz drummer who used to play with Stan Kenton. Phil would dream these percussion parts up at the session. They were his ideas. There were no formulas. I played percussion, chimes, orchestra bells. They weren't mixed way in the back.

"Vocalists. It would last all night. Background groups doubling and tripling so it would sound like two or three dozen voices. Phil would spend a lot of time with the singers. I would split and he'd still be working on lines with the singers. The rhythm section, and the horns were done together. Vocals and string parts were overdubbed later.

"Bass players. Jimmy Bond and Red Callender were on most of the dates. Ray Pohlman and Ray Brown as well. The bass parts were written out, and the players had to stick right with them. They were mixed way low in the back, almost a suggestive element to the song. No one really had a lot of room with those sessions. Really, only the drummer had any sort of freedom. They weren't R&B records.

"Guitarists. A lot of the guitarists were jazz players and weren't rock and roll players, like Howard Roberts, Joe Pass, Herb Ellis, Tommy

Tedesco, Barney Kessel, Dennis Budimar. A lot of the guitarists were good and well-known session players: Carol Kaye, Glen Campbell, Bill Pitman. Most the guitarists had to play eighth notes on Phil's records. There was a lot of acoustic guitar on the songs. It was hard for any of the guitarists to breathe or stretch out on the records.

"I was amazed how big Glen Campbell made it as a total entertainer. I knew he was a great guitarist. I never knew he would show up as a singer later. Billy Strange was good, too. I became aware of the 12-string guitar during the last Phil years. It was a new sound, and a new toy to play with."

In a 2007 lunch interview I conducted with Brian Wilson, he touted Campbell. "On 'Wouldn't It Be Nice,' Barney [Kessel] did the introduction to the song and Glen Campbell was also there. And, I said to myself, 'I'm going to have these guys play directly into the board instead of going out into the studio.' And they plugged their instruments into the recording console direct. That's how we got that sound."

During 1975 I interviewed Glen Campbell for *Melody Maker*.

"I played on a lot of Beach Boys records, 'Good Vibrations' and 'Dance, Dance, Dance', and some of the Jan and Dean albums. Being a studio cat proved a financially rewarding job. Before that I was in the Champs, which was really a studio group. We did 'Tequila,' and in that group were Jimmy Seals, Dash Croft and Jerry Cole."

Glen regularly appeared on the 1965-1966 television series *Shindig!* It wasn't impossible to see Glen in the *Shindig!* band. "We weren't struggling and there was always room to jam.

"I don't like any labels. Music is the most labelled, segregated and filed form in the US. I was cutting records six and seven years before 'Gentle On My Mind' and 'By The Time I Get To Phoenix' happened. I wasn't labelled then.

"It's a matter of feeling what you want to do and if you're good you'll be accepted. If you don't believe in yourself you don't have much chance of making it."

"I like to have all the musicians there at once," Phil Spector described during a 1976 interview I taped for the weekly *Melody Maker*. "I get everything on one track that I need. I put everything on twenty-four tracks just to see if it's plugged in. The finished track never ends up on more than one track. I don't wear a 'Back to Mono' button for no reason at all. I believe in it.

"The better the talent is around you, the better the people you have working with you. The more concerned, the better you're gonna come off as a producer, like a teacher in a class. The musicians I have never outdo me. I'm not in competition with them. I'm in complete accord with them. You need the ability, so you hire the best. I have the creativity. I know what I want.

"When you see a Kubrick movie, you tell me how many names you immediately remember in the cast. One? Two? It's the same with Fellini, and that's what I wanted to do when I directed a recording. Singers are instruments. They are tools to be worked with."

"Let me tell you a story," Brian Wilson disclosed to me in our 2007 interview. "I went to Gold Star and asked Larry Levine, the engineer, 'What is the secret of the Phil Spector echo trip?' 'Well, we have two echo chambers under the parking lot. Phil uses both the chambers at the same time.'

"So I tried that myself, and it worked. I also asked Larry Levine what Phil Spector did with his basses. Larry said Phil uses a standup and a Fender both at the same time. And the Fender guy used a pick. So I tried it out at my session, and it worked great! You also get a thicker sound putting the two basses together. I start with drums, bass, guitar and keyboards. Then we overdub the horns and the background voices."

"Gold Star was built for the songwriters," stressed the late Gold Star co-owner Stan Ross during a 2002 interview we conducted published in *Goldmine* magazine.

"They were fun, wonderful people to be around: Jimmy Van Heusen, Sammy Fain, Sonny Burke, Don Robertson, Johnny Mercer, Jimmy McHugh, Frank Loesser, Dimitri Tiomkin. We did song demos, voice-over work, radio and TV jingles.

"Our studio echo chamber gave it the wall of sound feel. Dave (Gold) built the equipment and echo chamber and personally hand-crafted the acoustical wall coating. We had so much fun with that echo chamber; it never sounded the same way twice. Gold Star brought a feeling, an emotional feeling. Gold Star was not a dead studio, but a live studio. The room was 30 X 40.

"It was all tubes," he instructed. "When you have tubes, you have expansion, and it doesn't distort so easy. We kept tubes on longer than anyone else. Because we understood that when a kick drum kicks into a tube it's not gonna distort. A tube can expand. The microphones with tubes were better than the ones without the tubes because if you don't have a tube and you hit heavy, suddenly it breaks ups. But when you have a tube, it's warm and emotional. It gets bigger and it expands. It allows for the impulse."

In August 2019, *33 1/3 - House of Dreams* a musical stage show on the landmark Gold Star Recording Studio premiered. Written by local San Diegans Jonathan Rosenberg and Brad Ross, with additional contributions by Steve Gunderson and Javier Velasco, the debut production chronicles the success of Gold Star Recording Studios through the history of rock 'n' roll.

33 1/3 - House of Dreams tells the story of Gold Star and its co-founder, engineer and hit maker Stan Ross. In Hollywood for 33 1/3 years, Gold Star was the birthplace of some of the greatest pop and rock hits of all time. Imagine a story featuring the music of a young Phil Spector and his Wall of Sound, the Beach Boys, Eddie Cochran, Sonny and Cher, Tina Turner, the Righteous Brothers, Ritchie Valens and many, many more.

"The creation of *33 1/3 - House of Dreams* is the culmination of efforts to share the story of what happened within the walls of Gold Star Recording Studios," shared writers and co-creators Jonathan Rosenberg and Brad Ross.

"Our musical is a way for us to honor the hit music and achievements through one of its co-owners, Stan Ross. He was the personality, lead engineer and mentor at Gold Star. His creative pioneering along with his partner's technical knowledge and studio design led them to develop Phil Spector's famous Wall of Sound productions. Stan's story is our story, and is still relevant today."

"After the death of my father in 2011, I took on the role of creating a production that would tell his life story," explained Ross. "As a producer and co-writer, I have spent the last four years researching and conducting video interviews with artists, songwriters, producers, arrangers, musicians and former employees that were involved in any aspect of Gold Star's existence as a mecca for the music industry from 1950-1984.

"These interviews have advanced both our projects: a music documentary and a theatrical musical stage play.

"In the play, we follow the path of Stan and his partner David Gold, reflecting on the creative events and significant moments that allowed the studio to become one of the most successful independent recording

267

studios in the world. Their creativity was recognized and promoted by Phil Spector in his Wall of Sound productions. He selected Gold Star due to its famous echo chamber and engineering techniques that allowed his unique production style to flourish. Gold Star was a place where any nationality, race, and faith could feel welcome to record and perform their music in a nurturing and welcome environment.

"What amazed me the most about this project was the reverence the music community still has for Stan Ross," remarked Jonathan Rosenberg. "The fact that Brad was Stan's son opened almost every door we knocked on. Brian Wilson, Bill Medley, Herb Alpert, Richie Furay, Mike Curb, and the Wrecking Crew musicians spent time with us recollecting their many great Gold Star memories.

"At that point, we realized that this was a story that has yet to be told. People don't think of Gold Star Recording Studios in the same way they think of Sun Studios, Motown, or Abbey Road. That's all going to change after they see *33 1/3 - House of Dreams*."

"It's an amazing story and should be told for the younger generation to follow," volunteered the late drummer/percussionist Hal Blaine.

I recorded at Gold Star with the Wrecking Crew a handful of times during 1976-1979. On one session I provided percussion and banged tambourine along with Rodney Bingenheimer and Phil Seymour on what many consider the last time Phil Spector assembled the Wrecking Crew.

"It was for a Paley Brothers recording track for 'Baby, Let's Stick Together.'" Larry Levine engineered.

In 2015, Andy Paley emailed me about that memorable evening.

"On the recording are Julius Wechter (vibraphone), Steve Douglas (sax), Jim Keltner (drums), Tommy Tedesco (guitar), Barry Goldberg (grand piano), Don Randi (baby grand piano), Dwight Twilley (percussion), Jay Migliori (sax), Richard Hyde (trombone), Jonathan Paley (acoustic guitar), Andy Paley (upright 'tack' piano), Hal Blaine (drums), Ray Pohlman (bass), you, Rodney and Phil Seymour (percussion), Dan and David Kessel (acoustic guitars with my brother Jonathan) and Phil Spector (percussion).

"The song was an up-tempo version of 'Baby, Let's Stick Together.' I sang lead . . . my brother Jonathan sang harmony. We got our vocals done very quick. Just a couple of takes. Phil really dug it.

"Phil kept Steve Douglas and Jay Migliori for another hour or so for some overdubs.

"Joey Ramone stopped by the session to say hi. He flipped! He called Seymour Stein in New York . . . held the phone up to the speakers in the control room, the studio . . . he was raving!

"About a month later the Ramones went into the studio with Phil. Darlene Love also showed up to say hi. It was the *last* session at Gold Star with all of those guys. He did other sessions with them after that but *not* at Gold Star."

I was the anointed food runner going to Canter's Delicatessen for the hungry throng. Rodney Bingenheimer and I also hand clapped during tracking dates on the Spector-produced *End of The Century* Ramones' album. In 2002 I penned the liner notes to a CD of *End of The Century*.

"I used to have a theory," the late Gold Star engineer Larry Levine expressed to me in 2002, "and I don't know if it's right or wrong, but part of the reason we took so long in actually recording the songs was that Phil needed to tire out the musicians, or they got to the point where they were tired enough so they weren't playing as individuals. But they would meld into the sound more that Phil had in his head.

"Good musicians start out and play as individuals and strive to play what Phil wants. As far as the room sound and the drum sound went, because the rooms were small, with low ceilings, the drum sound, unlike other studios with isolation, your drums sounded the way you wanted them to sound. They would change accordingly to whatever leakage was involved.

"As a matter of fact, Phil once said to me the bane of his recording existence was the drum sound. A lot of people attribute to echo what Phil was doing. The echo enhanced the melding of 'the wall of sound,' but it didn't create it. Within the room itself, all of this was happening and the echo was glue that kept it together."

"There was very little overdubbing done then," engineer/producer Al Schmitt mentioned at a 2002 interview session in Hollywood. "The nice thing about doing everything at one same time was that you knew exactly what it was going to sound like. When you started layering things you were never sure. Then a lot of experimenting came in and it took longer and longer to make records and the expenses went up."

"We were doing a job," admitted Hal Blaine to me in a 2008 interview. "We used to say: TTMAR. Take the money and run," Hal joked. "Nobody knew how long it would last.

"Larry Knechtel was on bass, and one of the great keyboardists. He played guitar, too. The guitarist Mike Deasy was a later day Wrecking Crew member. He was our mystical guru of guitar sounds when psychedelia entered the recording studio world.

"The Wrecking Crew could lock in with anybody. When we finished we had to go out and do another session. I might have had two other gigs that day. Our job was making hit records, and we loved it," enthused Blaine.

"After being a member of both Kaleidoscope and the Nitty Gritty Dirt Band, I began working as a sideman for Linda Ronstadt, John Stewart and Hoyt Axton," reminisced instrumentalist/songwriter Chris Darrow.

"During this period I ended up doing a lot of studio work in Hollywood and Los Angeles with Stewart and Axton as well as James Taylor, John Fahey and many others. As a member of the American Federation of Musicians, Local 47, I would have to call and see if the money from the sessions had come in. If so, I would drive to the office on Vine Street with copies of my W-2 forms and pick up the checks. Since I lived an hour away in Claremont, rush hour became an issue for me.

"One day I went to the Union and the check line was pretty short, so I was all ready to go visit a friend of mine until the traffic cleared.

Larry Knechtel, Jimmy Webb, Hal Blaine (Photo by Henry Diltz)

I was third in line and noticed that the person in front of me was the great drummer, Hal Blaine. The first guy in line picked up his check and was out in a flash. When it was Blaine's turn, he pulled out a big stack of W-2s and laid them out on the counter. It took over 20 minutes for him to go through all the checks he was going to get that day. That's how popular he was! I picked up my two checks and was out of there in no time."

During 2014, I did an extensive interview with Don Randi about the Wrecking Crew. Randi recorded for the Verve and Reprise labels, and for the last 45 years has been the proprietor of the jazz venue, The Baked Potato.

"Most of the times when we did those studio jobs we were asked to be somebody else. We were cloned. You know, if somebody wanted Floyd Cramer, you had to come out. If somebody wanted a more Ray Charles' sound you had to come up with it. If somebody wanted more of a Phil Spector sound, then I knew exactly what they wanted. Tommy Tedesco is the master guitarist of everybody, who had the capability of whatever he was doing sound better than what you ever expected.

"And, as great as it was, we were making up parts half the time. With Jack Nitzsche and Phil, I was able to go to Jack and he would translate what Phil wanted. There was camaraderie. You got to remember we all were together. Jack Nitzsche, Phil Spector, myself and Sonny Bono, who Jack knew from the late '50s at Specialty Records," announced Randi.

"You know what kills me, every time I hear Jack's 'The Lonely Surfer.' I'm on it. It still gives me chills because it's a great song. Jack wrote a great song. I didn't hear it until the day we went in. You know, we never rehearsed. (laughs). The composition. I'll tell you what gripped me was his brilliance. And the smart producers realized that, and they would put together some combinations that actually forced that because they wanted that edginess.

Don Randi
(Photo by Henry Diltz)

"Jack Nitzsche called me to play keyboard on some dates in 1967 at Sunset Sound. I picked out the piano for the studio, a guy who had a store on Beverly Boulevard. When I walked into Sunset Sound I didn't realize it was for Buffalo Springfield. I thought it was for a Neil Young [solo] album, 'cause that is what he was supposed to be breaking away from and going on his own. Hal Blaine and Jim Horn are on the track. I played piano and organ.

"When Jack and Neil asked me to play on the end part of 'Broken Arrow' they were both waiving me on to keep playing. I kept lookin' up at them, 'are you ever gonna tell me to stop?'

"Let me tell you something," emphasized Randi. "Jack really enjoyed working with Neil. This goes as well to 'Expecting to Fly.' Russ Titelman, Carole Kaye and Jim Gordon are on it. I'm on piano and harpsichord.

"Jack and I never judged artists by their voices. To me it didn't matter 'cause I loved the music so much. And Neil was able to sell it. There are some people you can't stand them on record until you see them live. And once you see them live you can understand their records. That doesn't happen a lot. But it does happen," Don maintained.

One other thing to consider about the praise that will now be heaped on the Wrecking Crew, are the nutritional aspects of the famed squad that never seem to get discussed or chronicled. On occasions, I was invited to join Phil Spector, Kim Fowley, Russ Regan, Jack Nitzsche, Hal Blaine and Don Randi for a dinner or lunch around their recording dates. More than once I heard the directive "don't get married in California!"

In the very early seventies, I'd nosh with session men, Mike Love, songwriter Stephen Kalinich, Rodney Bingenheimer, Brian Wilson. Del Shannon, Bobby Hart, Micky Dolenz, Danny Hutton, and music publisher Dan Bourgoise, who loved the avocado, sprouts, sunflower seed sandwich at a restaurant operated by Warren Stagg named H.E.L.P. (Health, Education, Love, Peace) located off the corner of 3rd Street and Fairfax Avenue.

It was only in the later part of the sixties that professional catering and available food on premises, often on record label budgets, and being delivered into the studios, became a part of the scene and collaboration. Frank Sinatra liked his sessions catered by Chasens.

Don Randi, who headed the house band at Sherry's cocktail bar on Sunset Boulevard from 1957-1970, revealed the Wrecking Crew's culinary habits and their favorite watering holes.

"Jack and I would go out to places like the Gaiety Delicatessen. Once in a while, Harry Nilsson would come to our table. He was still working at the Crocker Citizen Bank as a teller or had a job there. He might have made a record then.

"We loved Musso & Frank Grill on Hollywood Boulevard and Johnny's Steak House. That was my savior. I could go and have a three dollar meal in there with a Bone-In Ribeye, you know. Can't forget The Brown Derby. We went to Aldo's, great hamburgers. Sonny and Cher dug that place, Canter's, and once in a while, a coffee shop called Huff's. Taco-rama, and Pink's Hot Dogs on La Brea. Another tasty stop was The Dog House on Hollywood where you sat on stools right on the street.

"Chris Darrow reminded me of The Burrito King on Sunset Boulevard at Alvarado. The Flying Saucer. The best French Dip sandwiches in town. Near Wilshire. There was Young China, two doors down from radio station KFWB for fantastic Chinese. On Hollywood Boulevard. The best Won Ton soup. The Italian restaurant Miceli's was on Las Palmas.

"Dennis Wilson loved Ah Fong's restaurant. Delicious Chinese-American food. Gene Norman owned the Marquis restaurant on Sunset Strip, along with his Crescendo and Interlude clubs. I liked the Villa Capri. Mickey Cohen was there on a regular basis. I saw him at Sherry's as well. There was Hal's Nest, and The Speak, where all drinks were 39 cents. Phil and I went to The Cock'n Bull. The trout was incredible," exclaimed Randi. "Can't forget TAIL o' the PUP.

"The record company promo men all went to an Italian spot named Martoni's. Label owners like Norman Granz [Verve Records] enjoyed the Pacific Dining Car. Barney Kessel and his wife B.J. Baker requested their New York steaks cooked medium at Diamond Jim's in Hollywood.

"As you well know, we all went to the Hollywood Ranch Market. Are you kidding? The tater tots and the chicken gizzards! In the early sixties they had a donut machine there! [laughs]. I saw Lucille Ball one late night. In a full fur mink coat! She gave me the biggest smile. Rock bands, hookers, actors and hippies were at the counter, especially when there was a show at The Kaleidoscope or Hollywood Palladium.

TAIL o'the PUP (Photo by Henry Diltz)

"Myself, Jack, Neil [Young] and Denny Bruce also liked to eat at the House of Pancakes on La Cienega. They just closed Hamburger Hamlet on Sunset Boulevard!" Randi concluded, his voice conveying his wonder and dismay.

Allan Arkush on Martin Scorsese, Bill Graham, Roger Corman and the Ramones *Rock 'N' Roll High School*

Allan Arkush (Photo courtesy of Allan Arkush)

Allan Arkush was born in Jersey City, New Jersey in 1948 and graduated from Fort Lee High School which inspired his feature film directorial debut *Rock 'N' Roll High School*. During 1967-1970 Arkush attended New York University Film School. Martin Scorsese was his teacher and faculty adviser. Arkush's senior film, *Septuagenarian Substitute Ball*, starring John Ford Noonan, won third prize at the National Student Film Festival In 1970.

In his years at NYU, Arkush worked at Bill Graham's Fillmore East music venue as an usher and stage crew member. In 1970 he joined what was The Joshua Light Show-then renamed Joe's Lights, collaborating with numerous visiting acts including Fleetwood Mac, the Who, Grateful Dead, Santana, Allman Brothers, and Miles Davis.

In 1973, Allan was driving a taxi in New York City when he received a telephone call about coming to Hollywood.

Arkush relocated to Los Angeles in 1973 and got his start in the movie business in the trailer department for Roger Corman's New World Pictures where he cut trailers with Joe Dante.

The duo created telegenic campaigns and commercial spots for over 100 films including *Death Race 2000, Eat My Dust, Crazy Mama,* and *TNT Jackson.* In 1977 Arkush was a second unit director for Ron Howard on *Grand Theft Auto* and in 1978 appeared as an actor in Roger Corman's Hollywood's *Wild Angel.*

Allan Arkush Filmography:
Hollywood Boulevard (co-directed with Joe Dante) (1976)
Deathsport (1978)
Rock 'N' Roll High School (1979)
Heartbeeps (1981)
Get Crazy (1983)
Caddyshack II (1988)
Shake, Rattle and Rock! (1994)
Elvis Meets Nixon (1997)
The Temptations (1998)
Prince Charming (2001)

Arkush has produced 200 episodic television shows, directing 250, including *Fame, St. Elsewhere, Ally McBeal,* and *Nashville.* He directed a fourth of the *Moonlighting* episodes, receiving an Emmy nomination for *I Am Curious Maddie.* He's helmed videos for Elvis Costello, Christine McVie and Bette Midler/Mick Jagger, earning five MTV nominations. Arkush is a member of the DGA Mentor Program, and currently teaching the Narrative Workshop at the American Film Institute in Los Angeles. Allan continues to contribute commentary to the web series *Trailers From Hell.*

I first met Allan on the set of *Get Crazy* in the very early eighties. The location was the Wiltern Theater, built in 1931 at the intersection of Wilshire Blvd. and Western Ave. in Los Angeles. The movie was informed by the experiences of Arkush and screenwriter Danny Opatoshu when they worked at Bill Graham's Fillmore East venue in New York.

It starred Malcolm McDowell, Daniel Stern, Lou Reed, Howard Kaylan, John Densmore, Paul Bartel, Mary Woronov, Dick Miller, Fabian Forte, and poet/actor Ivan E. Roth portraying Electric Larry, based on a character Arkush encountered backstage at the Fillmore East when Jimi Hendrix cut the *Band of Gypsys* live album.

The next time Allan and I talked was in 1982 in the hallway at Roger Corman's New World Pictures on San Vincente Blvd. in Brentwood.

American International Films visionary and independent movie pioneer Corman had made *The Student Nurses, Caged Heat, White Line Fever*, and *Crazy Mama*, while helping launch the filmmaking careers of Jonathan Kaplan, Jonathan Demme, Paul Bartel, Ron Howard and Joe Dante. My friend, Harry E. Northup, had starred in *Fighting Mad* with Peter Fonda that Demme directed. Bruce Langhorne did the musical score.

Filmic visionary Corman acquired foreign movies for domestic exhibition from lauded directors Ingmar Bergman, *Cries and Whispers*, Federico Fellini's *Armacord*, as well as Uli Edel's *Christiane F.*

At the time I had a girlfriend who worked for Corman. She re-introduced me to Roger, Samuel Z. Arkoff and Paul Bartel at an AIP /New World Pictures tribute event at Melnitz Hall on the UCLA campus.

One afternoon, inside Corman's office, I mentioned the Gilmore Drive-In on 3rd street to Roger. He touted his AIP movies and New World's successful drive-in outdoor only scheduled films where he booked them with distributors as "ozone pictures."

I later ran into Allan Arkush in the late eighties on the Fox Studios back lot when he was directing an episode of *Moonlighting* with Eva Marie Saint as a guest star.

During 2019, director/producer Andrew Solt of SOFA Entertainment invited me to a special screening of *Heroes of Rock and Roll* at the Fine Arts Theatre in Beverly Hills, a 1979 two-hour ABC-TV special he produced, directed and wrote with Malcolm Leo hosted by Jeff Bridges. Jack Haley Jr. was the executive producer.

I attended their genre-changing premiere at the Plitt Century Plaza Theater. The rock documentary now had a new model. Solt and Leo had officially licensed master recordings of the last 25 years edited with video tape, newsreel footage, rare concert films, and trailers all sanctioned by rights holders and music publishing administrators.

When *Heroes* had its lone broadcast on ABC in 1979, I didn't have a Sony Betamax machine to tape it! It's never been available on VHS or DVD format. I was eagerly looking forward to watching it again on Wilshire Blvd.

I had a quick chat with Allan Arkush in the Fine Arts lobby about Jimi Hendrix. We exchanged digits. Allan had read me for years in the now defunct UK music weekly *Melody Maker* and owned one of my books. I arranged an interview to discuss Jimi and his *Rock 'N' Roll High School 40th Anniversary Edition*.

Arkush's movie debuted in August 1979, produced by Michael Finnell, screenplay by Richard Whitley, Russ Dvonch and Joseph McBride, from a story by Arkush and Joe Dante.

Lensed at a B-movie pace in 1979, Arkush shot *Rock 'N' Roll High School* in Los Angeles at Mount Carmel High School where *Rock Around the Clock* was filmed in 1956.

Special features on this anniversary product include a new 4K scan from the original camera negative, and a new feature-length documentary titled *Class Of '79: 40 Years Of Rock 'N' Roll High School* – featuring Interviews with director/story writer Allan Arkush, co-director/story writer Joe Dante, actress P.J. Soles, screenwriter Richard Whitley, screenwriter Russ Dvonch, cinematographer Dean Cundey, editor Larry Bock, and more.

There's also an interview with Roger Corman conducted by Leonard Maltin, original radio ads and TV spot, even audio outtakes from the Roxy Theater filming along with the theatrical trailer.

With musical performances from the Ramones, the outrageous candor of teenage angst and nostalgic reverie of a counterculture rock movement, *Rock 'N' Roll High School* has captured the hearts of many generations.

Rock 'N' Roll High School, executive produced by Corman and directed by Arkush, boasts performances by the Ramones and stars P.J. Soles (*Halloween*) in the lead role of Riff Randell, Vince Van Patten (*Hell Night*), Clint Howard (*Grand Theft Auto*), Dey Young (*Spaceballs*), Mary Woronov (*Death Race 2000*), Dick Miller (*Piranha*) and Paul Bartel (*Hollywood Boulevard*).

Based on Arkush's own high school fantasy, the 1979 cult film takes place at Vince Lombardi High School — the wildest, most rockin' high school around! That is, until a thug of a principal, Miss Togar, comes along and tries to make the school a totalitarian state. With the help of the Ramones, the students of Vince Lombardi battle Miss Togar's iron-fisted rule and take their battle to a rockin' conclusion!

Rock 'N' Roll High School quickly developed a devoted following after its release in 1979 and became a mainstay of the midnight movie cult circuit. As with films like *The Rocky Horror Picture Show*, audience members began to dress up like the cast and the Ramones for screenings.

In the Shout! Factory press materials provided, Arkush, the self-described "unabashed rock 'n' roll fanatic," explained why he chose the Ramones to star as the film's musical heroes, as he felt they epitomized pure rock 'n' roll.

"We staged a live, marathon show at the Roxy Theatre that consisted of 22 hours of nonstop Ramones," and the tireless quartet also wrote two songs for the film: 'I Want You Around' and 'Rock 'N' Roll School.' The Ramones were fans of Corman as well. Johnny Ramone said in an interview at the time, 'When we found out Roger Corman was behind the picture, we said, sure, we'll do it because we knew he had a reputation and we knew he made good movies.'"

"If you think things are polarized now, you should've seen (and heard) Toronto circa 1979," recalls old slash new waver Gary Gabba Gold. "The Summer of Hate still fresh in most hip teens' memories, it seems you just could no longer like, for example, both the Ramones *and* the Who. At the same time. And seeing as both *Rock 'N' Roll High School* and *The Kids Are Alright* shared a common distributor up in the Great Wide Northlands, both of those rockin' reelers shared a single, and singular Gala Premiere Event within a hitherto genteel movie palace just off Toronto's fabled Yonge Street Strip.

"That momentous night was my first of many, many viewings since of Johnny, Joey, Dee Dee and Marky's brat-beating silver screen debut and, in the grand tradition of *Carnival Rock, The World's Greatest Sinner* and even *Wild Guitar,* that first of what should have been a long loud string of Ramone-starring vehicles looks, and it goes without saying sounds every single frame as cinema-shaking and status-quo-quaking now as it did back in those distant days of, well, comparatively big-budget Who documentaries. Why, even poor P. J. Soles got her guy in the end, regardless of how many takes it took Dee Dee to get his lone line — 'Hey, pizza!' — safely onto celluloid. And where else, honestly, can you see gigantic lab rats frugging to 'Teenage Lobotomy' I ask you?

"So I still can't quite fathom why, as the end credits, not to mention Vince Lombardi High, crashed and burned to black that night in Toronto, practically every faux-leather-jacketed p-rocker in attendance

279

defiantly abandoned their seats to mock 'n' mosh all the Who fans streaming down the aisles to immediately replace them as *Kids* got queued up. Because K. Moon for one certainly would have enjoyed, not to mention thoroughly identified with his kindred spirits from Queens ...had he managed to live a year or so longer that is. And need I even mention none other than Pete Townshend himself eventually sang along with no less than 'Substitute' on that penultimate Ramones long-player?!

"Oh! And while we're on the subject: Would anyone out there happen to know whatever became of Marla Rosenfield? Just wondering..."

Harvey Kubernik and Allan Arkush Interview

HK: You have always been a music guy.

AA: I was a record collector and had been a deejay in college. I saw Bob Dylan go electric at Forrest Hills in New York with [Michael] Bloomfield on guitar, introduced by Murray the K. When Dylan sang "Ballad of a Thin Man," it was like an arrow pierced my heart. I caught the Blues Project a couple of times and was a huge fan, and the Mothers of Invention at the Garrick Theater. I saw the Yardbirds, Country Joe & the Fish and Janis [Joplin] when I was a film student in New York.

HK: Let's talk about Jimi Hendrix.

AA: I got tickets for Jimi Hendrix for his Friday night late show May 10, 1968. Opening act is Sly & the Family Stone. Jimi was great. And then something happened on stage that made it transcendent and one of the most amazing rock and roll moments I had ever witnessed.

He was playing the intro to 'Foxy Lady' in front of these giant Marshall amps with the big tops on them. And it just clicked off and overloaded. The roadies go crazy and then put two of 'em up there and now Jimi has twice as much power. And when he throws the switch to turn on his Fender this buzz happened and he starts laughing... He's mesmerizing and starts to walk toward the amp with his back to the audience and this feedback thing starts building up and this electromagnetic thing happening and it's vibrating and you feel it in your chest and he turns a knob, walks to an amp, catches this sound and twists it into the opening note of 'Foxy Lady.' And he backs up and slings it at us, like he's playing lacrosse. He takes that note of the

280

guitar and hurls it towards the audience. And the first note of 'Foxy Lady' you could hear it out on 2nd Avenue.

You know when you are at the beach, and you realize there is a giant breaker coming towards you, and it just hits you so hard you have no chance to move, that was what the opening chords of 'Foxy Lady' were like. It was a transcendent performance until end of set. The dexterity and the skill that he played with were so amazing, and his technical ability. Watching Jimi grab that note and moving it was like *Fantasia* in rock 'n' roll. He became the colors and sound of the music and the movement of the music.

HK: Martin Scorsese was your teacher and faculty adviser at NYU.
AA: On the first day the head of the film school sat down and played us a couple of student films. The best one was *It's Only You Murray*. The filmmaker was Martin Scorsese who eventually became my teacher at NYU.

Marty had in 1968 an American film history class, based on the auteur theory. There were only about six film schools in the country and the one textbook was Andrew Sarris' *American Film*.

The first movie Marty screened for us was *Shock Corridor* by director Sam Fuller. The next week was a real line in the sand when he showed us a movie with John Wayne, *The Searchers*. Then *The Big Heat* by Fritz Lang. And then imagine showing us Jerry Lewis' *The Nutty Professor*. He told us about Kenneth Anger's *Scorpio Rising* and Visconti's *The Dammed*. Scorsese would also suggest movies to see in New York and on TV. He'd show us *TV Guide* in the class.

I responded to it along with my passion for film history. Then Marty was my production teacher. I was so lucky. Not just because it's Marty, but to have the same person teaching me film history and production.

One day he said "I've seen a movie last night that will change everything forever. We will no longer look at action scenes and violence in movies the same way again. It opens this week, and it's called *The Wild Bunch*."

I went opening night. Half the class is in line with me. End of the movie we were so shaken we all went out to a bar and drank whisky and talked about what we had seen.

Marty knew I worked at the Fillmore East, and I would always tell him who was coming. And he would ask for tickets, and I thought he was amazing and just having him as my teacher. I had not seen *Who's that Knocking?* I would get him the same seats, fourth row, slightly on the left for him, Jay Cocks and two of their dates for different groups. Marty wanted to see Spooky Tooth. He wanted tickets for the Who, Grateful Dead but the group that he wanted tickets for than anything else, and he asked me almost every day about it was The Band. How was that for a connection?

On the night of the shows I'd come out and say hello. I certainly said hello on the night The Band played because there was no light show and I was on the stage crew. But I knew his connection to all this.

Allan Arkush (Photo courtesy Allan Arkush)

In fact on Thanksgiving of 1969, after Woodstock, he came down to the theater with [director] Michael Wadleigh and a whole bunch of other people and they did picture and sound system and ran us a couple of rough cut scenes of *Woodstock,* which was being edited to get the reaction of the real rock and roll people. [Scorsese edited Sha Na Na, Sly & the Family Stone and Santana].

So we had Thanksgiving dinner, saw those clips and I remember seeing Ritchie Havens, Canned Heat and some other people. To end the evening we all went up to Madison Square Garden to see the Rolling Stones. Jimi Hendrix and Janis Joplin are sitting behind the amps. On that show Terry Reid opened, B.B. King and the most awesome performance ever by Ike & Tina Turner and the Stones set that had 'Gimme Shelter.' How's that for a good day?

HK: A bio-regional relationship existed between NYU and Fillmore East.

AA: Whatever coincidence, six inches from the Fillmore East was the source of the genius that made the Fillmore East.

And that was the NYU Theater School, right next door. If you were at the NYU Theater School you were just like Scorsese and the people then. You were the theater version and these were the tech guys and they had no place to go after they graduated because Broadway was

282

dominated by older men and it was all about seniority. So you couldn't get a job. Or if you got a job you were the lowest of the low.

HK: Bill Graham understood the role of sound in all of his stage productions. In 1976 he told me "In the long run it's the public. I really sincerely feel this is the reason the relationship lasted over the years. We always had the same goal. We want to turn people on, and we want them to have a good time."

AA: Bill Graham did not just care about the sound. We took pride in having the best sound and lights in the world. And it's

Bill Graham (Photo by Henry Diltz)

a complete coincidence of geography that that happened. Bill wanted good sound and hired Hanley Sound because there was nobody doing sound for rock concerts. Bill Hanley installed a sound system at the Fillmore East.

All of a sudden this theater starts coming alive right next door and they go next door to see what is going on, and they get hired. All those people are the newest and the finest of the people who are starting to make the conversion. So they took Hanley Sound System with the help of Hanley and the technical knowledge they had and started building it week by week and month by month. And, as time went on, they started understanding the building and what was possible. And it was not unusual to come in on a Sunday night and help them set up the most advanced sound tracking equipment you can get. Where they were doing pink noise generators and white noise generators and putting up padding in different places and tuning the building.

It was around the time Jimi Hendrix was forming Band of Gypsys. And in 1969, I am on the stage crew at Fillmore East, as an usher, in the stage crew. Being on the stage crew was life changing.

HK: Later Roger Corman enters your life.

Allan Arkush (Photo courtesy Allan Arkush)

AA: I cut trailers for years with Joe Dante for Roger. We brought the spirit of rock 'n' roll as I knew it, into every aspect of the productions.

Roger and Bill Graham. Imagine going to film school and basically telling your parents you were not going to be a lawyer. Not happy. Now I'm in film school working at the Fillmore. All of a sudden I am surrounded by people who were older than me and responsible people.

So it was possible to be passionate about what you are doing and not be like my parents. And that was the example of what I got from Bill. He was driven. He had the responsibility for the business but he was so passionate about rock 'n' roll. You could talk to Bill and get to know him. He lent me the Fillmore East to do my student film. Can you imagine?

Bill Graham and Roger forged their own destinies. The thing where they are alike is that they are smart enough to trust the people that they hire. And they understand the territory to let the person in, beyond an employee. They had the ability to read who you are. They both bestowed on me the best of the information of their world because I asked. And, Roger made me understand how to direct.

And now when I teach at AFI, it's what I learned from Marty, Bill and Roger synthesized into my own course. So if you are in my course now you get the best of what I learned from those three men.

Allan Arkush (Photo courtesy Allan Arkush)

HK: How did your movie with the Ramones start? I handclapped with Rodney Bingenheimer on the "Rock 'N' Roll High School" recording session Phil Spector produced for the Ramones' LP *End of the Century*.

AA: The original idea of the film came in pieces when I was in high school. I was the kind of kid who did not apply himself, and I would stare out the window in class. I was bored, and I came up with this fantasy that a rock and roll band was going to come to my high school and play. And all the students would run out of class and watch this concert. And the band I chose for this just couldn't be any band in my fantasy. They had to have a certain fantasy. So here's the band I had in my mind: The Yardbirds, the Rolling Stones or the Kinks, because they all had that nasty sounding single sense.

This was early in my record collecting. I had that fantasy and an ongoing fantasy of the kids taking over the school and doing stuff like riding motorcycles up and down the hallway. And up and down the stairs. In my head, I had a race that took place in French class.

That was the first part of the fantasy. Then I thought I'd write something about this fantasy. Then I heard this Todd Rundgren song

'Heavy Metal Kids' in the early seventies, it really got to me. So I started writing a treatment of kid rock bands in schools.

And then I saw lots of rock bands at the Fillmore. Every classic rock band four or five times and did the lights. I talked to Roger Corman who was willing to let me do *Hollywood Blvd.* There was a high school comedy *Girls Gym* with Michael Finnell who worked at New World and was with me every step of the way from the beginning. He found the high school.

Joe McBride wrote the early draft of *Girls Gym*. Joe presented me with the idea of the students doing a walk out and going on strike, because that had happened with someone in his family. That was central. And then he suggested that the students blow up the high school at the end. I said no. I could not imagine that. And after about two weeks I turned to Joe and we went to Roger. "We want to blow up the high school at the end." He loved it. "That's a great point. Maybe we can sell the movie." Good. Because I wanted to get rid of the nude gymnastics that was scheduled for *Girls Gym*.

Roger didn't hate rock and roll but didn't know it. Not part of his daily life style. He didn't know the difference between disco music and rock music in terms of what it meant. But we were making *Girls Gym,* and I think maybe one of the girls was in a band, did that for a while. We were at a certain point in the script.

Then Roger asked me to save this movie *Deathsport* while I was working on *Girls Gym* but it was not going well. He said "why don't you save this movie? And I will make your high school musical."

Grease and disco movies like *Saturday Night Fever* were big at the time. And I said "absolutely." On the telephone he says "we'll call it *Disco High*." "That sounds great!" And in my mind it was never going to be called *Disco High*.

Mike and I had a script, but it wasn't funny enough. Then two guys, film students from Illinois contact New World, Richard Whitley and Russ Dvonch, who want New World to watch their student film. Joe Dante and I see it. *Deathsport* is in production. And there are lots of people in the New World lobby playing mutants in the movie, wannabees and budding filmmakers. The assistant director is getting names. Russ and Richard are in the lobby. "Are you here to be mutants?" "No. We're here to be writers." They get hired.

We have a meeting on the *Deathsport* set and they're pitching ideas at us. Mike and I make it a comedy. We ask them to write ten pages by Monday. "Re-write some parts." We're talking story with two mutants. OK. We get the pages by Monday. They invented characters and get hired to write jokes for *Disco High*. We confide to them it's now really a rock 'n' roll movie, and the only time disco is mentioned is on the title page. So the script and the movie changes and Mike and I go to Roger and break it to him.

HK: The direction and the name of the movie evolved.
AA: That's when I started thinking seriously about a group in it. And at some point, because of the genesis of "Heavy Metal Kids," and the fact I liked Todd Rundgren, Mike and I went up to San Franscisco to meet with Todd Rundgren. This is late spring or early summer 1978.

It didn't work out with Todd. And we also talked to Cheap Trick. Rodney, the KROQ-FM deejay was playing Cheap Trick's *Live at Budokan* album as an import LP. Rodney is a major source of the music heard during the making of this movie. It's very hard to find rock music that has humor in it and really rocks. Those things don't usually go together. The Who have it in places but there was no way I was gonna get the Who. Van Halen was suggested, a wild rock and roll band.

I got a meeting with the Ramones from a lawyer who worked at Warner Bros. Records, but was now working for Roger Corman, Paul Almond.

In the meeting I was explaining the difference between disco and hard rock, and demonstrating how the Who destroyed their instruments at the end of sets. You had to have that kind of feel. Roger listens. He has passion, is shrewd and turns to Paul Almond, who was from the music business, and said, "What do you think, Paul?" "He's absolutely right."

They like the new title. Paul then sets up a meeting with the head of A&R for Warner Bros. Records. We talked about Van Halen, I had heard them on Rodney's KROQ-FM radio show, and the thought was "they might be too uncontrollable."

We also saw the first videos of Devo. They were cool. It was already a complete thing. They had their costume and everything. Then we started talking about music in general and asked if I knew Sire Records. And I had the Talking Heads. I knew every band he talked about. And he's impressed. "What about the Ramones?"

I thought *Rocket to Russia* was one of the top ten albums ever made. At a certain age you find the music you love and end up with people who identify with this music and help define your own persona.

Seymour Stein at Sire Records was very active with us during the production sending us albums on Sire that he heard and felt were appropriate. We almost had the Clash's "White Riot." After we wrapped, Seymour took me into his office and played the Pretenders' "Stop Your Sobbing."

HK: What about after the movie was released?
AA: Let's be really honest here, it was a movie that nobody saw, except midnight movies. It had no profile.

The movie first opened in Texas! Johnny Ramone called me and asked "Why did you open the movie in Texas and New Mexico? We've sold about 150 copies there." The main distributor never liked the movie. He thought it was a commercial for the Ramones.

That movie was on a respirator until Siskel and Ebert reviewed it in Chicago. We were dead. It played in Chicago with two different movies *Grease* and *Dawn of the Dead*. The local distributor did well with Corman films. It played as a Midnight Movie. The audiences came out very satisfied. It did two weeks and started to travel to different territories screening at downtown theaters, drive-ins, grind house cinemas, and a few suburban theaters. The pattern developed: Atlanta, Boston and New York.

Then by sheer coincidence the Ramones are playing San Francisco, and I schlep up there with my wife. I'm still working in the trailer department at New World. Sire Records and their publicity people really get going. The movie does OK but not quite enough to be a hit.

Then it gets booked in New York City at an art house and plays on a Friday night with *The Rocky Horror Picture Show*. Joey and I did some radio shows. The screening in New York City is packed and they went nuts! It was one of the highlights of my life. Seymour Stein and his Sire Records label toss a party for us at The Mudd Club. The movie made its rounds.

HK: It had a life for a while on Betamax and video store rentals.
AA: It came out later on VHS, and I was really thankful because all of a sudden it's in all these stores. And people are taking a real interest in it, and then it went away through various deals, and it was nowhere for ten years. And people and fans were always asking me about it.

Roger's licensing deal with Warner Bros. expired. Roger sells the rights to Lumivision for a laserdisc. It had some new items we prepared for the package. A letter to the fans, reviews. Mike and I did a commentary for the laserdisc.

Then Roger sold it to Buena Vista. They didn't want past materials, and had self-imposed concerns about clearance rights on photos. They didn't even clean up the picture or the sound. The poster isn't on the box. There's a picture of a guitar. I did a lot of work for nothing and was upset with Buena Vista. I wrote a letter to Buena Vista and Roger. And Corman ends his deal with Buena Vista. Then Joey dies and later Johnny dies. The Ramones become bigger.

HK: And we have a 40th anniversary *Rock 'N' Roll High School* product.

AA: Earlier this decade Shout! Factory contacts me about a new DVD reissue. They bought the rights to the movie. We have a sit down meeting, and I got real respect. They do the definitive edition. The new DVD has new video interviews, commentary and every single photo from the crew. Someone found the original negative that was in a vault.

My goal was to make the viewers of 1979 and now in 2019 to feel the way I did on that first night when I saw *A Hard Day's Night* played.

There was a screening for it at Hollywood Forever, the cemetery in Hollywood. I noticed there were more women now in the audience than men. Everyone loves the Ramones. But it's the combination of the Ramones and Riff Randell who sustain the movie. Women in their forties and fifties come up to me and happily confess how much this movie meant to them when they were in Catholic school. They tell me stories of hiking up their dresses and singing Ramones' songs to the nuns.

So many young women and older women talk to me about what *Rock 'N' Roll High School* meant to them. And I realized that the movie would not be around if it wasn't for this magical chemical reaction between the female empowerment of Riff Randell and the Ramones music.

As far as this 40th anniversary DVD reissue, I can sum it up in one sentence: I was the kind of kid who used to read the back of the album. The more information I got the happier I was.

As a filmmaker this is a way for me to respond to people and the fans. And I've never talked to them. There is a group of people that this stuff is aimed at that I have a real debt too. And that goes back to Riff Randell.

Who was Riff Randell? And that's the kind of key to this reissue. After all this time, concerts, life, at this point, thousands of people have come up to me, they figure when they are working with me they look up my IMDB, they know who I am.

It's all about Riff Randell, who is composed of three young women who hung at the Fillmore East all the time, who I went to see the Stones at Madison Square Garden with: Gail, Diane and Janis. They were all pure rock fans, and so when I was making the movie that's how I wanted to embody the character to do.

It was made for a very loyal audience who have a story to tell me when I meet them about how this movie changed their life. Or, how they could be in control of themselves like Riff, and didn't take shit from anyone, and how the music accents this. And the choice of the Ramones fits so well into Riff's personality and the girl group influence on Joey, the lasting power of Riff Randell and now the lasting power of the Ramones fans.

Joey Ramone and Dee Dee Ramone (Photo by Heather Harris)

Quentin Tarantino:
Once Upon a Time... in Hollywood

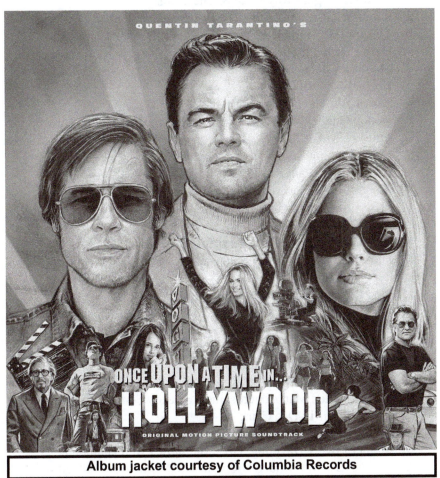

Album jacket courtesy of Columbia Records

The soundtrack for Quentin Tarantino's heavily anticipated music-laden film *Once Upon a Time... in Hollywood* is available now. The soundtrack released globally through Columbia Records in line with the nationwide film release.

Personally curated by Tarantino himself, the soundtrack is a love letter to the music of 1960s-era Hollywood. The *Once Upon a Time... in Hollywood* soundtrack features over 20 standout tracks from artists such as Paul Revere & the Raiders, Deep Purple, Jose Feliciano, and Neil Diamond, as well as vintage radio advertisements, creating a true time capsule of a golden era of filmmaking.

ONCE UPON A TIME... IN HOLLYWOOD Soundtrack Tracklist

1. Treat Her Right - Roy Head & The Traits
2. Ramblin' Gamblin' Man - The Bob Seger System

Boss Radio feat. Humble Harve:

3. Hush - Deep Purple
4. Mug Root Beer Advertisement
5. Hector - The Village Callers
6. Son of a Lovin' Man - Buchanan Brothers
7. Paxton Quigley's Had the Course (from the MGM film Three in the Attic) - Chad & Jeremy
8. Tanya Tanning Butter Advertisement
9. Good Thing - Paul Revere & The Raiders
10. Hungry - Paul Revere & the Raiders
11. Choo Choo Train - The Box Tops
12. Jenny Take a Ride - Mitch Ryder and the Detroit Wheels
13. Kentucky Woman - Deep Purple
14. The Circle Game - Buffy Sainte-Marie / Boss Radio featuring The Real Don Steele:
15. Mrs. Robinson - Simon & Garfunkel
16. Numero Uno Advertisement
17. Bring a Little Lovin' - Los Bravos
18. Suddenly / Heaven Sent Advertisement
19. Vagabond High School Reunion
20. KHJ Los Angeles Weather Report
21. The Illustrated Man Advertisement / Ready For Action
22. Hey Little Girl - Dee Clark
23. Summer Blonde Advertisement
24. Brother Love's Traveling Salvation Show - Neil Diamond
25. Don't Chase Me Around (from the MGM film GAS-S-S-S) - Robert Corff
26. Mr. Sun, Mr. Moon - Paul Revere & the Raiders (featuring Mark Lindsay)
27. California Dreamin' - Jose Feliciano
28. Dinamite Jim (English Version) - I Cantori Moderni di Alessandroni
29. You Keep Me Hangin' On (Quentin Tarantino Edit) - Vanilla Fudge
30. Miss Lily Langtry (cue from The Life and Times of Judge Roy Bean) - Maurice Jarre
31. KHJ Batman Promotion

Quentin Tarantino's *Once Upon a Time... in Hollywood* visits 1969 Los Angeles, where everything is changing, as TV star Rick Dalton (Leonardo DiCaprio) and his longtime stunt double Cliff Booth (Brad Pitt) make their way around an industry they hardly recognize anymore. The ninth film from the writer-director features a large ensemble cast and multiple storylines in a tribute to the final moments of Hollywood's golden age.

Written and Directed by Quentin Tarantino. The film also stars Margot Robbie as Sharon Tate plus Al Pacino, Emile Hirsch, Timothy Olyphant, Dakota Fanning, Bruce Dern, Lena Dunham, and more.

Highly effective on screen and in the stellar soundtrack are era-specific deejay intros from famed KHJ radio personalities The Real Don Steele and Humble Harve dovetailing product advertisements and weather reports from 1969.

There are several recordings broadcast in the movie but not incorporated in the soundtrack offering: Aretha Franklin's "The House that Jack Built," Otis Redding's 'I Can't Turn You Loose," "Soul Serenade" courtesy of Willie Mitchell, Billy Stewart's rendition of "Summertime" and the potent screen-only inclusion of The Rolling Stones' "Out of Time."

KHJ DJ The Real Don Steele
(Photo by Henry Diltz)

The impact of "Out of Time" was not lost on Sirius XM deejay Rodney Bingenheimer who programmed the Farlowe recording on his weekly shift, drawing attention to the 1966 UK smash, and revealing he was only faintly aware of this rare selection from *Metamorphosis* now re-discovered for *Once Upon a Time... in Hollywood* theater viewers and listeners.

The "Out of Time" heard in the movie's score takes on prophetic significance and is a telling musical sequence foreshadowing the celluloid tale's murderous task ending.

The initial media announcement earlier in 2019 of the *Once Upon a Time... in Hollywood* soundtrack album had listed the addition of the Rolling Stones' "Out of Time" culled from the epochal Stones' *Aftermath* UK edition, cut in Hollywood at RCA Studios in 1966, produced by their manager and liner note flapsmith, Andrew Loog Oldham. An edited version also appears on the Stones' 1967 album *Flowers*. The actual "Out of Time" eventually implemented in *Once Upon a Time... in Hollywood* is from their *Metamorphosis* compilation album of 1964-1970 outtakes and alternate versions, produced by Andrew Loog Oldham and Jimmy Miller, issued in June 1975 by ABKCO Records.

This "Out of Time," was done in England at Pye Studios April 27-30, 1966, produced by Mick Jagger for Oldham, featuring singer Chris Farlowe, for which Jagger recorded a reference vocal for the artist he was producing on a backing track comprised of English session musicians including guitarists Jimmy Page and Big Jim Sullivan, and overdubbed horn section assembled from the Ronnie Scott jazz club bandstand. The result featuring Chris Farlowe was a number one UK hit single for Oldham's Immediate Records label.

In July 2019 I interviewed Andrew Loog Oldham. He detailed both of his "Out of Time" studio endeavors.

"In one of my dreams that did not come true, Mick and Keith and I were gonna be Holland-Dozier-Holland for Immediate. That was the original idea. But it didn't work out. Everybody got extra busy, whatever. But that was one of the original thoughts behind it. Mick did a wonderful job on Chris Farlowe's 'Out of Time' and his album. Expensive. 12,000 pounds. A lot of money then. The price of a Rolls Royce Phantom V.

"It was also Mick's first production with me for my label. Immediate. The only reason Mick, Keith and I started to produce together was that we liked to do things the Beatles hadn't done.

"There came a settlement between the Rolling Stones and Allen Klein in the early seventies that I didn't know much about. In 1973 or '74. I was living in Paris with my wife, Esther. We got together with Mick and Bianca. Mick was meant to be settling with Allen Klein. Mick was gonna deliver great tracks and stuff that would make a great last album of the deal between the Stones and ABKCO. And then Mick and I were supposed to get together in New York to mix it and this was the album that would become *Metamorphosis*.

294

"I was not privy to what was going on. But Mick obviously changed his mind and delivered a bunch of lesser stuff to Allen Klein. It was just abysmal.

"In an attempt to not only rescue the album but make it complete, a full album, when I used to do Andrew Loog Oldham Orchestra recording sessions for Decca, when say. . . two hours and ten minutes was gone out of the three hours allotted, I would have done the tracks, whether it be a Four Seasons album, Beach Boys, Rolling Stones songbook, and I would have fifty minutes left with, you know, sixteen musicians. Which included Jimmy Page, John Paul Jones, and I would then record anything I wanted, something new I was working on, or more often than not, doing elaborate demos of songs that Mick and Keith had written.

"So that makes up five or six things that are on side one of *Metamorphosis*. The Rolling Stones are not playing on them. It's just Mick and Keith doing some vocals. Same is true of 'Out of Time.'

"Then I remembered that Mick had done a reference vocal for Chris Farlowe for 'Out of Time.' So I let Allen have it for *Metamorphosis* 'cause we needed a decent song. I mixed that and added a lot of people from Connecticut, bass players and background vocals that I used on a Donovan session. Same year. And that went onto the album with the Jimmy Miller-produced 'I Don't Know Why.'

"Stuff they worked on and not bothered to finish. For example, the version of Stevie Wonder's 'I Don't Know Why' which was recorded on the night Brian Jones died. The 'I Don't Know Why' that they recorded at Olympic, the night that dear Brian died, was like 1:30. Right?

"When I was putting together *Metamorphosis* in New York at the Record Plant in 1975, John Lennon was next door. Right? And I borrowed the horn people from Elephant's Memory. Stan Bronstein. And John Lennon said to me, 'Use him, man.' And I just suggested, 'I want a Jimmy Miller horn section.' (laughs).

"And they did that on 'I Don't Know Why.' And if you listen to it, Mick Jagger repeats the same verse and chorus three times. I just made it 3:40 with the addition of the horn section and the Connecticut musicians. And Allen Klein's classic words to me at the time were 'Don't worry Andrew. I've done the research. You could put shit on a Rolling Stones' record and it would still sell a quarter of a million in America alone.'

"As for the Stones' 'Out of Time' in this movie, maybe Quentin Tarantino is so vinyl-anal, he was familiar with *Metamorphosis*. Right? Good for him."

In a July 26, 2019 story on *Once Upon a Time... in Hollywood,* Armond White in *National Review*, contrasts the powerful exhibition of the Rolling Stones' 'Out of Time' off the UK *Aftermath* in an earlier film from director Hal Ashby with the 'Out of Time' employed for *Once Upon a Time... in Hollywood.*

"Tarantino's pop sadism vents the undigested frustration of the juvenile mentality. The hit parade of half-obscure pop tunes is a mere distraction, proof that Tarantino's understanding of pop music — like his understanding of movies — is far shallower than we imagined. The Mamas and the Papa's trenchant 'Twelve Thirty (Young Girls Are Coming to the Canyon)' has been used more felicitously elsewhere, as was The Rolling Stones' 'Out of Time,' which Hal Ashby scored in *Coming Home* so that it expressed the forgotten romance and regret behind Sixties political anxiety."

In a 2004 interview for my book *Hollywood Shack Job: Rock Music In Film and on Your Screen,* Loog Oldham was enthusiastic about the placement of the *Aftermath* master take in *Coming Home.*

"'Out Of Time' I love. It's used twice in the *Coming Home* movie. I do remember, we all have our way of looking at it, survival mode, I am sure I reached Hal Ashby outside the cinema. I got (producer) Lou Adler, who knew him, to connect me. 'I want you to hear me while I still have a lump in my throat. Great. You just blew me away....'

"Not like I had never been moved. I've had a moment that will be with me forever. The double use of 'Out Of Time' as a political statement and a love statement was just incredible.

"Hal was on location, and I reached him. If a piece of art has affected you like that either you want the person to see your eyes or the sound of your voice, and I was able to do it."

Around 1986 or 1987 I met Quentin Tarantino when he worked at a video store in Manhattan Beach, California, Video Archives. He was the buyer. I had a few memorable chats with him at the counter. It was quite apparent he was an AIP (American International Pictures) movie fan, collector and Samuel Z. Arkoff and James H. Nicholson catalog expert. He was also a scholar on Roger Corman's New World Pictures library. Chuck Kelly who founded Luxuria Internet radio worked at the store and later did some music supervision for Tarantino's films including *Jackie Brown* and *Kill Bill*.

The last time I talked to Quentin was in summer 1997 at the Los Angeles County Museum of Art at *Behind The Screen Roger Corman Tribute* held at the Bing Theater sitting with him and his date, actress Mira Sorvino.

On October 2, 2019 The Grammy Museum at L.A. Live in Los Angeles hosted a very special celebration around *Once Upon a Time... in Hollywood*. I was invited by a Columbia Records label publicist to cover the event and in attendance with Hal Lifson, former host of *Radio A Go-Go*. Writer-director Quentin Tarantino and Paul Revere & the Raiders co-founder / original lead singer Mark Lindsay were joined by music critic David Wild and Grammy Museum moderator Scott Goldman, who talked about the movie and its music. During the panel presentation, Mark Lindsay performed a couple of Raiders' songs from the soundtrack backed by a choral ensemble from Tesoro High School in San Juan, Capistrano who were terrific.

In December 2019, Sony Pictures Home Entertainment released a DVD and Blu-ray of the movie with 20 extra minutes of scenes. Tarantino provided insights in a question and answer session for fans, journalists, and tade magazine reporters on recordings licensed for his film and soundtrack album.

"I've heard a few people say that 'I think that a soundtrack should be complete. Every piece of music that was in the movie should be in the soundtrack.' I don't agree with that at all," Quentin cautioned.

"You want to go with the dramatic flow of the movie, so you probably aren't going to put a song from the last half hour in the first half hour of the album, he volunteered. "But we don't include 'Summertime' [by Billy Stewart"]. We don't include Joe Cocker ["The Letter"], because you can get that stuff anywhere," Tarantino explained to the devoted audience.

"These records were meant to be bought and played on 45s,"enthused Tarantino. During the talk, he also praised the impact and influence of famed Los Angeles-based radio station KHJ [93 AM]. Deejay introductions and station jingles from the late sixties are heard in his film.

KHJ DJs Frank Terry and Humble Harve on Santa Monica Beach (Photo by Henry Diltz, May 27, 1968)

"KHJ was able to give the entire soundtrack a personality and you can't break the personality.

"I made a couple different cassettes over the years of what I was thinking we could use in the movie," divulged Quentin. "I remember how everybody in Los Angeles listened to KHJ.

"It wasn't just me and the other kids at the elementary school. It was my mom, it was her brother and it was her brother's friends. Everybody's car was tuned in. If you were black, you listened to KGLH [102.3 FM in the Crenshaw District]. If you were white, you were listening to KHJ [located on Melrose Ave. in Hollywood].

"There's a Grammy Museum, but there's no KHJ Museum," he comically complained. "Like, 'what day of 1969 would you like to listen too? Oh, here's the tape for that day.' That shit doesn't exist…"

Thankfully, Tarantino and his production assistants were able to locate from sources radio air checks from uninterrupted programs of KHJ Boss Radio deejays/on-air personalities The Real Don Steele, Humble Harve [Miller], Frank Terry, Johnny Williams and Robert W. Morgan.

Quentin expressed how important the AM radio dial was to him as a youth living with his family in Los Angeles' South Bay beach community of Torrance.

298

"It made me remember just how constant the radio was. It was in your car. And when you got home, you'd also turn it on there. Hearing those shows was a revelation! Not just for the music, but for the deejays and ads as well."

Tarantino discussed one method he employed for the film's music lineup and soundtrack collection, after reviewing 14 hours of songs on tape.

Quentin cited "Snoopy vs. the Red Baron" as one of his favorite songs. It's spotlighted in a climax scene, but not included on the soundtrack.

"I was always a big fan of Paul Revere & the Raiders. In 1969, my favorite bands are gonna be Paul Revere & the Raiders and the Monkees," he proudly proclaimed as the crowd expressed their appreciation. "They were the ones that were speaking to me and talking to me. And they were funny. They were comedy, and they were cool. And because of their connection with Dick Clark, they were on TV all the time."

Tarantino frequented used record stores and picked up different Paul Revere albums.

"I had an assistant at the time. So I ended up making her a special Paul Revere & the Raiders cassette tape that she started listening to. And her enthusiasm got me even more enthusiastic about it, and so I kind of reacquainted myself with Mark and the boys' music."

"This soundtrack is the best driving music I've ever heard in my life," declared Mark Lindsay from the stage.

"What I'm looking for, I know it when I find it," replied Quentin to a question from the audience about recordings incorporated into his filmic ventures. "It depends on the movie. I usually have some sort of a deep-sea diving mission going on. For instance, if it's *Jackie Brown*, I'm listening to seventies soul music."

He referenced his love of the Batman theme and Barry Sadler's "Ballad of the Green Berets."

Tarantino informed Scott Goldman. the Grammy Museum executive director, in their exchange that his parents "got me one-by-one, all the Partridge Family records. I still think David Cassidy is one of the most underrated vocalists in the history of music to this day."

Quentin then mentioned the first two albums he purchased with his own money were George Carlin's *FM & AM* and Curtis Mayfield's soundtrack to *Superfly*.

Christopher Allport: *Emily or Oscar*

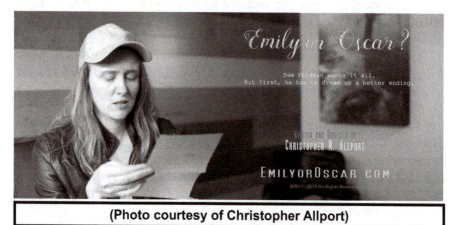

(Photo courtesy of Christopher Allport)

In spring 2020 I had the opportunity to interview Christopher Allport of Allport Production Studios International / Alpha Command Unit, a boutique video, music, audio, stage and event production company working with virtuoso musicians and well-known artists.

Christopher M. Allport is a veteran actor, director and musician/singer/composer with extensive credits as a writer/director/screenwriter and also a noted voiceover artist.

In 2000 Allport sang as back-up singer to Barbara Streisand in her *Timeless: Live in Concert* tour date at the Staples Center in Los Angeles. In 2012 Allport directed the motion picture and live broadcast from the Dorothy Chandler Pavilion in Los Angeles, of the Young Musicians Foundation Gala featuring conductors Michael Tilson Thomas, Joey Newman and John Williams, which is still broadcast on PBS-TV.

Allport has strong ties to the music community as a recording artist, composer and lyricist. Compact discs of his catalog are available. Composed for choir and orchestra, Allport's *Arise Awake O Christmas Day*, blends Hollywood studio soundtrack, chorale and the depths of Gregorian chant to celebrate the glory of Christmas. It's based on scripture from the books of Luke and Mathew. Another title is *Song of Solomon* (Solomon's Wedding Theme) for Jewish or Christian wedding celebration inspired by text from the Old Testament.

Also in retail release is his composition "Through the Windows on a Train" (a French Tryptich Excursion) orchestrated by David Fick and Jason Gamer. It's a virtuoso Concertino for piano and orchestra.

Through the Windows on a Train (Photo courtesy of Christopher Allport)

Currently in production, I was on the set of Allport's theatrical feature of *Emily or Oscar*. It's a true collaboration of artistic enlightenment, like an early United Artist movie. Poet and songwriter Stephen J. Kalinich plays the role of 'The Prophet,' who acts as a conscience to protagonist 'Sam Feldman,' played by the film's maker. Ingénue Casara Clark, in her breaking-out role, infuses 'Emily,' the female romantic lead, named in the film's title, with a juxtaposition of poise and quirky mannerisms. Susan Blakely offers her presence as 'The Agent,' while Susan Boyd Joyce (*Happy Days*) returns to the screen as an older 'Mary Pickford,' a muse to inspire 'Emily' to focus on her own desires.

Emily or Oscar features three ear-worm musical numbers, "Crashin' to the Other Side," "I Just Wanna Be Found" and "I've Lived a Thousand Lifetimes," by Allport, as well as a handful of other cues by singer/songwriter Susie Stevens (*The Simpsons*) and neo classical composer, Maria Newman. Dutch filmmaker, Ismaël Lotz also co-stars as 'The Mysterious Gentleman,' whom the audience is in for a big surprise when they discover who this character really was in the golden era.

Allport's production of *From: Manzanar-To: the Divided States of America,* with some narration by Martin Sheen, and commentary by George Takei, earned the title of Best Documentary Short, a 2017 L.A. Movie Award, while also winning the audience choice award the same year. This riveting portrait about World War II Japanese internment camps predicted the dark future of the 2016 US presidential election cycle which uprooted xenophobia thought to be of generations past.

Amazon Prime features another serious documentary, directed by Allport, is *All the Sins of the Past*, taking an in-depth look at the HIV and Apartheid Crises in South Africa.

Ranging from sacred and serious, through comedy and all the way to profane, Allport's mastery of a wide variety of genres also gave us *Fokking Short*, a fun satire that sarcastically flirts with pecking order dynamics of the ubiquitous Hollywood "totem pole."

The Young Musicians Foundation (YMF) and Allport Production Studios proudly presented Stephanie Vlahos' *Tristan und Isolde.* Based largely on the romance by Gottfried von Strassburg, Richard Wagner set the German libretto to an opera, with the stage production directed by Ms. Vlahos and the television production directed by Chris M. Allport.

Also rewarding is Allport's *Life Is Too Short To Sing Badly*, an award-winning, classic documentary short that examined the core, humanistic and musical teachings of Mary Breden, DMA, who is the protégée of the legendary Los Angeles Master Chorale Music Director Paul Salamunovich. Breden's inspirational approach to both classical and liturgical musical works teaches Loyola Marymount students about both music and life as she takes her chorale students on tour to Boston College, a sister School of Loyola Marymount (Los Angeles).

Chris Allport at the Hollywood Bowl (Photo courtesy of Christopher Allport)

302

HK: You went to Loyola Marymount University.

CA: I studied film at LMU. For two years I was the Perspective editor at *The Los Angeles Loyolan*. The greatest thing I learned was how to go against the system. I went to LMU specifically for their chorale music program, which was led by a really incredible music director, Mary Breden, even though I was going to major in film.

HK: You've cited the influence of music arrangers on your own music, TV and film work.

CA: I was listening to Carmen Dragon at age 3, who conducted the Hollywood Bowl Orchestra and Larry Grossman, who came out of Broadway. I knew Pete Rogolo who arrangements with Ella Fitzgerald and the score to *The Fugitive* TV series. Bill Byers, a distant cousin, was a major arranger for Herb Alpert. I love the arrangements on the Bee Gees albums, especially what Arif Mardin did on *Saturday Night Fever*. I love the vocal harmonies of Queen. Years ago Brian May, of Queen came to Disney to oversee some Queen vocals we were covering for *The Mighty Ducks,* when I was in as a kid. At the time I didn't really know who he was. What a treat that was, looking back.

I learned that the songwriters could write a lyric and jot down a melody, but it's the arranger who makes it work.

In 2006. I was the associate producer of the Richard Carpenter scholarship. To watch him and magic energy coming out of his ten fingers of his keyboard. Herb Alpert and his wife Lani Hall were slow dancing backstage. The vocal contractor that night was Morgan Ames and we were in tears.

When David Foster did some work at the Young Musicians Foundation, we were doing a big gala together, and I was actually directing the production when David came with Josh Groban.

HK: As a kid you also met and received some viable stage lessons from the legendary television team of director Gary Smith and producer Dwight Hemion Jr., who were known primarily for music-themed television programs of the 1960s and '70s. They understood the comedy and variety genre and always implemented visual musical elements in their TV work with Frank Sinatra, Barbra Streisand, Elvis Presley, Paul McCartney and Burt Bacharach.

CA: As a kid actor at Disney, I think I was about age 12, they took me aside at the Pantages Theater in Hollywood and taught me a lot of behind the scenes magic. Dwight showed me how a multi-camera set up worked. I will never forget it. I was getting to see how a stage, variety and theatrical event happened in front of a live audience while at the same time it was a live TV broadcast. They combined theater, live orchestra and television into one genre. It's now what I do.

HK: Background singing has always been a part of your life. In your recording ventures and stage work.
CA: You don't have a story unless you have the background singing that people believe. That's one of the magic sauces.

HK: And you've always understood the roles of the background and support singers coupled with the years of voice over jobs you've done.
CA: The legendary Stan Freberg was one of the first people who ever cast me for off camera character singing and voice word in radio. Commercial director, Jay Silverman, taught me a lot, too. Barbara Harris and Mickie McGowan taught me how vocal soundtrack details work in movies. There's so much voice over work in feature films that the audience isn't aware of. It's subconscious storytelling built into the sound design, score, and soundtrack. The sound carries the emotion of the film, while the picture carries the storyline.

You are there to make the stars shine. There are background singers on the tracks. I used to do a lot of background singing, a tool in my tool kit, so is improv. You don't have a complete project unless you have the background singers on it. Those are really cool backlines and harmonies that aren't on a lot of records anymore. The style of collaborative harmony we heard on the Von Trapp Family, the Beach Boys, Captain and Tennille.

HK: As a child actor you were in *Hook* directed by Steven Spielberg
CA: I learned from Spielberg the word discipline. A lot of other kids could have gotten the role. I met him at Glen Glen Sound. One of the reasons I was given the opportunity was that my mother agreed to have me within one hour of Todd A-O for any moment in a 90 day period and on-set tutoring. I did something for Steven. He called me 'one take-Allport.' Steven knew how to work with the psychology of a kid.

In his heart he is still a kid. And, like him, I never want to lose that inner adolescence. When I did *Hook* I had no idea how big the production was. Until we got invited to the *Hook* screening at Universal Studios. The whole cast and anyone who worked on the movie was there. The screen credits went on forever.

I did some voicing for Robin Williams. I met him at the *Disney American Teacher Awards* when he was presenting. The voice I did in his character was for the adult Peter Pan, who crows "cock-a-doodle-do" when he takes off and flies into the air for the first time after accepting himself as Peter Pan.

HK: Years ago you shot and directed video work for the Beach Boys.
CA: I met Beach Boys' archivist and reissue producer Alan Boyd through Maria Newman who I worked with at the Young Musicians Foundation. I've always done camera work, and Alan hired me to do camera for the video of the Beach Boys' "Child of Winter." We were in Grammy consideration for that video. It wasn't lost on me being at the Western studio where the Beach Boys and Brian did classic records. I recorded there at age 11.

Stephen [Kalinich] came up to me and said, "You are really talented kid, but kind of a pain in the ass." That line ends up in *Emily or Oscar*. Kalinich became my friend. He took me very seriously. We had a human connection. I knew he could work in film, and I cast him in *Emily or Oscar*. He's very comedic, and I knew what the challenges would be. He loves to riff and go off script. But I let him say things that needed to be said.

Chris Allport and Stephen J. Kalinich (Photo courtesy of Christopher Allport)

Stephen introduced me to Joe Wissert, and he saw some of the 13 videos I did for 13 Beach Boys songs. Joe said, after viewing *Arise Awake O Christmas Day*, "when I was at Columbia Records in A&R, we would have been starving for this at the label." High praise.

During my work with the Beach Boys Mike Love and I went over to Brian's house. He made me a sandwich. We worked very well together. Mike came over to my studio with his wife Jackie after his dad had passed, and he took some time to meditate near my olive tree.

I ask my clients what they want and giving them what they need as opposed to doing some stuff I work out on my own. I wanted to give my client what they need. Mike Love has the more quiet voice of all the Beach Boys but can do the more lower and more mellow tones.

I liked working with Bruce Johnson. One day we filmed at Paradise Cove at the beach and got the shot I needed with the Paradise Cove pier in the background. He reacted when he knew I had a classical music background. I talked with him about 'I Write the Songs' that Captain & Tennille and Barry Manilow covered.

Bruce initially wrote it as a commission for Daryl Dragon. A lot of people still think Barry Manilow wrote it because he sings it nightly. It's not from the singer's point of view. It's from the perspective of God when you realize that it's about the whole world singing. Or whatever God means to them. That is powerful. That's why the song Bruce wrote is a multi-decade anthem. I learned from him as well as David Foster. They get people to pull on their heart strings.

HK: And all this work had led to *Emily or Oscar*.

CA: It's a 'Hollywood golden era' throwback romantic comedy. With silent film references and Hollywood studio jokes, everyone is sure to get a laugh as they take a ride through screenwriter Sam Feldman's wild imagination. But what happens when a Hollywood director makes Sam choose between the Academy Award and the woman of his dreams? It embodies the feelings of growing up in Hollywood that I experienced. It embodies things that were said to me or things that I had heard. And the life styles of the way that people are in this town. How open they can be in many ways and also how closed off they can be in other ways.

It started three years ago. My collaborator in the Netherlands, Ismaël Lotz, and I made a little short film, *Fokking Short* that was well received. And he was back in Hollywood. 'Let's make another film.' I said 'I need to have a basic three act structure this time.' I've done a lot of short films. What's next? You have to have a satisfying ending. And we did the short, and I wasn't satisfied with the ending. 'What are you gonna do?' 'I'm going to turn it into a feature.' And he asked, 'How?' 'I'm gonna write it.' And I got together with Stephen J. Kalinich and Casara Clark. I had some notes my mom had left behind in her diaries. I know my mother would want me to be doing this. Drawing upon my experiences and my resources to create that which is true.

HK: Susan Blakely and Casara Clark are cast in *Emily or Oscar*.

CA: Susan Blakely played in a TV show with me 30 years ago and always showed me respect, even as a little kid. We had gotten together socially, and I needed a good tough female actress to portray an agent. I called her up. She read the script. "I think I can do this." No audition needed. Gave her top of the show billing. She's so talented and gracious.

Casara Clark. We had done a production of *Chicago*. I played the role of Billy Flynn. Great personality and has the ability to play and improv. I wrote a part for her and very grateful. *Emily or Oscar* is not all sunshine. There are some dark corners in this film. The questions asked are 'How do you go into those dark corners and come back? In one of the song lyrics I wrote there's a line, 'you and me, we've been through hell, and we've come out on the other side.'

The film is walking a tight rope between love and a career. And if you fall off you are dead in both. We all as human beings want to be loved. We want to share love. But what is love? How do you define it? For each person it is different. The media distorts it and makes it seem like there is only one way.

Emily or Oscar asks the questions of 'what is it for me? What is it for this character?'

Christopher Allport
(Photo courtesy of Christopher Allport)

And when entering into any relationship if you have the opportunity to discuss that with a potential partner of what it looks like for them, and for you, and to be able to accept those answers that are real. And build something off from that, which is honest. The title presents a choice between the girl and the gold. Various career decisions lead to moments in this movie musical. Yes, collaboration is very important. You have to stay on top of your vision and not just when you hand it off to somebody.

Colin Hanks, *All Things Must Pass*

Tower Records, Hollywood, 1972, (Photo by John Van Hamersveld)

All Things Must Pass is a feature documentary film directed by Colin Hanks exploring Tower Records.

Established in 1960, Tower Records was once a retail powerhouse with two hundred stores, in thirty countries, on five continents. From humble beginnings in a small-town drugstore in Sacramento, California, Tower Records eventually became the heart and soul of the music world, and a powerful force in the music industry.

I went to the 1970 opening of Tower Records on Sunset Boulevard in West Hollywood. The first LP I purchased was Jethro Tull's *Stand Up*. I knew the location already. Years earlier I frequented the same space formerly occupied by Earl "Madman" Muntz, who sold cars, installed stereo units and 8-track cartridge players in vehicles.

In 1999, Tower Records made $1 billion. In 2006, the company filed for bankruptcy. What went wrong? Everyone thinks they know what killed Tower Records: The Internet. But that's not the story. Hanks' movie investigates this iconic company's explosive trajectory, tragic demise, and legacy forged by its rebellious Sacramento, California-born founder, Russ Solomon. *All Things Must Pass* is essential viewing for anyone who ever found sound in a record store. It's a melodic, spiritual, retail and cautionary celluloid tale from filmmaker Colin Hanks.

Actor/director Hanks is a founding partner at Company Name with producer Sean Stuart, where he primarily directs and produces documentary films. He is one of the stars of the CBS-TV sitcom, *Life in Pieces*. The film's producer is cofounder Sean Stuart. Executive Producer Glen Zipper is a founding partner with Zipper Brothers Films and formerly the Head of Documentary Features for Exclusive Media's Spitfire Pictures. Glen was also the Executive in Charge of Production on Martin Scorsese's Emmy Award®-winning *George Harrison: Living in the Material World*.

Joe Elliott of Def Leppard remarked, "One of my ambitions when I first set foot on US soil was to visit Tower Records on Sunset Boulevard. As a kid growing up in England, we were always reading about these cool places in the states, CBGBs and The Bowery in New York, The Troubadour, The Roxy and Rainbow in L.A. and of course, Tower Records. This was also in the days before CDs, so it was a 'real' record store...
"When I did finally get there I couldn't believe it, it was so massive, one could spend an entire day in there and only get to see half of what

they had. It was essentially a toy shop for grownups, and boy did we come out of there with armfuls of records! It was a terrific experience, the likes of which I fear may have gone forever, but we live in hope."

Stanley Clarke, musician summarized "In L.A., I would go to Tower Records two to three times a week. Tower was the only place to get jazz, rock, fusion, classical and anything else, all in one place."

I interviewed Hanks in 2015 for *Record Collector News* magazine.

Harvey Kubernik: How did *All Things Must Pass* come together?
Colin Hanks: It's been a long journey, that's for sure. It started off at a dinner I was having around the time the stores were closing. Someone said, in passing, "Hard to believe that all started in that tiny little drugstore in Sacramento." It was like a light bulb went off. I knew the company had started in Sacramento. It had always been a source of civic pride.

HK: It's sort of a hometown movie.
CH: My mother had friends that worked at Tower in Sacramento. The hometown aspect is a really great byproduct of it. And obviously, the hometown connection for me, and my producing partner, Sean [Stuart] is undeniable. We sort of felt like we were incredibly lucky to have been raised in Sacramento so we inherently knew an important facet of the story is not only Russ Solomon, but also this group of people that are from Sacramento and got to go off and do this incredible thing around the world. And so we definitely felt that there was a part of that we understood, being from Sacramento.

Everything that Tower stood for was that sort of mom and pop vibe. That sort of hometown city vibe, no matter what city you lived in. Hopefully that Tower Records felt like it was from your hometown.

Some of my mother's close friends had even worked at both the Sacramento and San Francisco locations, but I didn't know about the beginnings of the company. That truly got my wheels spinning. I was dumbfounded that no one else had made a feature-length documentary on this amazing company.

HK: What are the fundamental elements/themes of the film in your opinion?
CH: The overall theme, really, is in the title: *All Things Must Pass*. All great rides have to come to an end sometime. It's like what they

yell out in the bar at closing time, you know? "You don't have to go home, but you can't stay here." That was an initial theme from the beginning. As we dug deeper and got to know the people involved, I was really struck by the family aspect, that bond. These people came together and did something truly special. They spent, in some cases, 30 years of their lives working on making Tower what it was. The fact that something as iconic as Tower Records started off in my hometown of Sacramento really resonated with me. The fact that this company took these people around the world, what that journey must have been like for them; that's a special thing. I really wanted to capture the fun and excitement of that. I also wanted to try and bring those stores back to life, in a sense.

I remember which stores I bought specific records from. I tried applying to two different Tower locations during college but I never heard back. As always, there was a long line of applicants in front of me.

I suppose this is a way of living out my fantasy of working at Tower. After becoming an actor, I still wanted to do something that involved the music business, I just didn't know what. I knew I was never really going to cut it as a musician. As I have gotten older, I have become obsessed with documentaries and hearing interesting stories from the people who actually lived them. So, naturally, combining the two and making a documentary about the music industry seemed like a natural progression for me.

HK: How did you first become interested in the Tower Records journey and focusing on Russ Solomon in particular?
CH: Once you meet Russ, it only takes about 0.03 seconds to know that he is a total character and just a great guy, but it started much earlier than that. I suppose growing up in Sacramento and going to Tower to buy my first cassettes and CDs was the starting point. I have a lot of memories of those stores as a kid. As I got older, going to other stores around the world and knowing that they were somehow connected, left some residual impression on me. Really it was that initial light bulb moment: hearing how the company started and witnessing how it was ending. That seemed like one hell of a ride that would probably make for an interesting film.

HK: What was the most surprising message from those featured in the film?

CH: How adamant Russ was that the success of Tower had very little to do with him. In one respect, he is being incredibly modest. Yet, he is also spot-on. The real reason why Tower was a success was because of all the people that worked in the stores. They made each store their own. Each location was truly unique; that attention to detail, by the people in the stores, and the awareness of the "higher ups" can't be overstated.

It's been a challenge making a music documentary that isn't focused on one band, or one star, but rather the guys and girls in the stores helping connect those people to the listeners. Those people, the clerks and employees, are not always the most celebrated people in rock and roll, but most of time, they are the ones you can relate to the most.

It's a documentary about a guy and his band of misfits who worked in the music business, who bonded together, took over the world, had the time of their lives thinking the party would never end, only to have someone flip on the lights and kick 'em out.

My hope is that those who were there will remember how great it was and what a unique moment in time it was when Tower first started opening their doors in Sacramento, San Francisco, and Los Angeles. For those who weren't around, I hope that they will wish they were!

At the end of the day, I hope it makes everyone want to go directly to their local record store and spend some time going through the bins. You never know who you might meet, or what cool new band or music you might discover.

HK: Tower Records had its own culture as well in addition to being a place music was sold.
CH: Yes. Definitely. You know, it was really in a strange way Tower Records was much more about the hang than about a business transaction. It was really about here was a place you could go and hang out. You could do nothing. You don't have to buy anything if you don't want, or if you can't, which is an important distinction. And, you know, there are people there that you can have conversations with. You can meet people in the store that are other customers or work in the store that are maybe gonna change the way you look at things.

It's a romantic or simplistic way of saying it, but I think it is kind of true, if someone can turn you on to a record or an artist that you have never heard about, and that ends up becoming "the record that changes your life," that's a big deal. And, I think that's a big reason why I

312

wanted to make the documentary even if I didn't know this while I was making it. But, that connection you make to the record. So many people ask about the personal connection, and are we missing stuff by not going to brick and mortar stores. Yes. I believe in all of that. But I really think at its core, we're talking about that personal connection you make with a record, or with a band. And you remember that. And, Tower was always like the residue of that exchange. You know what I mean?

HK: A lot of music documentaries are made by music lovers and fans. You're an actor who has done episodic television and big-budget movies, and one thing that struck me, maybe it was your budget or experience in front of other directors, or that you are a fan of documentaries as well as vinyl, that most of the interview subjects are so forthcoming and well lit.
 CH: I would like to take credit for all of the interviews. I can take credit for about half of them, really, because eventually we brought on a screenwriter, Steven Lekart who did a really great job of not only getting on the team but helping craft the story. Not only from the story perspective in terms of the beat we wanted to get throughout the course of 40 years. But also our interview style, it was incredibly beneficial for me as the director.

HK: Russ helped you find the narrative for the film?
CH: Absolutely. You know, the biggest saving grace, and it is really purely luck, was the fact that I somehow stumbled upon this idea of this documentary and then met the guy that was arguably responsible for it and that he just happened to be such a charismatic guy that he could talk for hours about any tiny detail about this company that existed for forty years. And he would be able to tell you stories about it. And they would be engaging stories that would be interesting. That not only have a beginning, middle and end, have color and flair to it.
　　That kind of personality is obviously beneficial to us as filmmakers. But obviously was incredibly beneficial to him as a businessman. Because that was how he was able to accomplish what he was able to do. The fact that he was a gregarious outgoing fun guy who was good at seeing a good idea and run with it. He was able to trust people. I love seeing him. I love sitting next to him and listening and talking to him. Because he's a fun guy to be around. And I learned so much from him from these past seven years. I just think the world of him. I just went

313

to his 90 birthday. And it was more fun than the majority of birthday parties I've been to put together.

HK: Let's talk about Russ Solomon. Working with him and how you wanted to present him.

CH: Russ was very adamant about being honest. I almost kind of laugh at my idea of what he was like prior to our first meeting with him. I was incredibly intrigued by this idea of this guy who starts off selling used records out of his father's drug store, 1940s Americana. Drug store pharmacy, and then ends up with this gigantic huge company. And we got this meeting with Russ, and a pre-conceived notion of who a CEO guy would be, and then you meet Russ and I mean, he's just the coolest guy in the world. He's very friendly, nice, sharp and funny. And he laughed at us at first. "Let's do it, but you guys are crazy. You're nuts and you're never gonna make any money." I'm still trying to prove him wrong on that one.

Russ was adamant about a couple of things: First he was adamant that no one would really want to see this documentary. And that's his modesty kicking in. He's one of the most modest people I've ever met in my life, which is incredible. And he was adamant that the story wasn't his story but really about the people who worked at the store. And he insisted we interview a handful of people and helped introduce us to those people. And that was really when the doc started to take on this other life of its own, and the story was really coming to us as opposed to the other way around.

Because Russ is the kind of guy who not only managed this way but he is this way. It's much more about the team. What everyone is able to do as a family as opposed to any one individual effort. And to have that point of view is incredible. And for us, to hear from the other people, saying Russ told me I should do this and Russ told me I should tell the truth from their perspective. That kind of assistance I can't even begin to describe how important that was. And we didn't even have to try and bring that out of people. Russ would say, "They're really good. You just tell them what you want. You tell them the truth and your opinions and let's help these kids out." Without that, this movie does not work. Without that we don't have a movie. *laughs.*

HK: Bruce Springsteen and Elton John are wonderful talking heads in the movie. Bruce and Elton John reinforced to me that they're record geeks and collectors. Like all of us.

CH: Absolutely. I knew very early on just from the stories that I had read and also been told, you know, from the Tower people, that Elton, has this very famous quote, that "if he had to do it all over again the job he would plug for the most was Tower Records." And I knew about his connection and passion for the store. I said, "If this is going to be the definitive Tower Records documentary, then we have to have Elton John." So we did everything we possibly could to get him in the documentary. And both Elton and his team were incredibly gracious to us in helping make that happen.

The same goes for Bruce. The funny thing about Bruce was, when he came to the interview, he actually said to me, "I don't know how many Tower stories I have." I said, "Don't worry about it. I'll just ask you some questions, and if you think there is anything you can't speak to, don't worry about it." I asked him one question, and he talked for about 15 minutes. Almost everything he said in the documentary was in those first 15 minutes. I asked him maybe five questions. That was the interview. He really came in.

The biggest thing about getting Elton and Bruce, those two, and I can't say this about Dave Grohl, because he worked at a Tower, and that was a very specific reason why I spoke with him, but with Bruce and Elton, they just shopped at the store. That was it. That was all they did. One bought prolifically from Tower Records in Los Angeles as well as Atlanta. And Bruce sort of seems to me the guy who hung out there a lot. And he kind of speaks to that.

Look, there's a reason why they are who they are. 'Cause when you get them in front of a camera and you ask them something, or a question about a subject matter that they are passionate about, which is music or buying records, they will give you the good quote. They will give you the goods. And they were both fantastic. And Elton said one line that he gave us that we actually didn't put in the film, that was very funny. He said "buying records was better than sex." I almost fought to keep that in. When they give you so much good stuff you kind of have to share something for the DVD. *laughs.*

HK: Your movie title is *All Things Must Pass*. And the *All Things Must Pass* George Harrison recording, produced with Phil Spector, runs over your end screen credits. Talk about the process securing licensing and permission for usage from Olivia and Dhani Harrison.
CH: *All Things Must Pass* was not always the title of the film. At the very early stages, and I was trying to make it, I obviously had an idea

of what I wanted the story to be. I didn't really know what the theme was. I was asked, "So what's like the theme of the film?" I still didn't have an answer for that. I talked a little about this in the Kickstarter video. But I went up to Sacramento on a lark and decided to drive by the old Tower store which was still there and intact. And that sign was still up. The *All Things Must Pass* Thanks Sacramento. And I just went, "Oh My Gosh! That's the theme."

Even the best parties have to end. And all things must pass. So that was really, for lack of a better phrase, that was a pretty obvious sign of what this thing needed to be called. And obviously it made perfect sense thematically. I really liked the fact it was a store employee that put that sign up. I thought there was some poetry in that. And, obviously, I wanted to do everything I could to use the song. But I'm also cognizant of the fact, very respectful of the fact, that that song is personal to George. And has a very deep meaning. And, so I'm very fortunate that I've met Olivia on numerous occasions and that I met George once a long time ago. He was an incredibly kind man. I sent her the film and said, "I would really like to be able to call this movie *All Things Must Pass*. I'd really like to be able to use the song. But know you have final say on this. And you can not hurt my feelings in anyway shape or form. We'd be really honored if you let us do this." We sent her the film. She came back to me after a weekend. "I've watched it twice. I love it. I can't believe this story. What an incredible story. Yes. Absolutely. Go right ahead."

'Cause I really wanted all of the songs in the movie to represent a different section of a Tower Records. And I didn't get them all. *laughs.* I didn't get every genre but I was able to get quite a few.

So when we were making the documentary, I came up with a list of a bunch of songs and artists that I like and slipped that to my editor. "Here's a bunch of music that I dig. By all means find out whatever works." And I talked about the idea of wanting to find music for not only the eras in which the movie is taking place, with the stories taking place, all the different genres that would fit within a Tower Records. Deep catalogues and every different type of music imaginable. I want to make sure we can represent that as much as possible in the film. And Darrin Roberts, our editor, who is also a big music fanatic, he found stuff I had never heard of before. And we were able to incorporate a lot of that in the doc as well. It was really, "Let's find the right stuff. 'Cause at the end of the day, especially with movies, it ends up kind of being music telling you how to feel. And it was fun to be able to do that. I hope we can do a soundtrack."

Marko Budgyk. Financial adviser for Transameria volunteered, "I lived there. I went every weekend to the Tower store on Sunset Blvd. from age 10 until age 18 until I graduated from Beverly Hills High School going through all the bins."

Brian Wilson Musician/Record producer observed, "Tower Records always had the most complete collection of music available to anyone at any time. Their inventory of every kind of music was just great. They were the best."

Rodney Bingenheimer, Sirius XM Radio DJ testified, "Tower Records was where I got a lot of my imports, especially for my glitter/ glam club Rodney's English Disco. When that club was happening in full swing in the 70's, there was a British Import record I forgot to bring to play that evening. I ran down to Tower Sunset to see if they had it, and lo and behold - they had it, I got it and ran back to the club and immediately started spinning it...On any given night, you might run into Brian Wilson of the Beach Boys in one aisle or Jane Wiedlin of the Go-Go's in another aisle. Because Tower was open 10-Midnight, Every Night -- it was one of the best places to shop anywhere, because of the late hours. Their book section was amazing as well. You could browse there all night until closing. It was always 'All Happening' at Tower Records Sunset."

Ron Lando: Music memorabilia collector reflected, "In the early 70's I would hang out at Tower Records, Columbus and Bay Street in San Francisco. I would go in at all hours of the day (and night) just searching for everything I didn't have. Tower had a fabulous import section second to none. It was like being a kid in a candy store. Wow, how I miss that."

Harvey Kubernik: What attracted you to the story of Russ Solomon and Tower?
Sean Stuart: You never know until you sit down with the person who is going to be your interview subject and five minutes into the first conversation with Russ, Colin and I kind of gave each other a look and realized this is a special person and special story. We also realized as much as this is a music doc it's an incredible human doc. We knew

317

it was gonna be worth our time and energy and worth the effort over seven years.

HK: The movie incorporates a lot of archival footage. I never really thought of the ongoing music media coverage Russ and the chain received over decades as well as trade magazines.

SS: Because Tower was such a beloved company to so many of the people who worked for it I think we had an easier time, because a lot of people kept the material. Tower employees really cherished what the company achieved and what it had become. So we were pretty lucky to find willing participants in regards to giving us access to their archives and their material. And that was across the board with the artists, too. We didn't have to twist Bruce or Elton or David Geffen or Dave Grohl's arms to sit down and talk to us. People were willing to sit down and give their time. They were generous to talk about the company and the stores because it meant so much to the industry.

HK: As you dived into this project, as it went along, what became more obvious to you about Russ Solomon and the impact of the Tower Records chain?

SS: What we as filmmakers hope to achieve is to find the story, to find the theme, to find that overriding umbrella of a concept, a music documentary, and make it bigger. And find other places where people can grab onto things that are broader and more interesting and more identifiable.

HK: You've screened the movie at some festivals and special events, and now, as it goes into theatrical release in the US during October, what has been the response and interactions from former Tower customers and music fans? Are feedback and kudos even better than you imagined? You guys touched a nerve with this one, dude.

SS: I think we're constantly amazed how like 90 per cent of the people we bump into the topic of Tower comes up, and they all have a story about Tower. They know exactly where their Tower store was. And they know exactly what it meant to them and how important it was to their lives and how they consume music. It constantly blows us away how relevant this company was to the populace. It is a revolving thing for us everywhere we go and every time we walk into any room, cocktail or dinner parties, business meetings. "Sherman Oaks was my store!" "I grew up in Chicago!" It's pretty remarkable and exciting to kind of see that fabric come together with people and they light up and kind of ignite the conversation when they tell you their stories of how music changed their lives and Tower changed their lives.

HK: Talk to me about the music in the movie.
SS: There are always going to be record labels who are initially difficult to crack the egg with. I think in general, when we went to major artists for Steve Miller, the Beach Boys and the Rolling Stones that they really got a little reminiscent at times as well too, and they saw it as our history and legacy, and we need to jump in and help with this 'cause it's going to be a great story. You've gotta have a starting point with the music and the soundtrack with something like this. We knew when we saw the Tower Records marquee in Sacramento with *All Things Must Pass* that it was going to be our central song. We really wanted to build a soundtrack in this movie that represented the decades this company existed, that took you on an adventure through those decades and represented as many aisles in that Tower Records as possible. Our major focus was to put stuff in there that would really prop up the store you went into that had 10,000 titles, From soundtracks to world music to westerns, hip hop and really try and create this very diverse and all inclusive sound for everyone who came to see the movie.

In approaching rights holders and record labels, I think in a way they understand the story. They lived the story. They know what story we're telling from a broader music industry standpoint. No one really needed to know what the movie was about. For the most part they understood what we were trying to achieve and trying to do. Colin and I were quite vocal and very descriptive with all of them about what this movie was and meant to be. Most people were pretty excited to have this story told.

Mick Garris, filmmaker and author proudly confessed, "I was employed in the San Diego and Westwood stores, and filled in several times in Hollywood. That was 1975-77. I spent my allowance and my Wonder Years at Tower Records before I became an employee and acolyte. It changed my life in more ways than anyone can imagine: it was the sun at the center of my personal solar system, opening my life to life, love, music and movies! For better or worse, I would not be who I am without having passed through the Tower Dimension."

Michael Des Barres, Sirius XM Radio pointed out, "There were two places in Los Angeles where I knew I could escape. One was the self-realization fellowship on Sunset Boulevard where Paramahansa Yogananda taught - and the other was Tower Records also on Sunset. Worlds apart but not really, searching for rock 'n' roll records and self-awareness is to me is almost the same thing... either way, in both places I felt at peace and inspired all at once."

Peter Frampton, musician, said, "It was such an iconic place. To go there was always a rush .... *The* record store! Then, to finally go in there and see my album being sold, stacked in huge piles was surreal!"

Neil Norman, GNP Crescendo Records enthused "When Tower opened up, it really helped esoteric and unusual independent record labels like our now 62-year old GNP Crescendo Records, because they would literally carry everything. And of course, Tower on Sunset Blvd. was my second home. I hung out there as GNP Crescendo was right up the street. My father Gene Norman and Russ Solomon went back to the early fifties, were good buddies, and had a wonderful relationship. Russ was, and is, a real gentleman. The Tower chain was dynamite and sold hundreds of thousands of our records. Congratulations on the documentary."

Harvey Kubernik: Russ, why did you consent to actively participate in this film? How was their pitch?
Russ Solomon: From time to time, people talked to me about doing a book on the company. And a couple of guys started but didn't get anywhere with it. It's a pretty arduous thing to do if you gotta have a real job. And then Colin and Sean had this idea they came up with. There was a third partner, and he was very good friends with my dentist, and the dentist fixed us up and we had a meeting. And, of course, I told them right off the bat they were nuts. "Why would anyone want to see a movie about a record store?" They persevered, and seven years later there it is…

What they did was get a writer and made a story out of it, And, they got a good editor, and the whole thing came together. At the end of the day, after initially thinking, "how are they gonna pull this thing off?" I enjoyed it, actually. And I think it got over the essence of what we were all about.

HK: I think your plan to open a San Francisco store in 1967 was a big factor in expanding the Tower visibility, image and brand. Did the

Summer of Love energy play a part in the expansion. You subsequently opened a store in 1968.

RS: Well, it was very serendipitous to say the least. Between 1952 and 1960 I had another little company simultaneously to having a retail store here in Sacramento. We had a company called Record Supply, which was one of the very early rack jobber companies and one stops. And we had an office, a warehouse, in San Francisco, over on Mission. First of all, I was born there. OK? But I never really lived there. But I always believed that was the place to go, and oddly enough, I don't know why, but it seemed that we shouldn't be downtown, the business district. We had to be somewhere else that was right. And the accident of finding that place was marvelous.

The independent labels that came out of the fifties and early sixties helped drive the retail environment. The independent guys were the ones who started it and drove it forward. They were pretty marvelous. That was the heyday. People like Syd Nathan at King Records, Gene Norman at GNP Crescendo Records, and the Chess Brothers. The whole history of the Chess Records operation in Chicago. I could see the parallel between the way that business developed, although I never worked in a bar in downtown Chicago, and the rise and demise of that. And, those guys were opportunistic as hell when it came to buying their acts.

On the other hand, they also paid their acts, too, so they made some money. Tower stocked their blues. Gave it floor space. I think "my people" knew about it and liked it. If we had a kid in the store who liked blues or country music, we had a lot of blues and country music in that store. You hunt around for somebody to hire who really knows and loves the music.

You gotta look at the timing. We really hit it at exactly the right time. We had all that experience of selling music that came out after World War II; 1946 to 1967, and the idea that the Summer of Love had happened down at Monterey, and then *Rolling Stone* starting in 1967, really got going in 1968, the Fillmore just kind of getting started a little before then, all through those formative years, and the kids in Sacramento were going into San Francisco on the weekends, dressing up in what would be now called hippie clothes, and hanging out and bringing back the whole culture that was happening down there.

Sacramento was not that at all. We were hanging on to the coat tails of that, but Tower and us moved into San Francisco and became part of that swirl. I like to say that we got on the wave, and we rode the damn thing until we ran ashore. And, it could not have been a more perfect spot. From a standpoint of timing, it was an accident. The combination of Bill Graham, the Fillmore, *Rolling Stone*, and us, in the very beginning, for a little while, we were their number one sales outlet. They could put a whole pile of magazines in, and they'd all get sold. Tower was a destination stop. People saw one of Graham's shows, then went into the store and got an album. Not from the headliner, but one of the opening acts.

HK: Your concept of management.
RS: I always belonged to what I call the "Tom Sawyer Theory of Management." He sat back and watched the other people paint the fence. That's a good idea. First of all, they know more than I do. And they are on the street with it. What am I gonna do? Press my word or my tastes and everything else on them? Not a good idea. It was just a natural thing. I was also lucky, growing up in the retail business, at my dad's drug store, I started working there when I was 13 years-old, and he was a loose kind of guy. He was not a micro-manager or anything. He went into business without any money at all and worked hard and made a good living out of it. To me the whole idea was natural. It wasn't learned anyplace, except intuitively, and probably a certain amount of laziness.

One of the sadder stories about this, and in the movie, later on, when we got into financial trouble and so on, and the banks put on inexperienced people who did micro-manage, who did go for central buying and things like that, which I felt was a terrible idea. I fought it but I got nowhere".

Joe Satriani, Guitar virtuoso observed, "If it weren't for Tower Records in Berkeley, CA, I wouldn't have had a solo career. The retail staff and especially the art department supported my records like no other store. I always considered the Berkeley Tower store to be what all record stores should have been like: fun, unpredictable, chill, vital, supportive, professional and responsive to their community."

Carol Schofield, MsMusic Productions, remembered, "Tower Records. The supreme music store for a few generations of collectors. Tower was the place to go for music and people watching or quick hookups. San Francisco's Bay and Columbus location was the go-to place for new releases and simply to find the record that most

322

other places didn't have. Also, after seeing a band at the Fillmore or Winterland, we would head to Tower before midnight to get the latest release of a band we had just heard live. And working there was even better for a record collector, as the saying goes, a kid in a candy store. I spent almost a year employed at the Bay & Columbus location. The only drawback was getting carried away with buying records and then when my paycheck arrived it was a big oops! Check was low due to buying many records that had been deducted from pay...

"There were on occasion sightings of celebrities in the store. I recall Iggy Pop and Dolly Parton passing through the Bay & Columbus store. Truly the Mutha of all record stores."

Joe Smith: President and CEO Capitol-EMI Music 1987-1993, Chairman of Elektra/Asylum Records 1975-1983, President of Warner Bros. Records 1972-1975 told me, "Russ Solomon was a head case… He had crazy plans and thoughts. The kicker was that he could and he did make most of them happen. When one of our records got piled up on the floor, it was a reason for celebration. A great story of a great adventure that we in the business believed would have a limited life when the new technology arrived. It did and the great ride ended."

Larry LeBlanc: Senior Writer, *Celebrity Access* reported "Tower Records made a brief foray into the Canadian marketplace when it opened a flagship location in Toronto in the Jamieson Building on the corner of Yonge and Queen streets in late 1995.

"Tower founder Russ Solomon told me in a phone conversation then, when I was Canadian editor of *Billboard* magazine, that by opening up down the street from such competitors as Sam The Record Man, HMV, Sunrise Records, Music World, and Records on Wheels— Toronto's Record Alley--would lead to Tower eventually providing competition to market leaders Sam The Record Man, and HMV elsewhere.

"That didn't happen due to the music market beginning to crumble in the early '90s with the advent of internet downloading and competition from other forms of entertainment.

"What Tower did do was provide a stark music retail difference in Canadian music retail. Its two stores spilled over with frontline product at competitive prices, but, importantly, there was the best selection available of imported CDs---LPs, EPs, and extended singles with tracks mostly unavailable elsewhere.

"These extended singles in particular. I would weekly cherry-pick for my weekend Q107-FM radio show *From The Vaults* that was centered on recorded rarities.

"The Tower locations also had superb selections of books focused on music and contemporary culture mostly unavailable elsewhere in Toronto.

"Through many conversations with him, I knew that Russ had his eye on the Sam the Record Man national chain which was emblematic of Canada's music industry for over 50 years. Prior to Sam the Record Man, operated by the Sniderman brothers, Sam and Sid, being forced into bankruptcy in 2001, Sam Sniderman had lobbied Russ for years to buy in full or a portion of the 250 store chain.

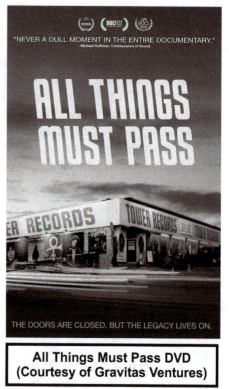

All Things Must Pass DVD
(Courtesy of Gravitas Ventures)

"Russ explained to me prior to coming to Toronto that many of the Sam retail locations were in malls with too high rents, and that the Sniderman family owned the real estate of the prime big city locations, so a buy-out was not in the cards. He'd go it alone by opening in Toronto, Montreal, and Vancouver.

"Tower Records never grew in Canada beyond the two outlets in Toronto which closed in 2001."

(After the chain's bankruptcy, Sam Sniderman's sons Jason and Robert took over the reins of the flagship Yonge St. store. The two men kept the store running until 2007.)

Trailblazing Pop Music Television:
Shindig! Shebang! and *Upbeat*

Jack Good: *Shindig!*

It's never been lost on me how important some daily and weekly local and national music television shows from the sixties impacted my life, setting the stage for me to watch and further investigate rock 'n' roll documentaries, now incorporating archival footage culled from *Shindig!, Shebang!* and *Upbeat.*

Jack Good, producer of the landmark *Shindig!* series passed away on September 24, 2017. Good also produced a very early TV special *Around the Beatles* in 1964.

Shindig! was a seminal pop and rock music series. It debuted September 1964, ran through 1965, and was shot in Los Angeles at the ABC Prospect Avenue studios in Hollywood. Initially it was a weekly half-hour spot that was extended to two weekly half hour episodes.

I went to live tapings as a teenager. I have a fond memory of the Four Tops in 1965. Singer Levi Stubbs and the group sung over a pre-recorded track by the *Shindig!* house band. The show might have been broadcast nationally in black and white, but what I saw was in living color. The Four Tops were clad in matching iridescent green suits, moving to "I Can't Help Myself (Sugar Pie Honey Bunch)."

Andrew Loog Oldham was the manager/record producer of the Rolling Stones 1963-1967 when his band secured a slot on *Shindig!* in 1965 that also showcased Howlin' Wolf.

During a 2004 interview for my book *Hollywood Shack Job: Rock Music In Film and on Your Screen*, Oldham told me, "The British fashion business was the first pop business. At the same time, poor British pop music had its moments, grand magical moments like Jack Good's TV shows, *Oh, Boy!* and *Boy Meets Girl*, but the music we had was hardly exportable. All that ever got out and onto *The Ed Sullivan Show* and the American airwaves was the one-offs and the freaks—Acker Bilk, Jackie Dennis and Laurie London.

"The music was shite-with a few exceptions, like Lonnie Donegan whose earnestness and belief was almost evangelical-the rest were a bunch of lame skiffers and jazz musicians who thought they were in a lamentable kindergarden, which they were.

"Yes, we had Eddie Cochran, Little Richard, Duane Eddy and Buddy Holly and the rest, but it had been a fight. How vaudeville and

World War II begot a middle class trad-jazz which begot skiffle and imitative well-meaning pop and eventually this little cluster of about 300 white kids with a passion for rhythm 'n' blues. How before the Beatles there was a Jack Good, Eddie Cochran, Little Richard, Buddy Holly, Billy Fury, Marty Wilde and Cliff Richard and the Shadows that ran that first all-important mile."

In my 2014 title, *Turn Up the Radio! Rock, Pop, and Roll in Los Angeles 1956–1972*, singer/pianist/songwriter Ian Whitcomb reflected on *Shindig!* (Jimmy O'Neill served as the host.)

"I had been a guest several times on producer Jack Good's TV series, *Shindig!* that was filmed in Hollywood at ABC-TV. Jack had a background in drama at Oxford. When he did the earlier *Oh Boy!* television music series in England, he had everything organized and synchronized. So Jack saw the dramatic potential of rock 'n' roll. To that point, it hadn't been exploited or explored in this country. You simply had teenage kids dancing with each other on the Dick Clark shows. Jack had this dramatic view. The *Shindig!* shows were done live, and some of the backing tracks of the music were done on Melrose Avenue at Nashville West, next to Nickodell Restaurant near Paramount Studios. It took a week to make a *Shindig!*"

In a 2000 interview I talked about *Shindig!* with keyboardist/ arranger/composer/and producer Jack Nitzsche.

"I spent a day with Howlin' Wolf on the set of *Shindig!* I went down there with the Stones, and Sonny & Cher were there, too. So Sonny introduced me to Howlin' Wolf, and I was speechless. He was imposing. There was a sweetness in there you could see. And anyway, we were sitting there for a long time, and he was sitting next to me ,and he had a friend with him who was a little older, and strange. He wore a cowboy hat, boots and a bolo tie. Western attire. We sat together, and I was content just to sit and not even speak. Just to be in the man's presence, ya know.

"So, after a while, we got to talking and he became more comfortable. So did I. He said, 'I didn't introduce you to my friend. Jack, this is Son House.'

"I'm sitting with Wolf and Son House. I saw the Stones sitting around Howlin' Wolf when he performed. You should have seen the take they stopped. They made him stop in the midst of a take. 'Cause he was like 300 pounds. Huge and he had a toy harmonica, a tiny harmonica that he would put in his mouth. He could hold it between his lips. Oh man. So, he got up there on stage to do his set and he

326

put that little harmonica in his mouth. That was the surprise. The band was playing, and it came time for the instrumental and he was kinda dancin' around when he came up again for air, he was playing harmonica and holding the microphone. It was theatrical and funny stuff for the fish fry.

"You could really hear Leon Russell play in the *Shindig!* television band. In 1964 I put him in the *TAMI Show* band, and he's all over the soundtrack. He was good."

Leon Russell in a 2010 interview with Jeff Tamarkin, displayed in 2020 on bestclassicbands.com, asked the multi-instrumentalist if he had fun in the *Shindig!* house band.

"Yeah, I guess so. It was something I'd never done before. Jack Good was the producer and he had, in my opinion, odd taste in music. He wanted to make me a star and wanted me to sing every week, and he wanted to film me walking up a ramp so the audience could see my limp."

**Shindig! producer, Jack Good
(Photo by Richard Furmanek)**

In 1985, I watched a Marvin Hagler and Thomas Hearns boxing match with Jack Nitzsche and Denny Bruce inside Bruce's Bel-Air home. That night Nitzsche touted and endorsed Good's vision for *Shindig!* but also bashed ABC-TV executives and programming censors who refused having race mixed recording artists vocalizing together on camera in their early 1964 pilot for *Shindig!*

Network brass didn't want Jack Nitzsche's Caucasian wife, Gracia, a studio background singer and a regular member of the Blossoms, *Shindig!* regulars, to appear on screen during the weekly series with them.

By January '66, Jack Good had his final argument with ABC management, splitting from *Shindig!* He went on to produce the locally lensed TV special *33 1/3 Revolutions per Monkee* that was broadcast on NBC-TV on April 14, 1969. Fats Domino, Little Richard, Jerry Lee Lewis, the Clara Ward Singers, the Buddy Miles Express and Brian Auger, Julie Driscoll and the Trinity were the guests.

Casey Kasem: *Shebang!*

When radio and television veteran Casey Kasem (April 27, 1932-June 15, 2014) died, *Billboard Magazine* asked me to write a tribute to him.

I first remember hearing the smooth, dulcet tones of Casey Kasem on the Pasadena, California-based radio station KRLA in the summer of 1963 while living in West Hollywood, where the disc jockey shared the dial with Bob Eubanks, Dave Hull and Jimmy O'Neill.

During his 1963-'69 tenure at the Top 40 powerhouse, Casey introduced us to the sounds of Sonny & Cher, the Bobby Fuller Four and Thee Midniters. He was an early advocate of the R&B music coming from East Los Angeles, spinning the Premiers' "Farmer John" and Cannibal and the Headhunters'

"Land of a 1000 Dances."

Gene Aguilera and Casey Kasem (Photo courtesy of Gene Aguilera)

In the '60s, I would see Casey at events in the San Fernando Valley or at the annual Teenage Fair held at the Hollywood Palladium. He was an accessible radio personality who had the rare ability to establish a firm connection to our ears. His vocals were perfectly attuned to our newly acquired transistor radios. Kasem's approach was not frenetic, like many of his peers, but pleasant, conversational and confessional. We trusted him when he was reading on-air spots for Coppertone suntan lotion.

On his afternoon shift, Casey would offer biographical information and anecdotes about each record. He'd mention who wrote or recorded the songs and their former occupations. His narrative glued us to the KRLA dial button just to hear what hit songs he would play next.

In early 1966, I danced for a few episodes on the KTLA television program *Shebang!*, a live daily afternoon teenage music show from Hollywood hosted by Kasem and produced by fellow DJ-turned-entrepreneur Dick Clark. During breaks off-camera, Casey would discuss current tunes on the Top 40 with the enthralled audience.

He told us how he originally wanted to be an actor. I really thought he was cool when I saw him in the 1967 outlaw biker movie *The Glory Stompers* with Dennis Hopper and Jock Mahoney at the Gilmore Drive-In.

The Doors, the Beau Brummels, the Seeds, Ian Whitcomb, the Turtles, Rudy Vallee and Brenton Wood all appeared on *Shebang!* Kasem and Clark introduced us to dancers like Famous Hooks and two-step king Buddy Schwimmer.

In 1970, Kasem, his friend Don Bustany, former KHJ program director Ron Jacobs, along with radio executive Tom Rounds, jointly created the American Top 40 syndicated format, where Casey served as host from 1970-'88.

In 1979, working as West Coast Director of A&R for MCA Records, I crossed paths with Casey. I was toying with the idea of producing spoken-word albums with Charles Bukowski and Allen Ginsberg. Various company employees frowned on the idea, but Casey was encouraging, and cited the Caedmon Records label, which released albums by poets Dylan Thomas and Robert Frost.

Kasem explained it all in that wonderful storytelling style that can only be compared to another local legend, Vin Scully, the Dodger announcer, describing the action on the baseball diamond.

Casey Kasem was just as influential as a figure in L.A. radio lore, a regional discovery who became a national treasure.

Don Webster: *Upbeat*

There are some things you need to write about.

Don Webster (May 6, 1939-December 13, 2018) died at the age of 79. Webster served as host of *Upbeat*, before embarking on a 35-year career which included a longtime meteorologist spot at News 5 in Cleveland. Don Webster was one of the original hosts of the long-running daily talk show *The Morning Exchange*, a former No. 1 rated program that subsequently influenced the launch of early morning programming like *Good Morning America*. He later hosted the quiz show *Academic Challenge*. In 1994 the Hamilton, Ontario-born Webster was inducted into the Broadcaster's Hall of Fame.

In 1964 Webster became the host of the music variety one hour TV program *Upbeat* that originated from WEWS-TV 5, an ABC-TV affiliate, in Cleveland that was broadcast on Saturdays 5-6:00 pm during 1964-1971 and syndicated in over 100 US markets. It was a black and white program during 1964-1967, and then produced in color from 1967 until the series demise in 1971.

By 1966, Hollywood still carried *The Lloyd Thaxton Show* on KCOP-TV, in daily national syndication from 1964-1968. Coach Earl Dean Smith, one of the Physical Education teachers from Fairfax High School, who cut records for independent labels and danced on *Shebang!* and *Thaxton*, took selected students to some *Thaxton* bookings. I'm still recovering from seeing James Brown, the Turtles and Major Lance.

But during 1966, *Hullabaloo* and *Shindig!*, weekly network music television programs had been cancelled. I was devastated. But the saving grace of live televised rock 'n' roll shows in the United States was *Upbeat*.

I relished *The Ed Sullivan Show* weekly Sunday night showcase of guests, and *American Bandstand* always booked live acts that lip-synced on fast and slow dance numbers for the viewers, but *Upbeat* featured eight to ten recording artists playing live. It was my ritual every Saturday afternoon from Cleveland ,Ohio that was thankfully broadcast in Hollywood.

Upbeat really made an impact on me. I cited it in my 2004 book *Hollywood Shack Job: Rock Music In Film and on Your Screen.*

In summer of 2017, I was an invited guest lecturer in the author series held at The Rock and Roll Hall of Fame Archives in Cleveland, discussing my just published *1967 A Complete Rock History of The Summer of Love.*

I must have spent 15 minutes just praising *Upbeat* to the highly receptive local crowd and acknowledging the efforts of producer Herman Spero.

I interviewed David Spero, son of Herman, for my *1967* book. David was a rock-radio fixture in the 1970s and for many years has been a very active music manager. He reflected on the *Upbeat* ground-breaking screen achievements with me.

"The whole purpose of the show and what my dad was trying to do at the time he watched *American Bandstand* and *Robin Seymour's Swingin' Time* show out in Detroit, *Ed Sullivan*, one artist two songs, and all the rest were dance numbers. And what he wanted to do was take Top 40 radio and put it on TV. And that was the goal with *Upbeat*."

Young Spero held up cue cards for Webster, wrote out questions for the host to answer on-air, and served "as the dancers' and artists' best friend" beginning at age 13.

Simon (right), Garfunkel (left) and host Don Webster (center)
(Photo courtesy of David Spero)

Simon and Garfunkel made their first-time-ever TV appearance on *Upbeat*. I could be watching Dizzy Gillespie and Gene Krupa alongside the Box Tops, Aretha Franklin, the Temptations, Jackie Wilson, Tommy James & the Shondells, Otis Redding, Terry Knight and the Pack, Jerry Butler, Bobby Goldsboro, the Yardbirds, Lesley Gore, Guess Who, Lou Christie, Davy Jones and Micky Dolenz, B.B. King, Gene Pitney, Smokey Robinson & the Miracles, Johnny Nash,

331

the Bar-Kays, Paul Revere and the Raiders, Sly & the Family Stone and Mitch Ryder. Webster interviewed the Beatles and the Rolling Stones.

"There were never any race meetings on *Upbeat*," Spero accented to me. 'Oh my God! The show is all black!' If that's what it was, that's what it was. There was never a meeting 'whose going to be our Motown act this week?' It was always the opposite.

"We were fortunate in Cleveland to have so much music coming through the town. Love, Simon and Garfunkel, the Velvet Underground did *Upbeat*.

"We had a place called Leo's Casino, and the only white group that ever played there was Wayne Cochran and the C.C. Riders. It was all Motown and Stax.

"Otis had been on the show six or seven times," recalled Spero. "He was like a member of the family. He was the first person I knew who died. Otis performed at Leo's Casino that night after doing the *Upbeat* show. He was leaving on Sunday. He had played cards with my dad on Friday or Saturday night. I do know I have a copy of the check; he signed it on the back because he had lost $209 to my dad playing cards and everyone playing cards and endorsed the check to my dad, which is why it wasn't in his pocket when he died.

"I literally spent four or five hours with Otis the day before. He was a young guy. He seemed much younger than he was."

Don Webster interviewing Tommy James (Photo courtesy of David Spero)

Don Webster and David Spero (Photo courtesy of David Spero)

Seymour Cassel,
Dispatches from the Celluloid Trenches

Photo of Seymour Cassel (Courtesy of Stars North)

American actor and storyteller Seymour Joseph Cassel, was born January 22, 1935 in Detroit, Michigan and died in Los Angeles, California April 7, 2019.

Over his 50-year film and television career Cassell was best known as a member of John Cassavetes' informal family of actors in addition to working with independent and veteran filmmakers.

Cassel was always involved with the regional Hollywood and Los Angeles musical community. Numerous movies he did utilized pop, jazz and rock music in the soundtracks.

As a tyke, Seymour traveled with his mother in a burlesque troupe and lived with her for several years in Panama, where his family owned a nightclub.

After a stint in the Navy, Cassel moved to New York City to pursue an acting career. He studied at the American Theatre Wing and with Lee Strasberg's famed Actors Studio.

Cassel then met Cassavetes at the future director's 46th Street acting workshop in 1957, eventually teaching alongside him and serving as associate producer on Cassavetes' 1960 landmark influential directorial debut, *Shadows*. During 1961 he then had a small role in Cassavetes' *Too Late Blues*. Credits in *Murder, Inc., Juke Box Racket*, Don Chaffey's *The Webster Boy* and Don Siegel's *The Killers* (1964) followed.

From 1961-1968 Cassel appeared in many episodic television programs: *Twelve O'Clock High, Combat!, The F.B.I., Burke's Law The Twilight Zone, Voyage to the Bottom of the Sea, The Fugitive* and *Batman*.

Seymour Cassel first achieved prominence as the hippie street hustler in Cassavetes' *Faces*. A movie that ushered in and positioned independent cinema into the retail marketplace. The 1968 feature earned Cassel an Academy Award nomination as Best Supporting Actor.

Cassel's most noticeable role for Cassavetes was when he was cast opposite the director's wife Gena Rowlands in the 1971 romantic comedy *Minnie and Moskowitz*. I remember eating at Pink's Hot Dogs on La Brea Ave. when Cassavetes filmed their scene on the premises with Seymour and Gena.

Cassel had support jobs in other Cassavetes endeavors *The Killing of a Chinese Bookie, Love Streams*, and a cameo moment in *Opening Night*, before choosing his screen time between major Hollywood pictures and independent ventures.

Seymour was in Barry Levinson's 1987 *Tin Men*, playing Cheese, and credited as Sam Catchem in Warren Beatty-directed *Dick Tracy*. Cassel appeared in director Andrew Bergman's *Honeymoon in Las Vegas* and *It Could Happen to You*. Seymour was then spotlighted in director Alexandre Rockwell's *In The Soup*.

Additional Cassel screen efforts include Adrian Lyne's *Indecent Proposal*, Steve Buscemi's *Trees Lounge* and a trilogy of Wes Anderson cinematic expeditions *Rushmore, The Royal Tenenbaums* and *The Life Aquatic with Steve Zissou*.

Cassel also starred with television actress Margaret Blye in *Time & Again*, a 35 mm short film written and directed by Todd Thompson.

In 2006, Seymour co-starred in the NBC TV series, *Heist*, and in four seasons of Tracey Ullman's *Tracey Takes On...* comedy series for HBO.

During 2007 and 2009, Seymour Cassel was a candidate for national president of the Screen Actors Guild, but lost both times.

In 2009, Cassel worked in *The Flight of the Conchords* and *Crash*.

Cassel has always been very supportive of the American independent film community, and following Cassavetes' death in 1989, Seymour with Gena Rowlands were often feted at national and global film festivals saluting Cassavetes' enduring legacy. Seymour is featured in filmmaker Michael Ventura's 1989 documentary *I'm Almost Not Crazy: John Cassavetes, the Man and His Work*. Writer and director Ventura chronicled Cassavetes in 1984 around the making of the last film he wrote and directed, *Love Streams*. The documentary is incorporated on the 2014 Criterion Collection release of *Love Streams* with a 2008 Cassel interview.

In 2010, I met up with Seymour Cassel one afternoon at the Rose Café in Venice, California. Over lunch we discussed his peripatetic acting career, John Cassavetes, Seymour's encounters with Dennis Hopper, Quinn Martin, Jimi Hendrix, Jim Morrison, Bob Dylan, Sam Pekinpah, and Slash over his last 50 years in Hollywood.

Harvey Kubernik: You grew up around the burlesque circuit as a kid traveling with your mother across the US in the late 1940s.
Seymour Cassel: Everybody loved me and I was the only kid. My mother was with Minsky's Burlesque. We'd travel to New York, Washington D.C., Kansas City and out to Los Angeles and Hollywood at the end of World War II. We pulled into the train station in downtown L.A. and I thought it was a cathedral. Because it had the great look. Taking the train from New York to L.A. and seeing all those Burma Shave signs.

HK: What was New York City like in the 1950's?
SC: I lived there as a kid. I'd wander around and no one would bother me. I could hear Billie Holiday, not see her, outside a music club on 52nd Street. I then saw Charles Mingus at The Five Spot and Birdland. I saw Lenny Bruce perform in New York.
As an actor, John Cassavetes was the best. I studied with Lonnie Chapman and Kirk Conway. But John, because we were friends,

and saw each other in New York when he was there cutting *Shadows*.

We'd go out together. I met everyone through him. Tennessee Williams and Budd Shulberg, who did *On the Waterfront* with Marlon Brando and Eva Marie Saint. I watched him in *On the Waterfront*. She was great. I almost did a movie with Marlon. Then I really got to know him out in L.A.

HK: Did working with John Cassavetes fortify your support for independent film?

SC: First of all, John was fed up with movies that weren't good. So, with *Shadows*, which was an experiment, that's where I met him.

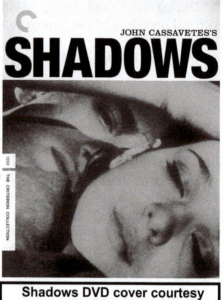

Shadows DVD cover courtesy of the Criterion Collection

HK: *Shadows,* which was released in November of 1959, was an improvisational film with a jazz score that captured interracial friendships and relationships around New York City. The actors included Lelia Goldoni, Ben Carruthers, Anthony Ray, Hugh Hurd, and Rupert Crosse. Rupert later lived in Laurel Canyon and was a friend of Robert Marchese and yourself.

SC: They had already started shooting *Shadows* the week before I met John. I initially encountered him at the 46th Street acting workshop in 1957. I talked to John and told him I was here for the free scholarship, and he asked me to come into an office. We talked in his office for 50 minutes. He wanted to know my background.

"My mother was a dancer with Minsky's." He said, "My partner, Burt Lane is teaching a class, and I got to go and shoot this movie." "Where?" "Here." "Can I watch?" "Sure."

So I went in the room and sat on a movie seat with hardwood. It was the set for *Shadows*, the kitchen, the dining room. Erich Kollmar was the cameraman that John had met. I set my watch and every time John would change the angle and want to shoot a scene, he had to unscrew the camera and take the camera to where it was gonna be and come back and get the tripod. So I just started helping. I was there until about 5 or 6 in the morning,

And John said, "What do you think? This is the way we do it." I said I had never seen anything like that. "When are you doing it again?" "Tonight." "Can I come back?" "Sure." I became associate producer of *Shadows*.

HK: You might have been one of the first New York actors to relocate to Hollywood in the very early '60s, but remained one of those transplanted New Yorkers who doesn't dislike the town or culture. Why have you remained here for 50 years?
SC: Because when I saw the film system out here and saw MGM and John taught me about movies, and not just American movies. Foreign movies. "Have you ever seen *La Terra Trema*? A Visconti film. What did you think?" "I didn't know who the actors were." "That's because they were mixed in with the real fishermen."

That was the whole thing. Acting should be a natural extension of your performance ability. It shouldn't be somebody acting for you.

HK: Did you know a new form of movie-making or an art form was being invented by watching and working with him?
SC: I became aware that the 4th wall was being eliminated. And I just realized I was becoming part of making that movie, and John's ideas were so independent and not collective thought.

HK: When you arrived you did black and white episodic television like *Twelve O'Clock High, Combat!, The F.B.I., Wagon Train*. I remember you from *The Twilight Zone* and *The Self-Improvement of Salvadore Ross*. In 1967 you appeared in the long-anticipated finale of *The Fugitive*. A lot of viewers checked out that Quinn Martin series.
SC: I did *Twelve O'Clock High* for director Leo Penn. I did a handful of those episodes and pilots. And whatever television I could. In 1961 I had already done the movie *Too Late Blues* for John (Cassavetes) and *The Lloyd Bridges Show*. I just did television for the work and to make the money, either a *Twilight Zone* or *Twelve O'Clock High*.

"I did *Combat!* with Vic Morrow. He was great, and *The Fugitive* conclusion episode, *The Judgement,* for producer Quinn Martin. *Twilight Zone's* Rod Serling was a bright guy. I knew writers like Paddy Chayefsky from New York. And directors from New York like

337

Sean Penn's father, Leo Penn. Leo was the best, because he understood actors and started in New York, and because his wife was an actress.

"John had done live television all during the fifties including *Johnny Staccato* in 1959 and '60. John didn't like doing television. Later when we were doing *Faces* and after we were done, he made a deal with Lew Wasserman who ran the Black Tower at Universal to do four pilots so he could pay back the money he spent on *Faces*, because he had mortgaged his house.

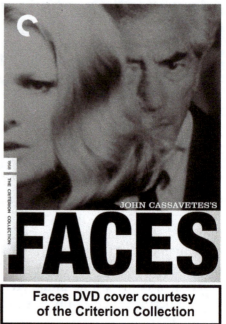

Faces DVD cover courtesy of the Criterion Collection

HK: What was the scene like in Laurel Canyon and Hollywood 1962-1972?

SC: In Laurel Canyon there was a lot of partying. I was living in Laurel Canyon under the Canyon Store. Early '60s. I was up there and the guy who had the restaurant next to the store, which is now the restaurant Pace, said there was an apartment for rent for $80.00 a month. The owner who had the store had the building, big huge living room. Kitchen, bedroom, and a shower. I took it.

I had two friends who worked as waiters in the restaurant, before I got married. They would bring me food. Laurel Canyon was great and it was before the musicians moved in, actors, beatniks and hippies.

HK: You also attended the '67 L.A. Love-Ins at Elysian Park and Griffith Park and up in San Francisco, as well as the Monterey International Pop Festival.

SC: In a way Monterey was just an extension of Elysian Park and all the things from Sunset Strip and Laurel Canyon. I had already seen girls without bras and the free love thing locally before I went up there. I went to The Monterey International Pop Festival in 1967 with my wife Betty and with our son who was about three or four at the time.

Lou Adler gave me a photographer's pass everyday. At first it was Alan Pariser's and Ben Shapiro's idea but the original concept changed. I bought Ben's house on King's Road. I used to go to his Renaissance Club. Alan's place in Laurel Canyon was a party house.

I met Jimi Hendrix at Monterey. I was in the photo pit and I got shots of him destroying the guitar. I was standing in the pit next to the stage and got some shots while he lit the guitar on fire. Tiny Tim was there. It was a new world at Monterey and L.A. We stayed in Big Sur at this little place, a little cabin by the river.

Otis Redding at Monterey...I saw him at the Whisky in 1966. I liked Jefferson Airplane and Janis (Joplin) at the festival. I met her up there and she moved down to Laurel Canyon. She was great, very free as a woman then. Her own thinker. Her performance at Monterey... She blew the festival away along with Otis and his band and Hendrix. Otis with that band...Life was great.

I later saw Jimi at the (Laurel) Canyon Store. I knew his music. He used to baby sit my son so my (then) wife Betty and I could go out. I loved Jimi, man. I saw him in '68 at a Shrine Auditorium concert. He had the most beautiful girlfriend. I tried to get some of his music in our film *Faces*.

As an actor Cassavetes really brought it out in me in *Faces*. I did all the music in the beginning because we couldn't get (Jimi) Hendrix. So I made up the songs. Or, when we couldn't use the Jimi Hendrix music in *Faces,* I just started to sing "put on the red meat mama." I just made it up. I could do that. And acting is performing.

I tried to get Jimmy Reed for the music. And so I took John to the Whisky a Go Go. We knew the owner Elmer Valentine, and Mario [Maglieri] who had the club. So we go to the Whisky, and I knew Jimmy from years earlier when I had taken some lessons from him at The Ash Grove. We didn't get to use his music.

Faces was written for me, when John gave me the script the first time under another title. And I started to read it. OK and I started to take it home. "Where are you going?" "Should I read it out loud?" "Read it here." I read it and thought it was great. "You're too old for that part, aren't you?" "You wrote that for me." We started it at the Whisky,

I did improv in *Faces* and *The Killing of a Chinese Bookie* because John knew me, and I never did something just to make me look good. I did it to make the actors enjoy me.

HK: One evening I saw you and Cassavetes in the late seventies doing a video shoot of Blondie at the Whisky a Go Go.

SC: I could always get into the Whisky because Elmer Valentine and Mario at the door took care of me. We gave Elmer a piece of the Cassavetes film *Faces* so we could shoot at the Whisky. We also plastered posters of *Faces* on Sunset Blvd.

HK: Bob Dylan was a fan of *Faces*.

SC: I knew The Band who worked with Dylan earlier when they played with Ronnie Hawkins. Levon (Helm) and Rick Danko. Cassavetes, Al Ruban, and I took the *Faces* movie and showed it free at midnight in three different places. Toronto, Montreal, and New York at the Capitol Theater. Bob (Dylan) had seen it there.

So, I'm in New York and about to go back home. And I get a call from Woodstock and asked to come up for a Fourth of July weekend. And all Bob wanted to know was how we shot the movie, what kind of cameras did we use?

He had seen *Faces* and wanted to make a movie. And I told him we only had two cameras, and we'd shoot with a crew of six and take turns. And John financed the whole thing. And that's what Bob went ahead and did. I know his sons.

HK: I would see you occasionally on Sunset Blvd. in the late 1960s and all through the '70s.

SC: There was a place where John liked to go, because he had a little more money, Cock 'N Bull, (director) Sam Pekinpah's watering hole. Sunset Strip when the open hippie thing happened with no bra. And nudie bars. I pulled three girls out of The Body Shop on Sunset Blvd. for *The Killing of a Chinese Bookie*. We hired them.

HK: You encountered Jim Morrison in Laurel Canyon and around Hollywood drinking and restaurant establishments. In 1969 you did a poetry reading with Jim, who was backed by Robby Krieger, at the Cinematheque 16 Theater. It was a fundraiser for Norman Mailer's bid for Mayor of New York City in 1969. The Doors' *Feast of Friends* and Andy Warhol's *I, a Man* films were screened. A live reading with Morrison, Michael McClure, Tom Baker, Mary Waronov, Michael C. Ford and Jamie Sanchez.

SC: Jim and I would read poetry on Sundays. I saw the Doors at the London Fog and the Whisky a Go Go. Jim had the same commitment to his art that Bob Dylan had. That any musician had. We would meet

340

and read poetry. The guy who ran the Cinematheque 16 later had the Tiffany Theater where *Faces* opened up, that was further up on Sunset Blvd. We had just met each other. It was a small town then. Jim was a big drinker. We all had become drinkers. He liked Jack Daniels. I know about the Love Street house. For this reading I did poems Jim gave me and drank beer.

I knew Gram Parsons. Members of the Flying Burrito Brothers lived next door to me on Weepah Way. I liked all the guys. Nobody bothered us up there. I remember when Gram died in Joshua Tree.

HK: The Guns N' Roses guitarist Slash (Saul Hudson) was a childhood friend of your son Matt. Slash has credited you with giving him the name "Slash." He recently told me, "I love Seymour. I had some crazy times with him over the years." I knew his mother, Ola, who was a terrific clothing designer. I would imagine long before his life with Guns N' Roses, you saw Slash gig on stage.

SC: See him on stage? He played at my house for my daughter's 16th birthday. Saul was friends with my son from school and Ola made the dress my wife wore to the Oscars when I was nominated for *Faces*. We became friends with her and her husband Tony. We would all see each other.

I had a house on Kings Road and Saul and Matt would run through the house as I would sit around, reading *The Los Angeles Times Sports* section, seeing how my Detroit teams like the Tigers, Red Wings and Lions were doing. I'd be reading the paper, and Saul and Matt, maybe age eight or nine then and later even at Fairfax High, they would chase each other around. I said, "Take it outside. You got two thirds of an acre and freedom. Hey Slash. Take out the breeze." "Why do you call me Slash?" "Cause you keep slashing in and out." So he took the name. I'd go to see Guns N' Roses at The Starwood. They played in our house. His hard work paid off. He's good.

HK: Does a film start with the story or the script?

SC: And the actors. Chemistry is important. I never had a part I couldn't contribute to. You give me something to read and I'm gonna play this. Because I know there is something to play in there and I just do it. And John loved it. He would bite his hand during takes to stop himself from laughing. He and I thought a lot alike. Because I was the brother he lost. And he became the brother I never had. We were so closely entwined, because of our sense of humor and the way we played.

341

HK: You have always said, I'm sure this extends to the Cassavetes library, you are a big proponent of shooting a movie in sequence.

SC: Yes. For the performance, it helps the actors continue their character, if you start at the beginning that is the way the script progresses. You don't shoot the end at the beginning. That's for some studio. That's why we shot our movies the way we did. And then John has the faith in each actor to give something, and they needed it and enjoyed it.

HK: Let me ask you about a couple of actors you know and have worked with: Jack Nicholson and Warren Beatty.

SC: I used to play softball with Jack Nicholson. We were on the Raincheck team. Jimmy Caan. Jack is a great actor, because he found out the joy of performing. Once you realize that you can look at the other person by listening to them, it's working. It's about engaging each other. It's like, if you go up and meet a girl. I've had a lot of practice in that. Warren Beatty is a dog and as big a dog as Marlon. He knew how to work the system. I give him credit as an actor as he became a really good actor and a director. I did *Dick Tracy* for him and Warren got us all to work for the same salary at $2,500.00 a week. But he has his vision and he knew the business.

HK: And the directors Don Siegel and Sam Pekinpah?

SC: Siegel was the coolest guy. Cassavetes one day said, "Come on. We're gonna hit golf balls." "I've never done that." "It will be fun. Just to do it." He takes us over to the Federal Building on Wilshire Blvd. that used to be a golfing drive. And there was no 405 Freeway and Don Siegel is showing us how to hit golf balls.

HK: You did the movie *Convoy* in 1978 with Sam Pekinpah?

SC: Sam was crazy. When we did *Convoy* in Albuquerque and it was hot and sunny outside, he'd come out with a bottle of Jack Daniels.

HK: For decades in TV and feature films it seemed early on you learned to accept character parts over lead parts in movies.

SC: They're the most fun. I just did the work. The idea is to work. That's why you're an actor. You're not gonna make anything in New York. You're not paid. You do television. You do films. John made the best films they could, and you can see the passion in the films and in the characters. And John never let an actor be bad.

342

HK: You and John got mugged one night in West Hollywood and the guy had a gun. I later heard the same dude got a job in a Cassavetes movie.

SC: It was behind this ice cream place, Will Wright's on Santa Monica Blvd. John gave his car away one night up on Vine Street. But this night we were going through the back alley and John loved their ice cream. And we're about to go in and this guy says, "Give me your money!" He had a gun, but I didn't know if it was loaded. So Cassavetes says to him, "What are you doing?" "I want your money." "I can't give you my money." "Then I'll shoot you." "Why would you shoot me? Come on, I'll get you an ice cream."

And I won't tell you the guy's name but he ended up working on the crew a bit and I don't know what happened. But John was so charismatic. He could talk a dog into walking backwards.

HK: When you and Gena Rowlands do these film festival tributes to John, what are the questions about? Why do his films hold up so well and are still so important? Is it because they emerged from independent thought and not collective or corporate machinations?

SC: We just screened *Faces* in Florida. And we're questioned about *Woman Under the Influence*. First of all, we're asked, "Why is this movie so real?" Because that's what you do to make it real. If it isn't real, you are not going to believe it. John would fight with his actors if they didn't really perform. "You can go home and shoot basketball." With me, I knew he had good faith and trust in my ability to contribute to the script. There will be more Cassavetes tributes, and I will always honor that because it was the best thing I ever did.

Bob Marley and the Wailers on your screen in 2020

In February 2020, Bob Marley's 75th birthday celebrations continued with the announcement of *Bob Marley: Legacy 75 Years A Legend,* a 12-part mini-documentary series, featuring a collection of intimate conversations and interviews with his family, friends and fans, woven together with his original music, remixes and covers. This unique YouTube series provides fans a refreshing and cinematic journey through the life, legacy and relevance Bob Marley still holds in this present day. The first episode, *MARLEY75* debuted in February on Bob Marley's official YouTube page.

Bob Marley 1979, San Diego Sports Arena
(Photo by Roger Steffens)

In January 2020, the Marley family, UMe and Island Records began to roll out their year-long *MARLEY75* commemorative plans in celebration of the cultural icon, with a stunning animated visual for the 40th anniversary of the timeless classic "Redemption Song." Created by French artists Octave Marsal and Theo De Gueltzl, the breathtaking animation, features 2,747 original drawings, using powerful symbols to amplify the magnitude of the song's timeless lyrics and importance in today's world.

In this digital era, Bob Marley remains one of the most followed posthumous artists on social media, and *MARLEY75* will serve to bring his music and message to the digital foreground, reaching new audiences and perspectives with innovative content and groundbreaking technology. Special live events, exclusive digital content, recordings, exhibitions, plus rare and unearthed treasures will also be revealed throughout the year. Bob Marley's music continues to inspire generation upon generation, as his legacy lives on through his message of love, justice and unity, a sentiment needed more than ever in 2020.

In conjunction with Tuff Gong and UMe, a division of the Universal Music Group, the Marley family will continue to ensure the highest quality, integrity and care is taken to honor Bob's legacy and to celebrate one of the 20th century's most important and influential figures.

The Marley family and Universal have teamed up for a Marley YouTube channel. Their initial offering is a first episode of what promises to be a total of twelve mini-docs involving family, friends and former co-workers of Bob Marley. Therein, we find folks like Jeff Walker, Marley's publicist at the time of the assassination attempt on his life in 1976, and Jeff's wife, the photographer Kim Gottlieb-Walker, who took some of the most famous images of the singer. Several of Marley's grandchildren, artists themselves, make emotional appearances. There are excerpts from live shows, and a soundtrack that promises unreleased music from deep in the vaults. The series will definitely be a must-see for all Bob's fans.

One episode in June 2020, *Rhythm of the Game*, explored Marley's well-known love of soccer and his longstanding connection between the game and his music. Delving deep into the archives, never before told anecdotes are revealed on Bob's life and his impact on the world.

The YouTube channel in spring 2020 also live-streamed *Bob Marley and the Wailers Live At The Rainbow*.

The *Rainbow* DVD demonstrates that it was one of the greatest shows of his life, and he was lucky to have it photographed so well. Marley, as warrior and messenger, unveiled and sang the whole first side of the *Exodus* album, which had only been available for a few days, so the excited throng had never heard any of these tunes before.

In 2007, the 30th anniversary edition of an expanded edition of Marley's *Exodus* was packaged for the first time in a "hardback" case. This configuration includes a separate DVD with 12 tracks from Marley's Rainbow Theatre concerts in July and August of 1977. Selections include "I Shot the Sheriff," "Exodus," "Jamming" and "Get Up, Stand Up." I witnessed Bob Marley and the Wailers numerous times during the mid and late 1970s live appearances and interviewed the band members in West Hollywood on Sunset Blvd. inside the Island Records office one smoky afternoon in 1977 for *Melody Maker*.

Reggae music scholar and Marley expert Roger Steffens is the author of S*o Much Things to Say: The Oral History of Bob Marley*, which *Rolling Stone* headlined, "Might Be the Best Bob Marley Book Ever."

Steffens, one of the men who introduced reggae to America, also underscores that crucial to the overall impact of the Wailers' concerts in 1977 was the presence of all the I Three.

"One or another would sometimes miss tours because of pregnancies. But at the Rainbow, Jamaica's female version of The Three Tenors - the magnificent trio of Jamaica's most precious songstresses, Judy Mowatt, Marcia Griffiths, and Marley's wife Rita - added an elegant visual and aural element. And when they sang, 'One day the bottom will drop out,' they bent their knees and shook their bottoms in girlish abandon."

The inspiring Rainbow shows, held over three nights in Finsbury Park, one of the most racially mixed neighborhoods of London, were the hottest ducat in town. The riotously received shows benefited from the imaginative and culture-shaping lighting of Wailers' art director Neville Garrick who also designed many of Marley's most famous album covers.

In a taped interview with director Neville Garrick, a UCLA graduate, he informed chronicler Steffens, "I think we had five cameras. We used the Paul Turner lighting company,

Harvey Kubernik, West Los Angeles (2017 Photo by Jan Kessel)

346

and I was the director. The camera doesn't see the way the eye sees, especially red, blue and green. If I had eight red lamps, I doubled it to 16 so it would be more intense and you could really see the colors. It was also the first time I had used a white overhead light on Bob, so that the photographers who used to complain that it was too dark to shoot Bob's face could see that the light created a more mystic shot because it cast shadows on his face like a mask. Drama. I used more spotlights than before, amber and straw colored. And when he sang lines like 'cold ground was my bed last night,' the stage became dark blue and cold. It was the only time on the tour that year I could do that grand a lighting scheme, because we couldn't afford it."

In 2019, Bob Marley was also the subject of a well-received Netflix's original documentary series, *ReMastered*, which investigated high-profile events affecting some of the most known names in music, presenting groundbreaking discoveries and insights beyond what's been previously reported. The 8-track series launched on October with *Who Shot the Sheriff?* directed by Kief Davidson. The violent political suppression of the roots reggae movement in Jamaica is told through an investigation into Jamaican politics and the CIA's involvement in the mysterious assassination attempt on Bob Marley's life in December 1976. Roger Steffens was featured.

"It's crucial in one very important regard," recalled Steffens, "because the man suspected of giving the order to eliminate Marley, the right-wing leader Edward Seaga, all but admitted in one of his final interviews that it was his people who came to kill Marley, but he always had at least two layers between himself and those who undertook actions he initiated, to shield him from guilt. Following the shooting, which wounded Bob in the chest and arm, Marley took refuge in London. He resumed touring six months later, including a run there at the Rainbow Theatre."

Bob Marley, a Rock and Roll Hall of Fame inductee, is notable not only as the man who put reggae on the global map, but as a statesman in his native Jamaica, who famously brought together the country's warring factions — symbolized by rival politicians Michael Manley and Edward Seaga joining hands on-stage -- during his legendary *One Love Peace Concert* in Kingston, which took place on April 22, 1978, less than six weeks before his Music Hall performance in Boston.

It was four years since Marley and the band arrived from Jamaica, with the 1977 release of *Exodus*, recorded in London just after an assassination attempt on his life, turned into not just a socio-political statement, but one which included such hits as the title track, "Waiting In Vain" and "One Love," paving the way for their next release, *Kaya,* and a world tour in '78. Together with his music's theme of liberation, Marley's own rags-to-riches story brought inspiration to subjugated people around the world, where he was revered as a larger-than-life leader.

Today, Bob Marley remains one of the 20th century's most important and influential entertainment icons. Marley's lifestyle and music continue to inspire new generations as his legacy lives on through his music. Kristian Mercado Figueroa just directed a "No Woman No Cry" video.

In the digital era, he has the second-highest social media following of any posthumous celebrity, with the official Bob Marley Facebook page drawing more than 74 million fans, ranking it among the Top 20 of all Facebook pages and Top 10 among celebrity pages. Marley's music catalog has sold millions of albums worldwide.

Bob Marley, 1976, Santa Monica Civic Auditorium
(Photo by Heather Harris)

Leslie Ann Coles: *Melody Makers* documentary

(Leslie Ann Coles photo by Joy Maxwell-Davis)

A new music documentary, *Melody Makers*, which had its theatrical premiere in December 2019, is now available on DVD via Cleopatra Entertainment. It chronicles the birth of rock, the ascent of musicians and *Melody Maker* magazine. Defining musical moments are captured at shutter speed by writer, director and producer, Leslie Ann Coles. It examines the start of music journalism in England during the birth of rock 'n' roll, and the world's oldest and longest standing *Melody Maker*.

Melody Makers features the very rare and largely unseen iconic black and white photographic archive by *Melody Makers'* Chief Contributing Photographer Barrie Wentzell (1965-1975), whose images often graced the front cover and forever informed rock photo journalism. *Melody Makers* reveals the cultural significance of the paper when rock was in its infancy, and it veered from a jazz musician's trade paper (est.1926) into a bible of rock 'n' roll. In 1975-1980 I wrote a weekly Los Angeles *MM* column.

Barrie Wentzell, deejays, journalists, managers, publicists, and noted musicians Eric Burdon, (The Animals), Ian Anderson, (Jethro Tull), Steve Howe, Chris Squire, Alan White of YES, Dave Cousins (The Strawbs), Judy Dyble (Fairport Convention), Nazareth (Pete Agnew and Dan McCafferty), Sonja Kristina, (Curved Air), Rick Buckler, (The Jam) and Steve Abbott (UK Decay) and other notable pundits along with the original staff of *Melody Maker* magazine provide their recollections.

The British music press, and *Melody Maker* in particular, are discussed on screen by *MM* veterans Christopher Welch, Chris Charlesworth, Alan Lewis, Allan Jones, and from archival footage, Richard Williams.

Music, film, art, and photography interviewees are also seen and heard: Chris Tsangarides, Glen Colson, Ian Grant, Jeff Dexter, Jill Furmanovsky, Edie Steiner, Keith Altham, Peter Whitehead, Roger Dean and Peter Blachley.

Leslie Ann Cole's movie has garnered a slew of awards, including *Winner Best Music Documentary Feature, 18th Bare Bones International Film Festival, Lois J. Weber Legacy Award, Bare Bones International Film Festival*, and *Winner Best International Documentary, 16th Garden State Film Festival*.

Melody Maker magazine was an internationally recognized "must read" for rock 'n' roll fans and musicians alike by the mid 1960's.

"When we entered the music biz at the start of the 60's in the UK we were blessed by the existence of the musical papers as a direct

350

route to the public we were all trying to reach," author, deejay and Canadian university lecturer Andrew Loog Oldham explained to me in a 2019 interview.

"The New Musical Express (NME) and *Melody Maker (MM)* were the leaders. *Record Mirror* and *Disc* followed.

"Melody Maker was founded by composer/publisher Lawrence Wright in 1926 to promote live bands. Promoter Maurice Kinn bought *NME* in 1952 for 1,000 pounds. *Record Mirror* was started by Sir Edward Lewis and Decca in 1954, headed by the superb writing team of Ian Dove, Peter Jones and Norman Jopling.

"Disc followed in 1958 and featured two great writers, Penny Valentine, who would go on to write the seminal bio of Dusty Springfield with *Ready, Steady Go!* alumni Vicki Wickham; and June Harris, with whom I witnessed Sam Cooke and Little Richard in 1962. I was doing PR for the tour. June went to the US in '68 with The Who, said 'who needs this,' met and married the man who singlehandedly changed the American road, Premier Talent's Frank Barcelona.

"In America you only had music magazines for the trade until the Beatles arrived and Gloria Stavers' *16 Magazine*. Jann Wenner came later with the American clash of music, drugs, Vietnam and FM radio.

"In the UK the four music papers post-Beatles would reach one million punters per week. We were read about and could read about ourselves. It was a direct and valuable link.

"Norman Jopling at the *Record Mirror* was the first to write about the Rolling Stones, and their editor, Peter Jones, suggested I go see them, and that is why I am here. The *MM's* Ray Coleman went on to ghost the Bill Wyman bio amongst others on the Beatles and Brian Epstein. Ray was to the word what the late Terry O'Neill was to pictures - they always had our back.

"I wrote a column for *Disc* or *Record Mirror* for a while, so did Jack Good and Jonathan King. Later writers would try to emulate the lifestyles of their subjects. I was lucky to welcome the first run when we were all welcomed into the game," volunteered Oldham, who in 2020 taught a full credit 13-week course in Canada at Thompson Rivers University in Kamloops, British Columbia, *Rock Dreams: A History, 1954-1984 Up Close and Personal* with Andrew Loog Oldham.

Bands were formed from the back page classified section, musicians gathered at the *Melody Maker* head office on Fleet Street, eager to be interviewed by *Melody Maker's* reporters with their new unreleased tracks in hand during this evolutionary period in rock 'n' roll. *Melody Makers* tells the story of the rise and fall of the most influential music publication in history, *Melody Maker* magazine, the primary source of exposure for up and coming musicians, and the ambitious young journalists who shared a common passion, the music. Contrary to the adversarial relationship that would later evolve between artist and the press, Barrie Wentzell and scribes were given editorial free reign and unprecedented access.

Melody Maker was a pop culture phenomenon and this was, to a great extent, due to its Chief Contributing Photographer, Barrie Wentzell and his black and white photos that blistered across the front cover weekly.

Filmmaker Coles met rock n' roll photographer Wentzell in 1996 at Canada Artscape, a work-live space for professional artists located in the heart of Queen St. West, Toronto. Over the years Wentzell regaled her with stories about his days with *Melody Maker* (1965-1975), when he unwittingly found himself intimately chronicling the birth of rock n' roll and amassed a unique collection of archival black and white photographs.

Cole's documentary replicates the style in which Barrie took photos back in the day when he worked with *Melody Maker*. These intimate moments between artist and image were suspended in time and stylistically integrated into the film during postproduction.

Actress, producer, writer, director Leslie Ann Coles dedicated 18 years to choreography and modern dance before transitioning into film and TV with her debut 2001 multiple-award-winning film *In The Refrigerator: Spirit of a Haunted Dancer*. Today she's engaged in theatrical features, non-scripted TV, documentary, and interactive digital media.

In tandem with the theatrical launch of *Melody Makers*, Leslie Ann created a special edition Interactive Digital Media / iBook. Designed for all mobile devices, the *Melody Makers* iBook will be available to drive exposure and sales for the feature film. The interconnected visual journey of the IDM contains a photo gallery, trailers, interactive rock trivia games, rock picture puzzles and embedded B roll. The VOD Canadian configuration implements the 95 minute director's Canadian 2019 cut supported by Telefilm Canada.

During December, 2019, I interviewed Leslie Ann Coles during a visit to Hollywood following a viewing of her movie inside a Sunset Blvd. screening room.

HK: Why did you decide to do this film?
LC: Barrie Wentzell and I met in 1996, as we both had studios in the same artists' building in Toronto. At the time, I was seeking a photographer for my dramatic short film, *In The Refrigerator*. Barrie took the photos, and we became fast friends. Photography has always intrigued me as a reflective medium; it triggers spontaneous memory and associations. It was Barrie's anecdotal stories behind his iconic rock photographs that inspired me to tell this story.

HK: Did you know and feel Barrie's photo catalog and available visuals could work and translate as the epicenter in a movie? As well as other photographers you present and display?
LC: Indeed, I did. It was through Barrie that I met other photographers which inspired the concept for a limited documentary series, *F-Stop*. It won a CTV Banff Fellowship but coincided with the onslaught of reality television at that time; no one was interested in a series that featured music photojournalists. I decided to forge ahead with a documentary film starring Barrie, the veteran photographer. There are two other photographers whose works are featured in *Melody Makers,* namely, Jill Furmanovsky (UK), and Edie Steiner (Canada). They were perfect additions in the telling of this story.

HK: What were the things that impressed you the most about his pictures and portraits?
LC: What blew me away about Barrie's work was his use of natural light and his unprecedented access to the musicians he photographed. Barrie took their photos not only during live performances, but also during the actual interviews. This would be unheard of today.

HK: The non-stage portraits?
LC: Barrie's more candid shots are my favourite. He captures the spirit of the artists. I was intrigued by his perspective and filmed large format photographs, contact sheets and even the negatives which are seen throughout the film. His images literally fill a 30 ft. screen!

HK: You had done film before, been a dancer and actress, what was the one thing from that journey that aided this film? Some of your crew worked with you before in dance productions.

LC: Having dedicated eighteen years to dance as a choreographer and performer, this played a role in the visual treatment of the documentary. I deliberately "choreographed" the images, the movements between the stills and subjects were something I paid close attention to. The crew members who worked with me previously were the DOP, Mark Bochsler, sound recordist Michael Cole, and still photographers Inger Whist and Liam McDonnell.

HK: You created your own process with Barrie's photos. Snaps during shooting were implemented in post-production, and they served as glue points.
LC: Yes, I wanted to replicate the style in which Barrie took his photos. So, I had a still photographer(s) taking snaps during the interviews. These were stylistically integrated in post-production. It is a blend of analogue and digital photography.

HK: What were some of the initial challenges? Did you have a script? Besides Barrie, did you get some commitments from the *MM* staff and assurances for involvement?
   LC: Originally, it was intended to be an intimate artist portrait within the context of a television series, so I did not have a script for a theatrical feature film. The treatment grew out of my conversations with Barrie.
   It was Barrie who insisted I go to London to interview his colleagues, so I pre-interviewed *Melody Maker* journalists, Chris Welch, Chris Charlesworth, Richard Williams and Mick Watts, and I spent time in the British Library researching the *Melody Maker* magazine archives. All of this informed me of a much bigger picture.

HK: Talk to me about the cinematographer and crew members.
LC: Mark Bochsler plays guitar and sings; he is a documentary filmmaker in his own right. Really, every crew member involved from Canada, London and the USA digs music and the visual arts. Everyone revered Barrie and trusted my vision.

HK: How long did it take to make the film? I would imagine at least a decade. How did the initial funding even happen?
LC: It took ten years if you include the development of the series concept. It took over eight years to make the feature documentary.

HK: What happened when you began the cinematic trek and then a slew of items were revealed? Perhaps it became more than a document of a photographer and the world of *Melody Maker*.

LC: So much was revealed to me along the way. Documentary filmmaking is like opening Pandora's Box, and this became most evident when I was researching and interviewing in London.

HK: What were some obstacles in the path?

LC: The cost of licensing the music was prohibitive, even though I created a prototype for an App to include the music, a photo gallery, and other interactive elements that could be monetized to benefit the creative partners and investors. It was a hard sell. I received development support and a pre-license from CBC to complete the project, but I never had production financing. Regardless, we completed the film and the *Melody Makers* App is available on Apple Books with the photos, embedded video, interactive picture puzzles and rock trivia games.

HK: Ian Anderson and Eric Burdon really shed some light on the impact of *MM* on them. Due to budget or time restrictions who else was approached but couldn't be scheduled to be lensed?

LC: I had Pete Townshend, Diana Ross, Ray Davies, Tina Turner, Joni Mitchell, Lou Reed, Elton John, and Bowie on my wish list. Regrettably some of them had become ill, and I danced around more than a few on occasion. Budgetary restrictions made it impossible to travel extensively, so I caught up with musicians on tour when they were in my territory, so to speak. All the musicians I interviewed gave me access to their music and Ian Anderson provided some archival video footage that features Barrie with the band.

HK: Bruce Cowley, Mark Sanders and Richard Hannett were essential members of your team.

LC: When the story evolved to include the history of *Melody Maker* magazine, Martin Harbury of the Film and Television Consultant for the Ontario Media Development Corporation entrusted me with $25,000 to go off to London to pre-screen and interview *Melody Maker* staff. Mark Sanders then came on board as a producer and he got us back to the UK to conduct the final interviews.

Then, Bruce Cowley, the Commissioning Editor for CBC, The Documentary Channel, licensed the film based on a rough cut. This

355

enabled me to complete the film. Richard Hanet, an entertainment lawyer, stuck with me from the start. He helped me navigate the contracts and clearances and wrangle the rights back to the project when I unwittingly entrusted the project to a pirate.

HK: Discuss your musical relationship with Walter "Chip" Yarwood.
LC: We've collaborated over the years on everything from art installations, modern dance, and film. Chip is multi- instrumental, and he happened to have a 1960's mixing board in his studio. He engaged local session musicians to do guitar and drum solos for the soundtrack. The documentary spans such an eclectic period in music. Chip brought it all together with the original and licensed music, sound design and the mix.

HK: Reflect on the script writing. Was some done before it started and expanded as the years went passing by?
LC: Barrie was the inspiration for the original story, and it continued to evolve when I met the journalists, musicians and others. I was fascinated to learn IPC, publishers of *Melody Maker*, had opened an office in New York during *MM's* prime, but it was short-lived because the newsstands were owned by the mob in the 70's. The Brits weren't inclined to pay the kickback to the mafia.

HK: There is no narrator. That's very refreshing. Was that planned in your pre-production?
LC: I was dead set on not having a narrator from the beginning. Barrie is at the heart of the story.

HK: Licensing the music we do hear in the film, director Peter Whitehead saved the day on some levels.
LC: Peter insisted on seeing my earlier work before he would agree to participate as a subject. Fortunately for me he loved *In The Refrigerator.* He then licensed his original footage of Pink Floyd playing at the UFO Club (circa 1965), and Roger Waters granted me the rights to the music that accompanied the footage. Peter's archival film footage in the film includes Allen Ginsberg, the Rolling Stones, and Pink Floyd.

HK: What about cameras, film stock, equipment? You've been in the frame game for a while and must have had some subject specific lenses, film stock and cameras to employ around directing.

LC: My early interviews with Barrie established the visual style and tone. That said, the film was shot over a lengthy period of time, so I worked with different camera operators, but it was all shot using high definition digital cameras.

HK: Do you now have a philosophy about shooting interview subjects?
LC: You must be engaged in listening. The best interviews are derived from establishing a sense of intimacy, and this stems from a place of trust. You have to forget about the camera and crew once you start rolling, and the interviewee will then do the same.

HK: When you edit these chats down, tell me about your editing process and method.
LC: I cut the film like a scripted feature. I enjoyed choreographing the interviews and the imagery in post-production. For example, there are two sequences whereby three different subjects are reminiscing about Keith Moon so I edited it as if there were three people at a party telling a different story about Moon simultaneously. The stories intersected thematically, and it worked. I layered the film using an A, B and C story line. "A" being Barrie's story; "B" is the trajectory of *Melody Maker* magazine, and "C" speaks to the changes in the music industry and the coinciding decline in *MM's* popularity. By the mid-seventies the music scene changed with the emergence of punk, and the industry was big business. With that came restrictions and limited access.

HK: How did you keep yourself motivated over the decade while working and securing additional funding, let alone representation for the title and distribution?
LC: There was definitely an ebb and a tide to this production. I loved the discoveries along the way, and this kept me motivated. I shelved the project on more than one occasion before I moved the needle again. I was entirely invested. I'm tenacious by nature. I also felt a duty to those I had interviewed, and I was committed to share their legacy. I believe it all came together at the right time.

Barrie Wentzell, unlike music photographers today, holds copyright to his photos following a grueling eight-year legal battle to regain ownership of his photo archive. His collection features virtually every notable artist that emerged between 1965-1975 namely, the Beatles, Led Zeppelin, Jimi Hendrix, the Who, David Bowie, the Kinks, Marianne Faithfull, the Rolling Stones, and Elton John, just to name a few."

During December, 2019, I interviewed Barrie Wentzell in Toronto about Jimi Hendrix and *Melody Makers*.

HK: Your philosophy on taking photos?
BW: I treated everybody the same and always wanted to put them in their best light. I was at *Top of the Pops,* and "Purple Haze" was out, and I asked Jimi Hendrix if I could take a few snaps at the BBC, and there was very little light. But one stairwell and I took some pictures there, a couple weeks before I had been photographing Cream and Eric Clapton. That's how I found the spot and the only place where I could get natural light, there was always people coming down the stairs interrupting us. But I told Jimi that a couple of weeks ago I took some pictures of Eric. "Oh man. He's my hero." And Eric was saying exactly the same thing about Jimi.

From an English point of view, anybody from the States was a legend already, from years earlier. Elvis Presley, Gene Vincent, Eddie Cochran, Jerry Lee Lewis and Buddy Holly were our heroes. And, then we heard the blues from Willie Dixon, Muddy Waters, Howlin' Wolf. We found out later that most Americans weren't listening to them, but we sure were.

An English producer in 1963 invited Bob Dylan to come over and do a TV play *Madhouse on Castle Street.* There was only one channel on a Sunday night back then [January 13, 1963], and everybody watched the play and there was Bob Dylan singing "Blowing in the Wind." "What!" Overnight sensation, you know. I think the same with Hendrix.

HK: Talk to me about the early days shooting music on stage or in portrait sessions.
BW: I did a lot of color shooting. There were times where I shot the Kinks and Cat Stevens sent them over and never got them back. You could judge a date by color. Black and white was timeless as it could be now or could have been 30, 50 years ago. There was no different technique, just a different film.

I started in 1964 and went to jazz and folk clubs. And I was the only person with a camera. And the lesson you learn is that you gotta know the door man. In the early days you could sneak a camera into the Royal Albert Hall. You could say *Melody Maker,* and you could get in most anywhere. There was hardly any trouble in the beginning, but the lighting was always so bad.

To get a picture was the first challenge. Early days it was come on in at the "photo pit." And you could move around. By the time there was a David Bowie concert, *Ziggy Stardust*, there were 20 photographers. I was interested in "Click, and got that."

I looked at live shows as a sharpshooter. You gotta be so ready. Usually I'd be hanging around at the bar or backstage whatever, walk around for the first three numbers and then you'd sort of get the feeling. And sometimes I'd get ready for the moment. You don't think about it. Just comes together. If you think, you've lost it. It's intuitive. It worked. But you really get into it. You are in a zone.

You can take pictures and be transported at the same time. Jimi Hendrix told me that. I remember asking him "sometimes I see you play and the guitar is playing you." "Yeah. Sometimes when you're in the groove as they call it, I'm not playing the guitar. It's the guitar playing me."

It's like being inspired by a different dimension or a different aspect of yourself to do that. It's infectious. And people get it. You're really into it. Not out of it. It's a magical bliss I guess like sex. That's what music can bring to life.

HK: Who were some of your favorite photography subjects?

BW: Pete Townshend, intelligent, always great in conversations. Frank Zappa. You'd talk to him, and he'd spend hours speaking about each track. You could have a long chat. He was the most intelligent right-on person. He only smoked cigarettes and drank lots of coffee. He hated drugs, and he was refreshing.

We'd run into many of the artists, band members and roadies at clubs like the Speakeasy and other late night places. So you'd have additional conversation and fun "after hours."

HK: Talk to me about participating in Leslie Ann's movie.

BW: When I was approached for the movie I said, "Well, Look. You just need a bigger picture." I was part of a group, a team at *Melody Maker*. It would be great to hear from some of them and some of the musicians while they're still on the planet. 'Cause we're all getting older. Just capture stuff.

I learned a lot. It started out with my snaps. And she was doing it on a shoe string and bloody good, 'cause you couldn't stop her. She had the tenacity. Well done. And it is whatever it is. It may entertain some or horrify others, but at least when I hear from others who have seen it,

"Wow. I wish we could have had that much fun." It was a happy time, which they don't have now, and maybe that's why nostalgia ain't what it used to be. But wasn't it better when you could go down and buy a 12 inch LP? Sit 'round and listen to it. Share it with friends.

I saw it for the first time and tried to watch it objectively. The pictures work all right. That's cool, and she interviewed all the characters which I hadn't heard before. It was like a team coming back together and these were the best days, lots of fun. It wasn't about the money. That was a great buzz and the musicians speaking. I wish there could have been a proper budget. It is what it is. I didn't expect it to be that much. No one booed. Some were stunned. "Wow man. That was fun." That's positive in this day and age. Good luck to her for that. The message got through.

The music continued and still works today, looking back at pictures. That's really cool. It worked back then and then it works now. Like Traffic's "Hole In My Shoe" or Hendrix's "Purple Haze" It still is like the first time you heard it. It's become a classical thing. It's a form that brings everybody together. It started back with cavemen hollering out to play the flute or the drum. That's culture. And it has a history and if it's personal, it works. When it's impersonal and mechanical, it's forgettable. The song is a poem. They're indelible. That's why it works.

Sandy Warren and John Anderson deliver
Horn From The Heart: The Paul Butterfield Story

Horn From The Heart: The Paul Butterfield Story is a feature-length documentary about the life and career of legendary blues musician Paul Butterfield. A white, teenage harmonica player from Chicago's South Side, Paul learned the blues from the original black masters performing nightly in his own back yard. Muddy Waters was Paul's mentor and lifelong friend, happy to share his wisdom and expertise with such a gifted young acolyte.

The interracial Paul Butterfield Blues Band, featuring the twin guitar sound of Michael Bloomfield and Elvin Bishop, the rhythm section of Sam Lay and Jerome Arnold and the keyboards of Mark Naftalin, added a rock edge to the Chicago blues, bringing an authenticity to its sound that struck a chord with the vast white rock audience and rejuvenated worldwide interest in the blues. The band's first LP, released in 1965, was named "#11 Blues Album of All Time" by *Downbeat*.

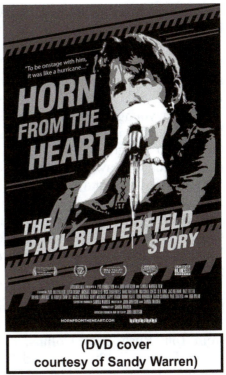

The only artist to perform at The Newport Folk Festival in 1965, The Monterey International Pop Festival in 1967 and the Woodstock Festival in 1969, Paul would continue to

(DVD cover courtesy of Sandy Warren)

break new ground in the blues, and to stand up for racial equality, until his death at age 44 in 1987 of a drug overdose. Through his music and words, along with first-hand accounts of his family, his band mates and those closest to him, *Horn From The Heart: The Paul Butterfield Story* tells the complex story of a man many call the greatest blues harmonica player of all time.

The Paul Butterfield Blues Band was inducted into the Rock and Roll Hall of Fame in 2015. Paul Butterfield is one of a handful of musicians inducted into both the Rock and Roll and Blues Halls of Fame, alongside other legendary artists including B.B. King, Chuck Berry, Billie Holiday and Eric Clapton.

Horn From The Heart: The Paul Butterfield Story is a revealing documentary about his life, blues crusade and ill-fated career.

Butterfield, Elvin Bishop, David Sanborn, Bonnie Raitt, B.B. King, Maria Muldaur, Jac Holzman, Sam Lay, Mark Naftalin, Marshall Chess, Michael Bloomfield, Al Kooper, Nick Gravenites, Buzz Feiten, Happy Traum, Clydie King, Geoff Muldaur, Jim Kweskin, Corky Siegel, Barry Goldberg, Paul Shaffer, James Montgomery,

361

Trevor Lawrence, Joe Boyd, Cindy Cashdollar, Todd Rundgren, Steve Madaio, Jim Rooney, and Bob Dylan are seen and heard in the movie.

I interviewed Sandy Warren, the executive producer, producer, and co-writer about the mission behind *Horn From The Heart: The Paul Butterfield Story.*

"As a young 'folkie' in the 60s who grew up with traditional folk music from the Pete Seeger songbook, my musical evolution took me to bluegrass music (such as the Greenbriar Boys); jug band music (such as Dave Van Ronk and the Ragtime Jug Stompers and the Kweskin Jug Band); "traditional" blues (such as Sonny Terry and Brownie McGhee); and to folk singers of the 60s, such as Phil Ochs, Joan Baez, Patrick Sky, Fred Neil early Donovan (*Catch the Wind*). I confess to having been among the folkie 'snobs' referred to by Maria Muldaur in *Horn From The Heart*, the purists who resisted music played on electric instruments.

"I used to buy a lot of records put out by Elektra – a label that released the folk music I was listening to – and one of them was the 'sampler' record called *Folksong '65*. That record included tracks from Tom Rush, Judy Collins, Koerner, Ray & Glover, Hamilton Camp, Fred Neil, Phil Ochs and Tom Paxton. And incongruously, it also included 'Born in Chicago' by the Paul Butterfield Blues Band.

"Of course, by 1965, music was exploding and beginning to define my generation. I was too young to go to the Newport Folk Festival that year, but I sure listened to *Folksong '65* and especially the Butterfield track. And after that, there was *What's Shakin'*, another Elektra sampler with amazing music including the Lovin' Spoonful, Al Kooper, Eric Clapton and more tracks from *The Paul Butterfield Blues Band*.

"There was no looking back. The electric blues played by the Paul Butterfield Blues Band captured me in a way that was different than the folk music I had been listening to. It was intense and pounding, totally immersive; sensual and challenging. For me, this opened up the musical floodgates. I listened to the first and then the second Butterfield records until they were so scratched up they popped and hissed. *East-West* was mind-blowing; it was a mesmerizing combination of rockin' thumping electric blues and San Francisco trippy rock.

"By 1966-1967, I was listening to Cream, the Yardbirds, Ten Years After and other British electric rock bands; Hendrix; the San Francisco bands like Jefferson Airplane, Moby Grape and Country

362

Joe and the Fish; and the Blues Project (I loved that band). But to my mind, Paul Butterfield was the guy who played electric blues first and opened up all these musical and other doors.

"I started going to Café Au Go Go around 1966 or 1967. Whenever the Butterfield band was playing there I was there too, after that same thing at the Filmore East. To this day, I think that the live performances by the Butterfield band are hard to surpass. Even the recordings, I think, didn't quite capture the excitement and intensity of the live performances.

"Roll forward decades....I happened to meet some of Butterfield's family in 2014, and the idea of making a documentary about him started to grow. The more I learned about Butterfield's life and the more I thought about his pivotal impact on rock and roll, the more I became convinced that his place in the history of pop music ought to be recognized and preserved. It seemed to me that he was disappearing into the dustbin of history. Because he died so young. And perhaps also because he did not self-promote, he spoke through his music and if you didn't get it, so be it, he didn't care. There is scant footage of him performing or even speaking, so his recordings and the memories of those of us lucky enough to have heard him live are his legacy. Thus this project was conceived and pursued."

Sandy Warren photo
(Courtesy of Sandy Warren)

Sandy Warren enlisted director, editor and co-writer John Anderson to capture the artistic and troubled world of Paul Butterfield.

When I discussed the film with John Anderson, he explained,"I saw Paul at The Atlantic City Pop Festival at 3 o'clock in the afternoon on August 2, 1969. The sheer power of his performance -- he had the five-piece horn section, including David Sanborn, Steve Madaio and Trevor Lawrence -- surpassed anything I'd ever heard. It was like an unstoppable train coming right at you for 60 minutes. It struck me

363

how intensely focused Paul was on the music and the band. He said little between songs and had his back to the audience much of the time. All that mattered to him was the music, an attitude that left a big impression.

"In 2014 Corky Siegel was asked who might make the film and he recommended me.

"Having worked on *Born In Chicago* and *Sam Lay In Bluesland* over the previous six years, I had a basic understanding of the Paul story and knew many of the key players. Through phone conversations with Paul's very generous friends, relatives and bandmates, the picture continued to fill in until we were able to determine who we needed to get on-camera, while keeping the main focus on the music.

"Given Paul's worldwide renown, there's remarkably little archival footage of him. He did few interviews and only a handful of complete live performances were committed to film or tape. David Hawkins at the blogspot *The Complete Paul Butterfield* was a tremendous resource.

John Anderson   (Photo courtesy of John Anderson)

"Paul's ex-wife Kathy and his brother Peter and Peter's family were very helpful in providing stills and in providing insight into this very humorous, talented and complex man.

"I love music, and the number of great music docs produced in the last 15 years is encouraging and inspiring. We hope this film brings to light not only Paul's importance to the history of popular music, but

364

also his key role in US race relations in the 60s and 70s. And what he got out of that little thing, as Sam Lay says, 'ain't even on it.'"

I loved the first three Paul Butterfield Blues Band LP's. I saw the group in the sixties. One time they shared the stage with Lee Michaels, Procul Harum, the Flying Burrito Brothers and John Mayall at the April 1969 Palm Springs Pop Festival held three miles east of Palm Springs in Cathedral City at the Sunair Drive-In.

Michael Bloomfield wasn't in that lineup but that outfit still delivered that very chilly night in the desert. The wail of Butterfield's harmonica solos were haunting instrumental signals that were heard loud and clear by 8,000 people. Shortly afterwards there was a riot that spilled throughout Palm Springs all the way to Taquitz Falls Park.

In 1978, I interviewed Michael Bloomfield for *Melody Maker*. I asked him about Butterfield and he told me "the one major thing that I learned from Paul was not to have any fear by watching him go further into the deepest sections of the south side Chicago world to see and play with the immortal bluesmen."

I was present on a couple of commercial recording sessions Paul Butterfield was hired to play harmonica on during 1986-1987. He was battling some severe health issues at the time. The 1986 session was in Hollywood and the second in Malibu the day before he died in North Hollywood. As this long overdue Butterfield documentary was booked across the US, I felt it appropriate to ask some folks who saw Paul in action, met him, dug his band's music and viewed this riveting cinematic portrait, and I've included some of their observation here.

"I loved *Dylan's Highway 61 Revisited* album. I loved Michael Bloomfield's guitar playing on that album and loved Bloomfield on the first *Paul Butterfield Blues Band* album," exclaimed Robby Krieger of the Doors.

"Bloomfield was my favorite for a while. To me he was the first white guy who could play blues better than the black guy. I liked *East-West*, the second Butterfield band LP, but the first one, oh my God…I wore the grooves out. He could play harmonica, and I got to know him later in life. I was really excited when we signed to Elektra and Paul Rothchild was going to produce our first album, and he had produced Paul Butterfield."

"Their Elektra debut was the first 'real' blues album I ever owned, at age 13," recalled Dr. James Cushing. "I had it in mono! I grew five inches in height that year, and the melodies and chords from those songs settled into the bones and sinew of the person I was growing into. And the lyrics! Before I ever fell in love with a girl, I knew that love could drift, that moneymakers could shake, and that last night a man lost the best friend he ever had. Paul Butterfield prepared me for adult life! At the same time, he prepared me for Muddy Waters, Howlin' Wolf, Little Walter, Chess Records, and this vast, great tradition of American music.

"The title track of their second Elektra album, *East-West*, is a prime example of what I call Stealth Jazz — jazz improvisation played in a rock venue on rock instruments. 'Spoonful' by Cream, 'King Kong' by Zappa, 'Machine Gun' by Jimi, and 'Flute Thing' by the Blues Project are other examples, and so Butterfield prepared me for Kenny Burrell, John Coltrane, Miles Davis, and another expansive, great musical tradition.

"The third Elektra album, *The Resurrection of Pigboy Crabshaw*, added horns and a soulful R&B coloration. A year later, he rejoined Mike Bloomfield on the *Muddy Waters Fathers and Sons* album for Chess, which closed the circle.

"I regret I never saw Butterfield live or met him. I did see Muddy Waters more than once, and I listen to blues regularly. This music is a part of my life, and that part is a great gift that Paul Butterfield gave me."

"In 1965 I interviewed Butterfield and he then played Massey Hall in Toronto on a Sunday night," remembered Canadian-based writer Larry LeBlanc. "I knew all about Butterfield via Jim Delehant in *Hit Parader* who wrote continually about him. So they play the Massey Hall show. Paul asks me where can we go for a drink. Toronto is closed down for liquor on Sunday night. Except for a few tourist designated areas. Sorta bullshit but there were a few. I knew one, the Palm Grove Lounge. So Butters, Mike Bloomfield and organist Mark Naftalin grab a cab. At the club it's a $5 charge. Paul pays for all. Performing is Chubby Checker. I kid you not. Mid-sized crowd in jackets and ties. We are all in hippie type clothing. Chubby is incredible. We get nicely inebriated. Fun evening. I worshiped Paul who could scare reporters. Not me. He was great. I was about 21, and I knew the blues. He was gracious and respectful. God bless anyone who messed with him though."

"From folk festivals to blues festivals and rock concerts, the Paul Butterfield Blues Band played a pivotal part in the integration of blues, rock, and psychedelic music," enthused multi-instrumentalist David Kessel, who helms cavehollywood.com.

"The band played Chicago blues with a jazz mentality that was really a needle and thread of the fabric of music going on at the time. Paul Butterfield really took the blues harp into a dimension transformed from Little Walter. They were so ahead of their time that the album *East-West* came out a month before the Beatles *Revolver* album."

"I was new to L.A. as I moved here in 1963 to attend a Junior College in the San Fernando Valley," revealed record producer and blues advocate, Denny Bruce. "No car. Little by little I got to meet people, especially girls who were friendly to me because I had what was considered long hair.

"Two of my girlfriends loved all the new groups now happening. The Byrds were everywhere on Top 40 radio in 1965, and so were Sonny and Cher. I finally got to go into Hollywood with the girls, and we saw the Byrds. I was impressed with their songs and harmonies. The Byrds were the jingle jangle folk rockers thanks to 'Mr. Tambourine Man,' they were hot.

"Nothing could have prepared me for my second trip to see the Byrds again at The Trip on Sunset Boulevard, in January, 1966. Because the group that opened for them, the Paul Butterfield Blues Band were no wannabe anything but who they were, a real blues band.

"They had an album out and the cover told you plenty," underlined Bruce. "An integrated bunch of guys representing the rough edges of Chicago, home of Muddy Waters, Buddy Guy, Junior Wells and many more who all knew and respected the Paul Butterfield Blues Band.

"They had been playing electric blues since junior high school. Now it was business for them.

"I have never seen or heard a band with this kind of power playing songs I was soon to hear for a long time, as it was so real. Paul Butterfield was the lead singer, and harmonica player. He had command of the band, so when it was Mike Bloomfield's time to play a solo it was because Paul nodded at him. Plus second guitarist, Elvin Bishop, could also solo. Mark Naftalin was the keyboard player who played perfect Chicago blues piano, as Otis Spann was his influence, as well as mentor.

"Their ensemble playing, with the harp, sounding like a much bigger band with a horn section," disclosed Denny. "They did play kinda loud, but they had to, as it was part of the sound. When they left the stage it seemed very quiet in the club.

"The Byrds were set up and ready to start. They started and it sounded like college guys who just put away their acoustic guitar, and plugged in their new electric instruments.

"The Butterfield Band were men and the Byrds now sounded like a bunch of boys. With a Bob Dylan song which was their silver platter welcome to become rock stars.

"In my humble opinion I wished that the PBB came back on and blew the roof off of this joint.

"I got to see the Butterfield Band play the Golden Bear in Huntington Beach a week later. Lines around the block. This time I went with two guys who knew the band. They were brilliant doing their thing in front of a packed house of blues lovers. They were so tight it felt as if the club was throbbing, like a big heart beat.

"The club owner told us he never had a band this good play here, and he has been doing this for a long time. He couldn't explain it, but he loved it.

"That is what happens when music is real. You feel it.

"Bob Dylan knew he wanted to add something to his set at the Newport Folk Festival. And he knew Mike Bloomfield, Jerome Arnold and Sam Lay from the Paul Butterfield Blues Band were some of the right guys to help him turn up the heat when he 'plugged in' and helped change the direction of music, big time.

"Dylan's *Highway 61 Revisited* album took him to the top of the pop charts with Michael Bloomfield's wild slide guitar playing, opening the door for blues rock to become a major fabric in what now made up the direction of acts being good studio players and even greater live acts."

"During the 1967 Berkeley Folk Festival, I got a chance to hang out with members of the James Cotton Band, including James himself," recounted multi-instrumentalist Chris Darrow. "James Cotton, to me, was the finest blues harmonica player alive at that time.

"One night, Jimmy Fadden, the harmonica player in the Nitty Gritty Dirt Band, and I, went to the Whisky a Go Go to see James Cotton play. Besides Jimmy, there was another famous player in the room, the great Chicago blues harpist, Paul Butterfield. Cotton, asked the two guys to join him up on stage, and they had at it. They had a friendly 'cutting session,' in the old jazz terminology. The band played a blues groove and then they took their turn in succession, until they were all playing together. It was a once in a lifetime experience."

During 2017, I conducted an interview with Jac Holzman, the founder and former owner of Elektra Records. In viewing the Butterfield documentary, we are reminded once again of Holzman's bold A&R acumen in his signing of the Paul Butterfield Blues Band to his label. This is the man who initially made it possible for all of us to hear and then purchase these precious platters of Paul and Co.

Jac Holzman told me, "I didn't listen to much of what was going around me except to hear the most contemporary of things so that I could kind of avoid it.

"Because it's like shooting a bird in the sky. If you want to shoot a bird you shoot ahead of the bird and the bird and buck shot gets there at the same time. So I always wanted to be out ahead and looking for things I hadn't heard before," explained Jac. "But there was a mood of those times. And the Summer of Love was also the summer of psychedelia and things of that nature.

"We did have Paul Butterfield, the Doors, we had Tim Buckley, *Goodbye and Hello*, which was very emblematic of that time, and Love's *Forever Changes*, their third album. But the whole label was me looking for something that I hadn't heard before. Or something that I had heard but it had a new face on it or it felt intrinsically different to me."

"I was the type of record collector that if I liked a cult label, such as Elektra, I would tend to buy everything they put out," confessed Gene Aguilera, East L.A. music historian and boxing book author (*Latino Boxing in Southern California,* Arcadia Publishing).

"And this is how I found *The Paul Butterfield Blues Band* first LP, in the used bins of Platterpuss Records in Long Beach for $1.99. They were a young interracial band from the south side of Chicago that played the blues at a break-neck pace. They played it fast, loud, and electric.

"I discovered Michael Bloomfield through this LP, and always preached to anyone who would listen that he was the best white blues guitarist around. I really liked how Butterfield played the harp and shared the vocal mic with drummer Sam Lay; and how everything clicked with future star guitarists Michael Bloomfield and Elvin

Bishop; and how these guys worshipped at the throne of Muddy Waters, Willie Dixon, and Robert Johnson. And that's the bottom line of any blues band worth their salt."

"There was a real buzz around Melbourne, Australia, about the Butterfield Blues Band's debut album," recollected writer and musician David N. Pepperell.

"It's hard to say where that buzz came from as there wasn't much music media available in town in 1965, yet it was all over that this was an album you had to have if you had any interest in the blues.

"Blues fans were a small coterie in those days, although growing day by day because of the influence of the Rolling Stones, and we all kind of knew each other from social gatherings and blues records nights at various people's houses.

"Elektra did not have a local record company licensee at that time, and we soon found that the only place to get the Butterfield's record was at a shop called Discurio run by Peter Mann who had somehow got a deal to bulk import Elektra records into Australia.

"Amazingly, he had started a list of people wanting the album and I put my name down, not really knowing anything about the record except it was going to 'shake the world.'

"The idea of young white Americans playing authentic blues was an exciting one and we all wondered how good the Butterfield Blues Band could be," admitted Pepperell.

"Finally I got a phone call from Peter saying my record was there, rushed into town, picked it up, rushed back home and put it on the turntable. From the opening harmonica trills of 'Born In Chicago' I was totally hooked. Paul B. was a knockout singer and harp player and the guitarist in the band, the then unknown to me Mike Bloomfield, seemed to have every blues guitar lick there was completely nailed down.

"I had the original versions of many of the songs – 'Shake Your Moneymaker,' 'Blues With A Feeling,' 'Got My Mojo Workin',' 'Mellow Down Easy' - but I loved the way Butterfield performed them with so much energy and passion, plus a band that rocked its socks off.

"What a record that was! The band originals all fitted into the mix along with the blues classics making it a totally remarkable, vibrant piece of work and I must have played it about ten times straight before I stopped for a break.

"I was singing in a sort of bluesy band at that time, but we didn't sound anything like the Butterfields - more like a poor man's Rolling Stones I think now - and to hear them wailing with all that authenticity was just mind boggling.

"Very few albums in my lifetime hit me like that the first time I played them and I still get a chill down my spine when I listen to *The Paul Butterfield Blues Band* even now.

"Regrettably neither the band nor Paul ever toured Australia, because they had thousands of fans here who would have given an arm, and maybe even a leg too, to see them," sighed Pepperell.

"Still their records live on, but their first album was a major event in my life and continues to be so. When *John Mayall's Bluesbreakers*, with a young Eric Clapton on lead guitar, released their eponymous album in 1966 it was another magic moment, but it could not compete with Butterfield and Bloomfield and Naftalin and Bishop and Lay and Arnold - they were as good as it could get!

"*Horn From The Heart* was a really fine documentary and told me so much I didn't know about Butterfield."

"*Horn From The Heart*, such an appropriate title," praised Sarah Kramer, a trumpet player and horn arranger. "The way Paul played and sounded was like an electric horn. His tone, phrasing and dynamic energy brought forth so much power and was mesmerizing every time he played! I love all of the live footage in this film, and the mention of his mentors and fellow luminaries. That gear, the vintage amps and those microphones... the Bullet mic and the Pistol Grip, brought his already fierce playing to such heights. Truly, he lived and breathed that music, and brought together and integrated so many people through his passion, through their own passion.

"What a gift he was, and such a treat to have so many of his friends and family lay out portions of his journey. Having lived up in that area, I especially loved the footage and interviews from Woodstock and Bearsville and the clip of him with John Sebastian (whose father was also a harmonica master!)."

"At the 1967 Monterey International Pop Festival, I saw the Paul Butterfield Blues Band," happily marveled Chris Hillman of the Byrds. "We had worked with Paul the one time when the Byrds really came to the plate. Which when we did a week [January 1966] at The Trip [in Hollywood] and Butterfield's original band, and they were so good.

Smoking. Michael Bloomfield doing answer solos with Butterfield on harmonica. They were so good.

"The one time in our whole career that we played every night at our peak. It wasn't a competition. It was two different kinds of music. We went 'Oh my God. We played good.'

"That was when the Byrds really jelled and really got together that week at The Trip. There were other times, but I always remember that so distinctly. Butterfield. Great band. I studied that first album. I got to know him a little bit," said the acclaimed singer/songwriter.

"I remember doing a music festival with him in 1969 in Palm Springs, with the Burrito Brothers. I remember walking with Paul Butterfield to the promoter's tent, and he's got his briefcase with a .38 Colt piece in it. I said to myself, 'this guy really did work on the south side of Chicago. Oh…Here we are in the peace and love scene and he's got his .38 Colt loaded, to go and collect his money!' This guy is real. A real blues guy!"

The Best of The Johnny Cash Show DVD

During the late '60s Johnny Cash was a box office attraction, selling concert tickets, appearing on national television and now entrenched in the spotlight partially owing to the commercial success of his *Johnny Cash at Folsom Prison* long player giving him increased visibility on the pop and rock music charts.

Granada, a UK TV channel then broadcast a documentary *Johnny Cash, The Man, His World, His Music* that garnered crucial US television along with print media attention. The Granada program directed by Robert Elfstrom triggered ABC-TV stateside to offer Cash an hour-long pilot as a summer replacement for their Saturday night variety show, *The Hollywood Palace*.

In June 1969, Columbia Records released *Johnny Cash at San Quentin* produced by Bob Johnston which yielded the LP's smash country and pop hit single "A Boy Named Sue." It convinced ABC, who then picked up the option on the Cash TV show for a full season.

"I would say there were many things that likely would not have happened were it not for [manager] Saul Holiff's influence on Johnny's career, but the San Quentin show and Johnny's television show are both ones that undoubtedly can be credited to Saul's vision for Johnny," observed author Julie Chadwick who penned *The Man Who Carried Cash Saul Holiff, Johnny Cash and the Making of an American Icon* (Dundurn Press).

"On the television front, there are dozens of letters that go back more than a decade in which he continually pitched the idea of getting Johnny on TV, which finally bore fruit when a Canadian named Stan Jacobson decided to do a CBC special on

Johnny Cash (Photo © 1994 by Jimmy Steinfeldt)

Johnny in 1967, which many regard as the predecessor to his television series."

A veteran of *The Wayne and Shuster Show* for several seasons, Jacobson had been a writer for *Country Hoedown* and writer/producer of the program *Music Hop*. In 1966 he wrote and directed the *Battle of Britain* documentary for the Canadian Broadcasting Company series *Telescope*, and in 1967, *The Legend of Johnny Cash*. During 1970-1971 Jacobson helmed the debut of the prime time Cash ABC-TV slot.

Bill Carruthers directed year 1969. He had previously directed both *The Soupy Sales Show* on station WXYZ-TV in Detroit and the Ernie Kovacs game show *Take a Good Look*, for ABC-TV. Carruthers subsequently directed *The Newlywed Game* and *The Dating Game*.

"My dad was the executive producer and director for the first year. It was his show," stressed Byl Carruthers, then Billy, the son of Bill

Carruthers, who today is a guitarist/songwriter in the roots music duo, Café R&B.

"The first show was a mindblower, as we all know, and the first season surprised ABC enough to pick it up. The sets were cheap, 'cause they had no money. The production issues they faced retro-fitting the Ryman Auditorium were immense," provided guitarist/songwriter Carruthers.

"For that year of pre-production and production, my dad and John were close. He showered my dad with gifts (among them a 1932 Martin Guitar, and a Civil War Colt Pistol). John had a pair of them with consecutive numbers. He gave my father one, and he kept one, so they'd each have one as symbol of their relationship."

The Johnny Cash Show debuted in June, 1969. Programs were done at Nashville's Ryman Auditorium, which back then was home to the Grand Ole Opry 1943-1974. Bill Walker was the musical director and arranger. June Carter Cash and the Carter Family, Carl Perkins, the Statler Brothers, and the Tennessee Three were screen regulars.

Among the Cash-invited performers: Louis Armstrong, Bill Monroe, Dusty Springfield, Judy Collins, the Monkees, Creedence Clearwater Revival, Stevie Wonder, Tony Joe White, Homer & Jethro, the Everly Brothers, Joni Mitchell, Neil Young, Derek and The Dominos, Roger Miller, Faron Young, Charley Pride, Loretta Lynn, Marty Robbins, Mickey Newbury, Neil Diamond, Conway Twitty, Tammy Wynette, Bob Dylan, Waylon Jennings, George Jones and Doug Kershaw.

"Dylan called my dad, before he and his staff left for Nashville," recalled Byl Carruthers. "I had gone to work with my dad that day. He had an overall deal with Screen Gems at the time, and had an office on their lot. He had said we were going to get lunch, and then his assistant beckoned him back to the office, saying it was important!

"Two full hours went by, and I had to wait. When he got off the phone, he came out and said that he had just gotten off the phone with Bob Dylan. I asked him what he was calling about, and he said that Johnny wanted Dylan to do the show. Johnny really wanted Bob to do the first episode, and told Bob that he would be in good hands with my dad, and he wouldn't have to do anything he didn't want to. My dad said Bob was 'feeling him out' on the phone.

"My dad was very cool about letting me hang when the musicians were there, and yes, I got to fetch coffee and stuff for Bob Dylan, in the hour or so before the taping...

"I distinctly remember Dylan having two very sedate western-style two-piece suits laid out, and he saying to my dad 'Bill, which one of these do you think would be best?' A few minutes later, my dad said to the assistant director, 'I can't believe Bob asked me what he should wear!'"

In his review of *The Johnny Cash Show* in the June 12, 1969 issue of *Great Speckled Bird*, the counterculture underground newspaper in Atlanta, Georgia, Gene Guerrero reviewed the ABC-TV/Screen Gems initial broadcast.

"TV CASHES IN. OCCASIONALLY, television gives the viewer a glimpse of its potential as a creative medium. Usually, as with *The Smothers Brothers Show*, it is a fleeting glimpse before the owners of the public airways get uptight or commercialism subverts the creativity. With the inauguration of the *Johnny Cash Show*, country music has finally made it to network television. One can only hope and pray that it will take a couple of seasons before these corrupting influences set in.

"Dylan sang a couple of songs off his new album including 'Girl From the North Country' which he sings with Cash. In a non-contrived way, Dylan and Cash singing together remind you of two kids practicing for their first recital. In this time of super-slick entertainers, that's very refreshing."

On August 16, 1975 forty miles from Los Angeles, California, I interviewed Johnny Cash for *Melody Maker* inside the Royal Inn Hotel in Anaheim. Cash's variety show TV program, along with his successful *Folsom Prison* and *San Quentin* albums ushered in today's acceptance of country music artists on national and cable television.

"One reason country music has expanded the way it has is that we haven't let ourselves become locked into any category. We do what we feel," stated Cash.

"I like to go into the studio with my own musicians and record my own songs," Johnny reminded me in our encounter. "I'm open to other songwriters. I like to do things different in my career."

However, Johnny said that TV obligations of his ABC-TV series hampered his creativity.

"It cut down on my touring, it became too confining. We stayed in Nashville for two-thirds of the time. I really didn't enjoy it all that much. If it was kept loose and spontaneous it could have been great. But we had to do the same song every eight or ten times before they would accept it. The show lost its feel and honesty. Consequently I lost a lot of interest in it."

In September 2006 a 2-disc DVD set of *The Best of the Johnny Cash Show*, hosted by Kris Kristofferson, was distributed by CMV/ Columbia Legacy, a division of Sony BMG Music Entertainment. The DVD restoration process was produced and directed by Michael B. Borofsky. Editor and Producer is Christine Mitsogiorgakis. Executive Producers are Lou Robin, Cash's longtime manager, and John Carter Cash, his son with June Carter Cash. Borofsky, whose video credits include *Stevie Ray Vaughan: Live At Montreux 1982 & 1985*, and *Johnny Cash At San Quentin*, also filmed all the original artist interviews for *No Direction Home*, the Martin Scorsese-directed documentary on Bob Dylan.

The four hour DVD incorporates 66 clips integrating highlights and select performances, plus new interviews with Tennessee Three bassist Marshall Grant, Hank Williams Jr., musical arranger Bill Walker, and hairstylist Penny Lane. The show's regulars included Johnny and June Cash, the Tennessee Three, Mother Maybelle and the Carter Sisters, Carl Perkins, and the Statler Brothers.

Most of the programs were recorded on two-inch quad videotape, a non-existent format these days, and in some cases a post-production "show master" was also available, or even joining the two together. Every master tape was baked like the audiotapes and played back on a machine to digitally process the material without tampering or colorization. The results were transferred for the final phase, and the creation of stereo mixes (where only mono recordings existed) and 5.1 Surround Sound.

In 2019 a documentary on Johnny Cash, *The Gift: The Journey of Johnny Cash* premiered at the South by Southwest festival in Austin, Texas.

Thom Zimny who directed *Elvis Presley: The Searcher* examines the live recording Cash and his band did in 1968 at Folsom Prison in California. That event serves as a central motif of the movie and features interviews with family and celebrated collaborators, "while the liner narrative of the Folsom Prison performances will anchor our film, each song in the set list will open a door into a nonlinear presentation of Cash's emotional, musical and personal development," Zimny posted on www.johnnycashonline.com. John Carter Cash, Frank Marshall, Ryan Suffern and Jeff Pollack are among the film's Executive Producers. Screenwriter is Warren Zanes. Mike McCready of Pearl Jam supplied the musical score.

Another Cash-themed documentary, *My Darling Vivian* from director Matt Riddlehoover was released in 2020. It was an official selection at SXSW. It traces the romantic and traumatic journey of Vivian Liberto, Johnny's first wife and mother of his four daughters. The film is produced by Dustin Tittle, the grandson of Vivian Liberto and Johnny Cash. The movie has exclusive, unprecedented access to never-before-seen footage and photographs and the participation of Vivian and Johnny's daughters-Rosanne Cash, Kathy Cash Tittle, Cindy Cash, and Tara Cash Schwoebel. The siblings share first hand, and for the first time, their story of love, career-obsession, isolation, fear, and survival.

Alison Ellwood's Two-part Series, *Laurel Canyon: A Place in Time*

Laurel Canyon: A Place In Time debuted in 2020 on television EPIX® channel on May 31st and concluded June 7th. EPIX®, an MGM company, is a premium television network delivering a broad line-up of original series and documentaries. EPIX® is available nationwide through cable, telco, satellite and emerging digital distribution platforms as well as through its EPIX NOW app, providing more movies than any other network.

Alison Ellwood is the writer and director of *Laurel Canyon: A Place in Time.* Her feature directing credits are *History of the Eagles, The Go-Go's,* and *Magic Trip: Ken Kesey's Search for a Kool Place.*

Ellwood's television directing credits include *Women of Troy* for HBO Sports and *Locked In: The Victoria Arlen Story* for ESPN's *30 for 30 Shorts.* She has produced and edited the documentaries *Gonzo: The Life and Work of Dr. Hunter S. Thompson* and the Oscar nominated *Enron: The Smartest Guys in the Room.*

Ellwood captures an intimate portrait of Laurel Canyon's cultural creatives during 1965-1975 in this big-budget, first class Hollywood

Writer/director Alison Ellwood (Courtesy of Alison Ellwood)

production implementing rare and newly unearthed footage mixed with audio recordings and photographs. The documentary features all-new interviews with Love co-founder Johnny Echols, Chris Hillman and Roger McGuinn of the Byrds, Little Feat's Paul Barrere, Sam Clayton and Bill Payne, Alice Cooper, Richie Furay, Michelle Phillips, Micky Dolenz, Graham Nash, Ray Manzarek and Robby Krieger of the Doors, the Turtles' Mark Volman, Jim Ladd, David Crosby, Bonnie Raitt, Don Henley, Jackson Browne, Bernie Leadon, Eliot Roberts, David Geffen, Russ Kunkel, Owen Elliot-Kugell, Mama Cass Elliot's daughter, Nurit Wilde's photographs along with photographer Henry Diltz, whose catalog work is spotlighted.

Executive produced by Frank Marshall, The Kennedy/Marshall Company; Darryl Frank and Justin Falvey, co-presidents of Steven Spielberg's Amblin Television; Craig Kallman and Mark Pinkus, Warner Music Group; Alex Gibney, Stacey Offman and Richard Perello, Jigsaw Productions; and Jeff Pollack. The film is produced by Ryan Suffern, The Kennedy/Marshall Company, and Erin Edeiken, Jigsaw Productions.

During 2019-2020, I served as a consultant on *Laurel Canyon: A Place in Time.*

In 2009, I wrote the book *Canyon of Dreams: The Magic and the Music of Laurel Canyon,* published in paperback edition in 2012. In 2013 photographer Henry Diltz, archivist/librarian Gary Strobl and I teamed with ABC-TV for their Emmy-winning one hour *Eye on L.A. Legends of Laurel Canyon* program hosted by Tina Malave.

Henry Diltz, Gary Strobl and I curated the 2014 Los Angeles-based Grammy Museum exhibition *California Dreamin': The Sounds of Laurel Canyon, 1965-1977.* Micky Dolenz of the Monkees, Gail Zappa, Art Podell, Joel Larson from the Grass Roots, Danny Hutton of Three Dog Night and I chaired a panel discussion on the community.

I graduated West Hollywood's Fairfax High School in 1969, taking my Driver's Education class lessons in Laurel Canyon. I am constantly encouraged to present a word's-eye-view history of the region. For cavehollywood.com and *Music Connection* I assembled oral histories for a multi-voice narrative text culled from my own 1974-2020 interviews with *Laurel Canyon: A Place in Time* screen participants.

Henry Diltz, photographer (Courtesy of Henry Diltz)

379

Henry Diltz told me, "I loved the Mamas and Papas. Michelle Phillips was very sweet as far as I could see. The camera loved her, a beautiful young girl and the ideal flower child.

"Mama Cass was a force of energy. She really was an earth mother and a great spirit at that time. Mama Cass was very intelligent, very funny, and she was very hip, and those three things together were amazing. And she was warm, open and wanted everybody to be friends. She and the group had the first money, big success. Many people came through and stayed at her house. You could go up there anytime and not know who would be there, you know. But that's the way the sixties were. People hung out for the afternoon, and then all go off somewhere else to a club. I loved the Mamas and Papas.

"The debut *Crosby, Stills and Nash* album along with *The Doors' Morrison Hotel* are the pictures I get asked to sign the most. I do them with a brown sharpie and do it on the back.

"As far as shooting musicians live, I prefer being to one side of the stage so the microphone is not in front of the person on stage. And you pick one side or another depending on which way the guitar looks the best. And you sort of get a side front ¾ view from either way. I like to have a

**Graham Nash
(Photo by Henry Diltz)**

nice telephoto lens so I can get them waist up and guitar up. And that fills the frame generally in a vertical way.

"It never occurred to me back in the '60s and '70s when I was really shooting all these things that it would ever be an archive, and that it would be a piece of

**Crosby, Stills and Nash
(Photo by Henry Diltz)**

social history. That's what it has turned out to be. And that was a total accident. The thought never occurred to me.

"Jim Morrison, Joni Mitchell and Cass Elliot were telegenic, as well as James Taylor and Jackson Browne. The Doors were interesting and weren't a guitar band. They came from a different place. It was that keyboard thing. They didn't have a bass. Ray Manzarek played bass on a keyboard with his left hand. It was a little more classical and jazz-oriented. And then you had Jim Morrison singing those words with that baritone voice. It was poetic and more like a beatnik thing. It was different. And Jim wrote all those deep lyrics. I took photos of them at the Hollywood Bowl in 1968 when they did a concert.

"Jim lived in Laurel Canyon. So did Robby Krieger and John Densmore. We were all friends in the area. I knew him as a musician just as I was first really taking photos. I did one day with the Doors in downtown L.A. for *Morrison Hotel* and got that picture. Then two days later they needed some black and white publicity pictures and we walked around the beach in Venice.

"I started taking photos and never thought one day I'll have an archive of history. I think it's great people can see, purchase and own signed limited editions of musicians. Portrait and concert shots. Wonderful days of peace, love and brotherhood. I'm glad I have this body of work that reflects those things. The fun of framing something up and pushing the button and capturing things that were lovely moments to me.

"My theory about the music of Laurel Canyon was that it was the flowering and the renaissance of the singer/songwriter. I think it had a lot to do with that change that it came from folk music. And then they started putting their own lyrics into it."

Graham Nash shared his memories. "You know, kid, the truth is there's a part of me that really believes none of this meeting David [Crosby] and Stephen [Stills] would have happened without Rodney Bingenheimer. Incredible music has been made from that moment. In 1966, Rodney told me about a Mamas and Papas recording session when we met at a Liberty Records label gathering for the Hollies.

"I only went with Rodney to see Michelle. But Michelle, Denny (Doherty) and John (Phillips) were doing an overdub in the studio, and Cass was outside the studio. I started talking to Cass.

"So then in the hallway down there at United Western studio, Cass said, 'What are you doing tomorrow?' 'Well, I don't think we're doing much.' We were staying in Hollywood at the Knickerbocker Hotel. And she picked me up around noon in her convertible Porsche. I said, 'where we going?' 'We'll be there in five minutes. Don't worry.' And drove me up to Laurel Canyon and I met Crosby. And once again, my life has never been the same.

"It's not lost on me that you can be in Laurel Canyon from Hollywood in five minutes. Not like in England where it's 90 minutes that's to get to the nearest bus stop. So I was in heaven. I was free. My first wife and I were getting divorced. I had already separated from Rose. I was a free man. And I must tell you that I took to the Laurel Canyon scene like a duck to water. It was just amazing to me that these people would be living in this kind of very rural area.

"I just felt so free. And more importantly, I felt appreciated. And that goes a long way with me. If you know what it is I can do and you appreciate that, I feel a lot better about things. And it seemed to be the Hollies' reputation in the Laurel Canyon scene was a big one.

"You gotta understand. David, Stephen and I came from harmony bands. I mean, we were harmony freaks. I've said before CS&N never had any claim on any of the notes that we sang. It's just when that sound happened it was instantly recognized by me, David and Stephen as something stunning.

"When I first went in to Wally Heider's studio on Cahuenga to record with engineer Bill Halverson, I thought. It was small, it was funky. I never met Bill Halverson. We got in Crosby's Volkswagen van and drove up to the studio and brought our guitars and amps out and started to make the records.

"It's not lost on me that I am coming from Laurel Canyon into Hollywood to record. And sometimes I would walk from Joni's house to the studio. I was in heaven. I was a musician making music with incredible people with a bunch of incredible songs.

"The neighborhood was Micky and Samantha Dolenz. They were close. Henry Diltz, his archive is a history of those times. David Blue, he was crashing at Elliot Robert's house, two houses up from Joan. We would go to the little Italian restaurant at the Laurel Canyon Country Store. We'd go to Art's Delicatessen, to Canter's Deli, Joni would cook dinner. We'd go to Greenblatt's Deli. Musso & Frank Grill.

"Joni loved Crosby, Stills and Nash as much as we did. She was the very first person on this planet to hear that sound. We did go and sing for Cass but the very first time was in Joni's living room. We knew that we had these songs to do. That if we got as live as possible, and as immediate as possible the very essence of the song down, and the expression is there and the emotion was there, and the slight retards and the slight speeding ups that you need within a piece of music sometimes, once we had that essence down, and we looked at it, and then added more voices to that, and then maybe added a guitar or something, it took on a life of its own.

Joni Mitchell (Photo by Henry Diltz)

"Living in Laurel Canyon. There's no way to describe it. My life was unbelievable on every level. Not only as a musician, but as a lover

383

as a friend, as a songwriter. My life was unbelievable at that point. I would be going and recording 'Suite: Judy Blue Eyes' with David and Stephen and then bringing tapes home and playing them for Joan and having her absolutely get it.

"I mean we would do normal stuff. But what was happening is that with Joni writing so much and me writing so much, and with Joni recording and me recording we didn't get a lot of time to socialize a lot. But people would come by the studio like Henry Diltz, who had an open invitation to come by at any point, you know.

"No formal rehearsals before we went into the studio. Our rehearsals consisted of private going through the tune, and then saying, 'let's go to (Peter) Fonda's house! Let's go to Paul Rothchild's house! Let's go to Alan Pariser's house! Let's go and sing them this shit!' Eventually we could sing that entire album on a couple of acoustic guitars and blow people's minds."

Richie Furay recollected, "The best time for Buffalo Springfield? As far as I'm concerned, it was right at the beginning when we were the house band at the Whisky (May-June 1966), with the five original guys--Steve and Neil, Bruce, Dewey and me—there was an undeniable magic. Whether or not we were the best musicians didn't matter; we had magic, and we all knew it. We had replacements later on when Bruce had his immigration troubles--and Jimmy Messina was the only one who came close--but that original group was our best.

Richie Furay of Buffalo Springfield
(Photo by Henry Diltz)

"Look, walking into Gold Star studio. I'm a young kid from Ohio. And to go in that studio, with all the history, and hear our music coming through those speakers, even though it's a four track, was bigger than life.

"Ahmet Ertegun also encouraged us to learn the board. So we'd go in, and we would record 'em like some of the vocals were going to be done. Ahmet had heart and soul for the band. 'Make these demos.

Do whatever you need to do to make the product.' Because of him the band got launched a lot quicker then maybe it could have. He definitely saw something in this band right away.

"Everything happened so fast. We were young. We were new, five young guys who brought five different elements together. When we put out stuff together, it was like 'here's what I want to contribute to your song, Stephen and Neil.' We took elements of folk, blues, and country and we established our own sound. We were pioneers, and I see that.

"People make bands a part of their life. We were always comfortable singing someone else's song early on. The first album and some of the second, you can hear the cohesiveness was a group effort, there was not the possessiveness of 'this is my song,' 'this is my baby, 'I'm singing it because I wrote it.' Early on there was this 'what does this sound like with you singing?' I know we tried 'Mr. Soul' with everybody singing, and it sounded best with Neil. The individual members brought their own take on what was being presented to the song. We liked the Beatles with John and Paul singing harmony. Stephen and I did a lot of that unison singing. That we picked up from the Beatles, but then there was a lot of experimentation.

"As far as why Buffalo Springfield's catalog still reaches people, it has to be the songs. Buffalo Springfield was very eclectic. I mean, we reached into so many genres. Look, the original five members of Buffalo Springfield couldn't be replaced. There were nine people out of the Springfield in two years. Jimmy Messina came in late in the game and did a fine job. I worked with him on *Last Time Around*.

"I think we're one of the most popular, mysterious American bands. The mystique has lasted for some reason. Two years, a monster anthem hit of the '60s, but no one really knew us. Neil has gone on to become an icon, Stephen has made enormous contributions, CS&N, and look at me into Poco, which I believe opened the doors for the contemporary country rock sound."

Roger McGuinn offered another perspective. "When I recorded the vocal on the Byrds' "Mr. Tambourine Man" I was trying to place it between Dylan and John Lennon. Dylan's stuff is brilliant. I coined the term that he was the 'Shakespeare of Our Time.' It was like knowing Shakespeare here. Dylan was carrying on [Jack] Kerouac and [Allen] Ginsberg. The baton had been passed. I remember Ginsberg said 'I think we're in good hands.'

"We did Dylan's 'Chimes of Freedom' at the International Monterey Pop Festival in June 1967. I loved the imagery. You can't pin it down as a peace song, or whatever, but it's got overtones of that. It's brilliant. I just identified with it and could relate to it. I love 'All I Really Want to Do.' It's kind of a simple little love song, you know, but it's got a really sarcastic whimsical attitude.

Allen Ginsberg & Harvey Kubernik (Photo by Suzan Carson!)

He doesn't want to be hassled. He just wants to be friends. We changed the arrangement from the 3/4 time to a 4/4 time. We became his 'unofficial, official' band for his stuff. I remember when Sonny & Cher got the hit with 'All I Really Want to Do,' Dylan went, 'Oh man, you let me down.' Normally, a writer would be happy to get a hit with his own songs. Who cares who did it? He was on our side."

"Chris Hillman and I knocked off 'So You Want to be a Rock 'n' Roll Star' in very late 1966 at his house in Laurel Canyon. It really wasn't about the Monkees. We were looking at a teen magazine, and noticing the big turnover in the rock business, and kinda chuckling

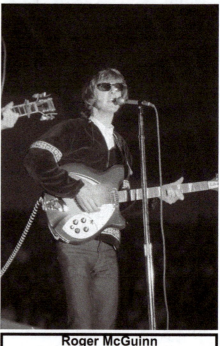

Roger McGuinn (Photo by Henry Diltz)

about it, you know, a guy was on the cover that we'd never seen before and we knew he was gonna be gone next issue. A funny little song. People didn't know how to take it. We just meant it as a satire. We got along well and we wrote well.

386

**Bob Dylan (center) with the Byrds at Ciro's
(Photo byJim Dickson, courtesy of the Henry Diltz Archives)**

"Actually, (David) Crosby and I wrote well too for a while together when we were writing, and so did Gene (Clark) and I. We had some good times writing songs. Chris Hillman played us 'Have You Seen Her Face' in the studio and we cut it. We weren't into making demos back then. Demos came along in the '80s. (laughs). Chris Hillman is a very gifted musician. The way he transitioned from mandolin to bass was amazing. I don't know if he was completely influenced by (Paul) McCartney, but he had this melodic thing, I guess more from being a lead player. He incorporated a lot of leads into his bass playing.

"David is an incredible singer for harmonies and he's written some wonderful songs as well. I also really appreciated his rhythm guitar work. I thought he had a great command of the rhythm part of it and also finding interesting chords and progressions.

"We sang together well. I give the credit to Crosby. He was brilliant at devising these harmony parts that were not strict third, fourth or fifth improvisational combination of the three. That's what makes the Byrds' harmonies. Most people think its three-part harmony, and its two-part harmony. Very seldom was there a third part on our harmonies.

"I was driving my Porsche up La Cienega Blvd. and got around to Sunset, and Jim Dickson, our former producer and manager, (he had been fired by the Byrds, shortly before that), he still liked us, or some of us, and he pulled up in his Porsche, and signaled for me to roll my window down. 'Hey Jim. You ought to record Dylan's 'My Back Pages.' I said, 'OK. Thanks.'

"The light changed, I drove back up into Laurel Canyon, and pulled out the Dylan album that had 'My Back Pages' and learned it. I then took it to the studio and showed it to the guys. And Crosby hated it because he was mostly upset because he wasn't getting his own songs on the album, and the reason why he left the band. There was a rift in the band, and he wasn't getting as many as some of us.

"So anyway, I liked 'My Back Pages' and don't remember any resistance from anybody else

Chris Hillman of the Byrds (Photo by Jim Dickson, courtesy of the Henry Diltz Archives)

in the band, just David. And it was a hit and a good tune. I'm real happy with it. It was Dickson's suggestion and I hadn't thought of it as a song for the Byrds' repertoire.

"I liked the wisdom of the song, and it's a very insightful song on the thing that happens when you think you're so knowledgeable and wise when you're real young. And then when you get a little older you realize what you didn't know.

"Gary Usher got the tune 'Goin' Back' to the Byrds and brought it to us in the studio and played it for us as a demo. I didn't know of Carole King, even though I had worked in the Brill Building earlier on. And, I had never heard of the Goffin/King songwriting team. But I loved the tune and thought it was really good.

"Gary explained that these were 'Tin Pan Alley' writers who had just kind of taken a sabbatical and come back and revamped their style to be more contemporary, like we were doing. So it really fit well I thought. We learned it and put a kind of dreamy quality into it."

Chris Hillman emphasized, "The music of the Byrds is melody and lyric. One thing I've said before, and what our manager, Jim Dickson, drilled into our heads, the greatest advice we ever got, and he said, 'Go for substance in the songs and go for depth. You want to make records you can listen to in forty years that you will be proud to listen to.' He was right.

"Here we were. Rejecting Dylan's 'Mr. Tambourine Man.' Mind you, I was the bass player and not a pivotal member. I was the kid who played the bass and a member of the band. Initially all five of us didn't like what we heard on the Bob Dylan demo with Ramblin' Jack Elliot. We were lucky. And Bob had written it like a country song. And Dickson said, 'Listen to the lyrics.' And then it finally got through to us and credit to McGuinn, mainly Jim arranged into a danceable beat. The Byrds do Dylan. It was a natural fit after 'Mr. Tambourine Man' was successful. Roger (then Jim) almost found his voice through Bob Dylan, in a way, literally voice-through Bob Dylan in a sense.

"Recording at Columbia studio. I remember that Columbia was a union room. The engineers had shirts and ties on. Mandatory breaks every three hours. Record producer Terry (Melcher) was a good guy. I didn't really get to know him. I was shy. Columbia was comfortable to record in there. Terry was good. I liked him. I will say this, and on the Byrds albums I was not mixed back. Sometimes it worked. And I do have to say all five of us were learning how to play. Once again, coming out of the folk thing and plugging in. And we were all learning. Roger was the most seasoned musician, and we all sort of worked off of Roger. He had impeccable time. Great sense of time. His style and that minimalist thing of playing that was so good. He played the melody.

"And then we start doing some Dylan stuff. 'Chimes of Freedom.' Great song. 'All I Really Want To Do.' At Monterey we included Dylan's 'Chimes of Freedom.' I didn't realize how beautiful that lyric was until years later. 'Chimes of Freedom' is a killer. It's just one of Dylan's beautiful songs. And he was just peaking then.

" 'Bells of Rhymney' is my all-time favorite Byrds' song. What song best describes the Byrds? I would say that, because of the vocals on it. The harmony, because of the way we approached the song and we had turned into a band. We had turned into a band with our own style.

"The *Younger Than Yesterday* album. I started really writing songs after Crosby and I were on a Hugh Masekela session that Hugh was doing with this South African gal Letta Umbulu. A wonderful singer. All the musicians were South African with the exception of Big Black. I played bass on a demo session. Such warm loving people. And David was a good rhythm guitarist. A pianist Cecil Bernard was very inspirational. I went home and wrote 'Time Between Us.' And 'Have You Seen Her Face' influenced by a blind date Crosby had set me up with along with other young ladies.

"The Byrds on *Turn! Turn! Turn!* album with 'Satisfied Mind,' which really was a Porter Wagner hit, and I think we had heard Hamilton Camp do it, but it's such a great song. And then, I still think 'Time Between' was our country rock song of the time. That's when we started doing that stuff. When we had Clarence White come in and played on *Younger Than Yesterday.* I'm not taking credit for any of that. Rick Nelson deserves credit in the country rock thing, too. Big credit. Way beyond anybody else. But you know how this business works.

"Gary Usher was an incredibly gifted producer to work with. Especially at the very end, and it was just McGuinn and I trying to finish *Notorious Byrds Brothers.* And Gary worked with us as another band member. Good ideas. Gary Usher brought us the Goffin and King 'Goin' Back.' I don't have a problem with that record. That was Gary bringing in a song that fit us like a glove. It was perfect, and it's Roger and I singing lead. It's a little too pretty but it's OK."

Micky Dolenz had another take on the community. "Before I even did the TV pilot for *The Monkees* in 1965, and the series started to air in 1966, I was at RCA studios every night watching the Wrecking Crew and the studio musicians, play with the singers and songwriters, on Mamas and Papas sessions, the Association songs, the Beach Boys songs. And these same musicians were playing on our songs. I was a singer, I sang. I can't express how important it was then, and now, to have songwriters. Before *The Monkees* I had recorded a couple

**Micky Dolenz
(Photo by Henry Diltz)**

of singles with the Wrecking Crew as a solo artist a year before I went on *The Monkees* audition.

"It was theater. It was probably the closest thing to musical theater in television. It was about this band that wanted to be famous, wanted to be the Beatles, and it represented in that sense all those garage bands around the country and the world. On *The Monkees* show the group was never famous, it was all about the struggle for success that made it so endearing I think to the public, anyway.

"In fact, one of the most important things, I think *The Monkees* show contributed to the culture was the idea that you could have longhair and wear bell bottoms, and you weren't committing crimes against nature. At the time the only time you saw people with longhair on television, they were being arrested, or treated as second class citizens. The people at Monterey, before and after, at my house were all the same people. Jim Morrison was up at the Laurel Canyon house all the time. I did some basement recordings with John Lennon. I had the first Moog synthesizer in town that I got from Paul Beaver."

The Turtles (Courtesy of SOFA Entertainment)

Mark Volman contributed "As far as the vocals and particularly the background vocals on the recordings of the Turtles, the basic overall philosophy of the vocal sound of the Turtles—and this goes back to the four of us: Chuck Portz, Jim Pons, Howard [Kaylan] and myself, and then narrowed down to the three of us, Jim, Howard and I—was that it was necessary to have complementary voices. One of the things that we learned going as far back as Westchester High School, was that the second tenor parts, which basically brought the melody, were important for the sound quality of the group. That was left to Howard and I. A lot of times when we would do a record, before Jim Pons became such an integral part of the singing, the backgrounds were done by me, Howard and Al Nichol. Jim Pons brought a lot to the table.

"Howard knew my strengths were in the quality of my voice. My voice got much more familiar to the Flo & Eddie fans, going back to the early Flo & Eddie records. I think there was always something about how we put together first and second tenor, a baritone and bass. I think there was a lot of thought in those background parts, a natural thing. As we became more and more in charge of our records and in arrangements the stuff that we brought became more and more obvious.

"But, you know, Howard understood that we had the songs and a friendly voice when we made records in the sixties. We had records and a familiar lead singer from song to song on the radio. That was very valuable, a familiar sound. Howard Kaylan of the Turtles or Micky Dolenz of the Monkees. We understood how important Howard was as a lead singer.

" 'Elenore' was written by Howard in a hotel room in Chicago as they [White Whale Records] wanted another 'Happy Together.' We sat down and shaped that song into the record that would eventually come out. Check out the second chorus. Chip Douglas produced it.

"Chip Douglas was now our producer. 'The Story of Rock and Roll' might be one of the greatest productions we have ever done and a powerful arrangement. Unbelievable. That whole high voice thing that we would eventually use on T-Rex records like 'Bang a Gong (Get It On)' and even with Zappa and Flo & Eddie.

" 'The Story of Rock & Roll' was the best recording we ever made. It also showcased for the first time the way sharing our vocals. Howard always had that control and that was the way it worked. You can argue that Howard is one of the best singers of that era or any era. He's still a great singer."

Howard Kaylan had more to say. "In the Turtles, I knew 'Happy Together' was going to be a big hit. We honed and developed it over months on the road. Wonderful fate. It was a luxury, and it's appreciated. I've never had the luxury to take something on the road for eight months and work it, re-work it and just fine-tune it.

"I did see Buffalo Springfield at the Whisky a Go Go. The band rehearsed in the house that Mark and I shared in Laurel Canyon on Lookout Mountain. Richie and Stephen slept on our floor. I moved out after a failed drug bust--didn't know if the house was being watched. Paranoid. Richie moved into my room and the group practiced and wrote there. We all knew well before they played show number one, that they would be stars. The Atco deal guaranteed it. In the canyon, we were used to our friends becoming stars.

"I was at the *Freak Out!* recording sessions with Frank Zappa. I saw the determination, but I didn't know the product. At the time it's not like I was aware until after the release of the record what a genius this guy was. I still just thought he was a freak. I was living in Laurel Canyon at the time. I might have gotten the album at Wallichs Music City. I get it, and we all love the album.

"Back in that era in 1966 and '67, before 'Happy Together' hit, and we were still L.A. street people working in the same clubs and stuff, there was enough of a camaraderie there, not only though our knowing Frank, but also through Herb Cohen and going to the Zappa Log Cabin.

"Nobody made distinctions in that canyon of dreams back then as to what type of music you were doing. If you were Lester Chambers and you were living in that canyon, Joni Mitchell didn't question what kind of music you were doing. Nobody did. Everybody was in there for themselves. To make their music shine for a minute while the bright stars were already living there. We didn't want to change things. We wanted so badly to be a part of it, that finding our place was so important. I'm not sure as Turtles we ever found our place, but as Mothers we sort of busted out of our comfort zone a little bit. I think the Turtles were comfortable for us."

Michelle Phillips put it this way. "First of all, the Mamas and Papas were a very unusual looking group. And it didn't have to be. Remember the name of the first album: *If You Can Believe Your Eyes and Ears* with Guy Webster's photo. If you believe your eyes, you're gonna look at that picture. And it doesn't matter if it's in color. It's fine in black and white. Because everyone is looking at this very overweight beautiful woman who sang like a bird, and then there was this tall thin blonde with long hair, and this beautiful Denny and this tall guy with a mink hat on. It was something that you just didn't look away from. You were gonna look at that picture and try to dissect who these people were. We were always very animated, too. So it wasn't a static pose. The pictures of the group all the way show that we were going through so much. We were always kind of living our drama as seen in many of those photographs.

"Why does our music still resonate and have influence? I'll tell you what I think. I think that we put a lot of energy into making the material great. John Phillips was such a perfectionist. And so was Lou Adler. That was a big romance. John and Lou were perfectly suited for each other. They bounced off each other. They really appreciated each other's gifts. John and I had

Michelle Phillips
(Photo by Henry Diltz)

never heard ourselves sing with anything more than one guitar when we went to audition for Lou Adler. So when Lou put together Hal Blaine, Joe Osborn, Larry Knechtel, and engineer Bones Howe, when we heard ourselves with a band it was amazing! It just inspired us more and more. And you know, I think we were very lucky that we picked a lot of good material.

"As far as the Mamas and the Papas always connecting. Years ago I came home one day and turned on the television and a special from Vietnam was being broadcast. The camera panned across this audience of soldiers and marines who were fighting in Vietnam. And there is such a look on their faces, this is like 1966, '67, just right in the middle of this horrendous war, and you can see it just etched on their faces. And the camera pans across them and there is this huge banner that says 'California Dreamin'. And, that just shook me to my core. It became a destination anthem. I'm the co-writer of that song. And there are still millions of people that hear the music of Los Angeles, and it represents their youth that was so tumultuous and so frightening and to so many of their friends and relatives.

"And in a way Mamas and Papas music is comforting to them. You know what I mean? They can go back into their childhood and say, 'That was the music of my era.' And, 'California Dreamin',' has surpassed any kind of era. And I think 'Dream a Little Dream of Me' has done the same thing.

"I think the Mamas and the Papas were kind of like a bubble. It was wonderful when that bubble was floating. And then the bubble popped. That was the Mamas and the Papas. When you think about it we were only together for two and a half years.

"I think *Monterey Pop* is a really wonderful film from the 1967 Monterey International Pop Festival. You get to see what the festival was really like, and how beautiful everyone felt in 1967, on June 16th, 17th and 18th, all bright sunny days. You see other festivals and they are rolling in the mud. *Monterey Pop* is so representative of the time."

Nurit Wilde (Photo by Henry Diltz)

Nurit Wilde offered a somewhat different perspective. "I lived in Canada from 1961-1965, and went to the Ontario College of Art. I worked as a waitress at the 5th Peg, and the Purple Onion. They started doing lights at the 5th Peg. There was a big art and music scene in Ontario.

"I came to Hollywood at the end of 1965. I was on the scene working at the Troubadour and the Whisky a Go Go doing lights

395

and sound. I met Barry Friedman. I was a little transient when I first got here and needed a place to stay. He had this great house in West Hollywood with a big Saint Bernard. There was a bathtub and shower in the living room. Barry was working for Doug Weston at The Troubadour. Earlier he had done publicity for KRLA DJ Bob Eubanks and the 1964 Beatles concert at the Hollywood Bowl. Barry always had various musicians around, like the Kaleidoscope. I was crashing at Barry's place and then Dickie Davis, another person whose couch I flopped on.

"I heard all the songs that were earmarked for Buffalo Springfield's debut LP. I loved their music. I went to Gold Star. But [there was] tension between Stephen and Neil. I think it was the competiveness. They continued that not only on stage with their guitar work, even though they were very different players, but they competed to hear whose song would be a single. They were both great writers and great musicians. And the music was the magic.

"I also went to some of the sessions for *Buffalo Springfield Again* at Sunset Sound. I took my camera. It's a different Neil at Sunset Sound primarily in the sense that he was now sitting at the control board. He was wearing a sweater. Jack Nitzsche was around. They had a thing going on. They would be at the side of the studio conferring.

"I lived at Peter Tork's house and Stephen would hang out a lot. And Stephen had bought Peter's house. I met Graham Nash at Cass Elliott's house. Lovely man. In 1969 Crosby, Stills and Nash make this great album. And I thought 'what in God's name are they doing now bringing Neil in?' I had seen a lot of tension in Buffalo Springfield. But maybe it helped the creative juices. To me the only way it made sense for Neil to join that band and because of his previous tension with Stephen, I think they were good foils for each other.

"That L.A. and Hollywood music scene in the mid to late sixties was such a great nurturing scene for real musicians.

"It is amazing to me that people today are so enamored with the sixties. And constantly want to know what it was like and what went on. When you are living it, you don't realize, you know, that it's a particularly special time, although the music was very special."

Ray Manzarek began his remarks with "I never lived in Laurel Canyon, but in Venice with my wife Dorothy.

"The sun and the beach and the light and the sand, it was all there. I lived with our father in the sky, the sun our mother, the ocean and the sand. Whenever we went to Laurel Canyon it was to visit someone like Paul Rothchild. John [Densmore] and Robby [Krieger] lived in Laurel Canyon. And Jim and Pam were overlooking the Canyon store.

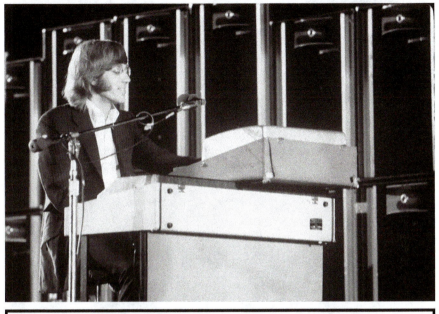

Ray Manzarek of the Doors (Photo by Henry Diltz)

"When Dorothy and I got married, Jim Morrison and Pamela [Courson] were with us, and we went down to City Hall to get married. And the bridesmaid was Pam and the best man was Jim. And we had our celebratory luncheon on Olvera Street, where we had enchiladas and margaritas. And the next night we played the Shrine Auditorium with the Grateful Dead. Psychedelic, man.

"Laurel Canyon was the natural place. In L.A. there were two places. One was the beach, where we were conceived, and Laurel Canyon was the more mature forest place where you were in touch with the earth and the sky, mainly the earth and the trees. The vegetation of Laurel Canyon was very conducive to songwriting. The Doors were always part of nature. It was always intense, closed in, locked in the four Doors entering that unified space that they occupied, of creativity. It didn't matter where we were. We could be in a Hollywood recording studio or Laurel Canyon, or the beach. It always had to do with the music and the submersion in the music. After you played your music, you stepped outside and you were with nature. It was always great. Laurel Canyon was a great place to join my fellow band members.

397

Harvey Kubernik and Ray Manzarek in Radio Tokyo Studio, Venice, California (Photo by Heather Harris)

"Our third album *Waiting For The Sun*. We loved that title. That's what we're all doing. That's what everybody is doing. Everyone is waiting for that sun of enlightenment, that blasting searing sun, the purity of the sunlight to be purified, to leave our closed circle bodies and expand into the light. 'Well let's call the album *Waiting For The Sun*.'

"That's how it happened. Songs were like that. Not how long they would take. You had to put them in the oven and bake them in the collective oven mind of the Doors. And some of them came out virtually.

"We were working in the future space. The Doors on their third album were in the future. And many things have come to pass that Jim Morrison wrote about.

"Robby was a different sort of lyric writer. You know, Robby might be the secret weapon of the Doors, we get this great guitar player who plays bottleneck, and all of a sudden he comes in and plays 'Light My Fire,' the first song he ever co-wrote with Jim. And then Robby

398

wrote 'Love Me, Two Times,' 'Love Her Madly.' 'Touch Me.' Lots of Doors' hit singles. Another guy with a high IQ."

Love at the Whisky a Go Go (Photo by Henry Diltz)

Johnny Echols illuminated Love's journey in the City of Angels. "*Forever Changes* could only happen in L.A. And could only happen at that particular point in time, because you did have that cosmopolitan freedom, you know, and you didn't have people necessarily put into little categories and boxes. You were able to go anywhere. In the L.A. area you could hear blues one night and go hear rock, experimental, avant-garde jazz, or whatever. So, right in the same area you are exposed to all these different cultures. If you listened to the radio then the DJ's were playing Herb Alpert & the Tijuana Brass, they were playing Dick Dale and Frank Sinatra. All on the same radio station. So you were exposed to whole different genres.

"And John Fleck and Michael Stewart were different players. Michael is one of the finest drummers on this planet. And he just knew exactly what to play. He's a percussionist, but a deft percussionist. He's not one playing all over the solo. (Don) Conka was one of the finest drummers I've ever known, but he could not have played *Forever Changes,* because he did not have the light touch Michael Stewart had, and John Fleckenstein, too, and Kenny Forssi a phenomenal bassist.

"My theory on why *Forever Changes* is so popular and in the top ten of all time, the magic of the record is that it is unexpected. It just came. All of a sudden there is the atom bomb. You are dealing with

399

regular TNT explosions, and all of a sudden you've got an atomic bomb. It just pushed the envelope so far outside of the mainstream, that it took a while. Now if it had been released in the last few years it would have done a whole lot better commercially, 'cause people are ready for that. But back then, people were just kind of stunned. All of a sudden you go from here to there and then stunning Arthur lyrics. Everything was just different. The way the horns were done. The way the jazz was blended in with folk music, was blended in with kind of show tunes and rock 'n' roll.

"It was all put together. But also because of the times we were living in. We had the civil rights movement. We had the Vietnam War, all of this turmoil and out of the turmoil there's a rose landed in all of this shit. There are assassinations. Martin Luther King, Jr. in Memphis. Robert F. Kennedy in Los Angeles on Wilshire Boulevard. And out of all that, a rose is blooming, and kind of permeating the air with sweetness."

50th Anniversary of the *Concert for Bangladesh*

August 1, 2021 will be the 50th anniversary of *The Concert for Bangladesh*, a pair of benefit shows organized by Ravi Shankar and George Harrison in New York City at Madison Square Garden that raised awareness and fund relief for East Pakistan refugees, after the Bangladesh Liberation War-related genocide.

It was in Los Angeles, California earlier that summer of '71 when Harrison was alerted to the scale of suffering his friend and sitar teacher Shankar was feeling about the struggle for independence from the ten million East Pakistani refugees who fled over the border from West Pakistan to neighboring India to escape mass starvation, hunger, and death.

Nearly three million people were killed. The crisis and dilemma was deepened when the Bhola cyclone and floods in 1970 devastated the region. At that period only small funds and help were made available from foreign governments.

Harrison, Ringo Starr, Bob Dylan, Leon Russell, Billy Preston, Eric Clapton, Jim Keltner, Jesse Ed Davis, Klaus Voorman, Badfinger, Claudia Lennear, Ravi Shankar, Ali Akbar Khan, Kamala Chakravarty, and Ustad Alla Rakha were among other recording artists who donated their services.

In June 1967 Shankar made a groundbreaking appearance at the Monterey International Pop Festival later spotlighted in the D.A. Pennebaker-directed documentary *Monterey Pop.*

"I knew when I saw Ravi Shankar we would have to end with that," asserted Oscar-winning filmmaker Pennebaker in a 2004 interview we conducted. "I remember sitting down at Max's Kansas City, and I wrote out a little thing on the back of a menu of what I thought the order of the music would be. And you know it was very close to what ended up being. It had to build from Canned Heat to Simon & Garfunkel to whatever it was, it had to be a history of popular music in some weird way that I didn't ever have to explain to anybody, 'cause I had music as a narration for the whole film so that just covered me."

In August 1969, Shankar performed at Woodstock. He then received an Academy Award nomination for his music in Richard Attenborough's *Gandhi.* Shankar recorded with conductors Andre Previn and Zubin Mehta.

During 1971, Shankar partnered with Harrison to produce the Concert for Bangladesh, which took place at Madison Square Garden in 1972 and raised funds for UNICEF. The live recording of the concert ultimately won the Grammy for Album of The Year.

It was in 1966 that Ravi Shankar initially met George Harrison. Harrison had first heard the sitar in April 1965, on the set of the Beatles' movie *Help!* Later in 1965, he would record with the instrument on John Lennon's "Norwegian Wood (This Bird Has Flown)."

In September 1966, Harrison traveled to Bombay and became one of Shankar's students. Subsequently, Harrison integrated the sitar into his own composition "Love You To" from The Beatles' *Revolver* album, as well as fusing sitar and Indian influences on his selection "Within You Without You," on the influential *Sgt. Pepper's Lonely Hearts Club Band* album and also on "The Inner Light," the B-side to the "Lady Madonna" single.

In 1997, I interviewed Harrison and Shankar in Southern California. Portions were first published in *HITS* magazine

George Harrison met Ravi Shankar at a dinner party for the North London Asian Music Circle decades earlier.

"His music was the reason I wanted to meet him," praised Harrison. "I liked it immediately, it intrigued me. I don't know why I was so into it -- I heard it, I liked it, and I had a gut feeling that I would meet him. Eventually a man from the Asian Music Circle in London arranged a meeting between Ravi and myself. Our meeting has made all the difference in my life."

Harrison reflected on his own sitar playing.

"I'm not a very good one, I'm afraid. The sitar is an instrument I've loved for a long time. For three or four years I practiced on it every day. But it's a very difficult instrument, and one that takes a toll on you physically. It even takes a year to just learn how to properly hold it. But I enjoyed playing it, even the punishing side of it, because it disciplined me so much, which was something I hadn't really experienced to a great extent before."

George went on to describe his earliest attempt at playing the sitar with the Beatles.

"Very rudimentary," he revealed. "I didn't know how to tune it properly, and it was a very cheap sitar to begin with. So 'Norwegian Wood' was very much an early experiment. By the time we recorded 'Love You To' I had made some strides."

In our exchange, Harrison put his sitar experiments with the Beatles in perspective.

"That was the environment in the band, everybody was very open to bringing in new ideas. We were listening to all sorts of things, Stockhausen, avante-garde music, whatever, and most of it made its way onto our records."

During my 1997 interview with Shankar at his home in Encinitas we discussed *The Concert for Bangladesh*.

"I told George, and George wanted to help me. The film *Raga* was ready, and it needed some finishing in which George helped. It was released later, I believe, in 1972.

"At the time I lived in Los Angeles and had a house on Highland Avenue. A beautiful Spanish villa and at that time, George was in town, and at that time I was planning to do a benefit concert for Bangladesh, because I was very hurt that this whole thing was going on. To help this refugee problem, I wanted to raise some money," explained Ravi.

"Everybody, every Indian, was thinking about doing that. And then, when I thought about it, I knew I could do more than any other Indian musician. Still, how much can you send? $20,000, $25,000, at the most?

Ravi Shankar, Kinnara School of Music, 1967 (Photo by Henry Diltz)

"At this time of turmoil I was having, George was there," Shankar disclosed. "He came to meet me, and I was sitting. George saw me.

"From 1966, whenever he came to town, we would meet. At that time, George was staying in L.A. for a couple of weeks. I told him what I was planning. You know, it's like a drop in the ocean. At the same time, I never wanted to take advantage of him. I did not want to say, 'Would you help me?' But, somehow, it came very naturally.

403

He was so sympathetic. 'Well, let's do something.' And you know, that made me feel so happy. What George did, he immediately started phoning and booking things up.

"His position naturally makes it quicker. He phoned and got Madison Square Garden in New York. Later he contacted Bob Dylan, Eric Clapton, Billy Preston, and a few of his friends. Somehow, it was done like that. Within three weeks or so, we gave a performance and it was sold out. So, they had to schedule a matinee.

"As you know, the first half was me. I called my guru's son Ali Akbar Khan who plays the sarod. Alla Rakha, now lives in Bombay, and he's running a school for himself. We were the first part. I composed the first lines for the items played, as we always do, and we improvised. And then intermission," remembered Ravi.

"There was no clapping when we were tuning, which is seen in the film and the people were so well-behaved, a lot of matches. It went beautifully. It was a young audience, especially because I had this existing audience already, who were mature listeners and who had come to Carnegie Hall. This audience was the same type of audience as Monterey, but they were very attentive and there was no problem at all. After our segment, I went to see the second half. Their program was very complimentary, because they chose the numbers that were very soulful in the sense that they weren't hard rock. 'My Sweet Lord' and 'That's The Way God Planned It.' Bob Dylan had his harmonica and did ballads. George sang 'Here Comes The Sun,' and the song he composed 'Bangladesh.' There was harmony, and it wasn't so different. It went off beautifully."

The Concert for Bangladesh was one of the first benefit concerts, along with the earlier 1967 Lou Adler and John Phillips produced Monterey International Pop Festival that brought together an extraordinary assemblage of major artists collaborating for a common humanitarian cause – setting the precedent that music could be used to serve a higher cause. *The Concert for Bangladesh* has been the inspiration and forerunner to the major global fundraising events of recent years, preceding *Live Aid* by 14 years.

Chris O'Dell of Apple Records was instrumental in helping George Harrison contact the musical talent for *The Concert for Bangladesh* in a Nichols Canyon house George rented with wife Pattie Boyd in the summer of 1971.

"The first line of thinking from George was 'Ravi has asked me to do something for him,'" offered O'Dell in a 2011 interview we did.

"That's about friendship. That was more important than where it was gonna go. Even in the lyric to the song 'Miss O'Dell,' George had mentioned 'the rice (that never made it) to Bombay.' George had told me about that situation earlier that summer.

"George was learning a lot from Ravi as time went by. So the idea of a concert didn't come up right off the bat. It came up later. Then it was, 'would you help me?' And it was little things. Don Nix came into town. George didn't know him. We all went to Catalina Island together. I knew him from Leon. From that came the background singers.

"I don't think we had any idea of what it could be. I mean, it was fairly apparent that if you put a Beatle on stage, with a successful album behind him, *All Things Must Pass*, that it would probably draw people especially. John & Yoko did their things, but George hadn't, and you make an assumption that with George involved it's gonna draw people.

"George said, 'I can't believe this is all coming together.' The whole thing just grew right before our eyes."

O'Dell also described Harrison's mission in securing Bob Dylan to the summit.

"That was part of the territory with him for a long time. And, you know, honestly, if George had an idol musically, that was it. So I think just having that piece there. George looked up to Bob in a way that there was that kind of esteem, and then the asking him to do something like that, and not wanting to let him down. George was really frightened by all this."

It was well documented that George, Pattie and Chris all had concerns about Bob Dylan even showing up at the Bangladesh gig, although all were immediately relieved when Dylan arrived at the rehearsal. O'Dell and Boyd were backstage for all the action and caught the second show in second row center-stage seats.

Nearly 40,000 people attended the two landmark benefit concerts at Madison Square Garden on August 1, 1971. It was coordinated by Allen Klein and ABKCO. The date was booked by Steve Leber who headed the musical division of the William Morris Agency.

"Really, it was Ravi Shankar's idea," answered Harrison in a press conference in July 1971. "He wanted to do something like this and was telling me about his concern and asking me if I had any suggestions.

405

Then, after an hour, he talked me into being on the show. It was a question really of phoning the friends that I knew and seeing who was available to turn up. I spent one month, the month of June and half of July just telephoning people."

Harrison subsequently organized two refugee relief charity concerts while composing, recording and releasing a studio single, "Bangla Desh," that was available before the heralded affair.

At Madison Square Garden, Harrison and his pals offered stellar renditions of 'Wah-Wah,' 'Here Comes The Sun,' 'Something,' 'While My Guitar Gently Weeps,' 'My Sweet Lord,' 'Just Like A Woman,' 'Blowin' In The Wind" and 'A Hard Rain's A-Gonna Fall.'

The two concerts generated proceeds for $243,418.50 eventually donated to UNICEF while also raising awareness and visibility for the organization around the world.

The shows were recorded by Phil Spector and engineer Gary Kellgren with the music produced by Spector and George Harrison.

American documentary film director and producer Saul Swimmer directed the movie produced by Harrison and Allen Klein which was distributed by 20th Century Fox in March 1972.

Swimmer had served as co-producer of the Neil Aspinall produced Beatles documentary *Let It Be* in 1970. Swimmer, a graduate of Carnegie Mellon University in Pittsburgh, Pennsylvania, in 1967 directed and produced the TV movie *Around the World of Mike Todd* narrated by Orson Welles, and previously directed the pop and rock musical 1968 comedy *Mrs. Brown, You've Got a Lovely Daughter* starring Herman's Hermits.

"I was at the Bangladesh sound check," mentioned photographer Henry Diltz, whose portrait of George Harrison graces the most recent *Concert for Bangladesh* CD box and DVD.

"I did not leave the perch, but walked around with a crew pass, so I was golden. I could not have a camera in my hand. I noticed Allen Klein of ABKCO sitting in the audience just up the side in the bleachers with couple of chauffer goon type guys. He had a cane and I saw him point his cane to someone on the floor. 'Who is that guy? Get him out!' And these goons went down and escorted whoever that was out. It was someone with a camera. They had very tight security. I could not get kicked out. I watched the rehearsal.

"I already had been at Woodstock and Monterey. I got the sense something monumental was being brewed up by important people in the music industry. Not the people I was hanging out with. Sound check was kind of boring.

"The show was amazing. I was in the wings. Not lost with me was George Harrison introducing Ravi Shankar. I saw Ravi at Monterey and Woodstock. I was very familiar with him and his music and loved it. I was tremendously moved by his mood. This was an inside facility, and I had always seen him outside in venues."

**George Harrison
(Photo by Henry Diltz)**

The Concert for Bangladesh, (originally titled *The Concert for Bangla Desh*) was a live, triple album, commercially released just before Christmas in 1971 in the US and after New Year's Day 1972 in the UK.

Richard Williams in the January 1, 1972 issue of *Melody Maker* proclaimed "If you buy one LP in 1972, make it this one." It immediately became a bestseller, landing at #2 for several weeks in the US charts and becoming George Harrison's second #1 UK album.

The multi-disc soundtrack set won the Grammy Award for Album of the Year of 1972 for music producers Harrison and Phil Spector.

George Harrison would set up his own charity foundation, The George Harrison Fund for UNICEF, after he became frustrated with red tape and bureaucracies that had slowed down the process of spreading monies intended for recipients.

The George Harrison Fund for UNICEF is a joint undertaking between the Harrison family and the U.S. Fund for UNICEF to support UNICEF programs that provide lifesaving assistance to children, including health, education, nutrition and emergency relief. In the tradition established by George Harrison and Ravi Shankar, The George Harrison Fund for UNICEF continues to support UNICEF programs in Bangladesh while expanding its influence to include other countries where children are in need.

Apple Corps/Capitol in October 2005 re-released *The Concert for Bangladesh-George Harrison and Friends* on CD and DVD to celebrate the 35th anniversary of this collaboration. The DVD includes the original 99-minute film restored and remixed in 5.1, as well as 72-minutes of extras.

There is also previously unseen footage: "If Not for You," with George and Bob Dylan from rehearsals, "Come On In My Kitchen," featuring George, Eric Clapton and Leon Russell at the sound check and a Bob Dylan performance from the afternoon show of "Love Minus Zero/No Limit," not included in the original film.

The extras feature a 45-minute documentary directed by Claire Ferguson and co-produced by Olivia Harrison. *The Concert for Bangladesh Revisited* with George Harrison and friends, with exclusive interviews and contributions from Sir Bob Geldof, and United Nations Secretary-General Kofi Annan, who stated, "George and his friends were pioneers."

In the documentary, Eric Clapton suggested, "This will always be remembered as a time that we could be proud of being musicians. We just weren't thinking of ourselves for five minutes." Ringo Starr added, "The beauty of the event came across and the audience was so great." Leon Russell added, "It was just one high level of experience from beginning to end."

"I first heard Ravi at age 19," volunteered drummer/percussionist Jim Keltner in a 2020 phone interview. "We used to sit around and listen to Ravi and Stravinsky in the days when we were trying to expand our consciousness. When Ralph J. Gleason wrote about Miles Davis he'd sometimes mention Ravi. I became well aware of him.

"And, then, years later to have actually recorded with him when George asked me to be part of his album *Shankar Family & Friends.* And to be on tour with George and watch Ravi in 1974 and the most amazing musicians on the planet every night was a thrill beyond. Every night on the plane I would sit next to Alla Rakha while he was having a Scotch. He didn't speak English at all and he would sing the tabla rhythms to me," Jim marveled.

"Over the decades I got to see George and Ravi a lot together. It was a father and son relationship in a way. He brought Ravi to the rest of the world in a very big way. One of my favorite things was being with George in the audience watching Ravi play."

I talked to Jim one evening over dinner at his home in Los Angeles for a 2002 *Goldmine* magazine interview.

"George was a very important teacher to me at that time. Georgie. My friend and my beautiful and wonderful brother. And I read these things about him being kind of anti-celebrity and all that. I guess he had enough of that with the Beatles, ya know, so that the Bangladesh event seems like a warm and wonderful cause that everyone turned out for.

"*The Concert for Bangladesh* concerts were in August, and the previous March, I did a couple of songs with Leon, Carl Radle, and Jesse Ed Davis for Bob Dylan, 'Watching The River Flow' and 'When I Paint My Masterpiece.'

"George called and said, 'Let's do a single.' So we went

Jim Keltner (Photo by Henry Diltz)

in to Wally Heider's studio 4 on Cahuenga in Hollywood and did 'Bangla Desh' with George and Phil Spector. Leon played and I think he helped arrange the song. The birth of the concert sort of started with this single. I loved the song."

For the Bangladesh booking, Keltner is double drumming with Ringo Starr, who was asked by George to play and accepted on the condition "but only if Keltner will do it with me."

Ringo Starr, Concert for Bangladesh   (Photo by Henry Diltz)

"Ringo was a little unsure, about playing live with a big band. He hadn't played live in a while, either. So, when they asked me I said 'of course, but I want to stay out of his way.'

"I didn't want to destroy anything of that great feel or his sound. When we actually sat down to play, I asked them to set me up in such a way that I could see his hi-hat hand. And after we played together at the sound check I had to decide on a few things. And one of the first decisions I made was to not play the hi-hat much. So I played the hi-hat like I had seen Levon (Helm) of The Band do, which was to pull the hand off the hi-hat for the two and four, so that it didn't come down with the backbeat at the same time. And that helped me stay out of Ringo's way.

"Ringo was a little on edge," admitted Jim. "He didn't fancy playing alone and was kind of unsure about his playing, which is amazing if you think about it. Ringo is one of rock's all-time great drummers. All you have to do is listen to the Beatles records, of course, especially, the *Live at the BBC*. Rock and roll drumming doesn't get any better than that. Earl Palmer, Hal Blaine, Gary Chester, Fred Below, and David 'Panama' Francis, great early rock and R&B drummers, and Ringo fit right in there with those guys. Listen to the *BBC* tapes and you'll hear what I'm saying. "Playing on *Bangladesh* was a really big deal for me. I made sure to stay completely out of Ringo's way and just played the bare minimum.

"For *Bangladesh* there was only one rehearsal," reaffirmed Jim. "The rehearsal was in a basement of a hotel, or near the hotel. George was beside himself trying to put together a set list and trying to find out if Eric (Clapton) was going to be able to make it, Where Bob (Dylan) was gonna make it. Plus, George was nervous because he hadn't played live for a long time. He was absolutely focused and fantastic as a leader. Of course, he had Leon in the band. And Leon helped with the arranging and all. I remember that everything seemed to be fine at the sound check. and that I didn't have too many concerns. When we started playing with the audience in the room it really did come alive.

"I remember loving the sound of Madison Square Garden. I heard Phil's voice over the speakers, but never really saw him at the actual show, except during sound check. He was in the Record Plant (recording) truck.

"Phil had his hands full and did a remarkable job if you really think about it. Horns, multiple singers, double drums, lots of guitars.

That was his forte, so he wasn't intimidated by two drummers and 14 background singers. On *Bangladesh,* George was very lucky to have had Phil on that set," underscored Jim.

In my 2004 book, *This Is Rebel Music,* Keltner revealed, "When George (Harrison) introduced Bob, I stood backstage and Dylan walked on. Jean jacket, kind of quiet the way Bob always is. Bob walked by me on his way to the stage. I had already recorded with him a couple of months earlier, and I sort of knew him.

Bob Dylan, Concert for Bangladesh, 1971
(Photo by Henry Diltz)

"He walks out there on the stage and puts the harp up to his mouth and starts singing and playing and chills up and down my arms. His voice and the command, it was awesome. And Leon decides to go up with his bass for 'Just Like a Woman,' and play with him. It was a tremendous moment. It was real dark on stage with a little light for them. Dylan was incredible. Standing in the back in the dark, it was great to see Leon have the guts to get up there with the bass and perform with him on 'Just Like a Woman.'

"George seemed very powerful that night. And the songs: 'My Sweet Lord,' 'Awaiting On You All,' 'Beware Of Darkness,' 'While

My Guitar Gently Weeps,' 'Wah-Wah,' and 'Bangla Desh.' Great stuff. And very appropriate for the suffering going on over there, and don't forget Billy Preston with 'That's The Way God Planned It.' I loved being a part of that with George. *Bangladesh* was a great little reunion. They loved playing with Ringo and me. Klaus Voorman was the principal bass player on *Bangladesh*. Phil loved the way Klaus played. He had a great way of stretching the time. Klaus is one of the greatest bass players I've ever played with.

"I was right in the back watching Ravi Shankar's set. The whole thing and being amazed and just how powerful it was. I had been listening to Ravi

George Harrison and Bob Dylan (Photo by Henry Diltz)

and Alla Rahka for years, and here I was seeing them up so close I could reach out and touch them. Alla Rakha and Ravi Shankar were telepathic. They played together for so many years, it was awesome to watch it. Ravi was at his peak in terms of technical proficiency. Alla Rakha was as well. It was dazzling. It is something that will always be with me.

"Between shows the hotel had an incredible hospitality room set up with delicious Indian food.

"Years later the cameraman on the *Bangladesh* movie told me, 'you really caused me some problems when I was editing that film because your hand coming up like that I could never tell whether I was on the cut.'

"In fact, one night at the Record Plant studio when somebody asked John [Lennon] did he see *The Concert for Bangladesh* movie John said he went to the premiere and when he saw my face on the screen for the first time he stood up and yelled 'Hey-that's me drummer!'

"I think it was Pythagoras who came up with the idea that music was this intangible thing that somehow connects the universe through the cosmos," singer and teacher Claudia Lennear told journalist Christian John Wikane in an interview he conducted with her for *Pop Matters* in June 2013.

"It just kind of made me think. This guy was onto something 2,500 years ago. In that particular band was Billy Preston, Leon Russell, Jim Keltner, and all of the wonderful singers in the choir. Everything just kind of came together. We never really rehearsed for that. All of us were about the same age and we came from similar influences. Maybe that's how it came together because Lord knows most people have to rehearse to get it right. We went through a couple of sound checks but that was it. To me it was cosmic," commented Lennear, one of the stars of director Morgan Neville's *20 Feet From Stardom*, the 2014 Oscar winning documentary.

"George may have always been the Quiet One," recalls lifelong Beatlemaniac Gary Pig Gold, "but today I think he would be called instead the Deep Beatle. Always grinning that sly, close-to-the-turtleneck smile, let's remember he always had just the right solo and diminished chord for the proceedings, plus was the first to fly highest when the Fabs splintered. Free as a bird.

"It's just no surprise then that such a kindred musical spirit as Ravi Shankar recognized this deep blueness within George Harrison, and duly approached him when his country called. Of course George being George, he put his guitar where most would put only their money, and when he made his own calls, all answered. Eric, Billy, Leon, Ringo, and even blue-jeaned Bob to name but the obvious.

"*The Concert for Bangladesh* made that first big helping splash, proving that rock 'n' roll trumped mere governments. And the world may not necessarily be a better place for it today, but it's definitely a wiser one.

"Of course George himself was *always* wise. And his heart was always as large as the spirit it carried, then and now. After all, isn't it usually the Quiet ones you have to watch?"

Dr. James Cushing in Morro Bay, California, supplied reflections on *The Concert for Bangladesh*.

"It might have been the first time in history that a major concert has begun with the star asking the audience to settle down instead of saying let's party. So, right away the tone is different."

"Something also needs to be said about how George Harrison is the most important non-Indian Indian. In the sense that the primary

413

association that Americans have with Indian culture is whatever George Harrison started them out with, unless they've actually met an Indian person. 'Norwegian Wood,' and 'Within You Without You.' The entire association that Harrison has with India. I think George Harrison is one of the reasons Indian cuisine has caught on in the United States," illustrates Cushing.

Dr. James Cushing   (Photo by Henry Diltz)

"There is, in Harrison's work, an extremely sincere and extremely devoted, extremely intent spiritual and religious interest. And that's been true from the very beginning. And that gives his work a certain power, focus and a certain respectability. But there is the B-side of that, which has to do with the weakness toward preaching and didacticism. And this sense for years and years humanity has been laboring along in the darkness and then, low and behold, here comes George Harrison to save us from the darkness by telling us what we need to do.

"There is a didactic element in Harrison and that in the concert for Bangladesh he seems to show an awareness of far high the didactic will and will not take you, because he is almost always deferring. You can hear it at the beginning. 'We've got a good show for you. I hope we do anyway.' I do not want to dismiss in any way the humanitarianism of it. I just want to say that humanitarianism is a message Ravi Shankar himself said, 'the concert has a message. We are not politicians. We are artists.'

"At *Bangladesh*, George Harrison is a voice of caution and fragility, a very interior kind of voice. We can tell and hear he is still a little nervous about the way this is going to go, like forgetting to introduce Billy Preston. It caused attention to how blissed out he's not. George, we love you.

"There is also a degree of humility here, essentially with Ravi Shankar and Alla Akbar Kahn, two of the greatest virtuosos in the history of playing stringed instruments opening up for Ringo and Leon Russell.

**Ravi Shankar, August 1, 1971, Concert for Bangladesh
(Photo by Henry Diltz)**

"In other words the old world having an ambivalent place in the new world. This music is a little bit more serious than our music.

"What Skankar and Ala Akbar do is very smart. Instead of doing a full raga performance, 35 minutes of just droning sitar and sarod. They start off with something with a bright, snappy tempo and they go. In other words, all the things that Americans who don't know much about Indian music they love about it they emphasize. There is also the touch of the feminine with the presence of Kamala Chakravarty.

"Shankar is treated as a kind of invocation of India," proposed Cushing. "And the concert at one level is about India, but on another level is not about India because Ringo Starr is singing 'It Don't Come

Easy' and Bob Dylan singing 'Mr. Tambourine Man,' and George Harrison doing 'Something' have nothing to do with Indian, really. But the concert has to do with India. So how to you assemble a concert of non-Indian music and make it relevant to India? There is only one way to get some authentic serious Indian stuff on the bill. Everybody knew who he was already."

"George Harrison's *Bangladesh* tour takes its white suburban audience to Bangladesh and then it takes us up to Watts for a while with Billy Preston with 'That's The Way God Planned It.' His authentic mastery of the gospel idiom and his willingness to find ways to find ways to work that gospel idiom into secular music. Billy also made the Beatles be on their best behavior when George invited him on the 'Get Back' recording sessions. Leon Russell and Billy Preston had played together earlier on the television series *Shindig!* in 1965.

"'Beware of Darkness' with Leon Russell and Jim Horn playing sax becomes more of a blessing," pondered Prof. Cushing.

"We have essentially an African-American gospel group with a British lead singer trying to get us into Hindu religious mythology. And this longhaired Oklahoma boy, Leon, drawls a country western take on the whole verse. So, we have India, plus England, plus religious devotion, plus Hari Krishna, plus rock super stardom. Only in America, the cultural salad bowl and head on collision.

"The fact that Leon Russell's 2nd LP has 'A Hard Rain's A Gonna-Fall' and 'It Takes A Lot To Laugh, It Takes A Train To Cry' in that order, and the *Bangladesh* set does those songs in that order in similar arrangements, needs to be pointed out. Russell's musicality anchors the 'superstar' vibe of Dylan and two Beatles; they are the steak potatoes and peas, but Russell is the plate and the table.

"Because two actual Beatles and a number of Beatles auxiliary members, Bob Dylan in the flesh, we don't have the Rolling Stones, but a very good instancing of Rolling Stones Dyanosian sexual rock energy with Leon doing 'Jumpin' Jack Flash.' All three of the '60s royalties and two of the forces that the '60s generation most bow down too.

"I do hope, though, that people recognize how important Leon Russell was to that Bangladesh band and to the rock scene during that whole 1969-72 period.

"This is the first time since 1965 that Dylan is singing his own material in New York and given how central the city is to his career. The surprises that it represented because no one at the arena or record business expected to hear or see him do something like this. Only in a sense is there a link to him performing at The March on Washington in 1963 where Dylan shows up to support an event for the larger good of a humanitarian cause. The March on Washington was much more explicitly political than *The Concert for Bangladesh*.

"The fact we get to hear George and Ringo and Bob, Bob Dylan and the Beatles singing together for the first time ever, kind of a thrill of uniqueness. All of the Dylan songs come from 1963-1966.

"Dylan had just turned age 30. He didn't perform any compositions from his recent albums of the time, *Nashville Skyline, Self Portrait* and *New Morning*. He was distancing people from the notion of Bob Dylan as the voice of his generation. So the gesture he makes in *Bangladesh*, and this is a very voice of a generation kind of move. Maybe because it is a special thing for Harrison and a special thing for *Bangladesh*, he'd be willing to do it just one more time.

"Plus, later in 1971, Dylan and Columbia Records release his *Greatest Hits Vol. 2* that has a cover photo and other pictures from his Bangladesh appearance.

"But let's not forget the next time Bob Dylan emerges

Bob Dylan (Photo by Henry Diltz)

he is a very different kind of performer with a different voice, a different haircut, a different set of arrangements for his *Before the Flood* tour."

George Harrison's efforts on *The Concert for Bangladesh* also had a life-altering directive on guitarist, singer/songwriter/producer, actor and deejay, Steven Van Zandt, a member of Bruce Springsteen and the E Street Band.

"Sun City," a 1985 protest song written by Van Zandt and produced by Van Zandt and Arthur Baker that was recorded by Artists United Against Apartheid to convey opposition to the existing South African policy of apartheid which ended in 1994.

"Well, it was directly related to George Harrison, of course," Van Zandt informed me in a 2002 interview. *The Concert for Bangladesh.* "No question about it.

"That was the first time where we connected those things together, man. Social concern and rock 'n' roll were two different things, man. And, that was big, and it stayed with me. That permanently affected me, and then when I had a chance to do it I did it."

In 2011, Steven emailed me from Lillehammer, Norway and amplified his bond to Harrison and the *Bangladesh* collaboration.

"The anti-apartheid *Sun City* project (single, album, video, documentary, book, teaching guide) was a high point and a rare clear-cut victory from the 10 years I spent immersed in the dark, murky, frustrating labyrinth of international liberation politics.

"It came in the middle of my five politically themed solo albums and had its roots, like all the charity and consciousness-raising multi-artist events that would follow, in *The Concert for Bangladesh.*

"One could go back seven years further to the work of Bob Dylan for the reason my generation had any political or social awareness at all. He would single-handedly bring the more personal, socially, and politically relevant lyrics previously confined to country blues, country, and folk music, to the pop and rock idiom. The fact that he probably did so to impress his girlfriend Suze at the time, rather than some grand megalomaniacal scheme to become the spokesperson of his generation, just makes him all the more human and likable and is probably the reason he's still around and still great.

"And it's not a coincidence that he's the one artist on both *Bangladesh* and *Sun City* 15 years later.

"But it was the *Concert for Bangladesh* that would be the beginning of all the multi-artist events bringing awareness to a cause and/or raising money.

"It would take the energy and focus of a Beatle, George Harrison, to bring the extraordinary necessary life-force to get the event organized and executed so quickly and with such high quality.

"The unfortunate financial complications that followed was the one thing that couldn't be foreseen by noble naïve artists trying to do the right thing in an emergency situation. The despicable, mindless, emotionless bureaucracy they would run into would later instruct all of us who followed.

"But that aside, it was a wonderful event and we all owe George our gratitude. All of us who have ever had the desire to use—and justify—our celebrity to do some good, as well as the tens of millions who have benefited from these events, all have him to thank. Him, and the generous heart of the legendary master musician Ravi Shankar, who came to his friend with the desire to bring aid and attention to a terrible, tragic situation.

"As far as history is concerned, we shouldn't take for granted the fact that these charity and awareness events exist, and that the rock world has done more than any other industry to help people in need. This was not some inevitable act of destiny or even a predictable evolution of what turned out to be a 25-year successful run of the music business.

"The idea had to start somewhere. The source is *The Concert for Bangladesh*."

David Leaf's Award-winning Documentaries on Rock Legends John Lennon, Brian Wilson, and James Brown

David Leaf is a Peabody and WGAW award-winning writer, director, producer and the creative visionary behind such critically acclaimed films and festival favorites as Focal Award winner *The Night James Brown Saved Boston, The U.S. vs. John Lennon* (winner of the Exhibitors' Award at The Venice Film Festival), the Grammy-nominated *Beautiful Dreamer: Brian Wilson and the Story of SMiLE, The Bee Gees: This Is Where I Came In*, and the forthcoming feature *Dion: Born To Cry*.

His television credits include being one of the writers on the Emmy-winning landmark 9/11, all-network telethon *America: A Tribute To Heroes*. That same year, Leaf wrote and produced *TNT's An-All Star Tribute To Brian Wilson*, a consultant on the long-running. A&E music series *Live By Request* and was a producer of the Emmy- nominated *Billy Joel: In His Own Words* (A&E).

419

Additionally, since 2010, David Leaf has been teaching undergraduate courses at the UCLA Herb Alpert School of Music in L.A. including courses on music documentary, hit songwriting (from the rock era to today) and the Beatles.

David Leaf (Photo by Juan Tallo © JuanTallo.com, courtesy of UCLA)

Harvey Kubernik: Hello Professor. Let's go back in time. What inspired *The U.S. vs. John Lennon*? Where did the concept for it come from? What are its roots and was it initially conceived of as a feature length movie?

David Leaf: The real roots of this film came from when I was a student at George Washington University. The south end of the campus was only three blocks from the White House, Because GW had become a staging area for those who were organizing the big anti-war demonstrations in D.C., the radical left reportedly called it "The most strategically located university in the country." That meant we were in the center of a cascading series of events.

I recall being chased by riot police and seeing the campus surrounded by military the morning *before* a demonstration began. So, ultimately, *The U.S. vs John Lennon* is kind of my revenge film against the disgraced President, the jailed Vice-President and the entire criminal enterprise that was the Nixon administration. I don't use that pejorative lightly. Because of activities related to the Watergate cover-up, the Attorney General, top White House officials and many more served jail time.

When I first conceived of the project, it was as part of a series I called *The Secret War Against...* which would feature separate films on subjects like the persecuted comedian Lenny Bruce. I called one episode *The Secret War against John Lennon.*

Then, after Jon Weiner's brilliant book *Gimme Some Truth* (published in 1999), revealed the unexpurgated government files about John, the name of the film had to change. It wasn't a *secret* war anymore. Anyway, after I had met Yoko and got her blessing to make it (which is quite a story unto itself), I still didn't have a new title. During a pitch when I was describing the film, I likened it to a heavyweight championship fight. In this corner, the United States. In that corner, John Lennon. *The U.S. vs. John Lennon.* The moment I said it out loud I knew that would be the title.

HK: What made you decide to blend music and politics initially, and after editing, why does the movie work musically, politically and spiritually?

DL: The blend of music and politics was inevitable, given my kind of bottomless disgust for how one president after another has lied us into war. President George W. Bush/Vice President Dick Cheney "scheme" to use the 9-11 attack to launch a war against Iraq -- the so-called non-existant "weapons of mass destruction" -- and the cowardly votes that approved it, felt to me so reminiscent of the lies that had been told and then revealed in *The Pentagon Papers*, I couldn't believe we were repeating the mistakes of the past. So the time seemed right for this movie.

The story resonated, to me at least, and once Yoko had agreed to participate, I went out to pitch it. Lionsgate said "yes."

As to using music, that had always been in my DNA, as an author, a writer/producer on TV series music specials and award shows, and as a producer/documentary maker, going all the way back to *You Can't Do That*, the documentary I wrote/produced about the making of the classic Beatles film, *A Hard Day's Night.*

I wrote *The Billboard Awards* and produced quite a few music projects, including retrospectives featuring Frank Sinatra, Nat "King" Cole, Dean Martin and Rosemary Clooney. Those, however, were celebrations of great artists from another generation.

That changed for me, beginning with the 2000 Bee Gees feature length biography we did for A&E. Since then, I've gotten the trust and been privileged to use the artist's own music...and as much as possible, *only* their music...as an integral part of the storytelling. Especially when it's the entire underscore, as it is in Brian Wilson, Bee Gees films, and *The U.S. vs. John Lennon,* it's a way of allowing the viewer to subliminally be "drenched" in the music of our subject.

For *The U.S. vs. John Lennon,* Yoko had her engineer give us "mix minus," versions of many masters. I think, thirty-six John Lennon masters without lead vocals. So instrumental versions of John's songs became the score for the movie. I think it was the first time that his solo catalogue could be heard in that way.

What that means is that even when we're providing historical context, which to me is essential to the storytelling, Lennon's music is always there.

As to why and how the movie "works," I'll leave that to other people to judge, but what works for me is the fact that through the use of music, archival audio and video, John is seen and heard telling his own story, and his enormous fearlessness, brilliance and charisma shines through. To the extent the movie feels timeless, I believe it is because the story is told through the prism of John Lennon's enduring greatness as an artist, a visionary and a revolutionary dreamer.

Regarding spirituality, I think there are unmissable hints of it in both *Beautiful Dreamer: Brian Wilson & The Story of SMiLE* and *The U.S. vs. John Lennon* because both artists were so in touch with what music means besides chart success.

When John sings "Imagine," and the lyric is about being a "dreamer," and Brian sings the first line of "Beautiful Dreamer,"they are both clearly expressing the "magic" that they have experienced when music comes through them.

And it's probably never been more front and center than in my almost-finished documentary of the legendary Rock and Roll Hall of Famer Dion. And thats because of him and the way he frames his life story; God is so central to who he is. The time certainly seems right for a film that connects music and humanity with a God who is forgiving.

HK: Can you see the relationship of your John Lennon movie mirroring today's climate of fear, paranoia, suspicion, and finger pointing?
DL: Sadly, yes. I can. I think it is all too relevant. What I wanted the film to do was tell John's story as it unfolded against the context of the times...as seen and experienced by the people who were there, who understood that era. His music is key; there is no voice-over

narration. The goal was to immerse the viewer in the very turbulent times of the late 1960s/early 1970s.

In my first meeting with Yoko, when I told her how I saw the opening of the movie, that began in discussion about Germany in the 1930s. And I truly, if naively, believed the film was to be something of a warning as, George Santayana said, "Those who cannot learn from history are doomed to repeat it."

It's never explicitly said in the film. Maybe it's only implicit in my head. Sadly, by the time the film was finished, I had come to see that we just seem to be condemned to repeat history. To me, we are now in enormously more turbulent times. Again, repeating the mistakes of the past, except this time on steroids.

I teach a UCLA course in music documentary; The Lennon film is part of that course as well as my class called *The Reel Beatles*. I guest lecture at Otis School of Design in their *Movies That Matter* course, and a course on *Politics in Film*, and I'm proud that the Lennon doc is always in their curricula, because it means it is seen by a lot of 20-year old students every year. It seems that the movie does resonate with audiences as, to use your phrase, in certain ways it is mirroring today's climate.

Regarding the "then vs. now" comparison you suggest about the film's release in 2006, while it was hardly an identical reflection with Iraq, in that both never-ending wars were very different, there are chilling moments in the film, such as an archival clip of a Nixon speech where he refuses to set a timetable for troop withdrawal from Vietnam.

At times, what was happening to John Lennon...and indeed, in the country... also sounds just like today's news. But I would say the valid comparison probably has mostly to do with how the administration conducts the secret business of governance and war and their response to dissent.

What we do see repeatedly is our failure to address what President Eisenhower warned, in his farewell address, to beware of "the Military-Industrial Complex. The potential for the disastrous rise of misplaced power exists and will persist." Sadly, tragically, Ike's admonition was never heeded. Trillions and trillions of dollars later, where are we?

HK: Bring me through the genesis of the Lennon project initially.
DL: As mentioned before, this was a project that had long been on my "short list." My "dream list" of projects, if you will. But I had no

idea how to get it done. So it wasn't until through a colleague (Steve Sterling at Eagle Vision), that I was introduced to Yoko's attorney, the late Peter Shukat. In 2001, it began to gather some momentum.

Meeting Peter and his colleague, Jonas Herbsman and their agreeing to talk with Yoko about it was a major step because from my point of view, the keys to this film being successful was going to be our ability to license John's music, get access to the Lennon photo and film archive, and, of course, interview Yoko. We couldn't do any of that without her permission and active participation.

I met with Yoko before I began pitching it to studios, way before production started. It was to explain how we intended to tell the story and how we wanted...needed...her to be on-camera as the "co-hero" of the film and off-camera with the music and archives. I can't speak for Yoko, but from our first meeting, she liked the *idea* I presented. Perhaps she just decided that the time was right for this story to be told.

Perhaps the next big step was a creative one. My film *Beautiful Dreamer: Brian Wilson and the Story of SMiLE* was released, and I think it was indicative of what kind of storytelling I could do in a feature documentary.

HK: Take me through the interview process you employed for this film. The artists and commentators who were chosen to participate. Explain your draft picks, and why so many wanted to endorse and support John Lennon's fight. List some of your favorite interviews that impacted you.

DL: We spent quite a long time putting together a very ambitious list of people we wanted to participate in the film. The main goal was to enlist a "cast" of interviewees who were from the era and/or genuinely understood the times, could contextualize the events of the Vietnam War, and understood the courage John had. Many of the people we interviewed either knew John or worked with him.

Greatest interview moments? We were so privileged on this film, and my co-director and I had to almost toss a coin as to who got to interview whom. My personal favorites included getting a "personal lecture" from Noam Chomsky, sitting with the great historian Gore Vidal, talking Constitutional law with Gov. Mario Cuomo. G. Gordon Liddy was quite unusual. And as you'll see in the movie, how about Senator George McGovern spontaneously breaking into "Give Peace A Chance"?

The Walter Cronkite interview was the last one I did, and what we got from that was both perfect and an hilarious experience.

HK: Why were so many influential media members and authors willing to chat about John Lennon and his plight? Why has this chilling story sort of been relegated to the "back of the bus" in terms of our cultural memory?
DL: Good question. I don't really know. Maybe it's as simple as the enormous media clutter and noise. Or just a lack of education. Part of my mision at UCLA, is to make great artists like John aren't fogotten. John Lennon was an extraordinary artist and a very courageous man. He and Yoko were willing to use their celebrity and art to fearlessly make the world a better place. And that can be a very dangerous threat to "the powers that be."

In the film, I think the challenge was to bring the story to the screen with a sense of visual excitement so it wouldn't just be "talking heads."

The themes addressed in the movie are big ones---war and peace, freedom of speech, dissent vs. disloyalty, governmental abuse of power, immigration. And while those are all political, the film is undeniably musical, with thirty-nine songs...three Beatles classics plus those from John's solo catalogue.

When the events of the movie happened, I was too naive to truly understand exactly what John and Yoko were doing, so in making the movie, my respect for what they accomplished grew exponentially.

I was reminded of how charismatic and how honest he was. What a sharp mind he had. Back in the day, I was so enthralled by the Beatles that I don't think I could appreciate either the gravity of the threat to John or the balls it took he and Yoko to stand up to power.

I also think that the film gave me even more respect for the purity and boldness of the art he and Yoko created during that time. For example, actually seeing Bagism, the light bulb goes on.

HK: This was a guy who loved the United States and yet, efforts were being made to monitor his actions. What were you trying to illustrate, and what does the film say to the audience and viewers?
DL: Another tough question. Maybe "watch your back?" A bigger theme to me is that great art and artistry is all that matters...all that survives through the ages. We generally know nothing about the Medici Popes, but the art they commissioned half a millennium ago by so many Renaissance-era greats including Michelangelo, DaVinci,

Raphael and Botticelli (in recent popular culture, with Donatello, known as *The Teenage Mutant Ninja Turtles*) still continues to enthrall the world. And perhaps that everything we need to know about the past can be seen and heard through the art of the times.

And perhaps, more naively on my part... and yet most relevant to today too... I think the film reminds us to be ever vigilant in defense of the Constitution. Trgically, even more relevant today.

HK: As a filmmaker, and a veteran of some seminal pop and rock music documentaries, can you expand on some cinematic areas that integrate picture and sound?

DL: Anything that enhances storytelling that remains true to the story is invaluable. In *The U.S. vs. John Lennon*, John's music is essential in giving us vital information, eliciting emotion and moving the story forward.

In regard to the visuals, in the film we used the most sophisticated graphics we could afford at the time. A great team at Sony Music Studios in New York (check out the film credits), helped bring a visual excitement and unity to the film. And our editor, Peter Lynch, has the talent to seamlessly combine visuals with music to help make films that hold up under repeated viewing... that almost demand repeated viewing, because there is so much happening on screen.

I love using archival footage, especially when the archival team can find footage that hasn't been overexposed. And in *The U.S. vs. John Lennon*, we had a lot of footage that will surprise even the most accomplished collectors. In part, that's because of my dear friend, the legendary archivasts Eric Kulberg, who knows where everything is. Without going into detail as to the source, thanks to a secret collector, there is a considerable amount of archival video and audio in the film that has either never been seen or heard before this production, some that hadn't been seen in 35 years or was never seen in the US.

Color footage is especially striking, especially when it comes from an era when color television was still something of a novelty. But generally, black and white footage is sharper and for some reason, feels more "historic," whatever that means.

Back in the day, John and Yoko had cameras or tape recorders around them constantly as if they were living a reality show. They were artists *and* documentarians. We were fortunate to have access to that archive itself.

What you see of the John Sinclair benefit concert they performed

426

at in 1971 was of a quality that had never been seen before. That's true of everything in the movie.

You have to have a great research team work around the world to get as close to the source material as possible. The goal is to insure that anything that is in the film is as good as it can be quality-wise. But the key to using rare footage is, "Is it part of the story?"

Our archivist found this spectacular Bagism press event from Austria that I don't think had ever been seen in the US. As I referred to earlier, we had heard the phrase "Bagism" in "Give Peace A Chance." We have sung along with the song for decades, most of us never even asking,"What *is* Bagism?"

So to see John and Yoko in the bag as it was happening at the time is extraordinary. To see John getting his green card, thrilling. Probably, no one had seen that footage since it was aired on the local New York news. That's now nearly fifty years ago.

I mentioned him a few moments ago. Peter Lynch edited the John Lennin, my James Brown and Brian Wilson features, our acclaimed Harry Nilsson doc (directed by John Scheinfeld), and I think all of the television specials (e.g. Norman Lear) Authorized Pictures made during the the first decade of the 21st Century. He's a brilliant young man with an extraordinary sensibility. Really can't sing his praises enough.

The reason my documentary class works in the music school at UCLA, is that music is an integral part of the movie from before the editing process begins. Music is vital to the storytelling, and as I teach my students every year, the challenge in each film is that to understand the story, one needs to understand the times in which it happened. In the Lennon and James Brown films especially, that was a particularly daunting challenge. To do that in a journalistically responsible way, we needed a lot of voices in the film, a lot of "talking heads" to give us the kaleidoscope of perspectives that existed back then. And now too.

But one of the keys to music docs, or any kind of film is *music.* With Phil Ramone, I produced a series called *The Score*, and we would show scenes from features both "wet" (meaning with music), and "dry" (meaning no music). Watching these great films without a score is almost a kind of slow torture. For my work, music is particularly vital to keeping the forward motion of a documentary.

I have learned from great writers and filmmakers that the key to a creatively successful movie is that you can only tell one story. Unless you're a Robert Altman or Quentin Tarantino.

427

In terms of staying "on story," what that meant for us was implicit in the title. We weren't producing a John Lennon anthology in four, six, or eight hours, which would have been a magnificent project to do. We were telling just *one* story.

So that's why there were aspects of John's life in the story that we either chose not to include in the film or dealt with as expeditiously as possible. Like virtually the entire Beatles saga.

More specifically, we had found footage of John and Yoko at a 1972 election night party, and they were upset that Nixon had won and George McGovern lost. But we decided that other than Nixon winning re-election, what happened that night wasn't relevant to telling the story of the battle at the forefront of *The U.S. vs. John Lennon.*

Story is king. It just is. If you don't tell your story well, you lose the audience. If you go "off story," you can lose them. The challenge is to draw them in quickly. You have to get the audience to sit with you and go on this ride for 90 minutes.

HK: Capitol Records issued a soundtrack to your movie. How were the Lennon songs selected? And why the three Beatles songs picked for inclusion? What is the mindset you had when constructing the soundtrack CD? Do the songs work away from the screen as a cohesive compilation?

DL: A lot of questions so I'll try to answer them all by giving you a sense of the process.

The folks at EMI (notably Herb Agner, Lisa Wohl and Cynthia Sexton), and the Lionsgate music team (headed up by Jay Faires), felt that the film merited a soundtrack. The soundtrack featured somewhere around 16-18 songs. The film itself has 39 music cues, including 36 Lennon (and Ono) solo works. The process of picking the songs is both musical and lyrical. Certain songs are essential to the story, and those are the ones that are featured both prominently in the movie and on the soundtrack.

Then, there are other songs that instrumentally have the right tempo, force, feel, etc. to drive a scene, and most of them were right for the soundtrack but we couldn't use them all.

The three Beatles songs---"All You Need Is Love," "Revolution" and "The Ballad Of John and Yoko"--- are the ones we felt were vital to showing John's evolution during those years. Apple and the Beatles very graciously allowed us to not only license those recordings but in the case of "All You Need Is Love" and "Revolution," the legendary world-wide premiere performance from 1967, the "Revolution" music video from 1968 and "The Ballad of John and Yoko" promo film too.

Picking the songs for the soundtrack was a group effort---the idea was to find the songs that were most important to the film, not just John's greatest hits, which have been well anthologized elsewhere. To a certain extent, the soundtrack is a "Best of" the political songs of John Lennon. It could almost be called "Power To The People."

Compilations are always tricky because if you have and know the original albums, no amount of brilliant sequencing can completely overcome your sense as to what song *should* come next. It's my belief that what makes this soundtrack so successful...both in the movie and on CD...is that it fulfills what could be a textbook definition of a great soundtrack---it sounds as if the songs were written for the movie.

We all felt that by putting together this particular group of John Lennon songs it would be a way to introduce him to an audience who only knew the greatest hits. Everybody who was integrally involved in the film---at Authorized Pictures and at Lionsgate---made suggestions. EMI had their ideas; Yoko, of course, had a strong point of view. Yoko has always taken very seriously her responsibility as the person who makes sure that John's legacy is properly respected and presented in all projects.

What I learned the most about working with her is how smart and savvy she is. And how consistent she is in her artistic approach to everything. When we made *The U.S. vs. John Lennon*, she was in her early seventies, as determined to express herself artistically as ever. That's very impressive.

She's a very smart artist. Which, as a woman, was always a challenge. Being of Japanese descent was another obstacle. We see in the film one of her most famous Fluxus-era creations, "Cut Piece." She and John met at her exhibit in London. And it became very clear to me during the making of the film that she was an enormous influence on John's art too.

Once she sets her mind on something, she is indomitable. So once she "signed on" to the movie and was happy with the final cut, she wanted to support it publicly. So she granted a number of interviews with the media for this film as well as press conference with us in New York, and on stage in Toronto for a post-screening question and answer session.

At one point, she was asked what she thought about the movie when I first approached her. She replied she was watching to see if we were going to do what we said we were going to do. She was more than cautious. Yoko is approached all the time about people wanting to make films about John. And to me the thing she said that was most meaningful was the ultimate compliment---that this movie was the one *John* would have loved.

HK: When the movie was released in August, you went to the Venice Film Festival, the Toronto Film Festival, a showing at Lincoln Center in New York City, and also several seminal high-profile screenings around Southern California.

DL: In New York, there was a screening and a press conference with Yoko. That two-week period where it was screened for the world for the first time was as gratifying a thing as I've ever experienced as a filmmaker.

In Venice in front of an international audience at one of the most prestigious film festivals in the world, in Toronto in a 1,500-seat theater, walking the red carpet with Yoko and posing for the paparazzi…the movie was received with such enthusiasm everywhere.

Those festival audiences wanted to see this movie, and they "got" it. They laughed, they applauded, and they cried in the right places. They just loved it.

The film won an official award at Venice---The Exhibitors Award--- which is a very significant thing to me in that it's the movie theater owners saying, "This is a movie we love." And when you've made a film and you want it to be seen all over the world, to go to a prestigious festival like Venice and be welcomed by the people who exhibit movies around the globe, that was very exciting.

There were two screenings at the London Film festival, and we held a Q&A afterwards. The film was extremely well-received by the people there too.

Before the movie was released, on three successive nights, we screened it in Los Angeles: an industry "insiders" event hosted by Jeff Ayeroff and Norman Lear, then for members of BAFTA and finally, at Leonard Maltin's film class at the University of Southern California.

Norman and Jeff had seen the movie previously and felt very strongly about it; they wanted to introduce it to people they knew in the industry. They wanted to make sure the movie was not overlooked. And Ayeroff was also instrumental in getting the "Rock The Vote people" to support it too.

In North America, at one point, it was playing theatrically in over

60 cities. People who went to see this movie in a theater shared in the experience. Even though it's a documentary and told through interviews and archival footage, it is John Lennon telling the story through audio, video and music. You don't feel like you're being preached to; there isn't an omnipresent narrator telling you what to think. And so it feels like a movie experience. And John is funny. So you want to be in a group with lots of people in a movie theater laughing. Because laughter is contagious.

Back to your original question: I wanted to make this movie as an allegory to what was going on in the world in 2006. But more importantly, it was created to tell the story of this great artist, an iconic figure, who through these beautiful dreams that he created--- "All You Need Is Love," "Give Peace A Chance" and "Imagine"--- found himself in the cross hairs of the Nixon administration.

That's the story we set out to tell and that's the story we told. The Iraq War is never mentioned in the film. That said, in watching the movie at the time, especially with younger people, I remember at one screening this woman (maybe she was 30) remarked that she almost got whiplash when Nixon appears on screen talking about Vietnam and a timetable for US withdrawal. She turned to me and said, "I can't believe I'm hearing this, and this happened 35 years ago, which is exactly the same 'script' we've been hearing [from the current administration] the last few years.

John Lennon was being watched (wire-tapped and spied upon), and in the early 2000s there was much talk and legislation in Washington, D.C. having to do with domestic spying and immigration. This is a story of immigration and deportation, so several of "the hot button" issues of the recent Presidential campaigns were part of John Lennon's story a long time ago.

HK: You saw John Lennon perform on stage with Elton John in 1974 at Madison Square Garden in New York. It was at that gig where John reunited with Yoko, and thirty years later, you end up collaborating with Yoko.

DL: Synchronicity? Thanksgiving night 1974, my younger brother went to the show thanks to a friend who got us tickets (the great rock concert promoter, producer, collector and archivist Jan Bridge who I had met in college).

Nearing the end of the concert, Elton brought John on stage for "Lucy In The Sky With Diamonds," "Whatever Gets You Through

431

The Night" and "I Saw Her Standing There," which John introduced as "Here's a song by an old estranged fiancé of mine called Paul."

You knew then (and know even more deeply now) about how lucky you were to be there. It was incredible. Think about it; the Beatles last concert in the United States was in San Francisco in the summer of 1966. After that, in terms of US concert stages, John was center stage for several benefits in 1969-1971. He did a few songs for a televised tribute for Sir Lew Grade. I think the only live concert appearance for which he wasn't the headliner was that show with Elton John. It would be his last night ever on a concert stage.

At the Garden that night people were going absolutely out of their minds. I know I was. It was John Lennon for God's sake. The Beatles were our Gods, so to see one in the flesh, it's beyond words. And it was John!

HK: You are obviously a big Beatles fan. How did you first connect with them?

DL: The journey for me begins strangely in late December of 1963. I was in seventh grade (or First Form as they called it) at this elite all-boys prep school in New York.

Anyway, at the "end of the semester" assembly, I first heard the Beatles played by a foreign exchange student. He had spent that fall in England. When the 11th grade student explained about a country going crazy for this group called "The Beatles," six hundred boys laughed. Same thing happened when he said teenager girls were screaming for them. We laughed again when he played a Beatles song on a tiny record player. It seemed ridiculous. (It was probably "She Loves You.")

But within less than a month, just about everyone was infected by Beatlemania. I was no exception.

From that point on, the Beatles were all I cared about in the sixties. That and sports. With a bit of politics too. In 1969, when I went to college in Washington, D.C., I was really politicized.

In the early fall of freshman year, I remember going to see Norman Mailer speak at Lafayette Park across from the White House (now infamous for the 2020 Trump photo op). After about a half hour of his speech, the sixty or so of us gathered were chased by the club-wielding CDU (Civil Disturbance Unit) of the Washington, D.C. Police department.

So while I was clueless when I went to college, it was only a matter of weeks before I began to wake up. There was "The March Against

Death" and the first Earth Day. Then, in 1971, early one morning on the day of a big May day demonstration, I remember opening the blinds in my dorm. We faced 21st and Pennsylvania Avenue. Shockingly, an airborne division of the Army was getting out of their vehicles to surround the campus. This was at 7:30. Hours before the demonstration had even begun. I turned to my roommate and said with disbelief, "What's going on? Are we living in Venezuela?"

I remember walking by Nixon's Committee To Re-Elect The President. The acronym on top of the building was CREEP. Saying to Mark Nadler, my friend and the editor of the school paper, "How appropriate."

So, this movie for me is the collision of my greatest youthful musical passion and the most important political time of my life. To then present a film about that time to the world was an incredible trip.

HK: When Fred Shuster, music editor for *The Daily News* wrote an article last decade on the enormous reggae music archive collection of writer/scholar Roger Steffens (that at the time was partially housed and displayed at the Queen Mary venue in Long Beach, California), Shuster wrote, "It may be the first museum exhibit you can dance to."

At the time I included that Shuster comment in my own *This Is Rebel Music* book profile on Steffens, adding, "the last time I talked to John Lennon was after a Wailers Roxy Theater show. I wish he could have seen and heard the reggae here."

I really wish John Lennon could have seen and heard the movie *The U.S. vs. John Lennon.*

DL: Me too. We can celebrate John for what he means to all of us. Even for a generation not born until this century, he matters. Goes back to what I said before. Great art may be all that survives. And John was a great artist.

HK: You produced the terrific making of *A Hard Day's Night* documentary that Phil Collins hosted. Can you offer some observations on the original film's producer Walter Shenson and his unique archive that was available to you? Any anecdotes about the project? I enjoyed seeing the movie's screenwriter, the late Alun Owen, on screen chat about his script.

DL: Arguably, it's the greatest narrative rock film ever made, so spending a lot of time watching and re-watching, well, let's just say it was a lot of fun to write and produce.

That was my first full-length music documentary---I named it *You Can't Do That: The Making of 'A Hard Day's Night'*. The late Mr. Shenson's archive was enhanced by one of the most legendary rock video/film researchers in the world, the producer who brought me on to the project, Ron Furmanek.

From the start of the project, I felt that a documentary on *A Hard Day's Night* needed to be funny and irreverent, in the spirit of the original movie. So what I decided might work was to use a trick similar to a TV show from the era called *Dream On*. I sat and watched *A Hard Day's Night* over and over and compiled a list of close-up "one liners" from the Beatles.

Then, as I was constructing the storyline of the documentary, I would use the Beatles comments from the movie to respond to what our interviewees would say. The idea was to give this documentary a sense of the Beatles irreverence that would work for the audience and wouldn't be viewed by Beatles' fans as sacrilegious.

One of my funniest memories of that experience was when Walter Shenson (who was executive producer of this doc) watched my first "rough cut" and dryly remarked, "Your documentary is longer than the movie." Needless to say, I cut about a half-hour out.

HK: I really enjoyed your documentary, *The Bee Gees: This Is Where I Came In*. Bring me through the development and production of that project. What were some of the essential elements that made this impressive film happen?

DL: When my Brian Wilson biography, *The Beach Boys and The California Myth*, was still in galleys, Jay Levy, an executive at RSO Records (the Bee Gees label), read it because they were looking for somebody to write the authorized biography of the Bee Gees. I think this was in the spring of 1978.

I got the job and flew to Miami that summer to begin work on it. I spent time interviewing all three Bee Gees, their wives, Robert Stigwood, Andy Gibb and their parents, wrote the book and it came out in 1979. Was my best-selling book by far.

Throughout the rest of the century, I worked with the Bee Gees on various projects, including, perhaps most significantly, their Rock and Roll Hall of Fame induction.

When I started to make all sorts of music docs and retrospectives in the 1990s, it was a natural for me to want to make one on the Bee Gees. I knew from the work I'd done with them that I had earned a measure of trust that is essential in every documentary.

Bee Gees sound check, Anaheim Convention Center January 1968
(Photo by Henry Diltz)

I think their then-manager Carol Peters might have brought the idea up originally and fortunately, A&E's *Biography* series thought this was a great subject for a two-hour special.

The timing was right. The Bee Gees were about to release what "insiders" felt would probably be their last album, if not forever then for a long time. And the title of the album, *This Is Where I Came In*, was a good name for a career-spanning documentary as well.

But, very simply, *This Is Where I Came In* works because the Bee Gees have one of the great family sagas in music history, one of the most-beloved bodies of work ever assembled and also have incredible on-camera presence and a way with an anecdote. You would have to be incompetent to make a bad Bee Gees biography, but I'll immodestly say that it is a very good one.

It's great that the film has won so many admirers, and love that those who weren't particularly big Bee Gees fans who watched it, said, "I couldn't turn it off." And then they told me that they had much more respect and admiration for the group than before.

That means a lot to me because one of my goals is that in creating these films of artists who I passionately care about appeal not just to

435

their hard-core fans but even more importantly, make new fans for them too.

HK: The Bee Gees were honest interview subjects. And you found some key archival clips in addition to an interview with their former manager, the reclusive Robert Stigwood. How important are the questions to the actual interview subjects to garner results? What do you do in terms of preparation in general for this documentary and your other work?

DL: It's important in an interview for a biographical film to have a general idea of the broad outline of the film and have key story points you need the subjects to talk about. But it's often even more important to listen, because answers sometimes take you down roads that are unexpected.

What can be even more vital is that listening gives the interview subject a chance to decide how much they are going to "give" in an interview. For this film, I had the advantage of my decades-long relationships with the Gibbs. And the brothers were competitive too; they wanted to get screen time. And the way to do that is offer a terrific insight or relate a very cool anecdote. That's unusual. Also really key is if that if your "subject" believes you will "protect" them in the editing room, they will be even more revealing in the interview.

Preparation in documentary making is no different from any other type of writing and reporting---simply, you need to know your subject better than anybody else. That said, I don't like to over-prepare for a specific interview, because I find that I can be more effective if I just take the conversation where it's naturally going, only returning to my prepared questions if and when necessary.

Some of the best stories I've gotten on tape are almost cosmic accidents. Part of the job is to create an environment in which the interviewee "forgets" there is a camera.

HK: You wrote and produced *An All-Star Tribute To Brian Wilson* concert and TV special in New York back in 2001. What was it like for you to witness and see Brian and his band over the last twenty years perform *Pet Sounds,* let alone *SMiLE* and then a new album like *That Lucky Old Sun* start to finish in concert settings?

DL: Given how long we've been fans, it was all unbelievable. You and I met in the summer of 1976 when we were sleeping overnight at the Santa Monica Civic box office for Springsteen tickets. That's when we discovered our mutual passion for not just Bruce but for Brian and the Beach Boys. Two years later, in your *Melody Maker* column, you were the first person in the rock press to write enthusiastically about my Brian Wilson biography. That same year, you, legendary L.A. DJ Rodney Bingenheimer and Brian came to my old West LA. apartment together. In so many conversations through decades, we never thought these legendary works would ever be presented live, let alone recreated in concert halls globally.

HK: Sometimes, through the years, it was you, me, Brian and your late wife Eva, eating at the Hamburger Hamlet. This was back in the early 1990s, all dreaming and hoping that Brian, who was listening to us, could eventually do some concerts and include some songs from his catalogue.

But this full-throttle big spectrum ride has been inspirational. And you may have written the most words on Brian and the Beach Boys in books, television specials, live events, concert programs and CD/ box set liner notes in popular culture history. And helming or consulting on several documentaries and other films and book projects about him.

DL: A grand obsession. By the time we presented the tribute concert in 2001 at Radio City Music Hall in New York, Brian had already done his first *Pet Sounds* tour. Which was an extraordinary experience because his band is so great, and Brian loves hearing and singing and playing that music. It was like going to see the best sermon you could have imagined, and on that tour, it unfolded every night in front of you and thousands of devotees.

There were close to 13,000 people at the Hollywood Bowl in 2000 when he performed *Pet Sounds* with the Los Angeles Philharmonic Orchestra. Not too long ago, there was another reprise of that, a tour of *Pet Sounds*, made easier because founding Beach Boys member Al Jardine had joined the Brian Wilson band.

The feeling of hearing it live has not changed anything. It's a celebration of a beloved album.

At first, in 2000, he was tentative, but pretty quickly, he began performing it with confidence and singing better and better leading up to the tribute.

I think *Pet Sounds*--- the album that Brian finished before his 24th birthday--- gets deeper and deeper as the years pass. We know that it was incredible and influential when it came out, and now, amazingly, over a half-century afterwards, even as contemporary popular music has moved in so many different directions, I still see the album mentioned by young artists as an important influence.

Given my history with Brian's story and the music, producing the Grammy-nominated *The Pet Sounds Sessions* with Brian (and engineer Mark Linett) and the *SMiLE* movie sometimes seems surreal in the extreme.

I would need to write an entire chapter in a book to explain the whole *SMiLE* adventure, how the film came about and how the completion of *SMiLE* affected Brian and (his *SMiLE* lyricist) Van Dyke Parks. But just listen to *That Lucky Old Sun*, and you'll get an idea.

I remember watching the show in England when *SMiLE* was played for the very first time; there was no question that this was an event that was emotionally fraught with a lifetime of baggage.

For all of us in the audience, we were psychically willing Brian on to do it. To me, it was a demonstration of the result of decades of "critical mass." That first night, it was like Muhammad Ali in Ali-Frazier III. Brian proved he was still the champ. He went out there and went the distance. And he got better and better as each show went on.

Imagine how you would feel if, like Brian and Van Dyke, when you're in your early twenties, you combine to create this extraordinary work of art and it never gets finished. It kind of comes out in bastardized, piecemeal form, and no one ever gets to ever hear it the way you know it was supposed to be. The way it was originally conceived and created. That's very painful for an artist.

So, there's a tremendous sense of gratitude and relief, especially on Van Dyke's part, that not only was it finally finished but it was received with such reverence, positivity and commercial success. It sold nearly a million CDs worldwide, and there was a website that showed that it was the best reviewed music of the 21st Century.

We live in a world where nothing lives up to the hype. How often in life does something *exceed* our expectations? The music of *SMiLE* did that and watching and documenting it and just being a small part of Brian's heroic journey to its completion is probably the most inspiring thing I've ever experienced. You and I are probably not going live to see anything we care about like this again.

On top of that, to be the one that Brian trusted to chronicle and bring the *SMiLE* movie out was a life-changing and career changing experience for both of us.

The *Pet Sounds* tour was an important step towards him reclaiming his musical legacy, and it was a key for him to viscerally understand that his band was capable of singing and playing the most complicated works he had ever composed, arranged and produced. They could do *anything.*

At the world premiere, in London, after the first 20-minute section ended, Brian was cautiously waiting to see how the audience was going to respond. When they burst into applause, all the apprehension and relief he had felt before walking on stage became joy and exultation. And that grew as the night and week went on.

For me, the biggest challenge in making a film about *SMiLE* was that he wasn't disappointed by it. Brian had already conquered his demons when we left London. In regard to *SMiLE,* he was finally on the back nine hitting it down the middle of the fairway. It was the biggest creative albatross in the world, and, suddenly, it was off his shoulders and out in the world. Brian became a much more confident person after all of that.

Brian has expressed his gratitude to me in a number of ways. And I have to thank him more than he has to thank me. He's allowed me to bring his many stories to the world.

Sir Paul McCartney, as is seen in the film, came to see him backstage before *SMiLE*. He wanted to offer encouragement. For Brian, that meant a lot; the Beatles are so important. When *Pet Sounds* came out, both John and Paul called Brian to tell him how much they loved the album. Can you imagine what that felt like in 1966?

Paul McCartney and Brian Wilson are like twin sons of different mothers in musical terms. They are born just two days apart. He loves Paul more than words can say. Ask Brian to list his favorite rock 'n' roll singers of all time and John Lennon is right at the top.

I got a kick out of the fact that Brian also loves *The U.S. vs John Lennon*. He's seen it a few times. The thing I think he connected with in the movie is that it gives us a chance to spend time *with* John Lennon. You sometimes forget about how much you love him, how much we miss him. And when you see him in this archival footage you are reminded *why* you love him. It's not about nostalgia. It's about taking a look about what matters to you and what matters in the world right now.

HK: Looking back on your Brian Wilson *SMiLE* movie and DVD now, you've had some time to reflect on the work. Talk to me about your initial concerns as you prepared to lens this "unfinished melodic journey" and how you view and felt and feel about how that film has been critically hailed.

What about the questions you prepared for this *SMiLE* movie? Or, was it finding some interview subjects that never had gone on camera that propelled this story? I would also think that your *SMiLE* movie helped bring you into some pitch meetings and film companies who wanted to know about the Lennon project, and had to be fans of *SMiLE* and wanted to do business with you and your production company.

DL: I'll take those in reverse order. I think that *Beautiful Dreamer* showed people what I could do as a director and may have also confirmed to the movie industry that I could make a musical documentary that was about much more than music. The head of Lionsgate told me that *Beautiful Dreamer* gave him the confidence to green light *The U.S. vs. John Lennon*.

The biggest concern I had in making the *SMiLE* doc was in trying to make a film that was worthy of Brian and Van Dyke's artistic creation, what is undoubtedly one of the greatest musical creations of the last century. I'm very proud of *Beautiful Dreamer* in telling the story, especially how it showcased Brian's courage in finishing *SMiLE* and finishing it so brilliantly.

HK: Viewers and fans and music lovers got to see the story behind the story of the fabled *SMiLE*.

DL: The people I interviewed for the film...some of whom have never spoken on-camera about that era...allowed us to get "inside" the story. And Brian's willingness to verbally share his feelings as he rode that emotional journey...a trip that lasted nearly 40 years...was so generous. I'm forever indebted to him for both encouraging me to do it, for inviting me inside the inner sanctum and for letting me make that movie. And what he said in the screening room the first time he saw it was unforgettable.

By the way, one of the things that made the experience even more remarkable is that Darian Sahanaja, Brian's bandleader for over twenty years was central to the completion of *SMiLE*. The synchronicity of that is he first read about *SMiLE* when he was in high school...in *my* book about Brian.

And he and the late (and sorely missed) Nick Walusko of The Wondermints once came to my old apartment in Santa Monica and listened to the outtakes I had.

This was before the *Good Vibrations* box I produced (again, with Mark Linett) in 1993 came out. That box included, with Brian's blessing, about an hour of music from the original *SMiLE* sessions. That was one of the reasons, I would say the main reason, it was one of the best-selling and most acclaimed box sets of the decade.

HK: You helmed a very important documentary on James Brown, *The Night James Brown Saved Boston*. That was a revealing portrait of a very fiery 1968 moment in America.

DL: I appreciate that. Shawn Amos (then of Shout! Factory) called and asked me if I thought there was a film to be made about the legendary concert James Brown had played at the Boston Garden the night after Dr. Martin Luther King, Jr. had been assassinated. I almost jumped through the phone with excitement.

It was the perfect follow-up for me after the John Lennon doc. More importantly, it was a challenging story to tell. I wanted to make sure it wasn't "paternalistic" --- a suburban, white boy liberal telling the story about one of the most important Africa-American artists at a crucial moment in American history.

I'm proud that I got out of the way in that film, let the story tell itself through key voices from various parts of African American music, culture, politics, and education. I knew I had been successful when I was doing publicity for it. A major African American talk show host was surprised to see that I was white. Maybe my greatest moment as a journalist and storyteller.

The film focuses on how James Brown bravely changed the world, his world and his artistry. It was done for the 40th anniversary of Dr. King's assassination, and it was made in a very short window---four months, from start to first screening.

James Brown on The Ed Sullivan Show (Courtesy of SOFA Entertainment)

I could tell you more about the process of making it, but that's for my students at UCLA to hear.

But all three of my films (on Brian Wilson, John Lennon and James Brown) that we study in the *Docs That Rock, Docs That Matter* course are about courage in the face of adversity.

442

HK: I'm also delighted to learn that you are in post-production of a documentary on Dion. Another fearless artist. I hope it will be finished and out before this book!

DL: Me too. Dion is a great artist, one of the most charismatic people you could ever meet. He is a remarkable, perhaps unparalleled storyteller.

At age 80, his fascinating artistic journey is still going with a new 2020 album that features Bruce Springsteen, Paul Simon, Jeff Beck, Van Morrison and many others. With liner notes by Bob Dylan!

Dion's life and career is an enormous subject for one film; his not being on the plane with Buddy Holly, ending up on the cover of *Sgt. Pepper* and in the Rock and Roll Hall of Fame, well, that alone would be a great film.

In my conversations with him, he revealed what the film had to be about. At least that is the way I heard it. Not a film just his music and his career but most importantly, *his soul*. He's probably the most religious person I've ever worked with. And focusing on that aspect of his life makes this the most spiritual film I've ever written and directed. And it happened because during my interviews with him, Dion opened his heart to our cameras. There is one powerful scene I can't wait for people to see; we shot it in his childhood church where Dion sings his great hymn, "The Truth Will Set You Free."

The fact that he and Susan, his teenage girlfriend and wife of nearly sixty years, love the documentary---well, that's all that matters to me.

But I know that anybody who sees it will be touched by Dion the way I was. Spending two hours with his music and on-screen presence---without my being profane---it's almost a religious experience, a kind of awakening.

HK: Since 2010, you have taught a very popular music documentary undergraduate class at UCLA. Tell me about it.

DL: I named my first course, *Docs That Rock, Docs That Matter*, because I wanted to teach music history through the medium I know best---music documentary. And I created it in the style of *Inside The Actor's Studio*, so each week, I have a filmmaker (producer, director, editor, writer) come to class, I interview them and we take my students on a ride, from the guest's origin story to their music documentary work to career advice.

We have been so blessed each year to have an amazing roster of guests. Here are just some of those who have joined me onstage at

UCLA; you can Google their names and see their credits: Academy Award winning documentary directors (Morgan Neville & Brett Morgen), Grammy award-winning producers (Nigel Sinclair), epic storytellers (Paul Justman), pioneers in the field (Steve Binder), contemporaries (Ryan Suffern, Paul Crowder, Jason Zeldes, A.J. Eaton) and people who have proven what it takes to make a dream come true (Denny Tedesco).

I also teach my films as well as focus on some of the most important music docs ever (*Dont Look Back*, et al.) and a more contemporary telling of Dylan's story (Martin Scorsese's *No Direction Home*.)

We also watch key music concert docs and events from an era when those events weren't commonplace (*The T.A.M.I. Show, Monterey Pop* and *Woodstock*) and one guest annually gives us a glimpse into one of the most famous superstar documentaries that never came out. My lips are sealed.

We even look at great films that are obviously not about the rock genre (e.g. *Johnny Cash, Pavarotti, Yo Yo Ma, Nina Simone, Romeo Is Burning*). And while the focus on the course is about the golden age of rock (basically, in my mind, 1955-1992), we include terrific documentaries about late legends (Kurt Cobain, Amy Winehouse), key figures in music history (Sam Phillips, Quincy Jones, Bob Marley) and punk (the Ramones, the Clash, the Sex Pistols, Green Day).

The list goes on and on: Chuck Berry, The Rolling Stones, Sam & Dave, Metallica, Radiohead, the Dixie Chicks, Queen, Madonna, Michael Jackson, David Crosby, Tom Petty, U-2, Little Richard, the Foo Fighters, Nilsson, ad infinitum. Of course, films about the Who are part of the course.

Studio stories like S*ound City*, unknown stories like *Searching for Sugarman*, faux documentaries like *The Rutles* and *This Is Spinal Tap* and a real one that feels unreal, *Anvil: The Story of Anvil*. And every year, we add more films to the curriculum.

My students have also gotten sneak previews of some very cool music docs, but I promised the filmmakers we would keep it secret.

Then, in my *Songwriters on Songwriting* class, besides getting master classes from so many members of the Rock and Roll Hall of Fame and the Songwriters Hall of Fame (e.g. Mike Stoller, Burt Bacharach, Jimmy Webb, Lamont Dozier, Randy Newman, Mann/ Weil, et al) we look at a lot of great films like *Troubadours*. And in my third course, *The Reel Beatles*, there are a bunch of Beatles films we study. Our in-class guests feature those who have worked with the

Beatles (including Peter Asher) and have included such fascinating directors as the legendary Michael Lindsay-Hogg (*Let It Be*).

HK: Do you have a theory about the current growth and interest in documentaries? Especially music-driven documentaries. I know Hulu, Netflix and production companies like Imagine starting documentary divisions all want content and there are more outlets for this genre. Streaming platforms etc.

A decade ago, networks and acquisition people veered away from these, partially owing to expensive music rights. The frame game has certainly changed. Do consumers want real deal movies about their music heroes?

DL: To me, there are at least three different answers to those questions.

The various networks (HBO, CNN, Showtime, Epix, et al) love music documentaries. As do the streaming platforms. They are relatively "inexpensive" quality content that keeps subscribers happy. I think that is a key for the streaming platforms like Netflix, Amazon, Apple music. And for superstar artists, like Taylor Swift, they are paying record-breaking prices.

I also think record companies are more interested than they were a decade ago because these films generate streaming income from old fans and especially new ones who might see a film about an artist their parents told them about. And then they might binge listen to an entire catalogue online. Or a box set. Or at least a greatest hits collection.

As streaming is such a key source of income for the major labels, my sense is it is one of the main reasons the record companies not only celebrate these films but sometimes co-finance or even finance them.

In your question as to whether fans, or as you call them, "consumers," want "real deal" movies about their heroes, that's a little bit more complicated.

They do. The David Crosby film is filled with unvarnished truth. But also, in recent years, I think aging baby boomers, who are disillusioned by so much in the world, don't want what one doc producer calls "a forensic look" at an artist so much as a celebration of their music. Their career.

I think that's one reason why the Linda Ronstadt doc in 2019 received so much positive attention. It's a terrific way to spend two hours with this great singer. Especially as she's not well enough to tour anymore.

And, of course, with the increasing success of narrative features (or biopics as the industry trades would call them), like *Rocketman* but going back to *The Buddy Holly Story, Ray,* et al, there seems to be no end to our desire to "live" with the artists and music that has been and still is central to our lives.

Those are my opinions. What matters to me is that I love telling the stories of great and legendary artists and their music. After all, it is the primary focus my life's work.

Text in this article, "David Leaf's Award-winning documentaries on Rock Legends John Lennon, Brian Wilson, and James Brown" © David Leaf

Publisher Travis Edward Pike on fifty years in and out of indie music and movie production

I've often interviewed Travis Edward Pike, Chairman Emeritus of the New Playwrights Foundation, mentor to promising writers, musicians, and familiar with the processes of filmmaking, founder of Otherworld Cottage Industries, winner of a 2018 LUXLife Global Entertainment Award, and a 2019 South East Star Lifetime Achievement Award. I wrote the Afterword to his generously illustrated *1964-1974: A Decade of Odd Tales and Wonders*, and the Foreword to his musical fantasy adventure, *Changeling's Return, a novel approach to the music.* My books this century, and 48 years of print and online articles, occasionally find their way into additional authors' efforts, university and college dissertations, indices, bibliographies and footnotes.

Once in a while, film school students, recent graduates, record collectors and bookworms seek advice, guidance, observations, and encouragement from me about the movie and music *Business*. The initial exchange often begins with a slew of questions usually about the music of the 60's and 70's, talent agents, managers, scripts and studio connections. My immediate answer to these queries from potential storytellers is "Have you ever heard of Travis E. Pike?"

446

The "Wikipedia children" always say no, and google his name, wanting to know more about him. I then suggest they investigate songwriters, arrangers, producers, writers, and filmmakers—outliers like Travis. They are the grinders, cultural creatives and multi-hyphenate artists who have logged over 50 years in the sound stages around Southern California, while still active in the arena.

I've known Pike for decades and worked with him on books. I've got a library card to his archives, in the Harvard Heights section of Los Angeles. It's right around the corner from Ray Charles' RPM Studios.

This is one person I don't have to worry about when it comes to finding photos, documents or visual artifacts—not just digital scans, or screen grabs, he's got original clippings and pictures from his artistic endeavors going all the way back to the Korean War, and being from Boston, Massachusetts, knows how to spiel over a meal, not preaching, but teaching, so I "Let Him Run Wild," as the Beach Boys' record demanded, so that scholars, scribes, and fans are sure to learn and earn valuable tips from the many trips he's taken.

Harvey Kubernik: Your early years are well documented in your memoir *1964-1974: A Decade of Odd Tales and Wonders*, focusing on music and film, that Lee Zimmerman, in his February 2019 Four Star *Goldmine* magazine review, called "...in every sense, a remarkable reservoir of craft and creativity," and was described in the March 2020 *Midwest Book Review, Small Press Bookwatch, the Biography Shelf* as "An inherently fascinating read and a 'must' for all Travis Pike fans, *1964-1974: A Decade of Odd Tales and Wonders* is a very special and unreservedly recommended addition to community and academic library Contemporary American Biography collections."

Travis Pike: And they also reported

Book cover courtesy of Otherworld Cottage Industries

"Harvey Kubernik, author of 14 music-related books including this year's *The Doors Summer's Gone,* published by Otherworld Cottage

447

Industries, wrote the Afterword to Travis's memoir, revealing the current impact of Travis's early works."

HK: I found it interesting that you first began thinking seriously about a career in music when you were in Germany, booked as the Twist sensation from the USA, singing with the international show band, the Five Beats. In Boston, you used to sing for tips in bars with live bands when you were a teenager.

TP: That band in Germany was put together especially for me, and the crowds loved us. We'd only been together about three months when I learned our soldout performances had come to the attention of the

The Five Beats international showband

Besetzung	
Teddy Pike USA	Twist and Show Sensation
Enriko Lombardi ITALIA	Gesang, Gitarre
Eddy Christers	Gesang, Gitarre, Klarrinetta, Baß
Charly Ross	Saxophon, Baß, Gesang
Ringo	Gesang, Schlagzeug
Chorty West	Gesang, Gitarre, Saxophon

Die Stationen dieser **Star~Palast~Kiel**
erfolgreichen Band **Studio 62**
waren: Eckernförde
Schützenhof
Rendsburg

Demnächst auch ⭐ *Star-Club*
Hamburg-St. Pauli

**Handbill courtesy
Travis Edward Pike archive**

---

powers that be at Polydor and Phillips Records. And that was about the same time, I received a flyer from home announcing my father's 28-minute crash action documentary *Demo Derby* had premiered on June 24th in downtown Boston's Paramount Theater with Frank Sinatra's *Robin and the Seven Hoods*, and in three other New England locations with Elvis Presley's *Viva Las Vagas*. That was when I learned a song I had hurriedly recorded while home on leave prior to going overseas, had been arranged and produced by Arthur Korb, recorded by the Rondels, and become the title song for Pike Productions *Demo Derby*.

HK: Were you writing songs back then?
TP: No. My repertoire consisted of covers of American hits that along with my wild leaps and strutting, really went over well with the Germans and Danes who lived in northern Germany and Jutland.

HK: Did you sing any Beatles tunes?
TP: No. The only Beatles songs I heard were *"Sie liebt dich,"* and *"Komm gib mir deine Hand,"* on the radio, played loud to help me stay awake as I drove home from performances that typically ended at 3:00 o'clock in the morning. A German girl group, the Sweetles had a hit with *"Ich wunsch mir zum Geburtstag einen Beatle,"* (I want a Beatle for my birthday.)

James A. Pike presents

DEMO DERBY

A 28 MINUTE FEATURETTE

with CRASH ACTION

filmed on location at Norwood Arena

with a music score that will ROCK YOU . . . featuring the sensational DEMO DERBY title song (Travis Pike - Arthur Korb) - recorded by the RONDELS.

(Flyer image courtesy Travis Edward Pike archive)

And then, like a cruel cosmic joke, in mid-July, I was seriously injured in an automobile accident. My Sunbeam Alpine was totalled by an oncoming *Bundeswehr* armored truck that skidded out of control on the freshly tarred road. The impact of that collision shortened my wheelbase, causing my steering column and motor to push through the firewall and invade the driver's compartment. The steering column hit me in the forehead, knocked me out, and my left ankle was fractured by the invasive motor.

I'd seen the safety belt behind the driver's seat when I put the top down. I rarely wore it, but that day, I buckled up. More cosmic humor?

I survived the wreck, but that was the end of the *Twistsensation aus USA*. My ankle failed to knit properly, and after a few months of walking around with a broken ankle, in October, nearly a year to the day after I arrived in Germany, I was sent Stateside to Chelsea Naval Hospital for reconstructive surgery.

(Photo courtesy Travis Edward Pike archive)

I choose not to recall the pain, but remember it was worse when one of the TV sets on the orthopedic ward began playing *American Bandstand, Hullaballoo,* or *Shindig!* Peering around my elevated left leg to watch those shows not only hurt my neck and back, but depressed the hell out of me. Other guys, no matter how deserving or underserving,were living the life I had once imagined would be mine, and that was hard to take.

One weekend, a bunch of teenagers showed up at the house and asked to see me. I didn't recognize any of them, but one introduced himself as the younger brother of the drummer in the Jesters, the first high school rock band I sang with when I was 14-years old. My father appeared and ushered us all into his screening room, probably to keep us from taking a tour of the house.

The drummer explained that the boys with him were all members the New Jesters. They didn't have a singer, and wanted me to sing at their High School Talent contest. My performance would disqualify them, but they wanted to win the popularity contest between themselves and the other teen band at their school.

I was mentally listing all the reasons I could refuse, starting with being barely ambulatory, when my father said my brother, Jimmy, had told him I was really popular in Northern Germany, and to my

450

astonishment, volunteered to drive me there and back, "so it really wouldn't be any trouble at all."

On the big night, we were last to go on, and the band before us finished with a creditable performance of the Cream hit "Sunshine of Your Love." A hush fell over the auditorium as I was hauled up on stage. The promised stool was too high, so I handed my crutches to one of the kids and, clinging to the microphone stand, without introduction, sang the opening line to "Heartbreak Hotel" and when the band entered with the famous double bang, the entire audience rose as one, and the screaming and whistling began. I did the three minute version, and as the crowd cheered, the band played the opening riff to "What'd I say?" My version of that Ray Charles hit brought the house down. Exhausted and with my ankle throbbing, my father and I escaped.

Between bone graft surgery, recovery, and rehabilitation, that winter I spent several months in the orthopedic ward at Chelsea Naval Hospital, where time hung heavily over us all. No lovely high school candy stripers got past the gate guards, but the infinitely kind, elderly, Red Cross volunteers who brought us books and magazines, surprised me one day with a guitar, to help pass the time. I was not much of a player, but with nothing else to do, I improved quickly. That's when I wrote "End of Summer," hoping, one day, to perform it in person for my German friends and fans.

Word of that composition got around the ward and one day, a Red Cross volunteer asked if I would play it for her. To my dismay, I choked up in the middle of the song I played so readily for my wardmates, and couldn't finish. She told me not to fret. It was a beautiful song, and she was sure my Lorelei (the girl's name mentioned in the lyrics), would wait for me. I didn't tell her there was no Lorelei. I took the name from Heinrich Heine's poem about the siren whose beauty so bewitched sailors that they failed to mind the rocks and shoals and were lost at sea.

I wrote a number of novelty songs and parodies of pop tunes to amuse my fellow cripples, and soon found myself being wheeled from ward to ward to entertain the other incapacitated shut-ins. On weekends when I was taken home, I began recording them on my old reel-to-reel at 7 ips. With no way to play them on the hospital ward, I left them at home. These must have been the songs my father took to New York City to run by the tunesmiths that he says convinced him to make his first widescreen, color, tongue-in-cheek response to the West Coast surfer comedies, *Feelin' Good*. That, and his success with *Demo Derby*, and the fact he didn't have to go far to get a singer-songwriter to play the lead, sealed the deal as far as he was concerned. In my defense, it's enough to know that *Feelin' Good* was my father's movie, and the songs were all selected to suit his movie, and not the other way around. Ultimately I wrote ten songs used in *Feelin' Good*, eight that I performed on screen and two performed by the Montclairs, winners of the First Masschusetts JayCees Battle of the Bands, a benefit of that victory being assured a part in the film.

I finally met Arthur Korb, the man whose arrangement and recording with the Rondels, turned my raw, original recording of "Demo Derby" into the title song for that extraordinarily successful 28-minute documentary. Arthur turned out to be wise, talented, gracious, caring, and allowed me to be present, when he recorded the orchestral score for *Feelin' Good*, which is not the same thing as the songs in the movie, at all, but the program music meant to underscore the emotions on screen. I had never been present at such a recording session before, and learned a great deal from it.

**Arthur Korb (left) and Travis Pike (right) at AAA, Boston
(Photo courtesy Travis Edward Pike archive)**

With me still in and out of hospitals, my role in the film had to be shot on weekends, but by the time the film premiered, I had been discharged from the Navy and was able to attend in person.

The stars arrive at the World Premiere of *Feelin' Good*
(Photo courtesy Travis Edward Pike archive)

The Montclairs meeting at their favorite pizzeria
(Photo courtesy Travis Edward Pike archive)

But *Feelin' Good* ran into an unforseen problem. The Montclairs, who won their roles, frequently had lunch at their favorite pizzeria. In keeping with the feeling of *cinéma vérité* my father filmed them where they were most comfortable, but seeing the band sitting together was enough to outrage some racists, and when the black and white hands began sharing pizza, Southern theater owners, fearing reprisals, refused to play the movie unless the scene was cut. My father refused, but lost interest in *Feelin' Good* when he lost the Southern distributors.

All the songs I sang in the movie were played by Oedipus and his Mothers, although in the film and on the "Don't Hurt Me Again" single, they were renamed the Brattle Street East, because three of them attended Harvard University in Cambridge, and Brattle Street adjoins that campus.

A clipping service kept me aware of *Feelin' Good* coverage in newspapers across New England. I wouldn't say I was a household name, but neither was I a complete unknown when I began playing my hospital repertoire and original material to small but receptive audiences in Greater Boston coffeehouses. It wasn't a living wage, but living at home, and doing a few shows a week brought in enough to get by. My picking, singing and original material was entertaining enough for intimate coffeehouse crowds, but I'd made more money singing pop tunes for tips in bars with house bands when I was a teenager than I did in coffeehouses.

On the other hand, I couldn't stand up long enough for a 45-minute set, and a second 45-minute set, 15 minutes later would be out of the question. At 22, my dreams of a career in music were fading, when Gordon Lightfoot (not the one you think), approached me between sets at a Saturday night hootenanny and asked if I would consider being the day manager at his state-of-the-art recording studio in Jamaica Plain (a Boston neighborhood having nothing to do with the Caribbean island).

My job would be minding the store during the day, and booking sessions for weekends and evenings. He couldn't pay me a salary, but I would earn a commission on each booking. With my Sunday Supplement reputation as a singer, songwriter and movie star, he thought I'd attract enough customers to make it worthwhile.

Not thrilled by the idea of minding a phone all day, and less sure than he that my reputation would attract bookings, he sweetened the pot. On weekends and evenings, if the studio wasn't booked, he'd record my songs. He was a folksinger, working as a carpenter by day, but hoped one day to be a full-time record producer. When asked if he had a studio band, he said he didn't, but knew musicians he could hire for sessions.

454

I told Gordon I'd been thinking about starting a rock band, and he lit up. He said I could rehearse the band in the studio, and he'd be happy to demo our songs just for the engineering practice, and if my band was good enough, he'd give us first refusal on recording gigs. With my local reputation, recruiting trained sight-readers from Boston's internationally famous Berklee School of Music, might be possible, but first I needed to see (and test) Gordon's studio. He gave me the address and for the first time in a long time, it seemed there was a light at the end of the tunnel that wasn't an on-coming train.

On Monday, armed with Lightfoot Studio's new demo recordings, I called Berklee, introduced myself, and to my delight, the Guidance Counselor recognized my name as the star of the Boston-made rock and roll movie *Feelin' Good*, but at mid-term, he only had one candidate to offer, a senior year classical guitar student, who'd been invited to go to Spain to study with Segovia, and was preparing to leave. He was happy to highly recommend this student for my purposes, but was doubtful he'd be interested. Karl Garrett agreed to meet, I played him my Lightfoot Studio demos, and that's how the incredibly accomplished and talented Karl Garrett became my friend, lead guitarist, and co-

Karl Garrett with his 1971 Oribe 10-string guitar, when he was the President of the Philadelphia Classical Guitar Society.
(Photo courtesy of Karl Garrett)

arranger from the beginning of Travis Pike and the Boston Massacre, right up to our final Travis Pike's Tea Party performance in Southern California.

With Karl on board, my ever-growing repertoire of original songs and a recording studio in which to rehearse and record our demos, the rest of the band came together quickly, but it still took several months of daily practice to master the 60 something songs we'd need to go public playing only original material.

Today, listening to some of our very early demos posted on my website, for our first demo of "Ali Baba Ben Jones," the intro Karl played, on his Gibson Les Paul, was in fact an excerpt from the classical guitar intro to Francisco Terrega's "Caprichio Arabe."

I asked Uncle Phil to play "camel music." His drum sound suggested two smallish kettle drums, mounted on either side of a camel's hump. Listening with closed eyes, I can almost see the Sheik arrive in his encampment greeted by scimitar-wielding guards at the entrance to his tent. And in "End of Summer," Karl's inspired lead guitar lines, alone and interwoven with my vocal, conjure images of falling autumn leaves, and his guitar harmonics conjure images of ice-encrusted twigs shimmering on the bare branches of trees in the dead of winter.

About a month later, the Cheetah Lounge in New York City responded to our demo album, saying that no matter how good we sounded, they'd never book a group calling itself "The Boston Massacre" into their venue for fear of causing a riot. The Cheetah was especially important because it was close to almost all of the record company home offices, so we decided to change our name.

The announcement first appeared in the *Boston Sunday Globe,* September 24, 1967, in its Record Time column, Sound in the Round titled "From the New Wave," where Ernie Santosuosso's final entry reported "Travis Pike and the Boston Massacre have changed their name to Travis Pike's Tea Party. They will appear Saturday Evening at Sydney Hill Country Club."

(We changed our name, six weeks after the WRKO Harbor Cruise. Three weeks later, MIT's campus newspaper *The Tech* Vol. 87, No. 45 Cambridge, Mass., reported on Tuesday, Nov. 14, 1967...

1500 attend mixer Saturday night: Music provided by Tea Party

In a November 22, 1967 letter we received from Jorge A. Romera, Vice-president of the Burton House Committee at MIT, he wrote "In behalf of the Burton House Committee, I would like to thank Travis Pike's Tea Party for their outstanding appearance at the mixer which Burton House sponsored jointly with Charlesgate Hall of Boston University, on Novemebr 11. On very few occasions before had the Sala de Puerto Rico of the MIT Student Center witnessed such a crowd. The success of this mixer, one of the most successful ever on the MIT campus, was in great part due to Travis Pike's Tea Party, who with their original music, kept a captive crowd of well over sixteen hundred college students from MIT, BU, and other schools in the Boston area."

BOSTON HERALD TRAVELER, FRIDAY, JANUARY 26, 1968

HUB-HUB

Boston Sound Stirs Interests

By JIM MORSE

The current Newsweek proclaims that the Boston Sound is "what's happening" in the music business today. Major recording companies have scouts here checking the sounds and the musicians making them. What amazes insiders is not the sudden recognition, but the fact that the talent has been here for years with no recognition, not even locally.

The Beacon Street Union, The Phluph, Orpheus, and The Ultimate Spinach are the names of local groups whose albums are being released this week. The next combo to be snapped up by a big label will be Travis Pike's Tea Party. It took eight months to put this outfit together, and six months of rehearsal to learn the 80 original songs the group performs.

Karl Garrett, lead guitarist in the Tea Party, is considered one of the outstanding classical guitarists in New England. Pike, who is from Newton, starred in the movie, "Feelin' Good," which was filmed here two years ago. The group has been featured at the Psychedelic Supermarket in Kenmore Square and the Unicorn Coffee House, where it's making a repeat appearance this week.

(Newspaper clipping courtesy Travis Edward Pike archive)

FIRST BOSTON ROCK FESTIVAL
MAY 10-18, 1968 (extended to MAY 25)

In a newspaper clipping from an unknown source, contributing critic William Phillips reported audiences were disappointing at the Boston Pop Festival, not for lack of talent, but for lack of local support, and elsewhere in his report, wrote of us, "Travis Pike's Tea Party performed in about every conceivable pop musical style from straight rock to psychedelic to folk to rinky-dinky ragtime. Aside from an excessive fondness for gimmickry and bad humor, they are pleasing and versatile entertainers."

We opened our festival show with "Till the End," our musical vampire blackout skit in which I was carried on stage in a coffin, climbed out, sang the song, complete with heinous laughter, bit my lovely victim's throat, left her pale corpse dead on stage, and staggered back into my coffin, "wishing I could find . . . a steady girl." Most young people found it funny, but it might strike some as in poor taste, but aside from that, pleasing and versatile entertainers . . .

We'd been hired to provide the music for a new WBZ-TV show. Karl Garrett and I were the Music Directors, and our band played the music for the first three episodes of a comedy-variety show that dealt satirically, and sometimes coarsely, with timely topics like drug abuse, interracial marriage, and the war in Vietnam war, all topics considered fair game by *Rowan and Martin's Laugh-In*, and *That Was the Week That Was*, and that might explain our jaded sense of humor.

But that Boston Pop Festival is where we introduced our new recording, playing both songs on our new Alma Records 45, "If I Didn't Love You Girl," and "The Likes of You," live on stage and shamelessly promoting the record during our performance, going so far as to ask the audience to call in to their favorite stations to request the songs be played, and apparently many, or if not so many, some fervid few dedicated fans, did call in and request the record be played.

Our TV show was put on hiatus for a few weeks, so we spent most of our time tuner surfing, trying to find someone—anyone, playing our songs, all to no avail, but I did get a strange call from a long-time friend from high school who said she and her friends had been calling WRKO, and had been rudely told, by someone claiming to be the program manager, to stop calling, and said Travis Pike's Tea Party's records would *never* be played on WRKO.

458

WRKO TOOK 500 LISTENERS ON A DOUBLE HEADER BOAT TRIP AROUND HISTORIC BOSTON HARBOR ABOARD TWO MASS. BAY LINES CRUISE SHIPS. LIVE MUSIC BY TRAVIS PIKE AND THE BOSTON MASSACRE AND THE RAMRODS, HONCHO PONCHOS FOR ALL AND THE WRKO JOCKS MADE THIS A PROMOTION THAT WAS GROOVY BECAUSE IT WAS WATERED DOWN. AGAIN, WRKO WENT TO THE LISTENERS . . . . AND THEY WALKED THE GANGPLANK HAPPILY.

68/WRKO

21 Brookline Ave. • Boston, Mass. 02215

CO 6-0800

(WRKO flyer courtesy Travis Edward Pike archive)

Sunday, August 6th, 1967: If you look closely at the names in the widest part of the ship's wheel, we were calling ourselves Travis Pike and the Boston Massacre when we were introduced on this Harbor Cruise by the aggressive, new, top 40 Boston radio station, WRKO. The WRKO radio listener contest ran for weeks, a huge promotion for us and for the Ramrods, who were on the other boat.

459

In 1967, WNAC had changed its call letters to WRKO, hired (and retired), WMEX's top disc jockey, Arnie "Woo Woo" Ginsburg, and set their sights on WBZ Radio 103, Boston's only remaining AM top 40 music station. Travis Pike's Tea Party had signed with producer Squire D. Rushnell to provide the music for WBZ-TV's *Here and Now* comedy-variety show. TV is TV and radio is radio, but the man in charge at WRKO saw it differently. His excuse for banning our records was that we'd "gone over to the enemy." Being banned from WRKO was bad, especially when WBZ Radio 103 switched its format to "adult contemporary music" . . . and then we received this letter.

WBZ-TV 4

1170 SOLDIERS FIELD ROAD BOSTON MASSACHUSETTS 02134 254-5670

WBZ · WBZ-TV BOSTON
WINS NEW YORK
KYW · KYW-TV PHILADELPHIA
WJZ-TV BALTIMORE
KDKA · KDKA-TV PITTSBURGH
WOWO FT WAYNE
WIND CHICAGO
KPIX SAN FRANCISCO
KFWB LOS ANGELES

GROUP W

WESTINGHOUSE BROADCASTING COMPANY INC

June 24, 1968

TO WHOM IT MAY CONCERN

This will inform you that Messrs. Travis Pike and Karl Garrett of "Travis Pike's Tea Party" served as music directors and arrangers for two television pilot programs here at WBZ-TV, Boston.

Their contributions were impressive. In addition to arranging and supervising the production of several "hit" songs performed on the programs, Travis Pike and Karl Garrett wrote and arranged theme music for instrumental bridges.

Should you require further information, please feel free to contact me at 617 254-5670.

Sincerely,

Squire D. Rushnell
Executive Producer

SDR:dz

June 24, 1968 cancellation notice and reference letter
(Courtesy of the Travis Edward Pike archive)

460

TRAVIS PIKE'S TEA PARTY POSITION UNTENABLE

Working on the TV show, we hadn't made any summer bookings, and the early fall college gigs were all booked up before the summer break, so we'd be lucky to get any meaningful work before the Christmas holidays. We'd given up our arrangement with Lightfoot Studios when we started taking gigs, and I suddenly felt the weight of responsibilty for everyone in the band, and I was wondering what I could do to get us back to work when Roger called.

Roger was a 40-something biker, a fan who'd become a friend before he relocated to California, back in town to pick up things he'd put in storage when he moved west. I invited him to come by and I'd give him a copy of our new record. He did. When I played the record, and told him our current situation, he immediately offered to take me to California. He rented a four bedroom house and would put me up until I was back on my feet, and thought we could easily

Roger La Chance
(Courtesy Travis Edward Pike archive)

line up gigs for Travis Pike's Tea Party in Southern California.

It was an easy sell. The Mamas and the Papas had me "California Dreaming" all winter. I asked when he'd be leaving, and he said whenever I was ready.

461

I needed at least a day to sort things out with the band, and he needed a day to load all his tools and other goods, so we agreed to meet the following day, and I'd let him know if I could take him up on his offer. I had most of the day to come up with a plan, tried to call George (rhythm guitar, vocals), got no answer, but got through to percussionist, Uncle Phil, who immediately started swearing at me for breaking up the band. I told him the band wasn't breaking up. I was going to California to try to generate some interest from record labels, and maybe even book some gigs before the end of the year, and if successful, I'd come back for everybody and we'd all go to California, together. He wanted to know what Karl thought. Karl was teaching, so I hadn't had a chance to tell him. I told Uncle Phil I'd fill him in as soon as I talked to Karl. He said, he'd rather hear directly from Karl.

When Mikey Joe and Karl, who shared an apartment on the top floor of the apartment building, came down to my tiny basement apartment and I filled them in on Roger's offer. My plan was to take prints from our photos taken on Old Ironsides, a fistful of flyers and newspaper clippings, and our Lightfoot Studio demo album and see if I could stir up some interest from the West Coast record companies in Los Angeles, and if not, maybe take a run up to San Francisco to check out our options there. Karl, who'd come with me for our presentation to Hy Mizrahi at Kama Sutra, Bhudda Records in New York City, knew I could handle the presentation, and was all in. I asked him to call Uncle Phil.

Roger had room in the truck, so Mikey Joe came west with me. Three days after arriving in La Puente, I was in Hollywood, meeting with Elmer Valentine, owner of the Whisky a Go Go. He looked at our clippings and photos, listened to our demo and liked what he saw and heard. Booked solid for the summer, he still relished the idea of introducing Travis Pike's Tea Party to the West Coast. He said to call him when I had everybody here, and he'd clear a week for us.

But only four of us made the trip. No one could find George, our rhythm guitarist and vocalist so crucial to our harmonies. Our goal was always to play only original material, but what made us unique, was also our Achilles heel. We could only play my original repertoire if we were all there. The new guy recruited to replace George knew all the top 40 tunes, but was slow as cold molasses when it came to learning our original repertoire. I suspect it was deliberate. To survive, we started playing top 40 in bars and dance halls. I owed it to the originals to help them get by, but I owed it to myself to move on, and quit the band in April, 1969. I kept writing songs, but I'd learned my lesson. I had to learn notation to enable me to hire the best musicians, and if one fell by the wayside, hire an equally talented sight-reader to take his place. Karl, Mikey Joe and the new guy decided to go on without me, but Uncle Phil went back to Boston, so they had to find a new drummer.

"What will you call yourself," I asked. "You can't call yourself Travis Pike's Tea Party any more." Mikey Joe asked me to help them come up with a new name. A few minutes later, I suggested "Quo Vadis." "Quo Wadis?" Mikey Joe asked, mimicing my correct Latin pronunciation. "What does it mean?" "I'm not sure," I lied, "but the movie was a spectacle, an epic masterpiece, eight Academy Award nominations!" "Cool!" he said, and asked me how to spell it.

IN RETROSPECT: WHAT WORKED, WHAT DIDN'T, AND WHY

My overseas experience and performances in Naval hospitals prepared me for coffeehouses, *Demo Derby* and *Feelin' Good* established my credentials as a prolific singer-songwriter, even though I didn't know how to read or write music, and at least one critic reported indirectly that I composed songs in "every conceivable pop musical style from straight rock to psychedelic to folk to rinky-dinky ragtime." Through Arthur Korb I'd experienced the thrill of seeing a studio orchestra at work, but I'd also learned that without material to record, they were all unemployed musicians with day jobs.

I finally had time to consider my accomplishments and failings and realized how lucky I had been. We all knew that the best original songs and performances could lead to recording careers and soldout concerts like Elvis Presley, Ray Charles, the Coasters and the Beatles, but to develop that sort of repertoire, a band had to have a place to arrange, rehearse, and showcase its material—a home room. Gordon Lightfoot provided all that for us, when he set me up as the day manger at Lightfoot Recording Studios—the best situation imaginable for developing a band dedicated to performing original material—a recording studio in which to rehearse during the day, and on nights when it was free, to record demos of our efforts, all for the price of the audio tape, allowing us to perfect our material before ever taking it public.

The third essential ingredient came in the person of Karl Garrett, a trained musician, arranger, and teacher, who kept everyone up to speed, crafting my songs as I introduced them. And because we rehearsed during the day, we were able to accept occasional work at special events, or in stop-gap situations when outside players were indisposed, and still enjoyed the possibility that Gordon Lightfoot would hire all or some of us for paid recording sessions. In California I never had that luxury.

I learned through my experience of creating and developing my band, to never again be held hostage by musicians. And now, I'd learn to write notation, arrange my own material, hire copyists as need be, and if a musician fell by the wayside, be able to replace him or her immediately with another equally talented sight-reader and be up to speed in days, rather than months.

Taking odd jobs to get by, in my spare time, I finished writing *The Red-backed, Scaly, Black-bellied, Tusked, Bat-winged Dragon*, the screenplay for an animated feature film I'd been working on since high school in 1961. I shopped it in Hollywood without success, but it led to a writing gig for Ray Arco, an indie filmmaker with ties to animation studios in Romania, for a screenplay we called *Caesar, the Sometimes Telepathic Lion,* and while I waited for that deal to come to fruition, I enrolled in the Communication Arts program at Cal Poly, Pomona, taking classes on documentary film, theater, and music.

Toward Christmas, I attended a party at the top of Nichols Canyon, where I was introduced to members of the Hollywood Foreign Press, presenters of the Golden Globe Awards. The hosts were German immigrants, so I sang "End of Summer" the song I wrote in German and English, intended for my German fans. Gerard Alcan, a filmmaker said it was the exact *Zeitgeist* he sought for the film he was co-producing with investigative reporter Ted Charach, about suppressed evidence in the investigation into the 1968 assassination of Robert Kennedy titled, *The Second Gun.* He couldn't know that Pike Productions filmed much of John F. Kennedy's campaign movie, but the irony wasn't lost on me.

I was 15-years-old, still adjusting to the huge house on Lake Avenue in Newton Centre, Massachusetts, when I met then State Senator John F. Kennedy. My father's crew was setting up lights in his office. He seldom filmed in the house, so I was standing in the doorway to the back hall, peering across the front of the house to see what was going on, when a voice from behind said, "Excuse me." I nearly jumped out of my skin, scrambling to get out of the way. The stranger, no doubt amused by my reaction, smiled and asked who I was. I told him I was Teddy Pike and I lived there. Still smiling, he said he had a brother named Teddy, and

464

then shook my hand and told me he was running for President. I don't remember what I said, but I do remember scurrying away before I could get caught snooping. I later learned that the film shot that day appeared in the Kennedy documentary, *A Time for Greatness*, shown at the 1960 Democratic National Convention.

I didn't want my song permanently linked to those tragedies, but allowed its music, without its lyrics, to be the theme for the entire film, but other than delivering the tracks, the music was edited and placed entirely by the filmmaker. *The Second Gun* (1973) was nominated, but did not win Best Documentary Feature at the 1974 Golden Globes.

THE SECOND GUN

The Second Gun, a shocking new film, makes the statement that the bullets in the gun of Sirhan did not kill Senator Kennedy, but that another gun 'A Second Gun' fired at point blank range behind Kennedy in the Ambassador Hotel Pantry -- did! The Second Gun stars the real life people who acted and reacted in this shocking episode of history.

Adapted and directed by	GERARD ALCAN
Based on the probe by	THEODORE CHARACH
Produced by	THEODORE CHARACH
	GERARD ALCAN
Music theme "The End of Summer" composed and performed by	TRAVIS E. PIKE
Art work	BILLY RASH
	MARC JOHNSON
Prologue voice	T. MIRATTI
Narrator	DEAN RANDALL
Re-enactments	RON GUIER and ROBERT MULLEN
Photographed and edited by	GERARD ALCAN
Additional photography	ELLEN HIBLER
Assistant director	GEORGE EDDY
Location sound	ZVI BOKER

Color by TECHNICOLOR
Title and Opticals CINEMA RESEARCH
"THE SECOND GUN"--All rights reserved
Copyright © 1973 by Theodore Charach and Gerard Alcan
AN AMERICAN FILMS, LTD. Release

The Lori 1973

Mark Roth, Richie Havens' partner in Stormy Forest Records, heard about *The Lori*, a concept album I was developing, and asked to meet me. We met at his house on Ogden Drive in Hollywood and I performed the rhyme, and played excerpts of the songs for him. He was interested and immediately scheduled me for a recording session at a tiny MGM recording studio on Fairfax Avenue. I recited the poem, played the songs and, excited by the concept, Mark asked if he could run it by some people at Universal. He thought it would make a great TV Special. Of course, I gave him my permission.

I drew these illustrations for The Lori when it appeared in CalPoly's OPUS 17, Spring, 1973, and in the style I later proposed for the Universal TV Special.

Mark told me the creative people at Universal Television loved it, but marketing turned it down. They didn't know how to sell it to sponsors. Maybe if we'd stuck with the idea of a concept album . . .

466

Changeling Troupe 1975-1976

Harvey Kubernik: So now, with the ability to write notation, you decided to form a new band you called the Changeling Troupe.

Travis Pike: In that "Age of Aquarius," especially in Hollywood, when you met anyone new, the first lines spoken in the conversation were inevitably an exchange of astrological signs. If they were incompatible, the conversation terminated quickly.

That popular occult mindset is what inspired me to compose my Faustian rock opera, *Changeling*, about a couple who playfully perform an occult ritual, neither believing it will have any efficacy, and their subsequent disorientation and terror, when its spell takes effect and they are unable to return to their previous reality.

I sought the needed players through Musician's Contact Service flyers at places like Wallichs Music City and Guitar Center on Sunset Boulevard in Hollywood. The best were quickly taken by bands with paying gigs, but I found a few who shared my vision, and with parental or matrimonial support, were able to commit to recording a master at my expense, that I would then attempt to market to a major label. As producer, I took the monetary risk, and promised that minimally, they'd all get some exciting tracks for their audition reels.

Unfortunately, I ran out of money before I could finish producing the album, and ended up with exactly what I had promised the nusicians if it didn't sell—some exciting tracks for my demo reel.

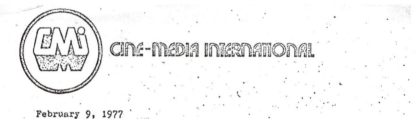

CINE-MEDIA INTERNATIONAL

February 9, 1977

Dear Travis,

    I'm going to put your property, "Changling," into our fall production schedule, based on an estimated budget of 2.5 million. With the music and the revised treatment, I'm going to go ahead and arrange the financing. As agreed, we'll work out the details of co-production upon funding approval.

Respectfully Yours,

J. Bond Johnson
President

MOTION PICTURE ALMANAC,
QUIGLEY PUBLISHING COMPANY, INC. 1992, page 523.

Cine-Media International, Ltd
  One Transglobal Square, P.O. Box 7005, Long Beach, CA 90807;
(213) 426-3622. Organized 1975. (Production and distribution of
theatrical motion pictures and television films.) A subsidiary of
Transglobal Industries and Subsidiaries, Inc.
PRESIDENT & CHIEF EXECUTIVE OFFICER
  J. Bond Johnson, Ph.D
VICE PRESIDENT
  Rudolph A. Maglin
SECRETARY
  Ruth Johnson
TREASURER
  Lenore Maglin
EXECUTIVE PRODUCER
  Frank Capra, Jr.
CREATIVE CONSULTANT
  Chester Dent
DIRECTOR OF PRODUCTION
  Travis Edward Pike
DIRECTOR OF FINANCE
  William A. Becker

HK: You became Director of Production for Cine-Media International.
TP: Cine-Media had just completed its first co-production, *Kingdom
of the Spiders*, and Bond was looking for their next project. Igo
Kanter, who in addition to producing *Kingdom of the Spiders*, was
the music coordinater for *The Monkees* TV series, invited Bond to
hear an "exciting musical project" brought to him for consideration.
Bond was awestruck by the *Changeling* music. He arranged a meeting
to learn more about me and the story behind the music, which led
to Bond's production proposal of 9 February 1977. Ultimately, when
Bond and I decided to prep a feature film, rather than a stage play,
Cine-Media was unable to secure the new multi-million dollar budget.
    Our continuing business relationship was established when Bond
asked me to write the Cine-Media screenplay adaptation of Mary
Stewart's novel, *Airs Above the Ground,* and when I delivered it in
February1980, he appointed me Cine-Media International's Director
of Production.

468

Bond's Cine-Media International-Neue Delta Film Produktion co-production for *Airs Above the Ground* collapsed when our first production window passed before we could close the deal, and without the cast we'd selected, the investors lost confidence and withdrew.

Fandango, 1981

HK: Travis was already a screenwriter, singer, songwriter, and record producer, but at Cine-Media, he also did script breakdowns, production scheduling, motion picture budgeting, location scouting, and learned how to structure Limited Partnership offerings. They came close a few times, and Travis wrote a number of screenplays, adaptations and treatments, but the tax shelter laws that had once favored motion picture investment were dried up by new tax shelter legislation, until, in 1981, Travis finally got to produce music for, and direct the filming of Cine-Media International's production of the pilot episode of a proposed country music variety TV Pilot titled *Fandango*, with special guest star, Barbi Benton, who was then a regular on the popular Country-Western TV Comedy Show, *Hee Haw*.

Guest star Barbi Benton and director Travis Pike on the set of *Fandango*
(1981 photo courtesy Travis Edward Pike archive)

Betsy and Thumper, 1982

Superbowl Sunday, February 6, 1982: David Pinto, left of center wearing a cap and leather jacket, counts bars of music as Betsy Baytos, (right) runs through her dance routine. Travis is the guy in the black shirt (far left), there to direct the session, hearing the playback and seeing the choreograpy for the first time. Between Travis and David is Betsy's brother Barry, her assistant choreographer, and the man half hidden by Travis, up against the wall, is Wolf Seeberg, in charge of music playback.

HK: In our 2020 conversation, you told me how you'd had to schedule a SFX shoot on Superbowl Sunday, and how you managed to wrap in time for everyone to get home for the game.

TP: Betsy Baytos, Eccentric Dancer and Disney artist, was producing a TV spot to promote that year's re-release of *Bambi*. The idea was that during her interview, she'd sketch the Disney characters, hold them up to show the people at home, and then, when she held up her live-on-camera drawing of Thumper suddenly pop into the sketch, and the audience would see Betsy and the bunny dance together in her drawing! My friend, David Pinto, composed the music for the sequence, but the technique of capturing it for animation and compositing were outside his comfort zone, so he recommended Betsy talk to me.

Betsy and I met to discuss her production, and what qualified me to direct it. I'd never done rotoscoping, but my neighbor, actress and choreographer Michele Hart, had been the rotoscoped model for the

470

Hanna-Barbera TV series, *Jana of the Jungle,* and I was familiar with the process. I'd also created 10 seconds of cel animation for a Duncan Yo-Yo national campaign when I was still in high school. That, and my musical background.

Betsy then explained her Disney assignment. Of course, I'd seen Dick Van Dyke dance with penguins in *Mary Poppins*, so having her dance with Thumper would be no problem for Disney's animators. The problem was how to get Betsy from her live TV appearance into the drawing of Thumper, and have them dance together on the TV show. I suggested that when she held up her Thumper sketch, instead of switching to a live studio camera, the studio could simply cut to a pre-recorded video clip, making it appear she had magically popped into her sketch and brought the bunny to life. That solved the "doing it on live TV" problem, and landed me the director's job.

My daughter Lisa took this photo of Betsy's dance rehearsal. The blurring you see in this action still, is what we need to eliminate for the animation. White space shows where Thumper will appear.

Normal cinematography captures blur in fast action sequences, but for animation, the images must be crisp, or the drawn character will be obscured by the blur, or in front of it, neither of which is acceptable. I asked Harry Mathias (1980 Academy Award Nominee for *Solly's Diner*), to film the sequence, and he accepted, with the stipulation that

471

I ask Disney's head of Special Effects Cinematography, what the best shutter angle would be for capturing the action to eliminate blur for the animation department. I had no idea what Harry was talking about, but I wrote down "shutter angle" and arranged a meeting with Director of Photography and Special Effects Supervisor Peter Anderson, then working on *Tron*, who talked to me as we hurried along the halls at Walt Disney Studios. After I explained what we were doing, he told me to tell Harry to set the shutter at 90 degrees. I didn't know what that meant, either, but I duly noted it, conveyed it to Harry, and the composite of Thumper's animation with Betsy's rotoscoped performance was superb.

Here, I'm calling the shots for Harry. The tall man is Steve St. John, Harry's focus puller. Harry is mostly hidden behind the camera. That morning, everything went exactly as planned, and I wrapped in time for everyone to get home for the Super Bowl. The truth is, I was more concerned about the budget. Sunday shoots are Golden Time, and the budget was for a weekday. Shooting only a half day, I stayed on budget.

**Betsy and Thumper shoot, February 6, 1972, Superbowl Sunday
(All photos in this article courtesy Travis Edward Pike archive)**

Orson Welles and Wagner e Venezia, 1983

HK: Once you were *"20 Feet From Stardom"* with Orson Welles.
TP: In 1983, the co-production by Filmarte Venezia (Italy), and Krátký Film Praha (Czechoslovakia), hired Orson Welles to read the voice of Richard Wagner for their production of *Wagner e Venezia,* then hired Sync, Ltd. to record the legendary director.

A pretty straight-forward voiceover assignment—no need to worry about lipsync, but working with Orson Welles is a very different matter. I was streamlining operations for Bran Arandjelovich, president of Sync. Ltd., a language dubbing service, when he suddenly asked me if I'd record Orson Welles. The entire project had arrived on film, and in his eyes, I was the only one in his organization with the experience and gravitas required to work with Orson Welles.

All that praise activated my radar, but it was an opportunity I couldn't ignore. Bran gave me the number of the studio Welles had selected . . . and the only studio Orson Welles would consider.

The blip on my rader grew a bit larger and sharper, but I called the number, and told the cranky old buzzard on the other end that I understood Orson Welles wanted me to use his studio, and I wanted to come by and see it. He said if I must, come now. He wasn't planning to hang around all day. I replied I'd be there shortly and he hung up. The blip kept getting larger.

The studio had a street number, but no signage, nothing but a plain steel door, and coming from the outside glare into the darkness inside had me groping my way through the clutter as he walked ahead of me to his control booth. He ascended, warning me to hang onto the handrail and come on up. On first glance, his gear was sophisticated enough for the job at hand, which was a simple dialogue recording, but as director, I had responsibilities, and I would have much preferred EFX Studios in Burbank. He threw a switch that turned on a light in a small isolation booth at floor level, a bit to the left of his elevated control booth.

"That's where Mr Welles will be," he said, and began laying down a litany of ground rules, beginning with "at no time will you speak directly to Mr. Welles. If you have anything to say, you'll say it to me, and I'll decide to pass it along or not." He showed me the talkback that would be *turned off* for the session, unless he turned it on. Mr. Welles would be in place before I'd be allowed in, and if any of these rules offended me, I could go elsewhere.

Safe enough for him to say, I thought. I was hired to direct and record *Mr Welles,* not get somebody else to read the part. I protested that I was the director assigned . . . and the cranky old sod cut me off. "Nobody directs the great director," he said. "Shall I cancel the session?"

I replied I hadn't scheduled a session, yet. He said the session had been scheduled and gave me a 3x5 card with the time and date, only a few days away.

I took the card, and returned to the Sync, Ltd. Office at 9000 Sunset Boulevard, where a large cardboard box containing 35mm film cans of *Wagner e Venezia* sound and picture reels awaited me. I had intended to tell Bran to get someone else, but seeing those film cans, I decided to view it, first. There was no way to view or listen to audio at Sync, Ltd., so I told Bran I had to rent a workspace to see what I was supposed to do with it all. He told me to go ahead, but be sure to get a receipt. I rented a room at Horizontal Editing in Burbank and went to work on a six plate Steenbeck flatbed editing table.

The English narration had been done, and I was following along, impressed by the excellent Music and Effects tracks (M&E), when the lady narrating the film completely derailed my train of thought with her horrible pronunciation of Wagner's theater at Bayreuth as "Bay-Ruth," making it sound like the capitol of Lebanon with a lisp, instead of a correct German pronunciation that would sound more like "Buy-Royt!" I was thinking about trying to replace the single word, when I was derailed again by "Tan-Howzer." It had to be replaced with "Tahn-Hoyzer." I called Bran, told him the narration was unacceptable and required a do-over. He authorized it, but again told me to be sure to get a receipt.

The original reading was unacceptable, but I wonder if my demand for an immediate do-over might also have been prompted by my feeling powerless in my dealings with Mr. Welles.

You'll remember I taught myself to do cel animation in high school. What wasn't mentioned was that in order to convey the emotions of the drawn characters, I spent hours in front of mirrors making faces, practicing making expressions that I thought would best convey happiness, foolishness, disappointment, anger, frustration, love and outrage, so I had pretty good control over my facial expressions.

When I arrived, I had to wait outside while Mr. Welles was made comfortable in the recording booth. I was not allowed to greet him, but did nod hello as I went to the control booth, where I discovered that from where he sat, Welles could see me, and I could see him.

474

His reading was spot on, right from the start, but I hung on every phrase like my life depended on it, and smiled when I thought the reading was excellent, and looked less enthusiastic if I wanted something more —and I got it! Welles watched me, and responded to my facial reactions, with second and third attempts at questionable lines. *I* established the *unspoken* rules, but kept my facial expressions subtle. Had I gone over the top, Welles might have been insulted, and whatever influence I might have, might be compromised. But I admit I was enjoying myself, wordlessly getting the readings I desired. And in the end, in editing, I assembled all his lines of dialogue exactly where I wanted them for the final mix.

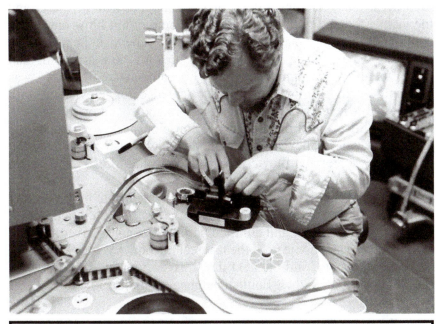

Travis cutting in Orson Welles' dialogue for *Wagner e Venezia*
(1983 photo courtesy Travis Edward Pike archive)

But the end of this story comes a few days later. The clients were flying into town to pick up the mixed English soundtrack, and Bran had booked a room where I could mix it to picture the night before they arrived. I had viewed the final cut with picture several times, and noted all the foot markings, for both the narrator and Orson Welles, and made notes regarding raising or lowering the levels as needed before the dialogue came up. We started on time, and were only a few minutes into the first reel, when the projection lamp burned out. That was unfortunate, because working in an analog environment, when

475

the projection lamp was replaced, we'd have to start over from the beginning of the reel. Then I was informed they did not have a spare projection lamp, and wouldn't be able to get one until the following day, and the room was booked solid the rest of the week. I couldn't believe my ears. How could he not have a spare projection lamp?

Of course, he was sorry. I saw the rest of his crew preparing to leave and hollered "Wait a minute. I have to deliver this soundtrack to the client tomorrow morning!" He began again to tell me how sorry he was, but I interrupted. "Screw the projection lamp." I said. "I'll mix it in the dark!" The looks on their faces were priceless. Mostly surprise, with a smattering of horror, but a few with rebellious twinkles in their eyes. They had never done such a thing, but with my notes and the visible footage flying by, if the desk lamp didn't blow out, I was confident I knew my material well enough to supervise the mix.

The fact is, music and motion pictures are both art forms that reveal themselves in time, something I became aware of when I was watching all those movies my father screened for television. On a subconscious level, as I previewed the film and sound on the flatbed, I suppose I'd married the two in my consciousness, so crazy as the idea may seem, I believed I had a good enough grasp of the material, to mentally screen the movie as I listened to the M&E. The studio manager drew up a release, and I signed it.

The projectionist and the engineer on the console in the mixing room were with me. I kept my notes under the desk lamp and announced each approaching entry and duration before the sound arrived. No one at the facility went home until the last reel ran out. Everyone cheered! We'd made history, and the next day, this story ended happily when the clients picked up their English language soundtrack.

Ingmar Bergman's Fanny and Alexander, 1983

HK: This sounds less exciting, but the ultimate reward was worth it.
TP: I was still director of production for Cine-Media International, but even writing, scouting, and prepping co-productions for Bond wasn't enough to keep me busy, much less bring in enough income to live on. I augmented my income by taking outside assignments. One such assignment was for Betty Givens' Lingo Tech Language Dubbing Service. I was the Technical Director responsible for selecting the facility, instructing the crew on our accepted procedures, and creating an accurate, feasible budget to dub the entire five hour and twelve minute director's cut of *Ingmar Bergman's Fanny and Alexander*.

476

In order to understand the scope of the assignment, I must first explain what ADR (Automated Dialogue Recording), is in reference to dubbing a film from its original language (in the case, Swedish), to another language (in this case, English).

The technical arrangements required for this incredibly long feature film, with a large cast of characters, for a director other than myself, although the designated dubbing director was to be Rudi Fehr, who had a long and impressive history as a feature film editor, and was a personal friend of Ingmar Bergman, was daunting, to say the least.

Assuming not all the readers of this book will be conversant with language dubbing techniques, here's a few basics to keep in mind. First, except in "local music" situations where the musician, band or orchestra plays on camera, (and sometimes even then), music soundtracks are recorded and mixed into the final, edited movie. On old school three stripe soundtracks, the stripes are music, effects and dialogue, all mounted on a 35mm reel for editing purposes. In ADR, when a film is to be dubbed from one language to another, M& E tracks are made, and a new dialogue track is created, all synced to the original film, and the dialogue is expected to be recorded and mixed with the same intensity and emotion as the original screen performance. The new dialogue recorded will then be transferred to the three stripe and from that, an optical sound track would be made and included on the new language prints of the film.

Ambient effects tracks are usually the first sound recorded during filming on location. The crew is ordered to be silent as the sound mixer records a sufficient sample of the environmental background noise in the location, to be used in a final mix as ambient sound for the scene on the screen. Consider a scene of two characters, shouting back and forth as they cross a crowded subway train platform. You'll film it, and record the location sound, knowing it will be useless except as a visual guide to replacing the dialogue in a studio environment. The characters still have to shout. We saw them shouting on screen. In the dub, if characters on screen step on each other's lines, the actors must record their lines separately, so they may step on each other's lines in a final mix. Done well, it will yield a final scene wherein we hear what our characters shout over subdued, rather than the live recording.

So much for the filmmaking side. In the 80's, for an ADR language dub, the film was first transferred to a timecoded Umatic 3/4" cassette, from which an adapter would capture the entry and exit timecode for each line, then write in a timecoded new language script trying to

477

match the mouth movements as closely as possible to hide the fact that the film is dubbed. The automation refers to the equipment and timecode allowing the image to fast-forward to each line, provide a ten second pre-roll to get the video cassette up to speed, and insert three beeps to signal the actor when to begin recording. As soon as an acceptable take is recorded, the equipment fast-forwards to the next timecode entry for that character and repeats the process. In this way, an actor hired to record one or more roles in a film may go quickly through all his lines for one character, rewind, and start again, as a completely different character, recording all the lines for the second character. Using ADR and carefully scheduling my actors, I once replaced the entire dialogue for a talky two-hour film in two days, and delivered the final mix on the third day.

For *Fanny and Alexander*, I selected the facility, explained our procedures, making sure the recording engineers understood my instructions with regard to saving takes. Saving half of a good take was acceptable, but only if, before moving on, it had been joined to its other half and saved as one complete take for that character's line, making the mix not a matter of selecting which take to use (there would only be one remaining), but what level the line should be in terms of the conversations around it. In my experience, my single take rule cuts mix time by more than two-thirds, and charged with creating a budget based on all the elements involved; character role hires, film runtime, and studio time to record, mix, and deliver the final product, making sure all the engineers likely to work on the project receive and follow my instructions (and call me if there is a problem), meant my job was done.

In 1983, the shorter theatrical release of *Fanny and Alexander* won four Academy Awards: Best Cinematography, Sven Nykvist; Best Art Direction-Set Direction, Anna Asp, Susanne Lingheim; Best Costume Design, Marik Vos-Lundh; and Best Foreign Language Film, Sweden. Ingmar Bergman was nominated for Best Director and for Best Writing, Screenplay Written Directly for the Screen, but won neither. On the other hand, his film did win another 22 awards worldwide.

That enormous undertaking came in ahead of time and under budget, and shortly after delivery of the English soundtrack, Betty Givens sent me a generous bonus check for the excellent job I'd done as her technical director. (And a few years later, when she retired, she gave her entire company, Lingo Tech Dubbing Services, to me.)

NASA'S 25TH ANNIVERSARY
AND SPACE OBSERVANCE WEEK
COMMEMORATIVE VIDEO, 1984

The Ventures ready for takeoff at the Conway Recording Studio shoot for *The Ventures - NASA 25TH ANNIVERSARY* album, (left to right) Nokie Edwards (lead guitar), Bob Bogle (rhythm guitar) Mel Taylor (drums) and Don Wilson (songwriter, rhythm and lead guitar).

The Ventures are the best selling instrumental rock band in music history, and their 1964 *Ventures In Space* album introduced special guitar effects, "reverse-tracking," and because of its ethereal space-like effects, is believed to have influenced the sixties San Francisco psychedelic evolution.

479

In 1984, David Carr asked me to co-produce a long-form music video, *The Ventures - NASA'S 25th Anniversary and Space Observance Week Commemorative* album for Award Records and Tapes, featuring "Also Sprach Zarathustra," "Theme for Sally" and "Telstar."

David Carr, one of the original Fortunes ("You've Got Your Troubles" and "Here Comes That Rainy Day Feeling Again,") was born and schooled in England, but had toured and recorded keyboards with the Ventures for several years, including the *Ventures in Space* album. In addition to co-producing it, he invited me to direct it. I secured the NASA footage seen in the video, and we shot the Ventures performance at Conway Recording Studios in Hollywood. David had played keyboards on the original album, and played keyboards on screen in the production. Nike provided the jump suits, so I had the studio engineering crew and David dress in maroon ones, and put the Ventures in blue ones, going for a sort of *Star Trek* look. David and I both supervised the video editing, intercutting the Ventures' studio performances with actual NASA footage.

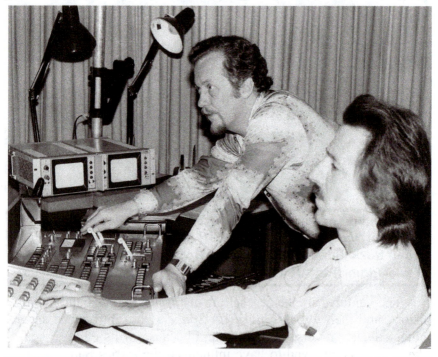

David Carr and Travis mix the Ventures long-form music video
(Photos courtesy Travis Edward Pike archive)

The shots of the studio engineers look like they are NASA mission controllers, plasma readers leap into action with the music, and a Studer, 2 inch, 24 track tape recorder starts remotely, spinning up to speed like a spinning satellite and they look great when cut together.

Morningstone, 1987

David Pinto mixes a reference recording for Travis
(Photo courtesy Travis Edward Pike archive)

David Pinto played and recorded most of the music to the original songs I composed and sang for the demo for my screenplay, *Morningstone*. David had previously played organ parts for "The Witch," with the Changeling Troupe at Conway studios, and gave me a rate on whatever we could record between us. David, a superb arranger and keyboard artist, played most of the parts on his emulator. I sang the male lead, hired a half dozen female vocalists, and managed to get the entire demo recorded in just over a month. My daughter, Lisa, produced the recordings. "In the end," she says, "it cost a small fortune, but I finally got to hear my dad's wonderful music."

481

In 1988, with the complete music demo recorded, I launched my production company, Otherworld Entertainment Corporation, hoping to secure funding for the *Morningstone* musical. Of course, my potential funding sources required references, and one of the first to reply was J. Bond Johnson, Executive Producer and Chief Executive Officer of Cine-Media International, who had optioned the original, *Changeling*, several years earlier.

 CINE-MEDIA INTERNATIONAL

November 10, 1988

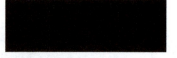

I am happy to respond to your request for an opinion and appraisal of Travis Edward Pike as to his capabilities to direct major motion picture films.

I have known Travis since 1977 at which time I was engaged in production of the feature film "Kingdom of the Spiders", which starred William Shatner (and which can be seen at 8 p.m. on next Thursday, November 17, on Channel 11). Since that time I have been most impressed with Travis on numerous levels.

Travis is that consummate film maker with the extraordinary skills of writer and director who has a realistic grasp and understanding of the financial requirements for each project. He is both imaginative and creative and at the same time careful with each detail--a rare combination. I have found him to be personable, impeccably fair, trustworthy, forthright and honest.

When I produced the "Fandango!" television pilot I did not consider any other writer-director than Travis. He approached this entire project with great skill and dedication. When in the midst of filming there arose serious equipment failures which threatened the entire project, Travis maintained his cool and wits and successfully "worked around" all the problems so that the project was completed both on time and within budget.

If I were to produce another feature film, regardless of difficulty or cost, I would seriously consider Travis both as writer and director. If you have any questions, please do not hesitate to call me.

Sincerely,

J. Bond Johnson
Executive Producer and
Chief Executive Officer

Post Office Box 7005 · Long Beach, California 90807 · (213) 426-3622

MOTION PICTURE PRE-PRODUCTION SERVICES

Featuring Screenplay Systems Software

SCRIPTOR™

MOVIE MAGIC™
SCHEDULING/BREAKDOWN

MOVIE MAGIC™
BUDGETING

Co-producing with my daughter, Lisa was a joy. Her management and technical skills, learned during her comprehensive internship while studying for her degree in Classical Civilization at UCLA, fully prepared her to be my co-producer.

Betty Givens presents Lingo Tech Dubbing Services' records and contacts to Travis. (Photos courtesy Travis Edward Pike archive)

George Johnsen (EFX), and Travis Edward Pike agree to co-venture

George's reply to a request for a reference for Mr. Pike tells the story.

As a facility owner, it is rare that I get the opportunity to review a client. Usually it is the other way around. As to my thoughts on Mr. Travis Pike, well, let's just say that I wish we could deal with more like him.

In a business that is also an art, it is hard for most producers and directors to keep track of these two distinctly different aspects of filmmaking. Too often, one aspect will rule the other-- either Art will become all consuming at the expense (literally), of the budget, or Cost control will reach a frenetic pitch with the result of the film being artistically stifled. Neither situation is movie making at its best.

Over the course of the last seven years, it has been our pleasure to work with Mr. Pike on a variety of Projects. He has shown the rare ability to be able to walk the line between art and

484

business. He has been able to take advantage of new technologies as they became available without becoming mired in the "technology for Technology's sake" syndrome. He has been able to deliver every project that we have been involved in on time and on budget (under in some cases!). It is refreshing to work with someone who asks your opinion, and actually uses the information offered to make a more informed decision.

Travis has the uncanny ability to direct the undirectable performer. We have seen quite a number of occasions where the client was sure he would have to replace an actor, but Travis was able to extract a performance that was seemingly impossible. Alternatively, when given a truly capable performer, he can respect their professionality, and use it to the project's best advantage.

Of the hundreds of producers and directors that have gone through this facility over the years, there is a small circle that are both dedicated to and qualified for the making of quality movies under controlled conditions. Travis Pike is one of those few.

If there are any questions I can answer, please call.
George Johnsen

Otherworld
Language Dubbing Services
Introduces

AUTOMATED DIGITAL DIALOGUE REPLACEMENT
by exclusive arrangement with

 Digital Technology

Until recently, most of the technological breakthroughs in **ADR** (automated dialogue replacement) had to do with high speed video tape to audio tape computer interlock. But in the rush for speed, all that audio tape racing back and forth over the recording heads built noise, and by the time 15-20 tracks were running open for a final mix, it began to sound like someone left the shower running!

Well, it's time to turn the shower off. The extra **"D"** in **ADDR** stands for digital (as in digital recording). What it means is that **all** the sound is stored in binary computer code and **nothing** is recorded to tape until the **final mix**. And that means no matter how many mix formats you need, each will be an original, **first generation soundtrack.**

Otherworld
Language Dubbing Services

OTHERWORLD's talent database lists the finest language experts in Los Angeles including former U.N interpreters, university language professors, and foreign nationals. Whatever language you may be going to, (or coming from), if your show needs translation, **OTHERWORLD** will do it for you!

OTHERWORLD's trained writers adapt the new language **ADDR** script to fit the on-screen lip movements, carefully maintaining the content and character of the original work.

OTHERWORLD's talent database also features a wide variety of experienced voice actors, including specialists for cartoon voices and childrens' roles. We can match, (or change, when desired), the voice quality of any on-screen performer.

OTHERWORLD's directors ensure that the voice actors' performances match the original characterizations. And we always have a qualified language expert in the **ADDR** studio during the dubbing session.

the bottom line

OTHERWORLD Language Dubbing **Services,** faster, better, and now exclusively digital, provides you with **first generation soundtracks in every language, every time!**

Bo Svenson utilized Otherworld Entertainment Pre-production Services for *A Spirit Rebellious*, his epic screenplay about the Finnish resistance during the 30 November 1939 to 13 March, 1940 Winter War between the Soviet Union and Finland. We reformatted his script, provided a script breakdown, shooting schedule and budget conversions displaying costs in the currencies of the international filming locations.

Lisa and Bo Svenson prepping *A Spirit Rebellious*

Travis and Bo Svenson finishing prepping *A Spirit Rebellious*
(1991 photos courtesy Travis Edward Pike archive)

Britt Lomond (left) was to be my Line Producer in my three picture package, (*Morningstone, Grumpuss,* and *Long-Grin*). Meanwhile I helped him prep his *Scapa Flow*, about the WWII German submarine that sank the Ark Royal harbored with the Home Fleet at Scapa Flow, and *Fokker*, about the brilliant aeronautical engineer, passed over by the British, subsequently employed by the Germans in WWI.

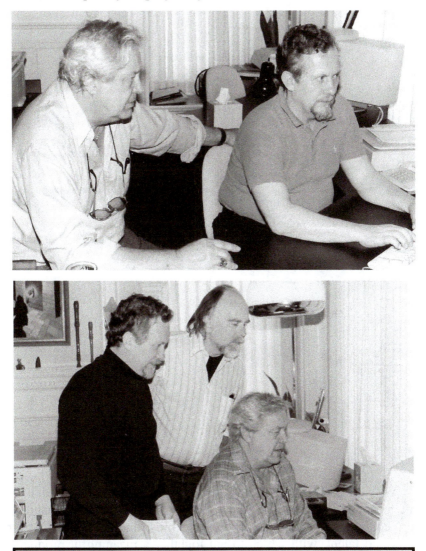

**Cinematographer Peter Anderson (center), and Line Producer Britt Lomond (right) helping prep *my three picture package.*
(Photos courtesy Travis Edward Pike archive)**

487

MOTION PICTURE BOND CO. INC.
MOTION PICTURE GUARANTORS LTD.

Los Angeles
1901 Avenue
of the Stars
Suite 1770
Los Angeles
CA 90067
(213) 203-8757
Fax: 203-0988

London
40 Clipstone St.
London W1P7EA
(01) 323-3220
Telex: 266075
Fax: 637-2590

Melbourne
75-83 High St.
Prahran
Vic. 3181
(3) 529-8852
Fax: 51-6449

Sydney
121 Bridge Road
Glebe, NSW 2037
Tel: (02) 660-3728
Fax: (02) 660-1091

Montreal
240 St. Jacques
Suite 700
Montreal
Quebec H2Y 1L9
(514) 288-2544
(514) 286-7063

Munich
Widenmeyer
Strasse. 39
8000 Munich 22
West Germany
(89) 222-165
Telex: 5212726
Fax: 291-3178

Berlin
Pariserstrasse 61
1000 Berlin 15
(49) 30-882-5967
Fax: (49) 30-882-5964

Toronto
14 Birch Ave.
Toronto, Ont.
Canada M4V 1C9
(416) 968-0577
Fax: 960-0474

Tel Aviv
61 Pinsker Ave.
Tel Aviv 63 568
Israel
(972 3) 293241
Fax: 293 243

October 21. 1991

Travis Pike
Otherworld Entertainment Corporation
1746 South Kingsley Drive
Los Angeles, CA
90006-5210

Dear Travis:

It was a pleasure to meet with you and Lisa last week. It was also an unexpected treat to receive a package that could not have been more complete. You deserve and Oscar for the planning alone.

I have enclosed a letter of intent for you in regards to "Morningstone". If you have any questions in regards to this letter, please give me a call.

Please remember that this quote is a preliminary one. I would imagine that given the experience of those that are involved in this film that we will be able to reduce the net premium once you go into production.

Sincerely,

Michael Strange

Reinsured at Lloyd's of London

With the promise of funding, the prep and Completion Bond, it was time to get over to the UK, find sound stages and get set constuction bids, equipment rental bids, processing bids, and costs for UK hire crews and talent, with which to put together a meaningful production board, schedule, and breakdown including travel time, per diems, day out of days for talent, equipment rentals, crews, processing—everything needed to commence production, and with the cooperation of the British Film Commisson, begin securing locations, crews and equipment, applying for whatever visas and permits my American department heads would need to work in the United Kingdom.

70 BAKER STREET · LONDON W1M 1DJ
TEL.: 071 224 5000 · FAX: 071 224 1013

Travis Edward Pike
President
Otherworld Entertainment Corporation
1746 South Kingsley Drive
Los Angeles California
90006-5210 USA

26th June 1992

Dear Travis

Re: Morningstone

Thank you very much for your letter of 15th June. The news contained within it is most heartening, and it all sounds very promising.

I would also like to reaffirm my appreciation of the constructive and supportive way you and Lisa raised the slight difficulties you had experienced during your visit and the useful suggestions you made to avoid any repetition in the future.

This was enormously valuable to us, and whilst I would rather not have encountered any such problems in the first place, I am grateful that they have not in any way dimmed your enthusiasm for the UK or willingness to continue to use the services of the BFC.

I listened to the cassette of the music the week-end following your visit and was most impressed. Here's hoping the rest of the project matches that quality - as I'm sure it will - and that we have the pleasure of seeing at least a portion of it made in the UK.

Thank you also for the scripts you sent of GRUMPUSS and LONG-GRIN. These will be retained for safe keeping ready - hopefully - for further action next year. I hope to read them myself in the not too distant future.

Kind regards,

ANDREW PATRICK
Chief Executive

Alas, it was not to be. All the Oscar-worthy preparation in the world amounted to nothing if there was no Oscar for prep. Similarly, if there is no money attached to an irrevocable letter of credit, all that translates to is that it is a promise that can never be unpromised, but doesn't strictly speaking, ever have to be fulfilled. Incomprehensible? Probably, but I'll try to give you some codewords that apply to transactions viewed through a financial looking glass.

When I was Director of Production for Cine-Media International, I was exposed to the myriad of non-commital commitments that are the substance of financial agreements. Co-production, co-financing, and limited partnership agreements are all about what hasn't been included in the agreement that provides the escape clause for the correspondent desiring to terminate the nebulously specific terminology, so carefully outlined in the language of the original agreement, implicitly understood to be included in the terms which invariably include either a non-circumvention agreement, or non-disclosure agreement, intended to limit the terms of the agreement agreed to by the parties, formulated by devious, suspicious, and/or criminal minds, reinforced by cadres of lawyers who wrote and interpret them so that no matter what they promise, there is an escape clause that renders the agreement nul and void, without penalty to the unreliable or dishonest partner not honoring the agreement. In other words, it's all boilerplate bullshit.

Now that you understand how financial agreements work (or don't work), it should be clear to anyone why I didn't know where the money was (or wasn't) coming from. Three times, I had agreements promising funding for *Morningstone*. Three times I alerted all my department heads not to take any long-term employment, because the following spring we'd be going into production, only to advise them, as spring approached, to try to get whatever work they could for the summer and fall, but to make sure they'd be available for the next window of opportunity, the following spring, because another funding agreement just as good as the previous one, was being hashed out, even as we spoke. It was true, and proved just as efficacious as the previous one, which is to say, it wasn't just smoke and mirrors—this one had sparkles.

I was always brutally honest when it came to saying the deal was off, but then, in 1997, I finally secured enough money to tell the story of the second property in my three picture deal, *Grumpuss*. Not enough to make the movie, but enough to tell the story, entirely in rhyme, for the benefit of the Save the Children Fund, which might get it on television, but did get us a lovely note from H.R.H. Princess Anne on Buckingham Palace stationery.

As President of Save the Children, I am delighted that Mr Travis Pike has chosen The Save the Children Fund as the beneficiary of tonight's World Premiere of Grumpuss.

Every day Save the Children provides practical assistance to children and their families, helping to alleviate the effects of poverty, war, and famine. The Fund is committed to giving children the best start in life, whether it is providing emergency food aid in Africa, implementing long-term health and education schemes in Asia, or challenging disadvantage and discrimination in this country.

I would like to take this opportunity to thank every company and individual for making this event such a success, and for supporting Save the Children. I send you all my best wishes for an enjoyable evening.

Anne

Actress Anna Scott, (Queen of the Sidh), posed in the forecourt of Blenheim Palace, birthplace of Sir Winston Churchill, home to the Duke of Marlborough, and the venue selected to stage the Save the Children Benefit Performance.

I wrote the epic, family-friendly rhyme, to be performed, live, in front of an audience, as such performances by bards of old were performed in front of royalty, nobility (and possibly some few bands of enlightened outlaws). For the Save the Children benefit performance, the audience would consist of up to thirty celebrity guests (there at my invitation and expense), to attract an audience of up to two hundred seventy guests (paying £1,000 each), for the privilege of attending the world premiere of the show, and after the show, being seated at the same table with one of the celebrities at a fabulous multi-course dinner in the Long Library at Blenheim Palace.

The poem was already written (and vetted by Buckingham Palace), and I had composed the music to underscore the production, my Otherworld Entertainment Corporation was producing it, and I intended to hire an actor to play the part of the bard telling the story, but no one I approached would even consider taking a part so demanding, a live, virtually uninterrupted performance, of a long story, to be told entirely from memory, and entirely in rhyme.

My friends (and investors), also balked at the cost of hiring an actor, because their investments were in the epic rhyme as performed by me on the demo tape each had heard. They argued that my style and interpretation was why they invested. One even argued that having written it, I was the only one who knew all the words. I did know all the words, but remembering the order in which they came, was more than daunting. At the end of the day, I really had no choice but to abandon the project—or do it myself.

I have worn many hats in my long career, but never before wore so many all at once. Writer, music composer, producer, director, and performer.

492

(Photo previous page left)
Music arranger/conductor David Carr
(Photo previous page right)
(Left to right) Master of Cermonies
Mr. Raymond P. Huggins, MBE,
Pipe Major Stephen Duffy
The Marquis of Blandford,
(now 12th Duke of Marlborough)
Extreme right, framed by greenery,
Actress Lynne Redgrave

(This page photo right)
City of Coventry Rhythmic Gymnasts
(bottom left,: Aimee Johnson); (top center
Yvonne Hill); (top right Rosy Merideth)
(Photo below, rhythmic gymnasts perform
during intermission. (Left, the orchestra
arranged and conducted by David Carr)
(Foreground, the audience.)

INTERCOM

INTERNATIONAL COMMUNICATIONS
COMPETITION

Silver Plaque Award

Special Achievement
Writing

Grumpuss

Travis Edward Pike
Otherworld Entertainment
Grumpuss Productions, L.P.

1999
INTERCOM

Judy Gaynor

Judy Gaynor
Executive Director

Michael J. Kutza
Founder and Artistic Director

Travis Edward Pike's *GRUMPUSS* World Premiere Benefit Performance, won a Silver Plaque for Special Achievement—Writing in the 1999 International Communications Film & Video Competition in Chicago, Illinois. It was the only award presented in this category that year and the previous year, no writing award was presented. To the best of our knowledge, this marks the first time in the 35-year history of the Chicago Film Festival, perhaps in the entire history of motion pictures and video productions, that an epic narrative rhyme was so honored.

Volunteers for Verdi
A Film by Jo Christensen & Travis Edward Pike
A New Playwrights Foundation Production

Jeff Bergquist, Artistic Director of the New Playwrights Foundation, approached Maestro Mario Leonetti, director of the Casa Italiana Opera Company, to pitch his idea for making a film about them. The Maestro agreed. Jeff recruited Danish-born director, Jo Christensen, with whom he had worked on previous New Playwrights Foundation productions, to produce and direct the project, and she began videotaping rehearsals, interviews and finally the performance, itself. But after completion of principal photography, the production stalled for lack of funds and it became clear that what was needed was a volunteer with the equipment, time and commitment to see it through to completion.

I had recently screened my 1997 VHS production of *Grumpuss* for our membership, so Jeff knew I had the hardware, software, talent and time, but I was wary about committing to a feature film about the inner workings of a community opera company—until Jo explained the movie was about the people, and she didn't want me to write a narrative. She wanted the principals to tell the story through their actions and in their own words, culled from the 55 hours of interviews, rehearsals and the performance already in the can.

It was an enormous undertaking, but together, over the next year and a half, meeting once or twice a week, we logged all the footage, captured and transcribed all the elements we hoped to use in the final cut, and managed to hone the potentially useful material down to just over six hours. The music might be different, but the problems and personalities were much like the ones I'd dealt with in rock 'n ' roll.

Finally, settling on simple chronology for the spine, we began weaving together the audio and visual elements, but as the program neared completion, there were still a few questions that needed answering, to which end Jo interviewed Jeff Bergquist and Phyllis Elliott, both attached to the Casa Italiana Opera Company, when the show was recorded, providing the answers to the last half-dozen questions I needed to finish what is now the 86-minute documentary, *Volunteers for Verdi* that won two Certificates of Excellence (feature length documentary and Arts: Performing Arts), at the U.S. International Film and Video Festival in 2006.

Located at the northernmost border of Los Angeles's Chinatown, the Casa Italiana is home to as eclectic a crowd as ever appeared in any major Hollywood production.

Drawn together by unflagging passion, dreadful tenacity and the notion that opera goes down better with a plate of spaghetti, these *Volunteers for Verdi* embody the rich cultural mix of Southern California, where America's melting pot continues to bubble and individual dreams can and do come true, even into the twilight years.

2006 US INTERNATIONAL FILM AND VIDEO FESTIVAL AWARD WINNER
Documentary 60:01-90:00 — Certificate of Creative Excellence
Arts: Performing Arts — Certificate of Creative Excellence

(above, right), *Volunteers for Verdi* DVD Cover (Courtesy New Playwrights Foundation)
Lee W. Gluckman, Jr., presented the Certificates of Excellence
to producers Jo Christebsen (center), and Travis Edward Pike (right).
(photo courtesy of US. INTERNATIONAL FILM AND VIDEO FESTIVAL)

EVERYTHING OLD IS NEW AGAIN

Harvey Kubernik: To the best of your knowledge, all the prints, interpositives and negatives to *Feelin' Good* were ruined when your father's film vault in Wakefield, Rhode Island was flooded.
Travis Pike: That's what I was told.

HK: But after your father passed, your brother Gregory, who lives in New Hampshire, drove down to Wakefield and discovered five rusty film cans labled *Feelin' Good* on a top shelf in the dried out film vault, and shipped them to you.
TP: When I saw the rusty cans, I thought he should have trashed them, rather than send them all the way to California for me to trash.

HK: So, why did you take them to Deluxe?
TP: Adam and I had just finished recording songs for albums from my back catalog, but I had no footage of me performing in the sixties. There was a slim possibility that the cans of film had been mislabeled, suggesting I might have a complete print of *Feelin' Good*, and maybe there was something there worth salvaging. I took it all to Deluxe to have them clean the film, and see what, if anything, was salvageable.

HK: And there was.
TP: Not what I hoped. The cans had not been mislabelled. Reels four and five from one print were useless, but Deluxe reported the last three reels from one print were historically salvageable, by which I mean, the film was warped, beyond having any commercial value, but the mono optical soundtrack was actually quite good. I was heartsick watching the sequence on reel five where I sang two songs with the Brattle Street East on the Charles River Esplanade, because the color kept changing. The Deluxe engineer screening it for me said it looked pretty good for a rock movie made in the sixties. "The color changes give it a psychedelic look." But it was made in 1966, and it was footage of me, performing "Watch Out Woman" on camera.

I had even dared to attempt a leap, expected of the *Twistsensation Aus USA*, taking off and landing on my good right foot, but barely cleared the height of the drum set.

HK: But that "Watch Out Woman" sequence led to the *Perlich Post* headline, "The best music video of 2016 was actually shot in 1966."

TP: Which led to an email from State Records, saying they'd like to re-issue it on a vinyl 45 in the UK. I wrote it couldn't be reissued, because it had never been released. But I had a mono optical soundtrack recording, complete with crowd noise. State Records was thrilled, and we signed.

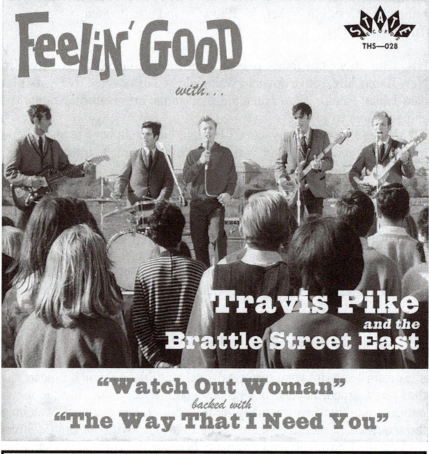

(2017 *Feelin' Good* record sleeve provided courtesy of State Records)

HK: This is not the first time one of your performances from more than a half century ago has, according to music reviewer Lenny Helsing in the *Shindig!* July 2017 issue #74, "had the '60s garage appreciation congregation all in a lather." Two of the eight original songs you performed in *Feelin' Good* in 1966, "Watch Out Woman' and "The Way That I Need You," released by State Records on a vinyl single in 2017, emerged as the number three single in *Shindig!* magazine's Best of 2017 issue #74. Then, Travis Pike's Tea Party's "If I Didn't Love You Girl" (Alma 1968), was listed in the 100th issue Collector's Edition of

498

Shindig!, in a four page editorial by Editor-In-Chief Jon "Mojo" Mills titled "The Hot 100. The Soundtrack Of Our Evolution," in which he presents one hundred Deep, Deep Cuts released on 45 and featured in the pages of *Shindig!*. Since its Alma release in 1968, "If I Didn't Love You Girl" has appeared on three separate compilation albums, and in 2019, was re-released in the UK on a Mousetrap 45, 28th Anniversary Single.

TP: The record never charted, and we broke up in California in 1969. However, as you said, in 1994, our recording of "If I Didn't Love You Girl" appeared on the *Sixties Rebellion* Vol. 7 (The Backyard Patio) LP compilation by Way Back Records (Germany), and in 1995, the song was included in the London Fog vinyl LP compilation, *Tougher Than Stains*, and most recently, in 2017, it appeared on *Le Beat Bespoké* 7 vinyl LP

compilation released by Detour Records, all dupes from the original Travis Pike's Tea Party cuts. Adam recorded it twice, once with *The Syrups* CD album, produced for them by Geoff Emerick, (*Revolver, Sgt. Pepper's Lonely Hearts Club Band*, and *Abbey Road*) and once with me for our *Travis Edward Pike's Tea Party Snack Platter* CD.

Publication, Preservation and Production

HK: But it wasn't just your sixties recordings that were making headlines. In the UK, Lenny Helsing placed an exclusive, in-depth, illustrated article celebrating your more than half-century in showbiz, with a focus, of course, on your music he called, "The Travis Edward Pike Story,*"* posted February 2018 on psychedelicbabymag.com, and in March-April 2018, Andy Pearson's fearandloathingfanzine.com posted "Travis Pike," his equally long, insightful and entertaining pictorial interview with you. TP: Yeah, but Harvey, you got there first with your six-page, timely interview, "Travis Pike: Feelin' Good" published in the Winter, 2016-2017 *Ugly Things,* and in December, 2018, you posted our long-form, in-depth interview you called "Travis Pike, Renaissance Man Revisited," on cavehollywood.com, taking readers from *Demo Derby* right up to the February 2018 release, *Travis Edward Pike's Grumpuss 20th*

Anniversary Platinum Edition DVD, and forecast my November 2019 publication of *Changeling's Return, a novel approach to the music.*

I'll be 76 by the time this book comes on market, and the likelihood that I will ever see my properties on the big screen is fading. One day, they may yet make it to the big screen, or whatever its equivalent may be, and starting in 2017, the release of the *Grumpuss 15th Anniversary Audio Theater Edition* preserved the source material that Rochelle O'Gorman's review (*The Boston Globe*, Sunday, August 18, 2000), called a "clever fairy tale...told completely in narrative rhyme. The language is rich and the presentation is exhilarating,

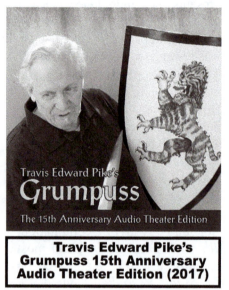

Travis Edward Pike's Grumpuss 15th Anniversary Audio Theater Edition (2017)

though too sophisticated for younger children...Underlying themes of courage and harmony are employed with a subtle hand." The release of the *Grumpuss 20th Anniversary Platinum Edition* DVD, makes it clear that an epic rhyme can hold live audiences of all ages in thrall. Imagine seeing that rich adventure unfold; the King's court, the knight, the dwarf, the Grumpuss (a CGI animated liger), and tell me that wouldn't draw and hold movie audiences enthralled.

HK: In our Winter 2017 *Ugly Things* interview, I concluded that your remastered DVD was in every way more potent and revealing than the reviews and testimonials for the 1998 VHS release claimed.

TP: *The Midwest Book Review*/Wisconsin Bookwatch/DVD Shelf reported, "Travis Edward Pike's Grumpuss 20th Anniversary Platinum Edition (1 hour, 38 min.) is the award-winning DVD of Pike's beloved narrative poem *Grumpuss* tranformed into an epic film performance. What exactly is a Grumpuss? It's a mythical beast that resembles an ill-tempered cat, "With tremendous paws and gigantic claws, and jaws that can crush armor flat!" A treasure sure to delight connoisseurs of classic British fantasy by authors such as J.R.R. Tolkien, Lewis Carroll, and C.S. Lewis, *Travis Edward Pike's Grumpuss 20th Anniversary Platinum Edition* is a choice pick for family movie night and public library collections.

"Bonus features include Travis Edward Pike's World Premiere Documentary, and three slideshows about the making of Grumpuss. Also highly recommended is the 2-CD set Travis Edward Pike's Grumpuss: The 15th Anniversary Audio Theater Edition (79 min. 9 sec), which allows one to listen to the marvelous adventure as a radio play."

When I presented *Grumpuss* to the studios, everyone loved it, but of course, they were not the *hoi polloi*. And while they would personally love to see it, it was cost prohibitive—unless, of course, it became a best seller, indicating it had an audience waiting and primed for the story to come to the screen.

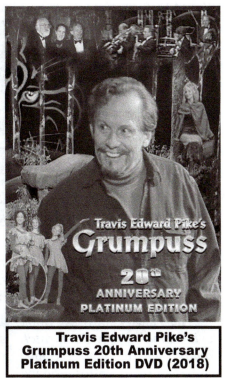

Travis Edward Pike's Grumpuss 20th Anniversary Platinum Edition DVD (2018)

HK: It would probably be huge as an oversized fully illustrated children's book for teachers, parents and grandparents to read to the kids.

TP: Possibly, but my intent has always been to put this fantasy adventure on screen, so the storytelling and theatrical presentations are more to the point, especially as far as filmmakers and investors are concerned. And preserved, these source materials will remain available to future producers, directors, and financiers. The risks involved in big-budget productions, are great, and distributors and investors want to see a broad-based, excited audience reaction before taking the plunge.

For all those reasons, I published *Changeling's Return, a novel approach to the music*, winner of a 2020 eLit Bronze Medal Award for Fine and Performing Arts, and *Changeling's Return, a novel musical concept* 53-minute music CD. In addition to preserving these fantasy adventures, they may now attract readers, listeners, and watchers who treasure these early incarnations. I expected them to do well in the UK, where these adventures are set, but now they're finding fans here (in the USA), as well.

HK: Mike Stax, in *Ugly Things* magazine set it up rather nicely when he wrote "Like Pike, the book's protagonist, Morgen, was raised in Boston and is the lead singer and songwriter of a band—not the Tea Party, but Beantown Home Cookin' —and the setting is not the sixties, but the present day . . . shades of *The Wicker Man* or HP Lovecraft."

TP: I particularly like the way he closed with "It's a compelling story with many surprising turns, and a powerful message about mankind's impact on the environment and the urgency of changing course."

The January *Midwest Book Review/Small Press Bookwatch Fantasy/Sci-Fi Shelf* critique may be more pertinent to music and film students: A unique literary and musical experience, the paperback edition of *Changeling's Return* can be significantly augmented by an accompanying CD of the same title that is comprised of eighteen original and thematically relevant musical numbers with a total running time of 53 minutes. Adapted from *Morningstone*, a screenplay by Travis Edward Pike, *Changeling's Return* is unreservedly recommended for community and academic library collections.

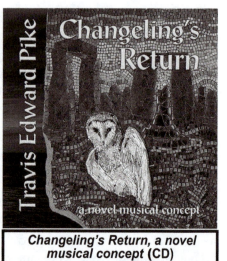

Changeling's Return, a novel musical concept (CD)

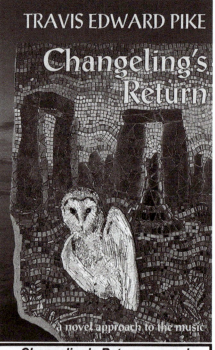

Changeling's Return, a novel approach to the music (BOOK)

Changeling's Return won a 2020 eLit Bronze Medal Award for
Fine and Performing Arts
(Music/Dance/Cinema/Theater/Photography)

502

HK: You've released two properties from your three-picture package, not as originally intended, but complete in themselves. I get it that there's terrific potential for cross-collateralization, but isn't that the same incentive you offered in 1975, and 1992? What has changed?

TP: Harvey, everything has changed in the more than quarter century since 1992. The world has changed. There's a whole new generation of filmmakers, a whole new generation of financiers and entrepreneurs looking to make a name for themselves in motion pictures and music, and while the names of the distributors and studios may seem constant, the ownership, production teams and mission of each has also changed. Humanity has changed too. No longer able to turn a blind eye to climate change, or the current global pandemic. My story has always been about living in harmony with nature, now more important than ever, as nature goes through this season of change.

I've changed too. I'm doing what the Hollywood movers and shakers asked me to do, getting my properties out to the public to see if they find an audience. Well, I can't say they've found an audience yet, but they've been winning awards, and for those Hollywood types who professed to love the story, but would never invest in an epic rhyme, I've shown an audience for such entertainment does exist, continues to grow, spellbound by the tale being told, by its complex, intriguing rhythms and exquisite language. Whether or not my new musical novel will find an audience, it's still early to say, but the reviews are promising, and until these unique properties are discovered and exploited, they remain backstage, eager to perform, waiting only to be called.

Harvey Kubernik visits Long-Grin in the Travis Edward Pike archive

HK: And what about the third picture in the package? Are you still planning to go forward with your *Long-Grin* saga?

TP: I'm already working on it. In fact I've been working on it since 1961, and the *Long-Grin Saga* has grown bigger, better, and more fascinating with each passing year. You've met the dragon lurking over me. Frankly, he's aging a lot better than I am, and now it's time for me to tell his story, lest it be lost forever.

James A. Pike's screening room in his house in Newton Centre, Massachusetts. (1966 photo courtesy Travis Edward Pike archive)

HK: I'm always impressed when you show me your scrapbooks and memorabilia.

TP: My wife, Judy's scrapbooks and memorabilia. This photo might interest you. It was my father's screening room when he lived in Newton Centre, Massachusetts. That's probably the same director's chair I sat in when I knocked out the song for *Demo Derby*. This is also where I first saw *Demo Derby*, in late 1964. And it's where my daughter, Lisa, and my ten year-old brother, Adam, saw *Feelin' Good*, when eleven year-old Lisa visited in 1975.

HK: Did your father ever screen anything besides his own films?

TP: Yes. All the time. I saw Steve Reeves in Joseph E. Levine's English-dubbed *Hercules* and *Hercules Unchained,* there.

HK: Joseph E. Levine, who was executive producer on *The Graduate, The Producers,* and *The Lion in Winter?*

TP: And *Zulu,* too, I think. He used to live in Chestnut Hill, an unincorporated part of Newton, Brookline, and Boston. He had no screening room, and used to bring his films to my father's house to view them.

HK: Did you ever meet Joseph E. Levine?

TP: No, I never met him, but until the summer of 1968, I saw all his movies in this screening room.

Levine had just released *A Bridge Too Far*, when my father visited me in 1977. He saw it was playing at the Egyptian theater in Hollywood, and invited me to see it with him. We went to the matinee, and the theater was practically deserted. We both thought the movie had everything it needed to be a blockbuster . . . except an audience. I don't think it glorifies war at all, but the war-weary American public wasn't having it.

HK: Joseph E. Levine was the subject of *Showman*, a 1963 documentary by Albert and David Maysles.

TP: There you go! I brought up language dubbing. You came back with the documentary. I'd say we're back on topic.

Harvey Kubernik native of Los Angeles and Fairfax High School alumnus earned an A.A. from West Los Angeles College, 1971; a B.A. Special Major (Health, Sociology, and Literature), from San Diego State University, 1973. Harvey Kubernik has been an active music journalist for over 48 years and is the author of 18 books. Kubernik is the head of editorial at *Record Collector News* magazine recordcollectornews.com and cavehollywood.com, for more than a decade. Select catalogue articles from Kubernik's catalogue are housed at rock'sbackpages.com, the online library of music writing.

Harvey's first book, *This Is Rebel Music* was published in 2002, and *Hollywood Shack Job: Rock Music In Film and on Your Screen* in 2004, were published by the University of New Mexico Press.

Harvey wrote the critically acclaimed *Canyon of Dreams: The Magic and the Music of Laurel Canyon*, published by Sterling/Barnes and Noble in 2009, and in a 2012 paperback edition. Ray Manzarek penned the introduction and Lou Adler the afterword.

Harvey is also a contributing writer of *That Lucky Old Sun*, a Genesis Publications limited edition (2009) title (signed), done in collaboration with Brian Wilson of the Beach Boys and Sir Peter Blake, designer of the Beatles' *Sgt. Pepper's Lonely Hearts Club Band* album cover.

Harvey Kubernik and his brother Kenneth, co-authored the highly regarded *A Perfect Haze: The Illustrated History of the Monterey International Pop Festival*, published in 2011 by Santa Monica Press.

In 2014, Otherworld Cottage Industries published Harvey Kubernik's *It Was Fifty Years Ago Today THE BEATLES Invade America and Hollywood*, and his *Turn Up the Radio! Rock, Pop and Roll in Los Angeles 1956-1972*, was published by Santa Monica Press and garnered global praise. Tom Petty wrote the introduction and Roger Steffens wrote the afterword.

Later that same year, Palazzo Editions published *Leonard Cohen: Everybody Knows*, a coffee-table-size volume with narrative and oral history written by Harvey Kubernik. Currently published in six foreign languages, in 2016, the title was also published in Chinese and Russian. In 2020, Harvey's book jacket endorsement for author Michael Posner's book, *Leonard Cohen, Untold Stories: The Early Years,* will be published by Simon & Schuster, Canada in fall 2020.

Harvey and Kenneth Kubernik's text and biographical portrait for legendary photographer Guy Webster's first book of music, movie and television photos for Insight Editions; *Big Shots: Rock Legends and Hollywood Icons: The Photography of Guy Webster*, with an introduction by Brian Wilson, was also published in 2014. In 2015, *Big Shots* won the Benjamin Franklin Gold Medal award in Art & Photography from the Independent Book Publishing Association Bronze Medal Award in the category of Photography.

Palazzo Editions arranged Harvey's music and recording study, an illustrated history book, *Neil Young, Heart of Gold* published in 2015, by Hal Leonard (US), Omnibus Press (UK), Monte Publishing (Canada), and Hardie Grant (Australia), coinciding with Young's 70th birthday. A German edition was published in 2016.

506

Sterling/Barnes and Noble published *1967, A Complete Rock Music History of the Summer of Love* in 2017. In July of that year, Harvey appeared at the Rock and Roll Hall of Fame in Cleveland, Ohio as part of their *Distinguished Author Series* discussing his *Summer of Love* book. July 2017 is also the month that Sterling/Barnes and Noble published Harvey and Kenneth Kubernik's *The Story of the Band From Big Pink to The Last Waltz* which chronicles The Band's influential musical career from 1966-1976.

Inside Cave Hollywood: The Harvey Kubernik Innerviews and InterViews Collection, Vol. 1 published by Cave Hollywood Books in 2017, is a compilation of interviews and essays culled from Harvey's online content at cavehollywood. com.

In 2018, Otherworld Cottage Industries published Harvey's multi-voice narrative book *The Doors Summer's Gone*, that in 2019 was nominated for an Association for Recorded Sound Collections Award for Excellence in Historical Recorded Sound Research.

Harvey and Kenneth recently signed a book deal with Sterling/Barnes and Noble for a hard cover illustrated text on Jimi Hendrix, slated for 2021 publication.

While writing all these books, Harvey kept up his journalist efforts and furthered his career as guest speaker and consultant on radio, television and motion picture productions.

In 1978 Kubernik co-produced and hosted *50/50*, a weekly television music and interview program from Theta Cable in Santa Monica broadcast on the milestone Z Channel in Los Angeles and Manhattan Cable in New York. Guests were Michael Lloyd, Todd Rundgren, Danny Sugerman and Murray the K.

Harvey was also a West Coast Director of A&R for MCA Records in 1978-1979 where he teamed engineer/producer Jimmy Iovine with Tom Petty for their *Damn The Torpedoes* and initiated the Del Shannon album *Drop Down and Get Me* which Petty produced.

Harvey produced the spoken word/poetry segments during 1983-1987 for *I.R.S. Records Presents: The Cutting Edge* music program that was broadcast monthly on MTV directed by Jonathan Dayton and Valerie Faris.

In July 1995 Kubernik served as co-producer and curator of the month-long *Rock 'n' Roll Literature Series* held at the MET Theatre in Hollywood. The three remaining members of the Doors reunited and performed during the engagement.

During 2007, Harvey Kubernik appeared on screen in the deluxe edition 40th anniversary DVD of *Jailhouse Rock* which starred Elvis Presley. He comments on the making of the infamous "Jailhouse Rock" musical number from the M-G-M Presley movie.

Kubernik served as Consulting Producer on the 2010 singer-songwriter documentary, *Troubadours* directed by Morgan Neville. The film was shown at the 2011 Sundance Film Festival in the documentary category. PBS-TV broadcast the movie in their *American Masters* series.

Kubernik appeared in director Matthew O'Casey's 2012 *Queen at 40* documentary broadcast on BBC Television, (released as a DVD *Queen: Days Of Our Lives* in 2014 via Eagle Rock Entertainment).

Harvey Kubernik, Henry Diltz and Gary Strobl collaborated with ABC-TV in 2013 for their Emmy-winning one hour *Eye on L.A. Legends of Laurel Canyon* hosted by Tina Malave.

Harvey Kubernik was also spotlighted for the 2013 BBC-TV documentary *Bobby Womack Across 110th Street,* directed by James Meycock. Womack, Ronnie Wood of the Rolling Stones, Damon Albarn of Blur, the Gorillaz, and actor Antonio Vargas participated.

In May 2014, filmmaker Matt O'Casey recorded Kubernik in his BBC-TV documentary on singer Meat Loaf, titled *Meat Loaf; In and Out of Hell,* broadcast in the US market in 2016 on the Showtime Cable TV channel.

In 2014, Kubernik was a consultant and interview subject for an hour-long examination of the musical legacy of Los Angeles for the Australian television series *Great Music Cities* for XYZ networks Pty Ltd www.xyznetworks.com.au. Slash, Brian Wilson, Steve Lukather and Keith Richards were also lensed for the project. Senior Producer is Wade Goring for Australian music television channel MAX www.maxtv.com.au.

Harvey Kubernik and author Jan Alan Henderson in 2014 were interview subjects for BBC Radio 4 and their documentary *California Dreaming, Laurel Canyon*, produced by Andy Parfitt, chronicling the California music scene of the late 1960s and early 1970.

During 2019, Harvey Kubernik served as consultant on a new 2-part, Alison Ellwood directed documentary *Laurel Canyon: A Place In Time* that debuted in 2020 on M-G-M's Premium network EPIX.

In summer, 2019, Harvey was featured on director Matt O'Casey's BBC4-TV digital arts channel *Christine McVie, Fleetwood Mac's Songbird.* The cast includes Christine McVie, Stan Webb of Chicken Shack, Mick Fleetwood, Stevie Nicks, John McVie, Christine's family members, Heart's Nancy Wilson, Mike Campbell, Neil Finn, and producer Richard Dashut.

In 2019 Harvey Kubernik appeared in the Chris Sibley & David Tourje-directed short documentary *John Van Hamersveld: Crazy World Ain't It.* Van Hamersveld designed the iconic Endless Summer visual image and album covers for the Beatles, the Rolling Stones, Jefferson Airplane, Grateful Dead, the Beach Boys, the Kaleidoscope, and Blondie.

This decade Harvey was filmed for the documentary about Gold Star Recording Studio and co-owner/engineer Stan Ross directed by Jonathan Rosenberg in which, Brian Wilson, Herb Alpert, Richie Furay, Darlene Love, Mike Curb, Chris Montez, Bill Medley, Don Randi, Hal Blaine, Don Peake, Marky Ramone, Artie Butler, David Kessel, and Steven Van Zandt appear.

Harvey Kubernik is the consulting producer and writer on a documentary examining Rock and Roll Hall of Fame inductee Del Shannon for Stars North production company. Todd Thompson and Mark Bentley are directing and producing. Dan Bourgoise, founder of the landmark Bug Music publishing company is Executive Producer. Bourgoise, for 35 years Shannon's best friend and personal manager oversees the Del Shannon estate.

Harvey Kubernik has lectured and conducted courses on the music business and film at UCLA and the University of Southern California. Today, Otherworld Cottage Industries hosts Kubernik's Korner at www.otherworldcottage.com.

CPSIA information can be obtained
at www.ICGtesting.com
Printed in the USA
LVHW021921091122
732755LV00001B/23

9 781892 900098